The Way We Lived

VOLUME I

The Way We Lived

Essays and Documents
in American Social History

Frederick M. Binder
City University of New York, College of Staten Island

David M. Reimers
New York University

D. C. HEATH AND COMPANY
Lexington, Massachusetts   Toronto

CREDITS

Cover painting: "Tammany Society Celebrating the Fourth of July, 1812" by W. P. Chappel (The New York Historical Society).
Chapter-opening photos: p. 4, Culver Pictures, Inc.; p. 23, Brown Brothers; p. 41, National Maritime Museum, Greenwich, Connecticut; p. 62, Fogg Art Museum, Harvard University, Harvard University Law Collection; p. 82, National Portrait Gallery, London; p. 100, The New York Historical Society; p. 117, The American Antiquarian Society; p. 142, The Bettmann Archive; p. 165, The Woolaroc Museum, Bartlesville, Oklahoma; p. 185, Denver Public Library, Western History Department; p. 205, The New York Historical Society; p. 226, The Library Company of Philadelphia: p. 244, The Library of Congress; p. 255, Chicago Historical Society; p. 279, The Library of Congress.

Published simultaneously in Canada.

Printed in the United States of America.

International Standard Book Number: 0-669-09030-1

Library of Congress Catalog Card Number: 87-81182

PREFACE

History courses have traditionally emphasized the momentous events of our past. Wars and laws, technological advances and economic crises, ideas and ideologies, and the roles of famous heroes and infamous villains have been central to these studies. Yet, what made events momentous is the impact they had on society at large, on people from all walks of life. The growing attention to social history is in part a recognition that knowledge of the experiences, values, and attitudes of these people is crucial to gaining an understanding of our past.

Thus America's history, as reflected in the everyday lives of its people, constitutes the focus of these volumes. In preparing a work of selected readings, we have had to make choices as to which episodes from our past to highlight. Each of those included, we believe, was significant in the shaping of our society. Each of the essays is followed by original documents that serve several purposes. They provide examples of the kinds of source materials used by social historians in their research; they help to illuminate and expand upon the subject dealt with in the essays; and they bring the reader into direct contact with the people of the past—people who helped shape, and people who were affected by, the "momentous events."

Our introduction to each essay and its accompanying documents is designed to set the historical scene and to call attention to particular points in the selections, raising questions for students to ponder as they read. A list of suggested readings has been included after each of the major divisions of the text. We trust that these volumes will prove to be what written history at its best can be—interesting and enlightening.

F. M. B.
D. M. R.

CONTENTS

PART I

Colonial Society, 1607–1783

1

ch. 5 pp. 96-101

Ch. 4 pp. 90-96

ch. 5 pp. 120-135

PART II

Social Life in a New Nation, 1783–1877

137

Ch. 9 p. 256

Contents

ch. 10 p. 284

Ch. 13   p. 356

ch. 11   p. 302

ch. 13

Ch. 11   p. 313

ix

Contents

The Way We Lived

PART I

Colonial Society

1607–1783

COLONIAL AMERICA WAS THE PRODUCT OF THE MIXING OF three distinct cultural groups: the Indians, who came thousands of years before the others; the Europeans; and finally the Africans. Not only did these groups differ widely in background and culture, but also within each there was significant variation in language, religion, and social customs. By the time of the European settlement of the New World, the Native American population consisted of hundreds of different and distinct tribes. Although the English played the major role in shaping colonial society, the British colonies included people from all parts of western and northern Europe. Cultural diversity also characterized the west Africans taken in bondage to the shores of America. The first three chapters introduce each of these groups and describe aspects of their culture, experiences, and interaction.

The Europeans, by sheer weight of numbers and superior technology, emerged as the dominant group in the seventeenth century. To a considerable extent, they tried to recreate their European life-style in the New World, but traditional institutions and attitudes often had to be modified in the face of new conditions. No element of their heritage was of greater significance to the European colonists than religion, which was characterized by a rich diversity of belief and practice during this period.

During the seventeenth and eighteenth centuries, the vast majority of colonists were farmers. Nevertheless, cities, as centers of commercial, political, social, and cultural life, were of vital importance in the making of American society. Like her peoples, America's cities had distinct personalities of their own and presented their inhabitants with a variety of life-styles, opportunities, and challenges.

The culminating episode of the colonial period, the American Revolution, brought disruptions, turmoil, and new opportunities. As with other aspects of colonial life, there were intense differences of opinion regarding the war, which often resulted in violence quite apart from the military conflict.

The chapters in Part I discuss Native American culture, the contrasting values of the Massachusetts and Virginia colonies, the sufferings of slaves and immigrants, family values in the Plymouth colony, religion and urban life in the early eighteenth century, and the impact of the American Revolution on the lives of the colonists.

CHAPTER 1

Indians and Europeans

Some 40,000 years before the establishment of England's New World colony of Jamestown in 1607, America's initial settlers had begun their migration, lasting thousands of years, across the Bering Sea. Drawn from a variety of Asiatic peoples, the hundreds of native tribes that had settled across America by the advent of European colonization differed profoundly in language, religion, economy, and social and political organization. These differences frequently were far greater than those separating settlers from the various European nations.

When they arrived, the European newcomers expected the Native Americans to give up their cultures and accept the "superior" ways of Western civilization. During the colonial era, both Indians and colonists adopted the goods and technology of the other culture that they found useful. However, this acceptance did not signal cultural surrender by either group. In the face of European encroachment, Native Americans held on to their life-styles as tenaciously as they defended their lands and, in the long run, with greater success.

The essay that follows, from Anthony Wallace's The Death and Rebirth of
the Seneca, *describes how one tribe, the Seneca, lived. The Seneca, along with
the Mohawk, Onondaga, Cayuga, and Oneida, belonged to the League of Iroquois—
a confederation founded by Hiawatha around 1570 and the only such union of tribes
that existed north of Mexico during this period. Their tribal homelands were located
in what today is New York State, between the Hudson River and Lake Erie, but
their hunting and war parties ranged as far as Hudson's Bay to the north, the
Mississippi River to the west, the Atlantic coast to the east, and the Carolinas to
the south. Their unity, courage, and military and diplomatic skills enabled them
to withstand European incursions for well over a hundred years, until their alliance
with the British during the Revolutionary War brought defeat. In reading the
Wallace essay, how do you, a twentieth-century observer, respond to Iroquois
attitudes and practices regarding the division of labor, status of the sexes, conduct
of war, treatment of prisoners, and child rearing? What evidence do you find in
the essay of European influences on the lives of Native Americans?*

*During the seventeenth and eighteenth centuries, a few Europeans kindly
disposed toward the Native Americans did get close enough to their villages to
observe and admire their customs. Such a man was John Lawson, an English-born
gentleman who came to North Carolina in 1701. A surveyor, he had occasion to
make a number of expeditions to the western area of settlement, where he came to
know the Indians quite well. The first document contains a favorable description
of Indian life from Lawson's* History of North Carolina *(1709).*

*A more common view held by the colonists saw the Indians as "barbarous"
and "savage." A typical expression of this view is found in the second document,
an excerpt from a letter to the* Freeman's Journal and North American Intelligencer. *What policy toward the Indians does the author, Henry Brackenridge,
propose? Might motives other than those stated have accounted for Brackenridge's
hatred of the Indians?*

*By the time of the final document, 1805, the once-mighty Iroquois shared the
fate of other Indians before them: encroachment on their lands and pressure to
abandon their religion and way of life. The document presents a speech by Red
Jacket, a Seneca warrior and subchief. Born in 1751, Red Jacket was old enough
to have been active during the years when Iroquois power and prestige were at their
height. Now he headed what detractors called the "pagan faction"—Iroquois who
sought to maintain their traditional culture and to keep European influences outside
the borders of their reservation. In this speech, Red Jacket is replying to missionary
Cram's suggestion that Native Americans convert to Christianity and accept European ways. What is Red Jacket's view of the European assault upon Indian life?*

5

ESSAY

The Seneca Nation of Indians
Anthony F. C. Wallace

A Seneca village in the eighteenth century was a few dozen houses scattered in a meadow. No plan of streets or central square defined a neat settlement pattern. The older men remembered days when towns were built between the forks of streams, protected by moats and palisades, and the dwellings within regularly spaced. But these fortified towns were no longer made, partly because of their earlier vulnerability to artillery and partly because times had become more peaceful anyway after the close of the fifty-odd years of war between 1649 and 1701. Now a village was simply an area within which individual families and kin groups built or abandoned their cabins at will; such focus as the area had for its several hundred inhabitants was provided by the council house (itself merely an enlarged dwelling), where the religious and political affairs of the community were transacted. Year by year the size of a village changed, depending on wars and rumors of war, the shifts of the fur trade, private feuds and family quarrels, the reputation of chiefs, the condition of the soil for corn culture, and the nearness of water and firewood. The same village might, over a hundred years' time, meander over a settlement area ten or fifteen miles square, increasing and decreasing in size, sometimes splitting up into several little settlements and sometimes coalescing into one, and even acquiring (and dropping) new names in addition to the generic name, which usually endured.

The traditional Iroquois dwelling unit was called a longhouse. It was a dark, noisy, smoke-filled family barracks; a rectangular, gable-roofed structure anywhere from fifty to seventy-five feet in length, constructed of sheets of elm bark lashed on stout poles, housing up to fifty or sixty people. The roof was slotted (sometimes with a sliding panel for rainy days) to let out some of the smoke that eddied about the ceiling. There was only one entrance, sometimes fitted with a wooden or bark door on wooden hinges, and sometimes merely curtained by a bearskin robe. Entering, one gazed in the half-light down a long, broad corridor or alleyway, in the center of which, every twelve or fifteen feet, smoldered a small fire. On opposite sides of each fire, facing one another, were double-decker bunks, six feet wide and about twelve feet long. An entire family— mother, father, children, and various other relatives—might occupy one or two of these compartments. They slept on soft furs in the lower bunks.

SOURCE: *The Death and Rebirth of the Seneca* by Anthony F. C. Wallace. Copyright © 1969 by Anthony F. C. Wallace. Reprinted by permission of Alfred A. Knopf, Inc.

[handwritten margin note: vermillion]

[handwritten margin note: beads made from shells]

Guns, masks, moccasins, clothing, cosmetic paint, wampum, knives, hatchet, food, and the rest of a Seneca family's paraphernalia were slung on the walls and on the upper bunk. Kettles, braided corn, and other suspendable items hung from the joists, which also supported pots over the fire. Each family had about as much room for permanent quarters as might be needed for all of them to lie down and sleep, cook their meals, and stow their gear. Privacy was not easily secured because other families lived in the longhouse; people were always coming and going, and the fires glowed all night. In cold or wet weather or when the snow lay two or three feet deep outside, doors and roof vents had to be closed, and the longhouses became intolerably stuffy—acrid with smoke and the reeking odors of leftover food and sweating flesh. Eyes burned and throats choked. But the people were nonetheless tolerably warm, dry, and (so it is said) cheerful.

The inhabitants of a longhouse were usually kinfolk. A multifamily longhouse was, theoretically, the residence of a maternal lineage: an old woman and her female descendants, together with unmarried sons, and the husbands and children of her married daughters. The totem animal of the clan to which the lineage belonged—Deer, Bear, Wolf, Snipe, or whatever it might be—was carved above the door and painted red. In this way directions were easier to give, and the stranger knew where to seek hospitality or aid. But often—especially in the middle of the eighteenth century—individual families chose to live by themselves in smaller cabins, only eighteen by twenty feet or so in size, with just one fire. As time went on, the old longhouses disintegrated and were abandoned, and by the middle of the century the Iroquois were making their houses of logs.

[handwritten margin note: a type of wading bird (usually in marshy areas)]

Around and among the houses lay the cornfields. Corn was a main food. Dried and pounded into meal and then boiled into a hot mush, baked into dumplings, or cooked in whole kernels together with beans and squash and pieces of meat in the thick soups that always hung in kettles over the fires, it kept the people fed. In season, meats, fresh fruits, herb teas, fried grasshoppers, and other delicacies added spice and flavor to the diet. But the Iroquois were a cornfed people. They consumed corn when it was fresh and stored it underground for the lean winter months. The Seneca nation alone raised as much as a million bushels of corn each year; the cornfields around a large village might stretch for miles, and even scattered clearings in the woods were cultivated. Squash, beans, and tobacco were raised in quantity, too. Domesticated animals were few, even after the middle of the century: some pigs, a few chickens, not many horses or cattle. The responsibility for carrying on this extensive agricultural establishment rested almost entirely on the women. Armed with crude wooden hoes and digging-sticks, they swarmed over the fields in gay, chattering work bees, proceeding from field to field to hoe, to plant, to weed, and to harvest. An individual woman might, if she wished, "own" a patch of corn, or an apple or peach orchard, but there was little reason for insisting on private tenure: the work was more happily done communally, and in the absence of a regular market, a surplus was of little personal advantage, especially if the winter were hard and other families needed corn. In such circumstances hoarding led only to hard feelings and strained relations as well as the possibility of future difficulty in getting corn for oneself and one's family. All land was national land; an individual could occupy and use a portion of it and maintain as much privacy in the tenure as he wished, but this usufruct title reverted to the nation when the land was abandoned. There was little reason to bother about individual ownership of real estate anyway: there was plenty of land. Economic security for both men and women lay in a proper recognition of one's obligation to family, clan, community, and nation, and in efficient and cooperative performance on team activities, such as working bees, war parties, and diplomatic missions.

If the clearing with its cornfields bounded the world of women, the forest was the realm of men. Most of the men hunted extensively, not only for deer, elk, and small game to use for food and clothing and miscellaneous household items, but for beaver, mink, and otter, the prime trade furs. Pelts were the gold of the woods. With them a man could buy guns, powder, lead, knives, hatchets, axes, needles and awls, scissors, kettles, traps, cloth, ready-made shirts, blankets, paint (for cosmetic purposes), and various notions: steel springs to pluck out disfiguring beard, scalp, and body hair; silver bracelets and armbands and tubes for coiling hair; rings to hang from nose and ears; mirrors; tinkling bells. Sometimes a tipsy hunter would give away his peltries for a keg of rum, treat his friends to a debauch, and wake up with a scolding wife and hungry children calling him a fool; another might, with equal improvidence, invest in a violin, or a horse, or a gaudy military uniform. But by and large, the products of the commercial hunt—generally conducted in the winter and often hundreds of miles from the home village, in the Ohio country or down the Susquehanna River—were exchanged for a limited range of European consumer goods, which had become, after five generations of contact with beaver-hungry French, Dutch, and English traders, economic necessities. Many of these goods were, indeed, designed to Indian specifications and manufactured solely for the Indian trade. An Iroquois man dressed in a linen breechcloth and calico shirt, with a woolen blanket over his shoulders, bedaubed with trade paint and adorned with trade armbands and earrings, carrying a steel knife, a steel hatchet, a clay pipe, and a rifled gun felt himself in no wise contaminated nor less an Indian than his stone-equipped great-great-grandfather. Iroquois culture had reached out and incorporated these things that Iroquois Indians wanted while at the same time Iroquois warriors chased off European missionaries, battled European soldiers to a standstill, and made obscene gestures when anyone suggested that they should emulate white society (made up, according to their information and experience, of slaves, cheating lawyers with pen and paper and ink, verbose politicians, hypocritical Christians, stingy tavern keepers, and thieving peddlers).

Behavior was governed not by published laws enforced by police, courts, and jails, but by oral tradition supported by a sense of duty, a fear of gossip, and a dread of retaliatory witchcraft. Theft, vandalism, armed robbery, were almost unknown. Public opinion, gently exercised, was sufficient to deter most persons from property crimes, for public opinion went straight to the heart of the matter: the *weakness* of the criminal. A young warrior steals someone else's cow—probably captured during a raid on a white settlement—and slaughters it to feed his hungry family. He does this at a time when other men are out fighting. No prosecution follows, no investigation, no sentence: the unhappy man is nonetheless severely punished, for the nickname "Cow-killer" is pinned to him, and he must drag it rattling behind him wherever he goes. People call him a coward behind his back and snicker when they tell white men, in his presence, a story of an unnamed Indian who killed cows when he should have been killing men. Such a curse was not generalized to the point of ostracism, however. The celebrated Red Jacket, about whom the "Cow-killer' story was told, vindicated his courage in later wars, became the principal spokesman for his nation, and was widely respected and revered. But he never lost the nickname.

Disputes between people rarely developed over property. Marital difficulties centering around infidelity, lack of support, or personal incompatibility were settled by mutual agreement. Commonly, in case of difficulty, the man left and the woman, with her children, remained with her mother. A few couples remained together for a lifetime; most had several marriages; a few changed mates almost with the season. Men might come to blows during drunken arguments over real or fancied slights to their masculine honor, over politics, or over the alleged mistreatment of their kinfolk. Such quarrels led at times to killings or to accusations of witchcraft. A murder (or its equivalent, the practice of witchcraft) was something to be settled by the victim's kinfolk; if they wished, they might kill the murderer or suspected witch without fear of retaliation from his family (provided that family agreed on his guilt). But usually a known killer would come to his senses, admit himself wrong, repent, and offer retribution in goods or services to the mourning family, who unless exceptionally embittered by an unprovoked and brutal killing were then expected to accept the blood money and end the matter.

Drunkenness was perhaps the most serious social problem. Two Moravian missionaries who visited the Iroquois country in 1750 had the misfortune to reach the Seneca towns at the end of June, when the men were just returning from Oswego, where they had sold their winter's furs, and were beginning to celebrate the start of summer leisure. Hard liquor was dissolving winter's inhibitions and regrets. At Canandaigua, the missionaries, who were guests at the house of a prominent warrior, had just explained the friendly nature of their errand when the rum arrived. "All the town was in a state of intoxication, and frequently rushed into our hut in this condition," complained the white men. "There was every reason to think that fighting might ensue, as there were many warriors among those who were perfectly mad with drink." After a sleepless night the missionaries traveled on, reaching the outskirts of Geneseo on the second of July. "The village," said the observers in surprise, "consisted of 40 or more large huts, and lies in a beautiful and pleasant region. A fine large plain, several miles in length and breadth, stretches out behind the village." But the kegs of rum had anticipated them. "When we caught sight of the town we heard a great noise of shouting and quarreling, from which we could infer that many of the inhabitants were intoxicated, and that we might expect to have an uncomfortable time. On entering the town we saw many drunken Indians, who looked mad with drink. . . ."

But such drunken debauches were only occasional rents in a fabric of polite social behavior. Other missionaries were more favorably impressed than the Moravians. The Seneca, said a Quaker scribe, "appear to be naturally as well calculated for social and rational enjoyment, as any people. They frequently visit each other in their houses, and spend much of their time in friendly intercourse. They are also mild and hospitable, not only among themselves, but to strangers, and good natured in the extreme, except when their natures are perverted by the inflammatory influence of spirituous liquors. In their social interviews, as well as public councils, they are careful not to interrupt one another in conversation, and generally make short speeches. This truly laudable mark of good manners, enables them to transact all their public business with decorum and regularity, and more strongly impresses on their mind and memory, the result of their deliberations." . . .

During the seventeenth and eighteenth centuries Iroquois men earned a reputation among the French and English colonists for being the most astute diplomatically and most dangerous militarily of all the Indians of the Northeast. Yet at the same time the Iroquois were famous for the "matriarchal" nature of their economic and social institutions. After the colonial era came to an end with the victory of the United States in the Revolutionary War, the traditional diplomatic and military role of the Iroquois men was sharply limited by the circumstances of reservation life. Simultaneously, the "matriarchal" character of certain of their economic, kinship, and political institutions was drastically diminished. These changes were codified by the prophet Handsome Lake. . . . The changes in kinship behavior that he recommended, and which to a considerable degree were carried out by his followers, amounted to a shift in dominance

10

from the mother-daughter relationship to that of the husband-wife. Handsome Lake's reforms thus were a sentence of doom upon the traditional quasi-matriarchal system of the Iroquois.

The Iroquois were described as matriarchal because of the important role women played in the formal political organization. The men were responsible for hunting, for warfare, and for diplomacy, all of which kept them away from their households for long periods of time, and all of which were essential to the survival of Iroquois society. An expedition of any kind was apt to take months or even years, for the fifteen thousand or so Iroquois in the seventeenth and eighteenth centuries ranged over an area of about a million square miles. It is not an exaggeration to say that the full-time business of an Iroquois man was travel, in order to hunt, trade, fight, and talk in council. But the women stayed at home. Thus, an Iroquois village might be regarded as a collection of strings, hundreds of years old, of successive generations of women, always domiciled in their longhouses near their cornfields in a clearing while their sons and husbands traveled in the forest on supportive errands of hunting and trapping, of trade, of war, and of diplomacy.

The women exercised political power in three main circumstances. First, whenever one of the forty-nine chiefs of the great intertribal League of the Iroquois died, the senior women of his lineage nominated his successor. Second, when tribal or village decisions had to be made, both men and women attended a kind of town meeting, and while men were the chiefs and normally did the public speaking, the women caucused behind the scenes and lobbied with the spokesmen. Third, a woman was entitled to demand publicly that a murdered kinsman or kinswoman be replaced by a captive from a non-Iroquois tribe, and her male relatives, particularly lineage kinsmen, were morally obligated to go out in a war party to secure captives, whom the bereaved woman might either adopt or consign to torture and death. Adoption was so frequent during the bloody centuries of the beaver wars and the colonial wars that some Iroquois villages were preponderantly composed of formally adopted war captives. In sum, Iroquois women were entitled formally to select chiefs, to participate in consensual politics, and to start wars.

Thus the Iroquois during the two centuries of the colonial period were a population divided, in effect, into two parts: sedentary females and nomadic males. The men were frequently absent in small or large groups for prolonged periods of time on hunting, trading, war, and diplomatic expeditions, simultaneously protecting the women from foreign attack and producing a cash crop of skins, furs, and scalps, which they exchanged for hardware and dry goods. These activities, peripheral in a geographical sense, were central to the economic and political welfare of the Six Nations. The preoccupation of Iroquois men with these tasks and the pride they took in their successful pursuit cannot be overestimated. But the system depended on a complementary role for women. They had to be economically self-sufficient through horticulture during the prolonged absences of men, and they maintained genealogical and political continuity in a matrilineal system in which the primary kin relationship (not necessarily the primary social relationship) was the one between mother and daughter.

Such a quasi-matriarchy, of course, had a certain validity in a situation where the division of labor between the sexes required that men be geographically peripheral to the households that they helped to support and did defend. Given the technological, economic, and military circumstances of the time, such an arrangement was a practical one. But it did have an incidental consequence: It made the relationship between husband and wife an extremely precarious one. Under these conditions it was convenient for the marital system to be based on virtually free sexual choice, the mutual satisfaction of spouses, and easy separation. Couples chose one another for personal reasons; free choice was limited, in effect, only by the prohibition of intraclan marriage. Marriages were apt to fray when a husband traveled too far, too frequently, for too long. On his return, drunken quarreling, spiteful gossip, parental irresponsibility, and flagrant infidelity might lead rapidly to the end of the relationship. The husband, away from the household for long periods of time, was apt in his travels to establish a liaison with a woman whose husband was also away. The wife, temporarily abandoned, might for the sake of comfort and economic convenience take up with a locally available man. Since such relationships were, in effect, in the interest of everyone in the longhouse, they readily tended to become recognized as marriages. The emotional complications introduced by these serial marriages were supposed to be resolved peacefully by the people concerned. The traveling husband who returned to find his wife living with someone else might try to recover her; if she preferred to remain with her new husband, however, he was not entitled to punish her or her new lover, but instead was encouraged to find another wife among the unmarried girls or wives with currently absent husbands. . . .

The basic ideal of manhood was that of "the good hunter." Such a man was self-disciplined, autonomous, responsible. He was a patient and efficient huntsman, a generous provider to his family and nation, and a loyal and thoughtful friend and clansman. He was also a stern and ruthless warrior in avenging any injury done to those under his care. And he was always stoical and indifferent to privation, pain, and even death. Special prominence could be achieved by those who, while adequate in all respects, were outstanding in one or another dimension of this ideal. The patient and thoughtful man with a skin "seven thumbs thick" (to make him indifferent to spiteful gossip, barbed wit, and social pressures generally) might become a sachem or a "distinguished name"—a "Pine Tree" chief. An eloquent man with a good memory and indestructible poise might be

chief

12

a council speaker and represent clan, nation, even the confederacy in far-flung diplomatic ventures. And the stern and ruthless warrior (always fighting, at least according to the theory, to avenge the death or insult of a blood relative or publicly avowed friend) might become a noted war-captain or an official war-chief. The war-captain ideal, open as it was to all youths, irrespective of clan and lineage or of special intellectual quali-fications, was perhaps the most emulated.

In the seventeenth century an Onondaga war-captain named Aharihon bore the reputation of being the greatest warrior of the country. He realized the ideal of autonomous responsibility to virtually pathological perfection. Let us note what is told of Aharihon in the *Jesuit Relations*.

Aharihon was a man of dignified appearance and imposing carriage, grave, polished in manner, and self-contained. His brother had been killed about 1654 in the wars with the Erie, a tribe westward of the Iroquois. As clansman and close relative, he was entitled—indeed obligated—either to avenge his brother's death by killing some Erie people or by adopting a war captive to take his place. Aharihon within a few years captured or had presented to him for adoption forty men. Each of them he burned to death over a slow fire, because, as he said, "he did not believe that there was any one worthy to occupy his [brother's] place." Father Lalemant [a Jesuit missionary] was present when another young man, newly captured, was given to Aharihon as a substitute for the deceased brother. Aharihon let the young man believe that he was adopted and need have no further fear, and "presented to him four dogs, upon which to hold his feast of adoption. In the middle of the feast, while he was rejoicing and singing to entertain the guests, Aharihon arose, and told the company that this man too must die in atonement for his brother's death. The poor lad was astounded at this, and turned toward the door to make his escape, but was stopped by two men who had orders to burn him. On the fourteenth of February, in the evening, they began with his feet, intending to roast him, at a slow fire, as far up as the waist, during the greater part of the night. After midnight, they were to let him rally his strength and sleep a little until daybreak, when they were to finish this fatal tragedy. In his torture, the poor man made the whole village resound with his cries and groans. He shed great tears, contrary to the usual custom, the victim commonly glo-rying to be burned limb by limb, and opening his lips only to sing; but, as this one had not expected death, he wept and cried in a way that touched even these Barbarians. One of Aharihon's relatives was so moved with pity, that he advised ending the sufferer's torments by plunging a knife into his breast—which would have been a deed of mercy, had the stab been mortal. However, they were induced to continue the burning without interruption, so that before day he ended both his sufferings and his life." Aharihon's career of death continued without interruption, and by 1663 he was able to boast that he had killed sixty men with his own hand and had burned fully eighty men over slow fire. He kept count by tattooing a mark on his thigh for each successive victim. He was known then as the Captain General of the Iroquois and was nicknamed Nero by the Frenchmen at Montreal because of his cruelty. . . .

But this voracious captain was not renowned among the Onondaga as a killer only. He was, on the contrary, also a trusted ambassador, dispatched on occasion to Montreal on missions of peace. He was, in a word, a noted man. He was a killer, but he was not an indiscriminate killer; he killed only those whom it was his right to kill, tortured only those whom he had the privilege of torturing, always as an expression of respect for his dead brother. And although his kinfolk sometimes felt he was a little extreme in his stern devotion to his brother's memory, they did not feel that he was any the less a fine man, or that they had a right to interfere with his impulses; they were willing to entrust the business of peace, as well as war, to his hand. . . .

With this sort of man serving as an ego-ideal, held up by sanction and by praise to youthful eyes, it is not remarkable that young men were ambitious to begin the practice of war. All had seen captives tortured to death; all had known relatives lost in war whose death demanded revenge or replacement. The young men went out on practice missions as soon as they were big enough to handle firearms; "infantile bands, armed with hatchets and guns which they can hardly carry, do not fail to spread fear and horror everywhere." Even as late as the middle of the eighteenth century, Handsome Lake and his brothers and nephews were still busy at the old business of war for the sake of war. Cornplanter became a noted war-captain; Blacksnake, his nephew, was one of the official war-chiefs of the Seneca nation; and Handsome Lake himself took part in the scalping-party pattern as a young man. But Handsome Lake became a sachem and later a prophet, and he never gloried in the numbers of men he killed as his brother Cornplanter (somewhat guiltily) did. "While I was in the use of arms I killed seven persons and took three and saved their lives," said Cornplanter. And Blacksnake, in later life, told with relish of his exploits as a warrior. "We had a good fight there," he would say. "I have killed how many I could not tell, for I pay no attention to or kept [no] account of it, it was great many, for I never have it at all my Battles to think about kepting account what I'd killed at one time. . . ."

The cultivation of the ideal of autonomous responsibility—and the suppression of it antinomy, dependency—began early in life. Iroquois children were carefully trained to think for themselves but to act for others. Parents were protective, permissive, and sparing of punishment; they encouraged children to play at imitating adult behavior but did not criticize or condemn fumbling early efforts; they maintained a cool detachment, both physically and verbally, avoiding the intense confrontations of love and anger between parent and child to which Europeans were accustomed.

n: contradiction between 2 apparently
reasonable laws or principles

Children did not so much live in a child's world as grow up freely in the interstices of an adult culture. The gain was an early self-reliance and enjoyment of responsibility; the cost, perhaps, was a lifelong difficulty in handling feelings of dependency.

The Seneca mother gave birth to her child in the privacy of the woods, where she retired for a few hours when her time came, either alone or in the company of an older woman who served as midwife and, if the weather was cold, built and tended a fire. She had prepared for this event by eating sparingly and exercising freely, which were believed (probably with good reason) to make the child stronger and the birth easier. The newborn infant was washed in cold water, or even in snow, immediately after parturition and then wrapped in skins or a blanket. If the birth were a normal one, the mother walked back to the village with her infant a few hours afterwards to take up the duties of housewife. The event was treated as the consummation of a healthful process rather than as an illness. The infant spent much of its first nine months swaddled from chin to toe and lashed to a cradleboard. The child's feet rested against a footboard; a block of wood was placed between the heels of a girl to mold her feet to an inward turn. Over its head stretched a hoop, which could be draped with a thin cloth to keep away flies or to protect the child from the cold. The board and its wrappings were often lavishly decorated with silver trinkets and beadwork embroidery. The mother was able to carry the child in the board, suspended against her back, by a tumpline around her forehead; the board could be hung from the limb of a tree while she hoed corn; and it could be converted into a crib by suspending it on a rack of poles laid horizontally on forks stuck in the ground. The mother was solicitous of the child's comfort, nursed it whenever it cried, and loosened it from the board several times a day to change the moss that served as a diaper and to give it a chance to romp. The children, however, tended to cry when released from the board, and their tranquility could often be restored only by putting them back. Babies were seldom heard crying.

The mother's feeling for her children was intense; indeed, to one early observer it appeared that "Parental Tenderness" was carried to a "dangerous Indulgence." Another early writer remarked, "The mothers love their children with an extreme passion, and although they do not reveal this in caresses, it is nevertheless real." Mothers were quick to express resentment of any restraint or injury or insult offered to the child by an outsider. During the first few years the child stayed almost constantly with the mother, in the house, in the fields, or on the trail, playing and performing small tasks under her direction. The mother's chief concern during this time was to provide for the child and to protect it, to "harden" it by baths in cold water, but not to punish. Weaning was not normally attempted until the age of three or four, and such control as the child obtained over its excretory functions was achieved voluntarily, not as a result of consistent punishment for mistakes. Early sexual curiosity and experimentation were regarded as a natural childish way of behaving, out of which it would, in due time, grow. Grandparents might complain that small children got into everything, but the small child was free to romp, to pry into things, to demand what it wanted, and to assault its parents, without more hazard of punishment than the exasperated mother's occasionally blowing water in its face or dunking it in a convenient river.

The years between about eight or nine and the onset of puberty were a time of easy and gradual learning. At the beginning of this period the beginnings of the differentiation of the roles of boys and girls were laid down. The girls were kept around the house, under the guidance of their mothers, and assigned to the lighter household duties and to helping in the fields. Boys were allowed to roam in gangs, playing at war, hunting with bows and arrows and toy hatchets, and competing at races, wrestling, and lacrosse. The first successes at hunting were greeted with praise and boasts of future greatness. Sometimes these roaming gangs spent days at a time away from the village, sleeping in the bush, eating wild roots and fruits, and hunting such small game as could be brought down by bow and arrow, blowgun, or snare. These gangs developed into war parties after the boys reached puberty. Among themselves, both in gangs and among siblings of the same family, the children's playgroups were not constantly supervised by parents and teachers, and the children governed themselves in good harmony. Said one close observer, "Children of the same family show strong attachments to each other, and are less liable to quarrel in their youthful days than is generally the case with white children."

The parents usually tried to maintain a calm moderation of behavior in dealing with their children, a lofty indifference alike to childish tantrums and seductive appeals for love. Hardihood, self-reliance, and independence of spirit were sedulously inculcated. When occasion presented itself, fathers, uncles, or other elder kinfolk instructed their sons in the techniques of travel, firemaking, the chase, war, and other essential arts of manhood, and the mothers correspondingly taught their daughters the way to hoe and plant the cornfields, how to butcher the meat, cook, braid corn, and other household tasks. But this instruction was presented, rather than enforced, as an opportunity rather than as a duty. On occasion the parent or other responsible adult talked to the child at length, "endeavoring," as a Quaker scribe gently put it, "to impress on its mind what it ought to do, and what to leave undone." If exhortation seemed inadequate in its effect, the mentor might ridicule the child for doing wrong, or gravely point out the folly of a certain course of action, or even warn him that he courted the rage of offended supernatural beings. Obedience as such was no virtue, however, and blows, whippings, or restraints of any kind, such as restriction to quarters, were rarely imposed, the faults of the child being left to his own reason and conscience to correct as he grew mature. With delicate perception the adults noted that childish faults "cannot be very great, before reason arrives at some degree of maturity."

Direct confrontation with the child was avoided, but when things got seriously out of hand, parents sometimes turned older children over to the gods for punishment. A troublesome child might be sent out into the dusk to meet Longnose, the legendary Seneca bogeyman. Longnose might even be impersonated in the flesh by a distraught parent. Longnose was a hungry cannibal who chased bad children when their parents were sleeping. He mimicked the child, crying loudly as he ran, but the parents would not wake up because Longnose had bewitched them. A child might be chased all night until he submitted and promised to behave. Theoretically, if a child remained stubborn, Longnose finally caught him and took him away in a huge pack-basket for a leisurely meal. And—although parents were not supposed to do this—an unusually stubborn infant *could* be threatened with punishment by the great False Faces themselves, who, when invoked for this purpose, might "poison" a child or "spoil his face." "I remember," recalled a Cayuga woman of her childhood, "how scared I was of the False-faces; I didn't know what they were. They are to scare away disease. They used to come into the house and up the stairs and I used to hide away under the covers. They even crawled under the bed and they made that awful sound. When I was bad my mother used to say the False-faces would get me. Once, I must have been only 4 or 5, because I was very little when I left Canada, but I remember it so well that when I think of it I can hear that cry now, and I was going along a road from my grandfather's; it was a straight road and I couldn't lose my way, but it was almost dark, and I had to pass through some timber and I heard that cry and that rattle. I ran like a flash of lightening and I can hear it yet."

At puberty some of the boys retired to the woods under the stewardship of an old man, where they fasted, abstained from any sort of sexual activity (which they had been free to indulge, to the limit of their powers, before), covered themselves with dirt, and mortified the flesh in various ways, such as bathing in ice water and bruising and gashing the shinbones with rocks. Dreams experienced during such periods of self-trial were apt to be regarded as visitations from supernatural spirits who might grant *orenda*, or magical power, to the dreamer, and who would maintain a special sort of guardianship over him. The person's connection with this supernatural being was maintained through a charm—such as a knife, a queerly shaped stone, or a bit of bone—which was connected with the dream through some association significant to the dreamer. Unlike many other tribes, however, the Iroquois apparently did not require these guardian-spirit visions for pubescent youths. Many youths were said not to have had their first vision until just before their first war party. Furthermore, any man could have a significant dream or vision at any time. Girls too went through a mild puberty ritual, retiring into the woods at first menstruation and paying particular attention to their dreams. With the termination of the menstrual period the girl returned to the household; but hereafter, whenever she menstruated, she would have to live apart in a hut, avoiding people, and being careful not to step on a path, or to cook and serve anyone's food, or (especially) to touch medicines, which would immediately lose their potency if she handled them.

The Europeans who observed this pattern of child experience were by no means unfavorably impressed although they were sometimes amazed. They commented, however, almost to a man, from early Jesuit to latter-day Quaker, on a consequence that stood out dramatically as they compared this "savage" maturation with "civilized." "There is nothing," wrote the Jesuit chronicler of the Iroquois mission in 1657, "for which these peoples have a greater horror than restraint. The very children cannot endure it, and live as they please in the houses of their parents, without fear of reprimand or chastisement." One hundred and fifty years later, the Quaker Halliday Jackson observed that "being indulged in most of their wishes, as they grow up, liberty, in its fullest extent, becomes their ruling passion." . . .

DOCUMENTS

The Indian as Noble Savage, 1709

The Victuals [diet] is common throughout the whole Kindred Relations [Family], and often the whole Town; especially when they are in Hunting-Quarters, then they all fare [eat] alike, whichsoever of them kills the Game. They are very kind and charitable to one another, but more especially to those of their own Nation; for if any one of them has suffered any Loss by Fire, or otherwise, they order the grieved person to make a Feast, and invite them all thereto, which, on the day appointed, they come to, and after every Man's Mess of Victuals is dealt to him, one of their Speakers, or grave old Men, makes an Harrangue, and acquaints the Company, That the Man's House has been burnt, wherein all his Goods were destroyed; That he and his Family very narrowly escaped; That he is every Man's Friend in that Company; and, That it is all their Duties to help him, as he would do to any of them had the like Misfortune befallen them. After this Oration is over, every Man, according to his Quality [status or rank], throws him down upon the Ground some Present. . . which very often amounts

SOURCE: John Lawson, *History of North Carolina* (Richmond: Garrett and Massie, 1951), 188–89, 208.

to treble the Loss he has suffered. The same Assistance they give to any man that wants to build a Cabin, or make a Canoe. They say it is our Duty thus to do; for there are several Works that one Man cannot effect, therefore we must give him our Help, otherwise our Society will fall, and we shall be deprived of those urgent Necessities which Life requires. They have no Fence to part one anothers Lots in their Corn-Fields, but every Man knows his own, and it scarce ever happens that they rob one another of so much as an Ear of Corn, which, if any is found to do, he is sentenced by the Elders to work and plant for him that was robbed, till he is recompensed for all the Damage he has suffered in his Corn-Field; and this is punctually performed, and the Thief held is Disgrace that steals from any of his Country-Folks. It often happens that a Woman is destitute of her Husband, and has a great many Children to maintain; such a Person they always help, and make their young men plant, reap, and do every thing that she is not capable of doing herself; yet they do not allow any one to be idle, but to employ themselves in some Work or other.

They never fight with one another unless drunk, nor do you ever hear any Scolding amongst them. They say the Europeans are always rangling and uneasy, and wonder they do not go out of this World, since they are so uneasy and discontented in it. All their Misfortunes and Losses end in Laughter; for if their Cabins take Fire, and all their Goods are burnt therein . . . yet such a Misfortune always ends in a hearty Fitt of Laughter, unless some of their Kinsfolks and Friends have lost their Lives. . . .

. . . there is one Vice very common everywhere, which I never found amongst them, which is, Envying other Men's happiness, because their station is not equal to, or above their Neighbors. Of this Sin I cannot say I ever saw an Example, though they are a People that set as great a Value upon themselves, as any sort of Men, in the World, upon which Account they find something Valuable in themselves above Riches. . . .

The Indian as Ruthless Savage, 1782

With regard to forming or making peace with this race [Indians], there are many ideas:

They have the shapes of men and may be of the human species, but certainly in their present state they approach nearer the character of Devils; take an Indian, is there any faith in him? Can you bind him by favors? Can you trust his word or confide in his promise? When he makes war upon you, when he takes you prisoner and has you in his power will he

SOURCE: Henry Brackenridge, letter to *Freeman's Journal and North American Intelligencer* (1782).

spare you? In this he departs from the law of nature, by which, according to Baron Montesquieu and every other man who thinks on the subject, it is unjustifiable to take away the life of him who submits; the conqueror in doing otherwise becomes a murderer, who ought to be put to death. On this principle are not the whole Indian nations murderers?

Many of them may have not had an opportunity of putting prisoners to death, but the sentiment which they entertain leads them invariably to this when they have it in their power or judge it expedient; these principles constitute them murderers, and they ought to be prevented from carrying them into execution, as we would prevent a common homicide, who should be mad enough to conceive himself justifiable in killing men.

The tortures which they exercise on the bodies of their prisoners, justify extermination. . . .

An Indian's View, 1805

Friend and brother, it was the will of the Great Spirit that we should meet together this day. He orders all things, and He has given us a fine day for our council. He has taken His garment from before the sun, and caused it to shine with brightness upon us; our eyes are opened, that we see clearly; our ears are unstopped, that we have been able to hear distinctly the words that you have spoken; for all these favours we thank the Great Spirit, and Him only. . . .

Brother, you say you want an answer to *your talk*, before you leave this place. It is right you should have one, as you are a great distance from home, and we do not wish to detain you; but we will first look back a little, and tell you what our fathers have told us, and what we have heard from the White people.

Brother, listen to what we say. There was a time when our forefathers owned this great land. Their seats extended from the rising to the setting sun. The Great Spirit had made it for the use of Indians. He had created the buffalo, the deer, and other animals for food. He made the bear and the beaver, and their skins served us for clothing. He had scattered them over the country, and taught us how to take them. He had caused the earth to produce corn for bread.

All this He had done for His Red children because he loved them. If we had any disputes about hunting grounds, they were generally settled without the shedding of much blood.

SOURCE: Red Jacket's reply to Missionary Cram at Buffalo, New York, in Samuel G. Goodrich, *Lives of Celebrated American Indians* (Boston: Bradbury, Soden and Co., 1843), 283–87.

But an evil day came upon us; your forefathers [the Europeans] crossed the great waters, and landed on this island. Their numbers were small; they found friends, and not enemies; they told us they had fled from their own country for fear of wicked men, and come here to enjoy their religion. They asked for a small seat; we took pity on them, granted their request, and they sat down amongst us; we gave them corn and meat; they gave us poison in return. The White people had now found our country, tidings were carried back, and more came amongst us; yet we did not fear them, we took them to be friends; they called us brothers; we believed them, and gave them a larger seat. At length their numbers had greatly increased; they wanted more land; they wanted our country. Our eyes were opened; and our minds became uneasy. Wars took place; Indians were hired to fight against Indians, and many of our people were destroyed. They also brought strong liquors among us; it was strong and powerful, and has slain thousands.

Brother, our seats were once large, and yours were very small; you have now become a great people, and we have scarcely a place left to spread our blankets; you have got our country, but are not satisfied; you want to force your religion upon us.

Brother, continue to listen. You say that you are sent to instruct us how to worship the Great Spirit agreeably to His mind, and if we do not take hold of the religion which you White people teach, we shall be unhappy hereafter; you say that you are right, and we are lost; how do we know this to be true? We understand that your religion is written in a book; if it was intended for us as well as you, why has not the Great Spirit given it to us, and not only to us, but why did He not give to our forefathers the knowledge of that book, with the means of understanding it rightly? We only know what you tell us about it; how shall we know when to believe, being so often deceived by the White people?

Brother, you say there is but one way to worship and serve the Great Spirit; if there is but one religion, why do you White people differ so much about it? Why not all agree, as you can all read the book?

Brother, we do not understand these things; we are told that your religion was given to your forefathers, and has been handed down from father to son. We also have a religion which was given to our forefathers, and has been handed down to us, their children. We worship that way. It teaches us to be thankful for all the favours we receive; to love each other, and to be united; we never quarrel about religion.

Brother, the Great Spirit has made us all; but He has made a great difference between His White and Red children; He has given us a different complexion and different customs; to you He has given the arts; to these He has not opened our eyes; we know these things to be true. Since He has made so great a difference between us in other things, why may we not conclude that He has given us a different religion according to our understanding? The Great Spirit does right; He knows what is best for his children; we are satisfied.

Brother, we do not wish to destroy your religion, or take it from you. We want only to enjoy our own.

Brother, you say you have not come to get our land or our money, but to enlighten our minds. I will now tell you that I have been at your meetings, and saw you collecting money from the meeting. I cannot tell what this money was intended for, but suppose it was for your minister, and if we should conform to your way of thinking, perhaps you may want some from us.

Brother, we are told that you have been preaching to White people in this place; these people are our neighbors, we are acquainted with them; we will wait a little while and see what effect your preaching has upon them. If we find it does them good, makes them honest, and less disposed to cheat Indians, we will then consider again what you have said.

Brother, you have now heard our answer to your talk, and this is all we have to say at present. As we are going to part, we will come and take you by the hand, and hope the Great Spirit will protect you on your journey, and return you safe to your friends.

CHAPTER 2

Conflicting Cultural Values
in Early America

European men and women constituted the second wave of permanent settlers on the shores of what today is the United States. As the essay "Looking Out for Number One" by T. H. Breen points out, there were significant differences among colonial settlements. Breen discusses early Virginia, a colony marked by greed and the exploitation of both people and natural resources.

The sharp contrast between Virginia and the New England colonies is illustrated in two documents following the essay. The first document, a letter written in 1623 by an indentured servant in Virginia to his parents in England, shows that the exploitation of human labor in Virginia was well underway at this early date.

The second document was written by John Winthrop, the first governor of the Massachusetts Bay Colony, during his journey to the New World in 1630. It clearly expresses the religious motives of the Puritan adventurers and sets forth the ideological goal that communal effort take precedence over individual ambition.

It is fascinating to contemplate how people from a common English background set off on such different paths of colonial development. In reading the essay and documents, consider how significant were the Virginians' hunger for profits and the Puritans' desire to establish a "Zion in the Wilderness" in determining the character of the two colonies. What did Winthrop mean by his declaration that "we shall be as a Citty upon a Hill"?

Winthrop, of course, was expressing an ideal. Within a generation of the founding of Virginia and Massachusetts, time and circumstances had done much to modify the original, and quite different, flavors of the two colonies. The Virginia colonists ultimately realized that their dreams of getting rich quickly were not to be fulfilled; eventually the expansion of agriculture contributed to the development of a more stable—but nonetheless prosperous—society. Massachusetts also represented a success story, though not the kind John Winthrop envisioned. By the end of the seventeenth century, profits from agriculture, fishing, and commerce had moved the eastern half of the colony beyond the "wilderness" status and diverted the attention of its citizens from the mission of creating a new Zion. Although the Puritan spirit would long continue to influence the Massachusetts population, its all-pervasive influence was broken.

ESSAY

Looking Out for Number One: Conflicting Cultural Values in Early Seventeenth-Century Virginia

T. H. Breen

Despite their common English background, the thousands of European men and women who migrated to Barbados, Virginia, and New England during the seventeenth century created strikingly different societies in the New World. . . .

This essay examines the creation of a distinct culture in Virginia roughly between 1617 and 1630. Although early Virginians shared certain general ideas, attitudes, and norms with other English migrants, their operative values were quite different from those that shaped social and institutional behavior in places such as Massachusetts Bay. Virginia's physical environment, its extensive network of navigable rivers, its rich soil, its

SOURCE: T. H. Breen, "Looking Out for Number One: Conflicting Cultural Values in Early Seventeenth Century Virginia," *South Atlantic Quarterly* 78 (Summer 1979): 342–360. Copyright © 1979 Duke University Press.

ability to produce large quantities of marketable tobacco, powerfully reinforced values which the first settlers carried to America. The interplay between a particular variant of Jacobean* culture and a specific New World setting determined the character of Virginia's institutions, habits of personal interaction, and patterns of group behavior that persisted long after the early adventurers had died or returned to the mother country. . . .

The early settlers in Virginia were an unusual group of Jacobeans. In no way did they represent a random sample of seventeenth-century English society or a cross section of English values. While little is known about the specific origins or backgrounds of most settlers, we do have a fairly clear idea of what sort of inducements persuaded men and women to move to Virginia. The colony's promotional literature emphasized economic opportunity, usually quick and easy riches. In his "True Relation of the State of Virginia" written in 1616, for example, John Rolfe pitied England's hard-working farmers who barely managed to make ends meet. "What happiness might they enjoy in Virginia," Rolfe mused, "where they may have ground for nothing, more than they can manure, reap more fruits and profits with half the labour." And in 1622 Peter Arundle, overlooking the colony's recent military setbacks at the hands of the Indians, assured English friends that "any laborious honest man may in a short time become rich in this Country." It was a compelling dream, one which certain Englishmen were all too willing to accept as truth. Indeed, so many persons apparently risked life and possessions in the illusive search for the main chance that John Harvey, a future Royal Governor of Virginia, begged men of integrity on both sides of the Atlantic to control "the rumors of plenty to be found at all tyme[s] in Virginia."

The lure of great wealth easily obtained held an especially strong appeal for a specific type of seventeenth-century Englishman, individuals who belonged to a distinct subculture within Jacobean society. By all accounts, early Virginia drew a disproportionately large number of street toughs, roughnecks fresh from the wars in Ireland, old soldiers looking for new glory, naive adventurers, mean-spirited sea captains, marginal persons attempting to recoup their losses. If contemporaries are to be believed, Virginia found itself burdened with "many unruly gallants packed thether by their friends to escape ill destinies." Even Sir Thomas Dale, himself a recent veteran of English military expeditions in Holland, was shocked by the colony's settlers, "so prophane, so riotous, so full of Mutenie and treasonable Intendments" that they provided little "testimonie beside their names that they are Christians."

Even if Dale exaggerated, there is no reason to question that the colonists were highly individualistic, motivated by the hope of material

[*The people and culture of England during the reign of James I, 1603–1625.]

gain, and in many cases, not only familiar with violence but also quite prepared to employ it to obtain their own ends in the New World. By and large, they appear to have been extremely competitive and suspicious of other men's motives. Mutiny and anarchy sometimes seemed more attractive than obeying someone else's orders. Few of the colonists showed substantial interest in creating a permanent settlement. For the adventurer, Virginia was not a new home, not a place to carry out a divine mission, but simply an area to be exploited for private gain. It was this "variant" strain of values—a sense of living only for the present or near future, a belief that the environment could and should be forced to yield quick financial returns, an assumption that everyone was looking out for number one and hence that cooperative ventures of all sorts were bound to fail— that help to account for the distinctive patterns of social and institutional behavior found in early Virginia.

The transfer of these variant values, of course, only partially explains Virginia's cultural development. The attitudes, beliefs, and ideas that the founders brought with them to the New World interacted with specific environmental conditions. The settlers' value system would certainly have withered in a physical setting that offered no natural resources capable of giving plausibility to the adventurers' original expectations. If by some chance the Virginians had landed in a cold, rocky, inhospitable country devoid of valuable marketable goods, then they would probably have given up the entire venture and like a defeated army, straggled home. That is exactly what happened in 1607 to the unfortunate men who settled in Sagadohoc, Maine, a tiny outpost that failed to produce instant wealth. Virginia almost went the way of Sagadohoc. The first decade of its history was filled with apathy and disappointment, and at several points, the entire enterprise seemed doomed. The privatistic values that the colonists had carried to Jamestown, a tough, exploitive competitive individualism were dysfunctional—even counter-productive—in an environment which offered up neither spices nor gold, neither passages to China nor a subject population easily subdued and exploited. In fact, before 1617 this value system generated only political faction and petty personal violence, things that a people struggling for survival could ill-afford.

The successful cultivation of tobacco altered the course of Virginia's cultural development. Clearly, in an economic sense, the crop saved the colony. What is less obvious but no less true, is that the discovery of a lucrative export preserved the founders' individualistic values. Suddenly, after ten years of error and failure, the adventurers' transported values were no longer at odds with their physical environment. The settlers belatedly stumbled across the payoff; the forests once so foreboding, so unpromising, could now be exploited with a reasonable expectation of quick return. By 1617 the process was well-advanced, and as one planter reported, "the streets, and all other spare places planted with To-bacco . . . The Colonie dispersed all about, planting *Tobacco.*"

The interplay between the settlers' value system and their environment involved more than economic considerations. Once a market for tobacco had been assured, people spread out along the James and York Rivers. Whenever possible, they formed what the directors of the Virginia Company* called private hundreds, small plantations frequently five or more miles apart which groups of adventurers developed for their own profit. By 1619 forty-four separate patents for private plantations had been issued, and by the early 1620's a dispersed settlement pattern, long to be a characteristic of Virginia society, was well established. The dispersion of the colony's population was a cultural phenomenon. It came about not simply because the Virginia soil was unusually well suited for growing tobacco or because its deep rivers provided easy access to the interior, but because men holding privatistic values regarded the land as an exploitable resource, and within their structure of priorities, the pursuit of private gain outranked the creation of corporate communities.

The scattering of men and women along the colony's waterways, their self-imposed isolation, obviously reduced the kind of ongoing face-to-face contacts that one associates with the villages of seventeenth-century New England. A migrant to Virginia tended to be highly competitive and to assume that other men would do unto him as he would do unto them— certainly an unpleasant prospect. Dispersion heightened this sense of suspicion. Because communication between private plantations was difficult, Virginians possessed no adequate means to distinguish the truth about their neighbors from malicious rumor, and lacking towns and well-developed voluntary organizations, without shared rituals, ceremonies, even market days, they drew increasingly distrustful of whatever lay beyond the perimeter of their own few acres.

The kind of human relationships that developed in colonial Virginia graphically reveal the effect of highly individualistic values upon social behavior. In this settlement only two meaningful social categories existed, a person was either free or dependent, either an exploiter or a resource. There was no middle ground. Those men who held positions of political and economic power treated indentured servants and slaves not as human beings, but as instruments to produce short-run profits. As a consequence of this outlook, life on the private plantations was a degrading experience for thousands of men and women who arrived in Virginia as bonded laborers. Whatever their expectations about the colony may have been before they migrated, the servants' reality consisted of poor food, meager

[*The private corporate body, headquartered in London, that organized and financed the early settlement of Virginia.

clothing, hard work, and more often than not, early death. The leading planters showed little interest in reforming these conditions. The servants were objects, things to be gambled away in games of chance, beaten or abused, and then, replaced when they wore out.

But dependence has another side. In Virginia dominance went hand in hand with fear, for no matter how tractable, how beaten down, the servants may have appeared, both masters and laborers recognized the potential for violence inherent in such relationships. In the early 1620's several worried planters complained that Captain John Martin, a long-standing troublemaker for the Virginia Company, "hath made his owne Territory there a receptacle of Vagabonds and bankerupts & other disorderly persons." Whether the rumors of Martin's activities were accurate is not the point. In such a society a gathering of "Vagabonds" represented a grave threat, a base from which the exploited could harass their former masters. The anxiety resurfaced in 1624 when the Virginia Company lost its charter and no one in the colony knew for certain who held legitimate authority. In shrill rhetoric that over the course of a century would become a regular feature of Virginia statute books, the colony's Assembly immediately ordered that "no person within this Colonie upon the rumor of supposed change and alterations [may] presume to be disobedient to the presente Government, nor servants to theire privatt officers masters or overseers, at their utmost perills."

The distrust that permeated Virginia society poisoned political institutions. Few colonists seem to have believed that local rulers would on their own initiative work for the public good. Instead, they assumed that persons in authority would use their office for personal gain. One settler called Governor George Yeardley, a man who grew rich directing public affairs, "the right worthy statesman for his own profit." William Capps, described simply as an old planter, referred to the governor as an "old smoker" and claimed that this official had "stood for a cypher whilst the Indians stood ripping open our guts." Cynicism about the motives of the colony's leaders meant that few citizens willingly sacrificed for the good of the state. In fact, Virginia planters seem to have regarded government orders as a threat to their independence, almost as a personal affront. William Strachey, secretary of the colony, condemned what he labeled the general "want of government." He reported, "every man overvaluing his owne worth, would be a Commander: every man underprising anothers value, denied to be commanded." Other colonists expressed agreement with Strachey's views. During the famous first meeting of the House of Burgesses in 1619, the representatives of the various plantations twice commented upon the weakness of Virginia's governing institutions. Toward the end of the session, they declared that whatever laws they passed in the future should go into immediate effect without special authorization from London, "for otherwise this people . . . would in a shorte time growe so insolent, as they would shake off all government, and there would be no living among them."

The colonists' achievements in education and religion were meager. From time to time, Virginians commented upon the importance of churches and schools in their society, but little was done to transform rhetoric into reality. Church buildings were in a perpetual state of decay; ministers were poorly supported by their parishioners. An ambitious plan for a college came to nothing, and schools for younger children seem to have been nonexistent. The large distances between plantations and the pressure to keep every able-bodied person working in the fields, no doubt discouraged the development of local schools and parish churches, but the colony's dispersed settlement plan does not in itself explain the absence of these institutions. A colonywide boarding school could have been constructed in Jamestown, a Harvard of Virginia, but the colony's planters were incapable of the sustained, cooperative effort that such a project would have required. They responded to general societal needs as individuals, not as groups. Later in the seventeenth century some successful planters sent their sons at great expense to universities in England and Scotland, but not until the end of the century did the colonists found a local college.

An examination of Virginia's military policies between 1617 and 1630 provides the clearest link between social values and institutional behavior. During this important transitional period, military affairs were far better recorded than were other social activities, and the historian can trace with a fair degree of confidence how particular military decisions reflected the colonists' value system. And second, in any society military efforts reveal a people's social priorities, their willingness to sacrifice for the common good, and their attitudes toward the allocation of community resources. Certainly, in early Virginia, maintaining a strong defense should have been a major consideration. Common sense alone seemed to dictate that a group of settlers confronted with a powerful Indian confederation and foreign marauders would, in military matters at least, cooperate for their own safety. But in point of fact, our common sense was not the rule of the seventeenth-century Virginian. The obsession with private profits was a more compelling force than was the desire to create a dependable system of self-defense. This destructive individualism disgusted John Pory, at one time the colony's secretary of state. In 1620 he reported that Governor Yeardley asked the men of Jamestown "to contribute some labor to a bridge, and to certaine platformes to mounte greate ordinance upon, being both for the use and defense of the same Citty, and so of themselves; yet they repyned as much as if all their goods had been taken from them."

Virginians paid dearly for their failure to work together. On March 22, 1622, the Indians of the region launched a coordinated attack on the scattered, poorly defended white settlements, and before the colonists could react, 347 of them had been killed. . . . The Massacre and the events of the months that followed provide rare insight into the workings of the Virginia culture. The shock of this defeat called into question previous institutional policies—not just military ones—and some colonists even saw the setback as an opportunity to reform society, to develop a new set of values.

Virginia's vulnerability revealed to some men the need to transform the privatistic culture into a more tightly knit, cooperative venture. Local rulers bravely announced that "this Massacre will prove much to the speedie advancement of the Colony and much to the benefitt of all those that shall nowe come thither." No longer would the planters live so far apart. Shortsighted dreams of tobacco fortunes would be laid aside, and the people would join together in the construction of genuine towns. And most important, the settlers would no longer evade their military responsibilities. As the members of the Virginia Council wrote only a month after the Massacre, "our first and princypall care should have beene for our safetie . . . yet its very necessarie for us yett at last, to laye a better and surer foundation for the tyme to come." But despite the death and destruction and despite the bold declarations about a new start, the colonists proceeded to repeat the very activities that contemporary commentators agreed had originally caused the people's immense suffering.

Even though the Indians remained a grave threat to security throughout the 1620's, the settlers continued to grumble about the burden of military service. Each person seemed to assess the tragedy only in personal terms—how, in other words, had the Indian Massacre affected his ability to turn a profit. By the end of the summer of 1622, there were unmistakable signs that many people no longer regarded the defeat of the Indians as a community responsibility. Few men talked of the common good; fewer still seemed prepared to sacrifice their lives or immediate earning power in order to preserve the colony from a second disaster.

Even as the governor and his council were weighing the various military alternatives, colonists were moving back to their isolated frontier plantations. The dispersion of fighting men, of course, seemed to invite new military defeats. But the danger from the Indians, although clearly perceived, was not sufficient to deter Virginians from taking up possessions which one person declared were "larger than 100 tymes their Nomber were able to Cultivate." In a poignant letter to his parents in England, a young servant, Richard Frethorne, captured the sense of doom that hung over the private plantations. "We are but 32 to fight against 3000 [Indians] if they should Come," he explained, "and the nighest helpe that Wee have is ten miles of us, and when the rogues overcame this place last [Martin's Hundred], they slew 80 Persons how then shall wee doe for wee lye even in their teeth, they may easily take us but that God is mercefull." Frethorne wrote this letter in March 1623, just twelve months after the Massacre had revealed to all the survivors the consequences of lying in the Indians' teeth.

The Virginia Council protested to colonial administrators in England, "It is noe smale difficultie and griefe unto us to maintaine a warr by unwillinge people, who . . . Crye out of the loss of Tyme against their Commanders, *in a warr where nothinge is to be gained.*" By contrast, the village militia in Massachusetts Bay provided an effective fighting force precisely because the soldiers trusted those persons who remained at home. In theory, at least, most New Englanders defined their lives in terms of the total community, not in terms of private advancement, and the troops had no reason to believe that their friends and neighbors would try to profit from their sacrifice. But in Virginia long before the massive enslavement of black Africans, human relationships were regarded as a matter of pounds and pence, and each day one man chased the Indians through the wilderness or helped build a fortification, another man grew richer growing tobacco. When William Capps in 1623 attempted to organize a raiding party of forty men to go against the indians, he was greeted with excuses and procrastination. Almost in disbelief, he informed an English correspondent of the planters' train of thought, "take away one of my men, there's 2000 Plantes gone, thates 500 waight of Tobacco, yea and what shall this man doe, runne after the Indians. . . . I have perhaps 10, perhaps 15, perhaps 20, men and am able to secure my owne Plantacion; how will they doe that are fewer? let them first be Crusht alittle and then perhaps they will themselves make up the Nomber for theire own safeties." Perhaps Frethorne's anxiety grew out of the knowledge that no one beyond Martin's Hundred really cared what the Indians might do to him and his comrades.

Such foot-dragging obviously did nothing to promote colonial security. Regardless of the planters' behavior, however, Virginia leaders felt compelled to deal with the Indians. After all, these appointed officials did not want to appear incompetent before the king and his councillors. But the Virginians soon discovered that in the absence of public-spirited citizen soldiers, their range of military responses was effectively reduced to three. The governor and his council could make the business of war so lucrative that Virginians would willingly leave the tobacco fields to fight, entrust private contractors with the responsibility of defending the entire population, or persuade the king to send English troops at his own expense to protect the colonists from their Indian enemies. Unfortunately, each of these alternatives presented specific drawbacks that rendered them essentially useless as military policies.

The first option was to make the conditions of service so profitable that the planters or in their place, the planters' servants, would join in subduing the common enemy. In times of military crisis, such as the one following the Great Massacre, both Company and Crown officials tried their best to persuade the settlers that warfare was not all hardship and sacrifice— indeed, that for some men, presumably not themselves, Indian fighting could be an economic opportunity. For the majority, however, such ar-

guments apparently rang hollow. The colonists had learned that local Indians made poor slaves, and in a spacious colony like Virginia, the offer
of free land was an inadequate incentive for risking one's life. The promise
of plunder drew few men away from the tobacco fields, and with typical
candor, Captain John Smith announced in 1624, "I would not give twenty
pound for all the pillage . . . to be got amongst the Salvages in twenty
yeeres."

A second possible solution for Virginia's military needs was to hire
someone to defend the colonists. The merits of this approach seemed
obvious. The state could simply transfer public funds to groups of enter-
prising individuals who in turn might construct forts along the rivers, build
palisades to ward off Indian attacks, and even in some cases, fight pitched
battles along the frontier. Unlike the New Englanders, who generally regarded matters of defense as a community responsibility, much like providing churches and schools, Virginians accepted the notion that private
contractors could serve as an adequate substitute for direct popular participation in military affairs.

In this belief the Virginians were mistaken. A stream of opportunists
came forward with schemes that would compensate for the colony's un-
reliable militia. Without exception, however, these plans drained the public
treasury but failed to produce lasting results. Indeed, Virginia's social values spawned a class of military adventurers—perhaps military profiteers
would be a more accurate description—who did their best to transform
warfare into a profitable private business.

Some of the private military schemes of the 1620's were bizarre, others
humorous, almost all misallocations of public revenues. In the summer of
1622 a sea captain named Samuel Each, whose military qualifications remain obscure, offered to construct a fort of oyster shells to guard the
mouth of the James River. Each's project seemed a convenient way to secure
the colony's shipping from possible foreign harassment. For his work, the
captain was promised a handsome reward, but as was so often to be the
case in the history of seventeenth-century Virginia, the contractor disappointed the settlers' expectations. The proposed site for the fortification
turned out to be under water at high tide and "at low water with everie
wynd washed over by the surges." One colonist sardonically described
Each's pile of sea shells as "a Castle in the aire" and suggested that the
captain had wisely died on the job "to save his Credit."

During the 1620's other adventurers followed, but their performance
was no more impressive than Each's had been. These men sometimes
couched their proposals in rhetoric about the common good. There was
no question, however, about what considerations motivated the contractors. In 1628, for example, two of the colony's most successful planters,
Samuel Mathews and William Claiborne, presented the king of England
with what they called "A Proposition Concerning the Winning of the For-

est." They humbly informed Charles I that their plan grew "not out of any private respects, or intent to gaine to our selves, but because in our owne mindes wee perceive [?] our selves bound to expend both our lives and fortunes in so good a service for this Plantation." One may be justly skeptical about the extent of their anticipated personal sacrifice, for in the next paragraph, the two Virginians demanded 1200 pounds "in readie monye" and 100 pounds sterling every year thereafter. Governor Francis Wyatt gave the project begrudging support. He explained that because of the planters' "too much affection to their private dividents" and their unwillingness to alter their pattern of settlement in the interest of defense, Mathews and Claiborne should be encouraged to construct a fortified wall running six miles between the Charles and James Rivers. The two men promised to build a palisade and staff it with their own armed servants. There is no record of what happened to this particular plan, but if it had been accepted, the servants most likely would have spent their days planting tobacco for two men already quite wealthy.

The reliance on military adventurers held dangers of which the Virginians of the 1620's were only dimly aware. As long as the price of tobacco remained relatively high, the colonists ignored much of the waste and favoritism associated with lucrative military contracts. But high taxes caused grumbling, even serious social unrest. In the early 1620's the members of the Virginia Council reported that when it came time to reimburse Captain Each, there was "a general unwillingness (not to say an opposition) in all almost but ourselves." As tobacco profits dropped over the course of the seventeenth century, small planters and landless freemen showed an increasing hostility to private military contractors, . . .

A second difficulty with the adventurers was no bigger than a man's hand during the 1620's. The colony needed every able-bodied defender that could be found, and no one seems to have worried much about arming indentured servants and poor freemen. But in later years, Virginians would have cause to reconsider the wisdom of creating mercenary bodies composed largely of impoverished recruits. The leading planters discovered, in fact, that one could not systematically exploit other human beings for private profit and then expect those same people to risk their lives fighting to preserve the society that tolerated such oppressive conditions. As privatism became the way of life, the colony's leading planters were less and less certain whether internal or external enemies posed a greater threat to Virginia's security.

A third possible solution to the settlement's early military needs lay in obtaining direct English assistance. During the 1620's Virginia leaders frequently petitioned the mother country for arms, men and supplies. In 1626—four years after the Massacre—the royal governor informed the Privy Council that the security of Virginia required "no less nombers then five hundred soldiers to be yearly sent over." On other occasions officials in

Virginia admitted that as few as 50 or 100 troops would do, but however many men England provided, the colonists expected the king to pay the bill. Free protection would remove the necessity for high taxes. Understandably, the English administrators never found the settlers' argument persuasive, and royal policy makers may well have wondered what several thousand colonists were doing to defend themselves.

Before the 1670's not a single English soldier was dispatched to Virginia. Nevertheless, despite repeated failures in gaining English assistance, the dream of acquiring a cheap, dependable military force remained strong. Had the colony's own citizens been more involved in Virginia's defense, more willing to live closer together, there would have been no reason to plead for outside support. But the spirit of excessive individualism ironically bred a habit of dependence upon the mother country, and as soon as internal problems threatened the peace, someone was sure to call for English regulars.

Virginia's military preparedness was no more impressive in 1630 than it had been a decade earlier. The colony's rulers still complained that the planters "utterly neglected eyther to stand upon their guard or to keepe their Armes fitt." The Council admitted helplessly that "neyther proclamations nor other strict orders have remedied the same." The settlers were incorrigible. Forts remained unbuilt; the great palisade neither kept the colonists in nor the Indians out. And in 1644 the local tribes launched a second, even more deadly attack, revealing once again the fundamental weakness of Virginia's military system.

Virginia's extreme individualism was not an ephemeral phenomenon, something associated only with the colony's founding or a peculiar boomtown atmosphere. Long after the 1620's, values originally brought to the New World by adventurers and opportunists influenced patterns of social and institutional behavior, and instead of providing Virginia with new direction or a new sense of mission, newcomers were assimilated into an established cultural system. Customs became statute law, habitual acts tradition. . . . seventeenth-century Virginians never succeeded in forming a coherent society. Despite their apparent homogeneity, they lacked cohesive group identity; they generated no positive symbols, no historical myths strong enough to overcome individual differences. As one might expect, such a social system proved extremely fragile, and throughout the seventeenth century Virginians experienced social unrest, even open rebellion.

Nor should the grand life style of the great eighteenth-century planters, the Byrds, the Carters, the Wormeleys, mislead one into thinking that their value system differed significantly from that of Virginia's early settlers. These first families of the early eighteenth century bore the same relationship to Captain John Smith and his generation as Cotton Mather and his contemporaries did to the founders of Massachusetts Bay. The apparent political tranquility of late colonial Virginia grew not out of a sense of community or new value-orientations, but out of more effective forms of human exploitation. The mass of tobacco field laborers were now black slaves, men and women who by legal definition could never become fully part of the privatistic culture. In Byrd's Virginia, voluntaristic associations remained weak; education lagged, churches stagnated, and towns never developed. The isolation of plantation life continued, and the extended visits and the elaborate balls of the period may well have served to obscure the competition that underlay planter relationships. As one anthropologist reminds us, "in a society in which everyone outside the nuclear family is immediately suspect, in which one is at every moment believed to be vulnerable to the underhanded attacks of others, reliability and trust can never be taken for granted." In the course of a century of cultural development, Virginians transformed an extreme form of individualism, a value system suited for soldiers and adventurers, into a set of regional virtues, a love of independence, an insistence upon personal liberty, a cult of manhood, and an uncompromising loyalty to family.

DOCUMENTS

The Experiences of an Indentured Servant, 1623

LOVING AND KIND FATHER AND MOTHER:

My most humble duty remembered to you, hoping in God of your good health, as I myself am at the making hereof. This is to let you understand that I your child am in a most heavy case by reason of the nature of the country, [which] is such that it causeth much sickness, [such] as the scurvy and the bloody flux and diverse other diseases, which maketh the body very poor and weak. And when we are sick there is nothing to comfort us; for since I came out of the ship I never ate anything but peas, and loblollie (that is, water gruel). As for deer or venison I never saw any since I came into this land. There is indeed some fowl, but we are not allowed to go and get it, but must work hard both early and late for a mess of water gruel and a mouthful of bread and beef. A mouthful of bread for a penny loaf must serve for four men which is most pitiful. [You would be grieved] if you did know as much as I [do], when people cry out day and night—Oh! that they were in England without their limbs—and would not

SOURCE: Richard Frethorne, Letter to his father and mother, March 20, April 2 & 3, 1623, in Susan M. Kingsbury, ed., *The Records of the Virginia Company of London* (Washington, D. C.: Government Printing Office, 1935), 4: 58–62.

care to lose any limb to be in England again, yea, though they beg from door to door. For we live in fear of the enemy every hour, yet we have had a combat with them . . . and we took two alive and made slaves of them. But it was by policy, for we are in great danger; for our plantation is very weak by reason of the death and sickness of our company. For we came but twenty for the merchants, and they are half dead just; and we look every hour when two more should go. Yet there came some four other men yet to live with us, of which there is but one alive; and our Lieutenant is dead, and [also] his father and his brother. And there was some five or six of the last year's twenty, of which there is but three left, so that we are fain to get other men to plant with us; and yet we are but 32 to fight against 3000 if they should come. And the nighest help that we have is ten miles of us, and when the rogues overcame this place [the] last [time] they slew 80 persons. How then shall we do, for we lie even in their teeth? They may easily take us, but [for the fact] that God is merciful and can save with few as well as with many, as he showed to Gilead. And like Gilead's soldiers, if they lapped water, we drink water which is but weak.

And I have nothing to comfort me, nor is there nothing to be gotten here but sickness and death, except [in the event] that one had money to lay out in some things for profit. But I have nothing at all—no, not a shirt to my back but two rags (2), nor no clothes but one poor suit, nor but one pair of shoes, but one pair of stockings, but one cap, [and] but two bands [collars]. My cloak is stolen by one of my own fellows, and to his dying hour [he] would not tell me what he did with it; but some of my fellows saw him have butter and beef out of a ship, which my cloak, I doubt [not], paid for. So that I have not a penny, nor a penny worth, to help me to either spice or sugar or strong waters, without the which one cannot live here. For as strong beer in England doth fatten and strengthen them, so water here doth wash and weaken these here [and] only keeps [their] life and soul together. But I am not half [of] a quarter so strong as I was in England, and all is for want of victuals; for I do protest unto you that I have eaten more in [one] day at home than I have allowed me here for a week. You have given more than my day's allowance to a beggar at the door; and if Mr. Jackson had not relieved me, I should be in a poor case. But he like a father and she like a loving mother doth still help me.

For when we go to Jamestown (that is 10 miles of us) there lie all the ships that come to land, and there they must deliver their goods. And when we went up to town [we would go], as it may be, on Monday at noon, and come there by night, [and] then load the next day by noon, and go home in the afternoon, and unload, and then away again in the night, and [we would] be up about midnight. Then if it rained or blowed never so hard, we must lie in the boat on the water and have nothing but a little bread. For when we go into the boat we [would] have a loaf allowed to two men, and it is all [we would get] if we stayed there two days, which is hard; and [we] must lie all that while in the boat. But that Goodman Jackson pitied me and made me a cabin to lie in always when I [would] come up, and he would give me some poor jacks [fish] [to take] home with me, which comforted me more than peas or water gruel. Oh, they be very godly folks, and love me very well, and will do anything for me. And he much marvelled that you would send me a servant to the Company; he saith I had been better knocked on the head. And indeed so I find it now, to my great grief and misery; and [I] saith that if you love me you will redeem me suddenly, for which I do entreat and beg. And if you cannot get the merchants to redeem me for some little money, then for God's sake get a gathering or entreat some good folks to lay out some little sum of money in meal and cheese and butter and beef. Any eating meat will yield great profit. Oil and vinegar is very good; but, father, there is great loss in leaking. But for God's sake send beef and cheese and butter, or the more of one sort and none of another. But if you send cheese, it must be very old cheese; and at the cheesemonger's you may buy very good cheese for twopence farthing or halfpenny, that will be liked very well. But if you send cheese, you must have a care how you pack it in barrels; and you must put cooper's chips between every cheese, or else the heat of the hold will rot them. And look whatsoever you send me—be it never so much— look, what[ever] I make of it, I will deal truly with you. I will send it over and beg the profit to redeem me; and if I die before it come, I have entreated Goodman Jackson to send you the worth of it, who hath promised he will. If you send, you must direct your letters to Goodman Jackson, at Jamestown, a gunsmith. (You must set down his freight, because there be more of his name there.) Good father, do not forget me, but have mercy and pity my miserable case. I know if you did but see me, you would weep to see me; for I have but one suit. (But [though] it is a strange one, it is very well guarded.) Wherefore, for God's sake, pity me. I pray you to remember my love to all my friends and kindred. I hope all my brothers and sisters are in good health, and as for my part I have set down my resolution that certainly will be; that is, that the answer of this letter will be life or death to me. Therefore, good father, send as soon as you can; and if you send me any thing let this be the mark.

ROT

RICHARD FRETHORNE,
MARTIN'S HUNDRED

"We shall be as a Citty upon a Hill," 1630

It rests now to make some applicacion of this discourse by the present designe which gave the occasion of writeing of it. Herein are 4 things to be propounded: first the persons, 2ly, the worke, 3ly, the end, 4ly the meanes.

1. For the persons, wee are a Company professing our selves fellow members of Christ, In which respect onely though wee were absent from eache other many miles, and had our imploymentes as farre distant, yet wee ought to account our selves knitt together by this bond of love, and live in the exercise of it, if wee would have comforte of our being in Christ, . . .

2ly. for the worke wee have in hand, it is by a mutuall consent through a speciall overruleing providence, and a more then an ordinary approbation of the Churches of Christ to seeke out a place of Cohabitation and Consorteshipp under a due forme of Government both civill and ecclesiasticall. In such cases as this the care of the publique must oversway all private respects, by which not onely conscience, but meare Civill policy doth binde us; for it is a true rule that perticuler estates cannott subsist in the ruine of the publique.

3ly. The end is to improve our lives to doe more service to the Lord the comforte and encrease of the body of christe whereof wee are members that our selves and posterity may be the better preserved from the Common corrupcions of this evill world to serve the Lord and worke out our Salvacion under the power and purity of his holy Ordinances.

4ly for the meanes whereby this must bee effected, they are 2fold, a Conformity with the worke and end wee aime at, these wee see are extraordinary, therefore wee must not content our selves with usuall ordinary meanes whatsoever wee did or ought to have done when wee lived in England, the same must wee doe and more allsoe where wee goe: That which the most in theire Churches maineteine as a truthe in profession onely, wee must bring into familiar and constant practise, as in this duty of love wee must love brotherly without dissimulation, wee must love one another with a pure hearte fervently wee must beare one anothers burthens, wee must not looke onely on our owne things, but allsoe on the things of our brethren, neither must wee think that the lord will beare with such faileings at our hands as hee dothe from those among whome wee have lived. . . . Thus stands the cause betweene God and us, wee are entered into Covenant with him for this worke, wee have taken out a

SOURCE: John Winthrop, "A Modell of Christian Charity," in *Winthrop Papers* (Boston: Massachusetts Historical Society, 1929), 2: 282–84.

Commission, the Lord hath given us leave to drawe our owne Articles wee have professed to enterprise these Accions upon these and these ends, wee have hereupon besought him of favour and blessing: Now if the Lord shall please to heare us, and bring us in peace to the place wee desire, then hath hee ratified this Covenant and sealed our Commission, [and] will expect a strickt performance of the Articles contained in it, but if wee shall neglect the observacion of these Articles which are the ends wee have propounded, and dissembling with our God, shall fall to embrace this present world and prosecute our carnall intencions, seekeing greate things for our selves and our posterity, the Lord will surely breake out in wrathe against us be revenged of such a periured people and make us knowe the price of the breache of such a Covenant.

Now the onely way to avoyde this shipwracke and to provide for our posterity is to followe the Counsell of Micah, to doe Justly, to love mercy, to walke humbly with our God, for this end, wee must be knitt together in this worke as one man, wee must entertaine each other in brotherly Afeccion, wee must be willing to abridge our selves of our superfluities, for the supply of others necessities, wee must uphold a familiar Commerce together in all meekenes, gentlenes, patience and liberallity, wee must delight in eache other, make others Condicions our owne reioyce together, mourne together, labour, and suffer together, allwayes haveing before our eyes our Commission and Community in the worke, our Community as members of the same body, soe shall wee keepe the unitie of the spirit in the bond of peace, the Lord will be our God and delight to dwell among us, as his owne people and will commaund a blessing upon us in all our wayes, soe that wee shall see much more of his wisdome power goodnes and truthe then formerly wee have beene acquainted with, wee shall finde that the God of Israell is among us, when tenn of us shall be able to resist a thousand of our enemies, when hee shall make us a prayse and glory, that men shall say of succeeding plantacions: the lord make it like that of New England: for wee must Consider that wee shall be as a Citty upon a Hill, the eies of all people are uppon us; soe that if wee shall deale falsely with our god in this worke wee have undertaken and soe cause him to withdrawe his present help from us, wee shall be made a story and a by-word through the world, wee shall open the mouthes of enemies to speake evill of the wayes of god and all professours for Gods sake; wee shall shame the faces of many of gods worthy servants, and cause theire prayers to be turned in Cursses upon us till wee be consumed out of the good land whether wee are goeing: And to shutt upp this discourse with that ex-hortacion of Moses that faithfull servant of the Lord in his last farewell to Israell Deut. 30. Beloved there is now sett before us life, and good, deathe and evill in that wee are Commaunded this day to love the Lord our God, and to love one another to walke in his wayes and to keepe his Com-maundements and his Ordinance, and his lawes, and the Articles of our

Covenant with him that wee may live and be multiplyed, and that the Lord our God may blesse us in the land whether wee goe to possesse it: But if our heartes shall turne away soe that wee will not obey, but shall be seduced and worshipp [serve cancelled] other Gods our pleasures, and proffitts, and serve them; it is propounded unto us this day; wee shall surely perishe out of the good Land whether wee passe over this vast Sea to possesse it;

Therefore lett us choose life,
that wee, and our Seede,
may live, by obeyeing his
voyce, and cleaveing to him,
for hee is our life, and
our prosperity.

CHAPTER 3

Crossing the Atlantic: The Experiences of Slaves and Servants

Africa was the third source of the population of the developing American colonies. Although the first blacks brought to Virginia in 1619 were forcibly removed from West Africa, they were probably not viewed as slaves by the English colonists; slavery at this date did not exist in the laws of the colonies. The fate of blacks brought to the colonies prior to the 1660s varied. Some, like white servants, eventually gained their freedom and obtained land and even servants of their own. Others spent their lives in servitude. But, as the need for labor became more acute, and as the advantages of the services of lifetime bondsmen over indentured servants (who served for a limited time) became apparent, the institution of slavery began to evolve in law and practice.

Gradually the colonists tightened the grip of slavery on blacks, making it ever more difficult for them to gain their freedom. Slavery existed in the northern colonies, though it was not crucial to their economies as it was in the south. Southern colonists depended upon slave labor to cultivate tobacco, rice, and indigo. By the eighteenth century, slaves were legally property—to be bought, maintained, and sold according to the whim and financial position of their masters.

Hundreds of thousands of Africans were ultimately uprooted and brought to the American colonies. Daniel Mannix's and Malcolm Cowley's essay "The Middle Passage" vividly describes the brutality of the slave trade. Many blacks perished resisting capture and on shipboard during the voyage to the New World. What do the practices of "loose packing" and "tight packing," discussed in the essay, reveal about the ship captains' attitudes?

Only a few slaves left reports of their experiences on the middle passage, as the voyage from Africa to the Americas was called. One who did was Gustavus Vasa, an excerpt from whose autobiography is presented in the first document.

The voyage to the colonies could also be filled with hardship for Europeans destined for servitude. Such was certainly the case for the German emigré Gottlieb Mittelberger, who recounts his experiences in the second document. Why would those in similar circumstances continue to come to America, despite Mittelberger's advice?

ESSAY

The Middle Passage
Daniel P. Mannix and Malcolm Cowley

As soon as an assortment of naked slaves was taken aboard a Guineaman [slave ship], the men were shackled two by two, the right wrist and ankle of one to the left wrist and ankle of another. Then they were sent to the hold or, at the end of the eighteenth century, to the "house" that the sailors had built on deck. The women—usually regarded as fair prey for the sailors—and the children were allowed to wander by day almost anywhere on the vessel, though they spent the night between decks in other rooms than the men. All the slaves were forced to sleep without covering on bare wooden floors, which were often constructed of unplaned boards. In a stormy passage the skin over their elbows might be worn away to the bare bones.

William Bosman says, writing in 1701, "You would really wonder to see how these slaves live on board; for though their number sometimes

SOURCE: *Black Cargoes: A History of the Atlantic Slave Trade, 1518–1865* by Daniel P. Mannix in collaboration with Malcolm Cowley. Copyright © 1962 by Daniel P. Mannix. Reprinted by permission of Viking Peguin Inc.

amounts to six or seven hundred, yet by careful management of our masters of ships"—the Dutch masters, that is—"they are so regulated that it seems incredible: And in this particular our nation exceeds all other Europeans; for as the French, Portuguese and English slave-ships are always foul and stinking; on the contrary ours are for the most part clean and neat." Slavers of every nation insisted that their own vessels were the best in the trade. . . .

There were two schools of thought among the Guinea captains, called the "loose-packers" and the "tight-packers." The former argued that by giving the slaves a little more room, with better food and a certain amount of liberty, they reduced the mortality among them and received a better price for each slave in the West Indies. The tight-packers answered that although the loss of life might be greater on each of their voyages, so too were the net receipts from a larger cargo. If many of the survivors were weak and emaciated, as was often the case, they could be fattened up in a West Indian slave yard before being offered for sale. The argument between the two schools continued as long as the trade itself, but for many years after 1750 the tight-packers were in the ascendant. So great was the profit on each slave landed alive in the West Indies that hardly a captain refrained from loading his vessel to her utmost capacity. The hold of a slaving vessel was usually about five feet high. That seemed like waste space to the Guinea merchants, so they built a shelf or platform in the middle of it, extending six feet from each side of the vessel. When the bottom of the hold was completely covered with flesh, another row of slaves was packed on the platform. If there was as much as six feet of vertical space in the hold, a second platform might be installed above the first, sometimes leaving only twenty inches of headroom for the slaves; they could not sit upright during the whole voyage. The Reverend John Newton writes from personal observation:

> The cargo of a vessel of a hundred tons or a little more is calculated to purchase from 220 to 250 slaves. Their lodging rooms below the deck which are three (for the men, the boys and the women) besides a place for the sick, are sometimes more than five feet high and sometimes less; and this height is divided toward the middle for the slaves lie in two rows, one above the other, on each side of the ship, close to each other like books upon a shelf. I have known them so close that the shelf would not easily contain one more.
>
> The poor creatures, thus cramped, are likewise in irons for the most part which makes it difficult for them to turn or move or attempt to rise or to lie down without hurting themselves or each other. Every morning, perhaps, more instances than one are found of the living and the dead fastened together.

Dr. Falconbridge stated . . . that "he made the most of the room," in stowing the slaves, "and wedged them in. They had not so much room as a man in his coffin either in length or breadth. When he had to enter the slave deck, he took off his shoes to avoid crushing the slaves as he was forced to crawl over them." Taking off shoes on entering the hold seems to have been a widespread custom among surgeons. Falconbridge "had the marks on his feet where [the slaves] bit and pinched him."

In 1788 Captain Parrey of the Royal Navy was sent to measure such of the slave vessels as were then lying at Liverpool and to make a report to the House of Commons. He discovered that the captains of many slavers possessed a chart showing the dimensions of the ship's half deck, lower deck, hold, platforms, gunroom, orlop, and great cabin, in fact of every crevice into which slaves might be wedged. Miniature black figures were drawn on some of the charts to illustrate the most effective method of packing in the cargo.

On the *Brookes*, which Captain Parrey considered to be typical, every man was allowed a space six feet long by sixteen inches wide (and usually about two feet, seven inches high); every woman, a space five feet, ten inches long by sixteen inches wide; every boy, five feet by fourteen inches; every girl, four feet, six inches by twelve inches. The *Brookes* was a vessel of 320 tons. By the law of 1788 it was permitted to carry 454 slaves, and the chart, which later became famous, showed how and where 451 of them could be stowed away. Captain Parrey failed to see how the captain could find room for three more. Nevertheless, Parliament was told by reliable witnesses, including Dr. Thomas Trotter, formerly surgeon of the *Brookes*, that before the new law was passed she had carried 600 slaves on one voyage and 609 on another.

Taking on slaves was a process that might be completed in a month or two at Bonny or Luanda. On the Gold Coast [present-day Ghana], where slaves were less plentiful, it might last from six months to a year or more. Meanwhile the captain was buying Negroes, sometimes one or two a day, sometimes a hundred or more in a single lot, while haggling over each purchase.

Those months when a slaver lay at anchor off the Guinea Coast, taking on her cargo, were the most dangerous stage of her triangular voyage. Not only was her crew exposed to African fevers and the revenge of angry natives; not only was there the chance of her being taken by pirates or by a hostile man-of-war; but also there was the constant threat of a slave mutiny. Captain Thomas Phillips says, in his account of a voyage made in 1693–1694:

When our slaves are aboard we shackle the men two and two, while we lie in port, and in sight of their own country, for 'tis then they attempt to make their escape, and mutiny; to prevent which we always keep centinels upon the hatchways, and have a chest full of small arms, ready loaden and prim'd, constantly lying at hand upon the quarter-deck, together with some granada shells; and two of our quarter-deck guns, pointing on the deck thence, and two more out of the steerage, the door of which is always kept shut, and well barr'd; they are fed twice a day, at 10 in the morning, and 4 in the evening, which is the time they are aptest to mutiny, being all upon deck; therefore all that time, what of our men are not employ'd in distributing their victuals to them, and settling them, stand to their arms; and some with lighted matches at the great guns that yaun upon them, loaden with partridge, till they have done and gone down to their kennels between decks.

. . . In spite of such precautions, mutinies were frequent on the coast, and some of them were successful. Even a failed mutiny might lead to heavy losses among the slaves and the sailors. James Barbot, Sr., of the *Albion-Frigate*, made the mistake of providing his slaves with knives so they could cut their meat. The slaves tore pieces of iron from the forecastle door, broke off their shackles, and killed the guard at the entrance to the hatchway. Before the mutiny was quelled, twenty-eight slaves either had been shot dead or had thrown themselves overboard. . . .

Mutinies were frequent during the years from 1750 to 1788, when Liverpool merchants were trying to save money by reducing the size of their crews. A small crew weakened by fever was no match for the slaves, especially if it had to withstand a simultaneous attack from the shore. On January 11, 1769, the *Nancy* out of Liverpool, Captain Williams, was lying at anchor off New Calabar. She had 132 slaves on board, who managed to break their shackles and assail the crew. The slaves were unarmed, but "it was with great difficulty, though [the crew] attacked them sword in hand, to make them submit." Meanwhile the natives on shore heard the fighting and swarmed aboard the *Nancy* from their canoes. They seized the slaves (whom they later resold to other ships . . .) and looted the cargo. There was a wild scene of plunder, with black men running through the vessel, breaching rum casks, throwing ships' biscuit and salt beef into the canoes, and robbing the sailors of everything they possessed. Afterward they cut the cables and set the *Nancy* adrift. Another slaver lying in the river sent a boat to rescue Captain Williams and the surviving seamen. The vessel, however, was wrecked. . . .

There are fairly detailed accounts of fifty-five mutinies on slavers from 1699 to 1845, not to mention passing references to more than a hundred others. The list of ships "cut off" by the natives—often in revenge for the kidnaping of freemen—is almost as long. On the record it does not seem that Africans submitted tamely to being carried across the Atlantic like chained beasts. Edward Long, the Jamaica planter and historian, justified the cruel punishments inflicted on slaves by saying, "The many acts of violence they have committed by murdering whole crews and destroying ships when they had it in their power to do so have made these rigors wholly chargeable on their own bloody and malicious disposition which calls for the same confinement as if they were wolves or wild boars." For "wolves or wild boars" a modern reader might substitute "men who would rather die than be enslaved."

As long as a vessel lay at anchor, the slaves could dream of seizing it. If they managed to kill the crew, as they did in perhaps one mutiny out of ten, they could cut the anchor cable and let the vessel drift ashore. That opportunity was lost as soon as the vessel put to sea. Ignorant of navigation, which they regarded as white man's magic, the slaves were at the mercy of the captain. They could still die, but not with any hope of regaining their freedom.

The captain, for his part, had finished the most dangerous leg of his triangular voyage. Now he had to face only the ordinary perils of the sea, most of which were covered by his owners' insurance against fire, shipwreck, pirates and rovers, letters of mart and counter-mart, barratry, jettison, and foreign men-of-war. Among the risks not covered by insurance, the greatest was that the cargo might be swept away by disease. The underwriters refused to issue such policies, arguing that they would expose the captain to an unholy temptation. If insured against disease among his slaves, he might take no precautions against it and might try to make his profit out of the insurance. . . .

On a canvas of heroic size, Thomas Stothard, Esq., of the Royal Academy, depicted "The Voyage of the Sable Venus from Angola to the West Indies." His painting is handsomely reproduced in the second volume of Bryan Edwards' *History of the West Indies*, where is appears beside a poem on the same allegorical subject by an unnamed Jamaican author, perhaps Edwards himself. In the painting the ship that carries the Sable Venus is an immense scallop shell, in which she sits upright on a velvet throne. Except for bracelets, anklets, and a collar of pearls, she wears nothing but a narrow embroidered girdle. Her look is soft and sensuous, and in grace she yields nothing—so the poem insists—to Botticelli's white Venus,

> In FLORENCE, where she's seen;
> Both just alike, except the white,
> No difference, no—none at night
> The beauteous dames between.

The joint message of the poem and the painting is simple to the point of coarseness: that slave women are preferable to English girls at night, being passionate and accessible; but the message is embellished with a wealth of classical details, to show the painter's learning. Two legendary dolphins draw the bark of Venus toward the West. Triton leads one of them, while blowing his wreathèd horn. Two mischievous loves gambol about the other dolphin. There are cherubs above the woolly head of Venus, fanning her with ostrich plumes. In the calm distance a grampus discharges his column of spray. Cupid, from above, is shooting an arrow at Neptune, who strides ahead bearing the Union Jack. As the poet (who calls the dolphins "winged fish") describes the idyllic scene:

> The winged fish, in purple trace
> The chariot drew; with easy grace
>   Their azure rein she guides:
> And now they fly, and now they swim;
> Now o'er the wave they lightly skim,
>   Or dart beneath the tides.

Meanwhile the Sable Venus, if she was a living woman borne from Angola to the West Indies, was roaming the deck of a ship that stank of excrement, so that, as with any slaver, "You could smell it five miles down wind." She had been torn from her husband and her children, she had been branded on the left buttock, and she had been carried to the ship bound hand and foot, lying in the bilge at the bottom of a dugout canoe. Now she was the prey of the ship's officers, in danger of being flogged to death if she resisted them. Her reward if she yielded was a handful of beads or a sailor's kerchief to tie around her waist.

Here is how she and her shipmates spent the day.

If the weather was clear, they were brought on deck at eight o'clock in the morning. The men were attached by their leg irons to the great chain that ran along the bulwarks on both sides of the ship; the women and half-grown boys were allowed to wander at will. About nine o'clock the slaves were served their first meal of the day. If they were from the Windward Coast, the fare consisted of boiled rice, millet, or cornmeal, which might be cooked with a few lumps of salt beef abstracted from the sailors' rations. If they were from the Bight of Biafra, they were fed stewed yams, but the Congos and the Angolans preferred manioc or plantains. With the food they were all given half a pint of water, served out in a pannikin [a small pan or cup].

After the morning meal came a joyless ceremony called "dancing the slaves." "Those who were in irons," says Dr. Thomas Trotter, surgeon of the *Brookes* in 1783, "were ordered to stand up and make what motions they could, leaving a passage for such as were out of irons to dance around the deck." Dancing was prescribed as a therapeutic measure, a specific against suicidal melancholy, and also against scurvy—although in the latter case it was a useless torture for men with swollen limbs. While sailors paraded the deck, each with a cat-o'-nine-tails in his right hand, the men slaves "jumped in their irons" until their ankles were bleeding flesh. One

47

sailor told Parliament, "I was employed to dance the men, while another person danced the women." Music was provided by a slave thumping on a broken drum or an upturned kettle, or by an African banjo, if there was one aboard, or perhaps by a sailor with a bagpipe or a fiddle. Slaving captains sometimes advertised for "A person that can play on the Bagpipes, for a Guinea ship." The slaves were also told to sing. Said Dr. Claxton after his voyage in the *Young Hero*, "They sing, but not for their amusement. The captain ordered them to sing, and they sang songs of sorrow. Their sickness, fear of being beaten, their hunger, and the memory of their country, &c, are the usual subjects."

While some of the sailors were dancing the slaves, others were sent below to scrape and swab out the sleeping rooms. It was a sickening task, and it was not well performed unless the captain imposed an iron discipline. James Barbot, Sr., was proud of the discipline maintained on the *Albion-Frigate*. "We were very nice," he says, "in keeping the places where the slaves lay clean and neat, appointing some of the ship's crew to do that office constantly and thrice a week we perfumed betwixt decks with a quantity of good vinegar in pails, and red-hot iron bullets in them, to expel the bad air, after the place had been well washed and scrubbed with brooms." Captain Hugh Crow, the last legal English slaver, was famous for his housekeeping. "I always took great pains," he says, "to promote the health and comfort of all on board, by proper diet, regularity, exercise, and cleanliness, for I considered that on keeping the ship clean and orderly, which was always my hobby, the success of our voyage mainly depended." Consistently he lost fewer slaves in the Middle Passage than the other captains, some of whom had the filth in the hold cleaned out only once a week. A few left their slaves to wallow in excrement during the whole Atlantic passage.

At three or four in the afternoon the slaves were fed their second meal, often a repetition of the first. Sometimes, instead of African food, they were given horse beans, the cheapest provender from Europe. The beans were boiled to a pulp, then covered with a mixture of palm oil, flour, water, and red pepper, which the sailors called "slabber sauce." Most of the slaves detested horse beans, especially if they were used to eating yams or manioc. Instead of eating the pulp, they would, unless carefully watched, pick it up by handfuls and throw it in each other's faces. That second meal was the end of their day. As soon as it was finished they were sent below, under the guard of sailors charged with stowing them away on their bare floors and platforms. The tallest men were placed amidships, where the vessel was the widest; the shorter ones were tumbled into the stern. Usually there was only room for them to sleep on their sides, "spoon fashion." Captain William Littleton told Parliament that slaves in the ships on which he sailed might lie on their backs if they wished—"though perhaps," he conceded, "it might be difficult all at the same time."

After stowing their cargo, the sailors climbed out of the hatchway, each clutching his cat-o'-nine-tails: then the hatchway gratings were closed and barred. Sometimes in the night, as the sailors lay on deck and tried to sleep, they heard from below "an howling melancholy noise, expressive of extreme anguish." When Dr. Trotter told his interpreter, a slave woman, to inquire about the cause of the noise, "she discovered it to be owing to their having dreamt they were in their own country, and finding themselves when awake, in the hold of a slave ship." . . .

In squalls or rainy weather, the slaves were never brought on deck. They were served their two meals in the hold, where the air became too thick and poisonous to breathe. Says Dr. Falconbridge, "For the purpose of admitting fresh air, most of the ships in the slave-trade are provided, between the decks, with five or six airports on each side of the ship, of about six inches in length and four in breadth; in addition to which, some few ships, but not one in twenty, have what they denominate wind-sails." These were funnels made of canvas and so placed as to direct a current of air into the hold. "But whenever the sea is rough and the rain heavy," Falconbridge continues, "it becomes necessary to shut these and every other conveyance by which the air is admitted. . . . The negroes' rooms very soon become intolerably hot. The confined air, rendered noxious by the effluvia exhaled from their bodies and by being repeatedly breathed, soon produces fevers and fluxes which generally carry off great numbers of them."

Dr. Trotter says that when tarpaulins were thrown over the gratings, the slaves would cry, "Kickeraboo, kickeraboo, we are dying, we are dying." "I have known," says Henry Ellison, a sailor before the mast, "in the Middle Passage, in rains, slaves confined below for some time. I have frequently seen them faint through heat, the steam coming through the gratings, like a furnace." . . .

Not surprisingly, the slaves often went mad. Falconbridge mentions a woman on the *Emilia* who had to be chained to the deck. She had lucid intervals, however, and during one of these she was sold to a planter in Jamaica. Men who went insane might be flogged to death, to make sure that they were not malingering. Some were simply clubbed on the head and thrown overboard.

While the slaves were on deck they had to be watched at all times to keep them from committing suicide. Says Captain Phillips of the *Hannibal*, "We had about 12 negroes did wilfully drown themselves, and others starv'd themselves to death; for," he explained, " 'tis their belief that when they die they return home to their own country and friends again." This belief was reported from various regions, at various periods of the trade, but it seems to have been especially prevalent among the Ibo of eastern Nigeria. In 1788, nearly a hundred years after the *Hannibal's* voyage, Ecroide Claxton was the surgeon who attended a shipload of Ibo. "Some of the slaves," he testified, "wished to die on an idea that they should then get back to their own country. The captain in order to obviate this idea, thought of an expedient viz. to cut off the heads of those who died intimating to them that if determined to go, they must return without heads. The slaves were accordingly brought up to witness the operation. One of them by a violent exertion got loose and flying to the place where the nettings had been unloosed in order to empty the tubs, he darted overboard. The ship brought to, a man was placed in the main chains to catch him which he perceiving, made signs which words cannot express expressive of his happiness in escaping. He then went down and was seen no more."

Dr. Isaac Wilson, a surgeon in the Royal Navy, made a Guinea voyage on the *Elizabeth*, Captain John Smith, who was said to be very humane. Nevertheless, Wilson was assigned the duty of whipping the slaves. "Even in the act of chastisement," Wilson says, "I have seen them look up at me with a smile, and, in their own language, say, 'presently we shall be no more.' " One woman on the *Elizabeth* found some rope yarn, which she tied to the armorer's vise; she fastened the other end round her neck and was found dead in the morning. On the *Brookes* when Thomas Trotter was her surgeon, there was a man who, after being accused of witchcraft, had been sold into slavery with his whole family. During his first night on shipboard he tried to cut his throat. Dr. Trotter sewed up the wound, but on the following night the man not only tore out the sutures but tried to cut his throat on the other side. From the ragged edges of the wound and the blood on his fingers, he seemed to have used his nails as the only available instrument. His hands were tied together after the second wound, but he then refused all food, and he died of hunger in eight or ten days.

"Upon the negroes refusing to take food," says Falconbridge, "I have seen coals of fire, glowing hot, put on a shovel and placed so near their lips as to scorch and burn them. And this has been accompanied with threats of forcing them to swallow the coals if they persisted in refusing to eat. This generally had the required effect"; but if the Negroes still refused, they were flogged day after day. Lest flogging prove ineffective, every Guineaman was provided with a special instrument called the "speculum oris," or mouth opener. It looked like a pair of dividers with notched legs and with a thumbscrew at the blunt end. The legs were closed and the notches were hammered between the slave's teeth. When the thumbscrew was tightened, the legs of the instrument separated, forcing open the slave's mouth; then food was poured into it through a funnel. . . .

One deadly scourge of the Guinea cargoes was a phenomenon called "fixed melancholy." Even slaves who were well fed, treated with kindness, and kept under relatively sanitary conditions would often die one after another for no apparent reason; they simply had no wish to live. Fixed melancholy seems to have been especially rife among the Ibo and among the food-gathering tribes of the Gaboon, but no Negro nation was immune to it. Although the disease was noted from the earliest days of the trade, perhaps the best description of it was written by George Howe, an American medical student who shipped on an illegal slaver in 1859:

> Notwithstanding their apparent good health [Howe says] each morning three or four dead would be found, brought upon deck, taken by the arms and heels, and tossed overboard as unceremoniously as an empty bottle. Of what did they die? And [why] always at night? In the barracoons it was known that if a Negro was not amused and kept in motion, he would mope, squat down with his chin on his knees and arms clasped about his legs and in a very short time die. Among civilized races it is thought almost impossible to hold one's breath until death follows. It is thought the African can do so. They had no means of concealing anything and certainly did not kill each other. One of the duties of the slave-captains was when they found a slave sitting with knees up and head drooping, to start them up, run them about the deck, give them a small ration of rum, and divert them until in a normal condition.

It is impossible for a human being to hold his breath until he dies. Once he loses consciousness, his lungs fill with air and he recovers. The simplest explanation for the slaves' ability to "will themselves dead" is that they were in a state of shock as a result of their being carried through the terrifying surf into the totally unfamiliar surroundings of the ship. In certain conditions shock can be as fatal as physical injury. There may, however, be another explanation. The communal life of many tribes was so highly organized by a system of customs, relationships, taboos, and religious ceremonies that there was practically nothing a man or a woman could do that was not prescribed by tribal law. To separate an individual from this complex system of interrelationships and suddenly place him, naked and friendless, in a completely hostile environment was in some respects a greater shock than any amount of physical brutality.

Dr. Wilson believed that fixed melancholy was responsible for the loss of two-thirds of the slaves who died on the *Elizabeth*. "No one who had it was ever cured," he says; "whereas those who had it not and yet were ill, recovered. The symptoms are a lowness of spirits and despondency. Hence they refuse food. This only increases the symptoms. The stomach afterwards got weak. Hence the belly ached, fluxes ensued, and they were carried off." But flux, or dysentery, is an infectious disease spread chiefly by food prepared in unsanitary conditions. The slaves, after being forced to wallow in filth, were also forced to eat with their fingers. In spite of the real losses from fixed melancholy, the high death rate on Guinea ships was due to somatic more than to psychic afflictions.

Along with their human cargoes, crowded, filthy, undernourished, and terrified out of the wish to live, the ships also carried an invisible cargo of microbes, bacilli, spirochetes, viruses, and intestinal worms from one continent to another; the Middle Passage was a crossroads and marketplace of diseases. From Europe came smallpox, measles (less deadly to Africans than to American Indians), gonorrhea, and syphilis (which last Columbus's sailors had carried from America to Europe). The African diseases were yellow fever (to which the natives were more resistant than white men), dengue, blackwater fever, and malaria (which was not specifically African, but which most of the slaves carried in their bloodstreams). If anopheles mosquitoes were present, malaria spread from the slaves through any new territories to which they were carried. Other African diseases were amoebic and various forms of bacillary dysentery (all known as "the bloody flux"), Guinea worms, hookworm (possibly African in origin, but soon endemic in the warmer parts of the New World), yaws, elephantiasis, and leprosy.

The particular affliction of the white sailors after escaping from the fevers of the Guinea Coast was scurvy, a deficiency disease to which they were exposed by their monotonous rations of salt beef and sea biscuits. The daily tot of lime juice (originally lemon juice) that prevented scurvy was almost never served on merchantmen during the days of the legal slave trade, and in fact was not prescribed in the Royal Navy until 1795. Although the slaves were also subject to scurvy, they fared better in this respect than the sailors, partly because they made only one leg of the triangular voyage and partly because their rough diet was sometimes richer in vitamins. But sailors and slaves alike were swept away by smallpox and "the bloody flux," and sometimes they went blind from various forms of ophthalmia, the worst of which seems to have been a gonorrheal infection of the eyes.

Smallpox was feared more than other diseases, since the surgeons had no means of combating it until the end of the eighteenth century. One man with smallpox infected a whole vessel, unless—as sometimes happened—he was tossed overboard when the first scabs appeared. Captain Wilson of the *Briton* lost more than half his cargo of 375 slaves by not listening to his surgeon. It was the last slave brought on board who had the disease, says Henry Ellison, who made the voyage. "The doctor told Mr. Wilson it was the small-pox," Ellison continues. "He would not believe it, but said he would keep him, as he was a fine man. It soon broke out amongst the slaves. I have seen the platform one continued scab. We hauled up eight or ten slaves dead of a morning. The flesh and skin peeled off their wrists when taken hold of, being entirely mortified." But dysentery, though not so much feared, could cause as many deaths. Ellison testifies that he made two voyages on the *Nightingale*, Captain Carter. On the first voyage the slaves were so crowded that thirty boys "messed and slept in the long boat all through the Middle Passage, there being no room below"; and still the vessel lost only five or six slaves in all, out of a cargo of 270. On the second voyage, however, the *Nightingale* buried "about 150, chiefly of fevers and flux. We had 250 when we left the coast.". . .

The average mortality in the Middle Passage is impossible to state accurately from the surviving records. Some famous voyages were made without the loss of a single slave, as notably by Captains John Newton, William Macintosh, and Hugh Crow. On one group of nine voyages between 1766 and 1780, selected at random, the vessels carried 2362 slaves and there were no epidemics of disease. The total loss of slaves was 154, or about 6½ per cent. On another list of twenty voyages compiled by Thomas Clarkson the abolitionist, the vessels carried 7904 slaves and lost 2053, or 26 per cent. Balancing high and low figures together, the English Privy Council in 1789 arrived at an estimate of 12½ per cent for the average mortality in the Middle Passage. That comes close to the percentage reckoned long afterward from the manifests of French vessels sailing from Nantes. Between 1748 and 1782 the Nantes slavers bought 146,799 slaves and sold 127,133 on the other side of the Atlantic. The difference of 19,666 would indicate a loss of 13 per cent in the voyage.

Of course there were further losses. To the mortality in the Middle Passage, the Privy Council added 4½ per cent for the deaths of slaves in harbors before they were sold, and 33 per cent for deaths during the seasoning process, making a total of 50 per cent. If those figures are correct (U. B. Phillips, the author of *American Negro Slavery*, thinks they are somewhat high), then only one slave was added to the New World labor force for every two purchased on the Guinea Coast.

To keep the figures in perspective, it might be added that the mortality among slaves in the Middle Passage was possibly no greater than that of white indentured servants or even of free Irish, Scottish, and German immigrants in the North Atlantic crossing. On the better commanded Guineamen it was probably much less, and for a simple economic reason. There was no profit in a slaving voyage until the Negroes were landed alive and sold; therefore the better captains took care of their cargoes. If the Negroes died in spite of good care, the captains regarded their deaths as a personal affront. . . .

After leaving the Portuguese island of São Thomé—if he had watered there—a slaving captain bore westward along the equator for a thousand miles, and then northwestward toward the Cape Verde Islands. This was the tedious part of the Middle Passage. Along the equator the vessel might be delayed for weeks by calms or storms; sometimes it had to return to the African coast for fresh provisions. Then, "on leaving the Gulf of Guinea," says the author of a *Universal Geography* published in the early nineteenth century, ". . . that part of the ocean must be traversed, so fatal to navigators, where long calms detain the ships under a sky charged with electric clouds, pouring down by turns torrents of rain and of fire. This *sea of thunder*, being a focus of mortal diseases, is avoided as much as possible, both in approaching the coasts of Africa and those of America." It was not until reaching the latitude of the Cape Verde Islands that the vessel fell in with the Northeast Trades and was able to make a swift passage to the West Indies.

Ecroide Claxton's ship, the *Young Hero*, was one of those delayed for weeks before reaching the trade winds. "We were so streightened for provisions," he testified, "that if we had been ten more days at sea, we must either have eaten the slaves that died, or have made the living slaves *walk the plank*," a term, he explained, that was widely used by Guinea captains. There are no authenticated records of cannibalism in the Middle Passage, but there are many accounts of slaves killed for various reasons. English captains believed that French vessels carried poison in their medicine chests, "with which they can destroy their negroes in a calm, contagious sickness, or short provisions." They told the story of a Frenchman from Brest who had a long passage and had to poison his slaves; only twenty of them reached Haiti out of five hundred. Even the cruelest English captains regarded this practice as Latin, depraved, and uncovered by their insurance policies. In an emergency they simply jettisoned part of their cargo.

The most famous case involving jettisoned slaves was that of the *Zong* out of Liverpool, Luke Collingwood master. The *Zong* had left São Thomé on September 6, 1781, with a cargo of four hundred and forty slaves and a white crew of seventeen. There was sickness aboard during a slow passage; more than sixty Negroes died, with seven of the seamen, and many of the remaining slaves were so weakened by dysentery that it was a question whether they could be sold in Jamaica. On November 29, after they had already sighted land in the West Indies, Captain Collingwood called his officers together. He announced that there were only two hundred gallons of fresh water left in the casks, not enough for the remainder of the voyage. If the slaves died of thirst or illness, he explained, the loss would fall on the owners of the vessel; but if they were thrown into the sea it would be a legal jettison, covered by insurance. "It would not be so cruel to throw the poor sick wretches into the sea," he argued, "as to suffer them to linger out a few days under the disorders to which they were afflicted."

The mate, James Kelsal, demurred at first, saying there was "no present want of water to justify such a measure," but the captain outtalked him. To quote from a legal document, "The said Luke Collingwood picked, or caused to be picked out, from the cargo of the same ship, one hundred and thirty-three slaves, all or most of whom were sick or weak, and not likely to live; and ordered the crew by turns to throw them into the sea;

which most inhuman order was cruelly complied with." A first "parcel," as the sailors called them, of fifty-four slaves went overboard that same day, November 29. A second parcel, this time of forty-two, followed them on December 1, still leaving thirty-six slaves out of those condemned to be jettisoned. (One man seems to have died from natural causes.) Also on December 1 there was a heavy rain and the sailors collected six casks of water, enough to carry the vessel into port. But Collingwood stuck to his plan, and the last parcel of condemned slaves was brought on deck a few days later. Twenty-six of them were handcuffed, then swung into the sea. The last ten refused to let the sailors come near them; instead they vaulted over the bulwarks and were drowned like the others.

On December 22 the *Zong* dropped anchor in Kingston harbor after a passage of three months and sixteen days. Collingwood sold the remainder of his slaves, then sailed his vessel to England, where his owners claimed thirty pounds of insurance money for each of the one hundred and thirty-two jettisoned slaves. The underwriters refused to pay, and the case was taken to court. At a first trial the jury found for the owners, since "they had no doubt . . . that the case of slaves was the same as if horses had been thrown overboard." The underwriters appealed to the Court of Exchequer, and Lord Mansfield presided. After admitting that the law supported the owners of the *Zong*, he went on to say that "a higher law [applies to] this very shocking case." He found for the underwriters. It was the first case in which an English court ruled that a cargo of slaves could not be treated simply as merchandise. . . .

. . . Usually the last two or three days of the Middle Passage were a comparatively happy period. All the slaves, or all but a few, might be released from their irons. Where there was a remaining stock of provisions, the slaves were given bigger meals—to fatten them for market—and as much water as they could drink. Sometimes on the last day—if the ship was commanded by an easy-going captain—there was a sort of costume party on deck, with the women slaves dancing in the sailors' cast-off clothing. Then the captain was rowed ashore to arrange for the disposition of his cargo.

There were several fashions of selling the slaves. In a few instances the whole cargo was consigned to a single rich planter, or to a group of planters. More often a West Indian factor* took charge of retail sales, for a commission of 15 per cent on the gross amount and 5 per cent more on the net proceeds. When the captain himself had to sell his slaves, he ferried them ashore, had them drawn up in a ragged line of march, and paraded

[*a middleman between the suppliers and purchasers of slaves] them through town with bagpipes playing, before exposing them to buyers in the public square. J. G. Stedman, a young officer in the Scots Brigade employed as a mercenary by the Dutch in their obstinate efforts to suppress the slave revolts in Surinam, witnessed such a parade. "The whole party was," he says, ". . . a resurrection of skin and bones . . . risen from the grave or escaped from Surgeon's Hall." The slaves exposed for sale were "walking skeletons covered over with a piece of tanned leather."

But the commonest method of selling a cargo was a combination of the "scramble"—to be described presently—and the vendue or public auction "by inch of candle." First the captain, probably with the West Indian factor at his side, went over the cargo and picked out the slaves who were maimed or diseased. These were carried to a tavern and auctioned off, with a lighted candle beside the auctioneer; bids were received until an inch of candle had burned. The price of these "refuse" slaves sold at auction was usually less than half of that paid for a healthy Negro; sometimes it was as little as five or six dollars a head. "I was informed by a mulatto woman," Falconbridge says, "that she purchased a sick slave at Grenada, upon speculation, for the small sum of one dollar, as the poor wretch was apparently dying of the flux." There were some slaves who could not be sold for even a dollar, and they were often left to die on the wharfs without food or water.

There were horse traders' methods of hiding the presence of disease. Yaws, for example, could be concealed by a mixture of iron rust and gunpowder, a practice which Edward Long, the Jamaica historian, denounces as a "wicked fraud." Falconbridge tells of a Liverpool captain who "boasted of his having cheated some Jews by the following stratagem: A lot of slaves, afflicted with the flux, being about to be landed for sale, he directed the surgeon to stop the anus of each of them with oakum. . . . The Jews, when they examine them, oblige them to stand up, in order to see if there be any discharge; and when they do not perceive this appearance, they consider it as a symptom of recovery. In the present instance, such an appearance being prevented, the bargain was struck, and they were accordingly sold. But it was not long before a discovery ensued. The excruciating pain which the prevention of a discharge of such an acrimonious nature occasioned, not being to be borne by the poor wretches, the temporary obstruction was removed, and the deluded purchasers were speedily convinced of the imposition."

The healthy slaves remaining after an auction were sold by "scramble," that is, at standard prices for each man, each woman, each boy, and each girl in the cargo. The prices were agreed upon with the purchasers, who then scrambled for their pick of the slaves. During his four voyages Falconbridge was present at a number of scrambles. "In the *Emilia*," he says, "at Jamaica, the ship was darkened with sails, and covered round. The men slaves were placed on the main deck, and the women on the quarter deck. The purchasers on shore were informed a gun would be fired when they were ready to open the sale. A great number of people came on board with tallies or cards in their hands, with their own names upon them, and rushed through the barricado door with the ferocity of brutes. Some had three or four handkerchiefs tied together, to encircle as many as they thought fit for their purpose." For the slaves, many of whom thought they were about to be eaten, it was the terrifying climax of a terrifying voyage. Another of Falconbridge's ships, the *Alexander*, sold its cargo by scramble in a slave yard at Grenada. The women, he says, were frightened out of their wits. Several of them climbed over the fence and ran about Saint George's town as if they were mad. In his second voyage, while lying in Kingston harbor, he saw a sale by scramble on board the *Tyral*, Captain Macdonald. Forty or fifty of the slaves jumped overboard—"all of which, however," Falconbridge told the House of Commons, "he believes were taken up again."

DOCUMENTS

Voyage From Africa, 1756

The first object which saluted my eyes when I arrived on the coast was the sea, and a slaveship, which was then riding at anchor, and waiting for its cargo. These filled me with astonishment, which was soon converted into terror, which I am yet at a loss to describe, nor the then feelings of my mind. When I was carried on board I was immediately handled, and tossed up, to see if I were sound, by some of the crew; and I was now persuaded that I had got into a world of bad spirits, and that they were going to kill me. . . .

I was not long suffered to indulge my grief; I was soon put down under the decks, and there I received such a salutation in my nostrils as I had never experienced in my life; so that, with the loathsomeness of the stench, and crying together, I became so sick and low that I was not able to eat, nor had I the least desire to taste anything . . . but soon, to my grief, two of the white men offered me eatables; and, on my refusing to eat, one of them held me fast by the hands, and laid me across, I think, the windlass, and tied my feet, while the other flogged me severely. . . .

SOURCE: Gustavus Vasa, *The Interesting Narrative of the Life of Olandah Equiano or Gustavus Vasa, Written by Himself* (London: Printed and sold by the author, 1793), 46–53.

In a little time after, amongst the poor chained men, I found some of my own nation, which in a small degree gave ease to my mind. I inquired of them what was to be done with us? they gave me to understand we were to be carried to these white people's country to work for them. I then was a little revived, and thought, if it were no worse than working, my situation was not so desperate: but still I feared I should be put to death, the white people looked and acted, as I thought, in so savage a manner; for I had never seen among any people such instances of brutal cruelty; and this not only shewn towards us blacks, but also to some of the whites themselves. One white man in particular I saw, when we were permitted to be on deck, flogged so unmercifully with a large rope near the foremast, that he died in consequence of it; and they tossed him over the side as they would have done a brute. This made me fear these people the more; and I expected nothing less than to be treated in the same manner. . . .

The stench of the hold while we were on the coast, was so intolerably loathsome, that it was dangerous to remain there for any time, and some of us had been permitted to stay on the deck for the fresh air; but now that the whole ship's cargo were confined together, it became absolutely pestilential. The closeness of the place, and the heat of the climate, added to the number in the ship, which was so crowded that each had scarcely room to turn himself, almost suffocated us. . . .

The shrieks of the women, and the groans of the dying, rendered the whole a scene of horror almost inconceivable. Happily perhaps for myself I was soon reduced so low here that it was thought necessary to keep me almost always on deck; and from my extreme youth I was not put in fetters. In this situation I expected every hour to share the fate of my companions, some of whom were almost daily brought upon deck at the point of death which I began to hope would soon put an end to my miseries. . . .

One day, when we had a smooth sea, and moderate wind, two of my wearied countrymen, who were chained together (I was near them at the time), preferring death to such a life of misery, somehow made through the nettings, and jumped into the sea; immediately another quite dejected fellow, who, on account of his illness, was suffered to be out of irons, also followed their example; and I believe many more would very soon have done the same, if they had not been prevented by the ship's crew, who were instantly alarmed. Those of us that were the most active were in a moment put down under the deck; and there was such a noise and confusion amongst the people of the ship as I never heard before, to stop her, and get the boat out to go after the slaves. However, two of the wretches were drowned, but they got the other, and afterwards flogged him unmercifully, for thus attempting to prefer death to slavery. In this manner we continued to undergo more hardships than I can now relate. . . .

An Immigrant's Journey, 1750

Both in Rotterdam and in Amsterdam the people are packed densely, like herrings so to say, in the large sea vessels. One person receives a place of scarcely 2 feet width and 6 feet length in the bedstead, while many a ship carries four to six hundred souls; not to mention the innumerable implements, tools, provisions, water-barrels and other things which likewise occupy much space.

On account of contrary winds it takes the ships sometimes 2, 3 and 4 weeks to make the trip from Holland to Kaupp [Cowes] in England. But when the wind is good, they get there in 8 days or even sooner. Everything is examined there and the custom-duties paid, whence it comes that the ships ride there 8, 10 to 14 days and even longer at anchor, till they have taken in their full cargoes. During that time every one is compelled to spend his last remaining money and to consume his little stock of provisions which had been reserved for the sea; so that most passengers, finding themselves on the ocean where they would be in greater need of them, must greatly suffer from hunger and want. Many suffer want already on the water between Holland and Old England.

When the ships have for the last time weighed their anchors near the city of Kaupp [Cowes] in Old England, the real misery begins with the long voyage. For from there the ships, unless they have good wind, must often sail 8, 9, 10 to 12 weeks before they reach Philadelphia. But even with the best wind the voyage lasts 7 weeks.

But during the voyage there is on board these ships terrible misery, stench, fumes, horror, vomiting, many kinds of seasickness, fever, dysentery, headache, heat, constipation, boils, scurvy, cancer, mouth-rot, and the like, all of which come from old and sharply salted food and meat, also from very bad and foul water, so that many die miserably.

Add to this want of provisions, hunger, thirst, frost, heat, dampness, anxiety, want, afflictions and lamentations, together with other trouble, as c. v. the lice abound so frightfully, especially on sick people, that they can be scraped off the body. The misery reaches the climax when a gale rages for 2 or 3 nights and days, so that every one believes that the ship will go to the bottom with all human beings on board. In such a visitation the people cry and pray most piteously. . . .

Many sigh and cry: "Oh, that I were at home again, and if I had to lie in my pig-sty!" Or they say: "O God, if I only had a piece of good bread,

SOURCE: Gottlieb Mittelberger, *Journey to Pennsylvania in the Year 1750 and Return to Germany in the Year 1754*, trans. Carl Theo. Eben (Philadelphia: John Jos McVey, 1898), 19–20, 22, 24–31.

or a good fresh drop of water." Many people whimper, sigh and cry piteously for their homes; most of them get home-sick. Many hundred people necessarily die and perish in such misery and must be cast into the sea, which drives their relatives or those who persuaded them to undertake the journey, to such despair that it is almost impossible to pacify and console them. In a word, the sighing and crying and lamenting on board the ship continues night and day so as to cause the hearts even of the most hardened to bleed when they hear it. . . .

At length, when, after a long and tedious voyage, the ships come in sight of land, so that the promontories can be seen, which the people were so eager and anxious to see, all creep from below on deck to see the land from afar, and they weep for joy, and pray and sing, thanking and praising God. The sight of the land makes the people on board the ship, especially the sick and the half-dead, alive again, so that their hearts leap within them; they shout and rejoice, and are content to bear their misery in patience, in the hope that they may soon reach the land in safety. But alas!

When the ships have landed at Philadelphia after their long voyage, no one is permitted to leave them except those who pay for their passage or can give good security; the others, who cannot pay, must remain on board the ships till they are purchased, and are released from the ships by their purchasers. The sick always fare the worst, for the healthy are naturally preferred and purchased first; and so the sick and wretched must often remain on board in front of the city for 2 or 3 weeks, and frequently die, whereas many a one, if he could pay his debt and were permitted to leave the ship immediately, might recover and remain alive. . . .

The sale of human beings in the market on board the ship is carried on thus: Every day Englishmen, Dutchmen and High-German people come from the city of Philadelphia and other places, in part from a great distance, say 20, 30, or 40 hours away, and go on board the newly arrived ship that has brought and offers for sale passengers from Europe, and select among the healthy persons such as they deem suitable for their business, and bargain with them how long they will serve for their passage money, which most of them are still in debt for. When they have come to an agreement, it happens that adult persons bind themselves in writing to serve 3, 4, 5 or 6 years for the amount due by them, according to their age and strength. But very young people, from 10 to 15 years, must serve till they are 21 years old.

Many parents must sell and trade away their children like so many head of cattle; for if their children take the debt upon themselves, the parents can leave the ship free and unrestrained; but as the parents often do not know where and to what people their children are going, it often happens that such parents and children, after leaving the ship, do not see each other again for many years, perhaps no more in all their lives. . . .

It often happens that whole families, husband, wife, and children, are separated by being sold to different purchasers, especially when they have not paid any part of their passage money.

When a husband or wife has died at sea, when the ship has made more than half of her trip, the survivor must pay or serve not only for himself or herself, but also for the deceased.

When both parents have died over half-way at sea, their children, especially when they are young and have nothing to pawn or to pay, must stand for their own and their parents' passage, and serve till they are 21 years old. When one has served his or her term, he or she is entitled to a new suit of clothes at parting; and if it has been so stipulated, a man gets in addition a horse, a woman, a cow. . . .

If some one in this country runs away from his master, who has treated him harshly, he cannot get far. Good provision has been made for such cases, so that a runaway is soon recovered. He who detains or returns a deserter receives a good reward.

If such a runaway has been away from his master one day, he must serve for it as a punishment a week, for a week a month, and for a month half a year. But if the master will not keep the runaway after he has got him back, he may sell him for so many years as he would have to serve him yet. . . .

However hard he may be compelled to work in his fatherland, he will surely find it quite as hard, if not harder, in the new country. Besides, there is not only the long and arduous journey lasting half a year, during which he has to suffer, more than with the hardest work; he has also spent about 200 florins which no one will refund to him. If he has so much money, it will slip out of his hands; if he has it not, he must work his debt off as a slave and poor serf. Therefore let every one stay in his own country and support himself and his family honestly. Besides I say that those who suffer themselves to be persuaded and enticed away by the man-thieves, are very foolish if they believe that roasted pigeons will fly into their mouths in America or Pennsylvania without their working for them.

CHAPTER 4

Husbands and Wives, Parents and Children in Puritan Society

The colonists wanted to live in the New World as Europeans. Thus, in addition to material necessities, they brought with them the languages, religions, political and social institutions, values, and attitudes of their native lands. But the European traditions were transformed as the settlers responded to their new surroundings and experiences, ultimately producing a distinctive colonial American culture.

The phenomenon of cultural continuity and modification is explored in the essay from John Demos's A Little Commonwealth: Family Life in Plymouth Colony. The author discusses patterns of interpersonal relationship in seventeenth-century Plymouth, Massachusetts, instances in which women's behavior differed from the traditional norms. What factors might have contributed to the relatively improved status of women in the colonies? Is the author convincing when he speaks *of Plymouth as a society not "characterized by a really pervasive, and operational, norm of male dominance"?*

In discussing feelings of warmth and love in Plymouth marriages, Demos acknowledges the difficulty of drawing conclusions from the available sources: court records, wills, and other legal documents. Although, as he points out, literary materials from Plymouth Colony are scarce, we are fortunate to have the poems of Anne Bradstreet of the neighboring Puritan colony of Massachusetts Bay. Bradstreet was the first important woman writer in colonial America. The first document presents two of her poems, "To My Dear and Loving Husband" and "Before the Birth of One of Her Children"—works that evoke a sense of deep and abiding love in a Puritan marriage. The poet's husband, Simon Bradstreet, served two terms as colonial governor of Massachusetts (1679–86, 1689–92).

The concept of reciprocal obligations between parents and children that Demos describes was of central importance to Puritans. The establishment in Massachusetts in 1647 of the first system of public schooling in the British Empire was a reflection of the Puritans' concern for education, and of their belief that the state had a role to play in ensuring that family obligations were fulfilled. The second document is from the New England Primer *(1727 edition), the first school book published in America. It sets forth the Puritan concept of the "Duty of Children Toward Their Parents."*

The final document is an excerpt from Eleazer Moody's The School of Good Manners, *a well-known book of eighteenth-century children's literature. Which of the fifty-two dicta Moody lists might be considered valid by today's parents? Which, if any, would be rejected? What general conclusions can be drawn regarding differences in attitudes toward children's behavior today and in colonial New England?*

ESSAY

Husbands and Wives, Parents and Children in Plymouth Colony

John Demos

No aspect of the Puritan household was more vital than the relationship of husband and wife: But the study of this relationship raises at once certain larger questions of sex differentiation: What were the relative positions of men and women in Plymouth Colony? What attributes, and what overall valuation, were thought appropriate to each sex?

SOURCE: *A Little Commonwealth: Family Life in Plymouth Colony* by John Demos. Reprinted by permission of the author and Oxford University Press, Inc.

We know in a general way that male dominance was an accepted principle all over the Western World in the seventeenth century. The fundamental Puritan sentiment on this matter was expressed by Milton in a famous line in *Paradise Lost:* "he for God only, she for God in him"; and there is no reason to suspect that the people of Plymouth would have put it any differently. The world of public affairs was nowhere open to women—in Plymouth only males were eligible to become "freemen."* Within the family the husband was always regarded as the "head"—and the Old Colony provided no exceptions to this pattern. Moreover, the culture at large maintained a deep and primitive kind of suspicion of women, solely on account of their sex. Some basic taint of corruption was thought to be inherent in the feminine constitution—a belief rationalized, of course, by the story of Eve's initial treachery in the Garden of Eden. It was no coincidence that in both the Old and the New World witches were mostly women. Only two allegations of witchcraft turn up in the official records of Plymouth, but other bits of evidence point in the same general direction. There are, for example, the quoted words of a mother beginning an emotional plea to her son: "if you would beleive a woman beleive mee. . . ." And why *not* believe a woman?

The views of the Pilgrim pastor John Robinson are also interesting in this connection. He opposed, in the first place, any tendency to regard women as "necessary evils" and greatly regretted the currency of such opinions among "not only heathen poets . . . but also wanton Christians." The Lord had created both man and woman of an equal perfection, and "neither is she, since the creation more degenerated than he from the primitive goodness." Still, in marriage some principles of authority were essential, since "differences will arise and be seen, and so the one must give way, and apply unto the other; this, God and nature layeth upon the woman, rather than upon the man." Hence the proper attitude of a wife towards her husband was "a reverend subjection."

However, in a later discussion of the same matter Robinson developed a more complex line of argument which stressed certain attributes of inferiority assumed to be inherently feminine. Women, he wrote, were under two different kinds of subjection. The first was framed "in innocency" and implied no "grief" or "wrong" whatsoever. It reflected simply the woman's character as "the weaker vessel"—weaker, most obviously, with respect to intelligence or "understanding." For this was a gift "which God hath . . . afforded [the man], and means of obtaining it, above the woman, that he might guide and go before her." Robinson also recognized that some men abused their position of authority and oppressed their wives most unfairly. But *even so*—and this was his central point—resistance was not admissible. Here he affirmed the second kind of subjection laid upon woman, a subjection undeniably "grievous" but

[*those with full rights of citizenship, including the franchise] justified by her "being first in transgression." In this way—by invoking the specter of Eve corrupting Adam in paradise—Robinson arrived in the end at a position which closely approximated the popular assumption of woman's basic moral weakness.

Yet within this general framework of masculine superiority there were a number of rather contrary indications. They seem especially evident in certain areas of the law. Richard B. Morris has written a most interesting essay on this matter, arguing the improved legal status of colonial women by comparison to what still obtained in the mother country. Many of his conclusions seem to make a good fit with conditions in Plymouth Colony. The baseline here is the common law tradition of England, which at this time accorded to women only the most marginal sort of recognition. The married woman, indeed, was largely subsumed under the legal personality of her husband; she was virtually without rights to own property, make contracts, or sue for damages on her own account. But in the New World this situation was perceptibly altered.

Consider, for example, the evidence bearing on the property rights of Plymouth Colony wives. The law explicitly recognized their part in the accumulation of a family's estate, by the procedures it established for the treatment of widows. It was a basic principle of inheritance in this period—on both sides of the Atlantic—that a widow should have the use or profits of one-third of the land owned by her husband at the time of his death and full title to one-third of his movable property. But at least in Plymouth, and perhaps in other colonies as well, this expressed more than the widow's need for an adequate living allowance. For the laws also prescribed that "if any man do make an irrational and unrighteous Will, whereby he deprives his Wife of her reasonable allowance for her subsistencey," the Court may "relieve her out of the estate, notwithstanding by Will it were otherwise disposed; especially in such case where the Wife brought with her good part of the Estate in Marriage, or hath by her diligence and industry done her part in the getting of the Estate, and was otherwise well deserving." Occasionally the Court saw fit to alter the terms of a will on this account. In 1663, for example, it awarded to widow Naomi Silvester a larger share of her late husband's estate than the "inconsiderable pte" he had left her, since she had been "a frugall and laborious woman in the procuring of the said estate." In short, the widow's customary "thirds" was not a mere dole; it was her *due*.

But there is more still. In seventeenth-century England women were denied the right to make contracts, save in certain very exceptional instances. In Plymouth Colony, by contrast, one finds the Court sustaining certain kinds of contracts involving women on a fairly regular basis. The most common case of this type was the agreement of a widow and a new husband, made *before* marriage, about the future disposition of their respective properties. The contract drawn up by John Phillips of Marshfield and widow Faith Doty of Plymouth in 1667 was fairly standard. It stipulated that "the said Faith Dotey is to enjoy all her house and land, goods and cattles, that shee is now possessed of, to her owne proper use, to dispose of them att her owne free will from time to time, and att any time, as shee shall see cause." Moreover this principle of separate control extended beyond the realm of personal property. Phillips and widow Doty each had young children by their previous marriages, and their agreement was "that the children of both the said pties shall remaine att the free and proper and onely dispose of theire owne naturall parents, as they shall see good to dispose of them." Any woman entering marriage on terms such as these would seem virtually an equal partner, at least from a legal standpoint. Much rarer, but no less significant, were contracts made by women *after* marriage. When Dorothy Clarke wished to be free of her husband Nathaniel in 1686, the Court refused a divorce but allowed a separation. Their estate was then carefully divided up by contract to which the wife was formally a party. Once again, no clear precedents for this procedure can be found in contemporary English law.

The specific terms of some wills also help to confirm the rights of women to a limited kind of ownership even within marrige. No husband ever included his wife's clothing, for example, among the property to be disposed of after his death. And consider, on the other side, a will like that of Mistress Sarah Jenny, drawn up at Plymouth in 1655. Her husband had died just a few months earlier, and she wished simply to "Despose of som smale thingss that is my owne proper goods leaveing my husbands will to take place according to the true Intent and meaning thereof." The "smale thinges" included not only her wardrobe, but also a bed, some books, a mare, some cattle and sheep. Unfortunately, married women did not usually leave wills of their own (unless they had been previously widowed); and it is necessary to infer that in most cases there was some sort of informal arrangement for the transfer of their personal possessions. One final indication of these same patterns comes from wills which made bequests to a husband and wife separately. Thus, for example, Richard Sealis of Scituate conferred most of his personal possessions on the families of two married daughters, carefully specifying which items should go to the daughters themselves and which to their husbands. Thomas Rickard, also of Scituate, had no family of his own and chose therefore to distribute his property among a variety of friends. Once again spouses were treated separately: "I give unto Thomas Pincin my bedd and Rugg one paire of sheets and pilloty . . . I give and bequeath unto Joane the wife of the aforsaid Thomas Princin my bason and fouer sheets . . . I give and bequeath unto Joane Stanlacke my Chest . . . unto Richard Stanlacke my Chest . . . unto Richard Stanlacke my best briches and Dublit and ould Coate."

The questions of property rights and of the overall distribution of authority within a marriage do not necessarily coincide; and modern sociologists interested in the latter subject usually emphasize the process of decision-making. Of course, their use of live samples gives them a very great advantage; they can ask their informants, through questionnaires or interviews, which spouse decides where to go on vacation, what kind of car to buy, how to discipline the children, when to have company in, and so forth. The historian simply cannot draw out this kind of detail, nor can he contrive any substantial equivalent. But he is able sometimes to make a beginning in this direction; for example, the records of Plymouth do throw light on two sorts of family decisions of the very greatest importance. One of these involves the transfer of land and illustrates further the whole trend toward an expansion of the rights of married women to hold property. The point finds tangible expression in a law passed by the General Court in 1646: "It is enacted &c. That the Assistants or any of them shall have full power to take the acknowledgment of a bargaine and sale of houses and lands . . . And that the wyfe hereafter come in & consent and acknowledg the sale also; but that all bargaines and sales of houses and lands made before this day to remayne firm to the buyer notwithstanding the wife did not acknowledge the same." The words "come in" merit special attention: the authorities wished to confront the wife personally (and even, perhaps, privately?) in order to minimize the possibility that her husband might exert undue pressure in securing her agreement to a sale.

The second area of decision-making in which both spouses shared an important *joint* responsibility was the "putting out" of children into foster families.* For this there was no statute prescribing a set line of procedure, but the various written documents from specific cases make the point clearly enough. Thus in 1660 "An Agreement appointed to bee Recorded" affirmed that "Richard Berry of Yarmouth with his wifes Concent and other frinds; hath given unto Gorge Crispe of Eastham and his; wife theire son Samuell Berry; to bee att the ordering and Disposing of the said Gorge and his wife as if hee were theire owne Child." The practice of formally declaring the wife's consent is evident in all such instances, when both parents were living. Another piece of legal evidence describes an actual deathbed scene in which the same issue had to be faced. It is the testimony of a mother confirming the adoption of her son, and it is worth quoting in some detail. "These prsents Witnesse that the 20th of march 1657–8 Judith the wife of William Peaks acknowlidged that her former husband Lawrance Lichfeild lying on his Death bedd sent for John Allin and Ann his wife and Desired to give and bequeath unto them his youngest son Josias Lichfeild if they would accept of him and take him as theire Child; then they Desired to know how long they should have him and the said Lawrance said for

---

* Concern that parental love and affection might inhibit the proper, disciplined upbringing of children was a frequent cause of the decision to "put out" a son or daughter.

ever; but the mother of the child was not willing then; but in a short time after willingly Concented to her husbands will in the thinge." That the wife finally agreed is less important here than the way in which her initial reluctance sufficed to block the child's adoption, in spite of the clear wishes of her husband.

Another reflection of this pattern of mutual responsibility appears in certain types of business activity—for instance, the management of inns and taverns ("ordinaries" in the language of the day). All such establishments were licensed by the General Court; hence their history can be followed, to a limited degree, in the official Colony Records. It is interesting to learn that one man's license was revoked because he had recently "buryed his wife, and in that respect not being soe capeable of keeping a publicke house." In other cases the evidence is less explicit but still revealing. For many years James Cole ran the principal ordinary in the town of Plymouth, and from time to time the Court found it necessary to censure and punish certain violations of proper decorum that occurred there. In some of these cases Cole's wife Mary was directly implicated. In March 1669 a substantial fine was imposed "for that the said Mary Cole suffered divers psons after named to stay drinking on the Lords day . . . in the time of publicke worshipp." Indeed the role of women in all aspects of this episode is striking, since two of the four drinking customers, the "divers psons after named," turned out to be female. Perhaps, then, women had considerable freedom to move on roughly the same terms with men even into some of the darker byways of Old Colony life.

The Court occasionally granted liquor licenses directly to women. Husbands were not mentioned, though it is of course possible that all of the women involved were widows. In some cases the terms of these permits suggest retail houses rather than regular inns or taverns. Thus in 1663 "Mistris Lydia Garrett" of Scituate was licensed to "sell liquors, alwaies provided . . . that shee sell none but to house keepers, and not lesse than a gallon att a time;" and the agreement with another Scituate lady, Margaret Muffee, twenty years later, was quite similar. But meanwhile in Middlebury one "Mistress Mary Combe" seems to have operated an ordinary of the standard type. Can we proceed from these specific data on liquor licensing to some more general conclusion about the participation of women in the whole field of economic production and exchange? Unfortunately there is little additional hard evidence on one side or the other. The Court Records do not often mention other types of business activity, with the single exception of milling; and no woman was ever named in connection with this particular enterprise. A few more wills could be cited—for instance, the one made by Elizabeth Poole, a wealthy spinster in Taunton, leaving "my pte in the Iron workes" to a favorite nephew. But this does not add up to very much. The economy of Plymouth was, after all, essentially simple—indeed "underdeveloped"—in most important respects. Farming claimed the energies of all but a tiny portion of the populace; there was relatively little opportunity for anyone, man *or* woman, to develop a more commercial orientation. It is known that in the next century women played quite a significant role in the business life of many parts of New England, and one can view this pattern as simply the full development of possibilities that were latent even among the first generations of settlers. But there is no way to fashion an extended chain of proof.

Much of what has been said so far belongs to the general category of the rights and privileges of the respective partners to a marriage. But what of their duties, their basic responsibilities to one another? Here, surely, is another area of major importance in any assessment of the character of married life. The writings of John Robinson help us to make a start with these questions, and especially to recover the framework of ideals within which most couples of Plymouth Colony must have tried to hammer out a meaningful day-to-day relationship. We have noted already that Robinson prescribed "subjection" as the basic duty of a wife to her husband. No woman deserved praise, "how well endowed soever otherwise, except she frame, and compose herself, what may be, unto her husband, in conformity of manners." From the man, by contrast, two things were particularly required: "love . . . and wisdom." His love for his wife must be "like Christ's to his church: holy for quality, and great for quantity," and it must stand firm even where "her failings and faults be great." His wisdom was essential to the role of family "head"; without it neither spouse was likely to find the way to true piety, and eventually to salvation.

It is a long descent from the spiritual counsel of John Robinson to the details of domestic conflict as noted in the Colony Records. But the Records are really the only available source of information about the workings of actual marriages in this period. They are, to be sure, a negative type of source; that is, they reveal only those cases which seemed sufficiently deviant and sufficiently important to warrant the attention of the authorities. But it is possible by a kind of reverse inference to use them to reconstruct the norms which the community at large particularly wished to protect. This effort serves to isolate three basic obligations in which both husband and wife were thought to share.

There was, first and most simply, the obligation of regular and exclusive cohabitation. No married person was permitted to live apart from his spouse except in very unusual and temporary circumstances (as when a sailor was gone to sea). The Court stood ready as a last resort to force separated couples to come together again, though it was not often necessary to deal with the problem in such an official way. One of the few recorded cases of this type occurred in 1659. The defendant was a certain Goodwife Spring, married to a resident of Watertown in the Bay Colony and formerly the wife and widow of Thomas Hatch of Scituate. She had, it seems, returned to Scituate some three or four years earlier, and had been living "from her husband" ever since. The Court ordered that "shee either repaire to her husband with all convenient speed, . . . or . . . give a reason why shee doth not." Exactly how this matter turned out cannot be determined, but it seems likely that the ultimate sanction was banishment from the Colony. The government of Massachusetts Bay is known to have imposed this penalty in a number of similar cases. None of the extant records describe such action being taken at Plymouth, but presumably the possibility was always there.

Moreover, the willful desertion of one spouse by the other over a period of several years was one of the few legitimate grounds for divorce. In 1670, for example, the Court granted the divorce plea of James Skiffe "haveing received sufficient testimony that the late wife of James Skiffe hath unlawfully forsaken her lawfull husband . . . and is gone to Roanoke, in or att Verginnia, and there hath taken another man for to be her husband." Of course, bigamy was always sufficient reason in itself for terminating a marriage. Thus in 1680 Elizabeth Stevens obtained a divorce from her husband when it was proved that he had three other wives already, one each in Boston, Barbadoes, and a town in England not specified.

But it was not enough that married persons should simply live together on a regular basis; their relationship must be relatively peaceful and harmonious. Once again the Court reserved the right to interfere in cases where the situation had become especially difficult. Occasionally both husband and wife were judged to be at fault, as when George and Anna Barlow were "severly reproved for theire most ungodly liveing in contension one with the other, and admonished to live otherwise." But much more often one or the other was singled out for the Court's particular attention. One man was punished for "abusing his wife by kiking her of from a stoole into the fier," and another for "drawing his wife in an uncivell manor on the snow." A more serious case was that of John Dunham, convicted of "abusive carriage towards his wife in continuall tiranising over her, and in pticulare for his late abusive and uncivill carryage in endeavoring to beate her in a deboist manor." The Court ordered a whipping as just punishment for these cruelties, but the sentence was then suspended at the request of Dunham's wife. Sometimes the situation was reversed and the woman was the guilty party. In 1655, for example, Joan Miller of Taunton was charged with "beating and reviling her husband, and egging her children to healp her, bidding them knock him in the head, and wishing his victuals might coak him." A few years later the wife of Samuel Halloway (also of Taunton) was admonished for "carryage towards her husband . . . soe turbulend and wild, both in words and actions, as hee could not live with her but in danger of his life or limbs."

It would serve no real purpose to cite more of these unhappy episodes—and it might indeed create an erroneous impression that marital conflict was particularly endemic among the people of the Old Colony.

But two general observations are in order. First, the Court's chief aim in this type of case was to [restore] the couple in question to something approaching tranquility. The assumption was that a little force applied from the outside might be useful, whether it came in the form of an "admonition" or in some kind of actual punishment. Only once did the Court have to recognize that the situation might be so bad as to make a final reconciliation impossible. This happened in 1665 when John Williams, Jr., of Scituate, was charged with a long series of "abusive and harsh carriages" toward his wife Elizabeth, "in speciall his sequestration of himselfe from the marriage bed, and his accusation of her to bee a whore, and that especially in reference unto a child lately borne of his said wife by him denied to bee legittimate." The case was frequently before the Court during the next two years, and eventually all hope of a settlement was abandoned. When Williams persisted in his "abuses," and when too he had "himself . . . [declared] his insufficency for converse with weomen," a formal separation was allowed—though not a full divorce. In fact, it may be that his impotence, not his habitual cruelty, was the decisive factor in finally persuading the Court to go this far. For in another case, some years later, a separation was granted on the former grounds alone.

The second noteworthy aspect of all these situations is the equality they seem to imply between the sexes. In some societies and indeed in many parts of Europe at this time, a wife was quite literally at the mercy of her husband—his prerogatives extended even to the random use of physical violence. But clearly this was not the situation at Plymouth. It is, for example, instructive to break down these charges of "abusive carriage" according to sex: one finds that wives were accused just about as often as husbands. Consider, too, those cases of conflict in which the chief parties were of opposite sex but not married to one another. Once again the women seem to have held their own. Thus we have, on the one side, Samuel Norman punished for "strikeing Lydia, the wife of Henery Taylor," and John Dunham for "abusive speeches and carriages" toward Sarah, wife of Benjamin Eaton; and, on the other side, the complaint of Abraham Jackson against "Rose, the wife of Thomas Morton, . . . that the said Rose, as hee came from worke, did abuse him by calling of him lying rascall and rogue." In short, this does *not* seem to have been a society characterized by a really pervasive, and operational, norm of male dominance. There is no evidence at all of habitual patterns of deference in the relations between the sexes. John Robinson, and many others, too, may have assumed that woman was "the weaker vessel" and that "subjection" was her natural role. But as so often happens with respect to such matters, actual behavior was another story altogether.

The third of the major obligations incumbent on the married pair was a normal and exclusive sexual union. . . . Impotence in the husband was one of the few circumstances that might warrant a divorce. The reasoning behind this is nowhere made explicit, but most likely it reflected the felt necessity that a marriage produce children. It is worth noting in this connection some of the words used in a divorce hearing of 1686 which centered on the issue of a man's impotence. He was, according to his wife, "always unable to perform the act of generation." The latter phrase implies a particular view of the nature and significance of the sexual act, one which must have been widely held in this culture. Of course, there were other infertile marriages in the same period which held together. But perhaps the cause of the problem had to be obvious—as with impotence—for the people involved to consider divorce. Where the sexual function appeared normal in both spouses, there was always the hope that the Lord might one day grant the blessing of children. Doubtless for some couples this way of thinking meant year after year of deep personal disappointment.

The problem of adultery was more common—and, in a general sense, more troublesome. For adultery loomed as the most serious possible distortion of the whole sexual and reproductive side of marriage. John Robinson called it "that most foul and filthy sin, . . . the disease of marriage," and concluded that divorce was its necessary "medicine." In fact, most of the divorces granted in the Old Colony stemmed from this one cause alone. But adultery was not only a strong *prima facie* reason for divorce; it was also an act that would bring heavy punishment to the guilty parties. The law decreed that "whosoever shall Commit Adultery with a Married Woman or one Betrothed to another Man, both of them shall be severely punished, by whipping two several times . . . and likewise to wear two Capital Letters A.D. cut out in cloth and sewed on their uppermost Garments . . . and if at any time they shall be found without the said Letters so worne . . . to be forthwith taken and publickly whipt, and so from time to time as often as they are found not to wear them."

But quite apart from the severity of the prescribed punishments, this statute is interesting for its definition of adultery by reference to a married (or bethrothed) *woman*. Here, for the first time, we find some indication of difference in the conduct expected of men and women. The picture can be filled out somewhat by examining the specific cases of adultery prosecuted before the General Court down through the years. To be sure, the man involved in any given instance was judged together with the woman, and when convicted their punishments were the same. But there is another point to consider as well. All of the adulterous couples mentioned in the records can be classified in one of two categories: a married woman and a married man, or a married woman and a single man. There was, on the other hand, no case involving a married man and a single woman. This pattern seems to imply that the chief concern, the essential element of sin, was the woman's infidelity to her husband. A married man would be punished for his part in this aspect of the affair—rather than for any wrong done to his own wife.

However, this does not mean that a man's infidelities were wholly beyond reproach. The records, for example, include one divorce plea in which the wife adduced as her chief complaint "an act of uncleanes" by her husband with another woman. There was no move to prosecute and punish the husband—apparently since the other woman was unmarried. But the divorce was granted, and the wife received a most favorable settlement. We can, then, conclude the following. The adultery of a wife was treated as both a violation of her marriage (hence grounds for divorce) *and* an offense against the community (hence cause for legal prosecution). But for comparable behavior by husbands only the former consideration applied. In this somewhat limited sense the people of Plymouth Colony do seem to have maintained a "double standard" of sexual morality.

. . . Very little has been said here of love, affection, understanding—a whole range of positive feelings and impulses—between husbands and wives. Indeed the need to rely so heavily on Court Records has tended to weight the balance quite conspicuously on the side of conflict and failure. The fact is that the sum total of actions of divorce, prosecutions for adultery, "admonitions" against habitual quarreling, does not seem terribly large. In order to make a proper assessment of their meaning several contingent factors must be recognized; the long span of time they cover, the steady growth of the Colony's population (to something like 10,000 by the end of the century), the extensive jurisdiction of the Court over many areas of domestic life. Given this overall context, it is clear that the vast majority of Plymouth Colony families never once required the attention of the authorities. Elements of disharmony were, at the least, controlled and confined within certain limits.

But again, can the issue be approached in a more directly affirmative way? Just how, and how much, did feelings of warmth and love fit into the marriages of the Old Colony? Unfortunately our source materials have almost nothing to say in response to such questions. But this is only to be expected in the case of legal documents, physical remains, and so forth. The wills often refer to "my loveing wife"—but it would be foolish to read anything into such obvious set phrases. The records of Court cases are completely mute on this score. Other studies of "Puritan" ideals about marriage and the family have drawn heavily on literary materials—and this, of course, is the biggest gap in the sources that have come down from Plymouth Colony. Perhaps, though, a certain degree of extrapolation is permissible here; and if so, we must imagine that love was quite central to these marriages. If, as [Edmund] Morgan has shown, this was the case in Massachusetts Bay, surely it was also true for the people of Plymouth.

There are, finally, just a few scraps of concrete evidence on this point. . . . John Robinson wrote lavishly about the importance of love to a marriage—though he associated it chiefly with the role of the husband. And the wills should be drawn in once again, especially those clauses in which a man left specific instructions regarding the care of his widow. Sometimes the curtain of legal terms and style seems to rise for a moment and behind it one glimpses a deep tenderness and concern. There is, for example, the will written by Walter Briggs in 1676. Briggs's instructions in this regard embraced all of the usual matters—rooms, bedding, cooking utensils, "lyberty to make use of ye two gardens." And he ended with a particular request that his executors "allow my said wife a gentle horse or mare to ride to meeting or any other occasion she may have, & that Jemy, ye neger, catch it for her." Surely this kind of thoughtfulness reflected a larger instinct of love—one which, nourished in life, would not cease to be effective even in the face of death itself. . . .

Egalitarianism formed no part of seventeenth-century assumptions about the proper relationship of parents and children. But at Plymouth this relationship involved a set of *reciprocal* obligations.

From the standpoint of the child, the Biblical commandment to "Honor thy father and mother" was fundamental—and the force of law stood behind it. The relevant statute directed that "If any Childe or Children above sixteen years old, and of competent Understanding, shall Curse or Smite their Natural Father or Mother; he or they shall be put to Death, unless it can be sufficiently testified that the Parents have been very Unchristianly negligent in the Education of such Children, or so provoked them by extreme and cruel Correction, that they have been forced thereunto, to preserve themselves from Death or Maiming." A corollary order prescribed similar punishment for behavior that was simply "Stubborn or Rebellious"—or indeed, for any sort of habitual disobedience.

The rightful authority of the parents is clear enough here, but it should also be noted that this authority was limited in several ways. In the first place, a child less than sixteen years old was excluded from these prescriptions; he was not mature enough to be held finally responsible for his actions. Disobedience and disrespect on the part of younger children were surely punished, but on an informal basis and within the family itself. In such cases, presumably, the purpose of punishment was to form right habits; it was part of a whole pattern of learning. But for children of more than sixteen different assumptions applied. Ultimate responsibility could now be imputed, and an offense against one's parents was also an offense against the basic values of the community. Hence the full retributive process of the laws might properly be invoked.

The clause relating to "extreme and cruel correction" implied a second limitation on parental power. The child did have the right to protect his own person from any action that threatened "Death or Maiming." Finally, it seems significant that the arbiter of *all* such questions was not the parental couple directly involved but rather the constituted authorities of the Colony as a whole. The correct response to gross disobedience in a child was as follows: "his Father and Mother, . . . [shall] lay hold on him, and bring him before the Magistrates assembled in Court, and testifie unto them, that their Son is Stubborn and Rebellious, and will not obey their voice and chastisement." This may sound rather menacing, but it did imply an important kind of negative. The parents shall *not* take matters completely into their own hands. The child shall also have *his* say in Court; and presumably he may try, if he wishes, to show that his behavior was provoked by some cruelty on the part of his parents.

It must be said that only a few cases of youthful disobedience to parents actually reached the Courts, and that these few are not very revealing. Certainly the death penalty was never invoked on such grounds; only once, in fact, was it even mentioned as a possibility. In 1679 "Edward Bumpus for stricking and abusing his parents, was whipt att the post; his punishment was alleviated in regard hee was crasey brained, otherwise hee had bine put to death or otherwise sharply punished." In other instances the Court's function was to mediate between the affected parties or to ratify an agreement which had already been worked out on an informal basis. In 1669, for instance, it heard various testimonies about the "crewell, unnaturall, and extreame passionate carriages" of one Mary Morey toward her son Benjamin, and his own "unbeseeming" response. The situation was described as being so "turbulent . . . that severall of the naighbours feared murder would be in the issue of it." Yet in the end the Court took no action beyond admonishing both principals and making them "promise reformation." Some years earlier Thomas Lumbert of Barnstable complained formally that "Jedediah, his sone, hath carryed stuburnly against his said father," and proposed that the boy be "freed, provided hee doe dispose himselfe in some honest family with his fathers consent." The Court merely recorded this arrangement and decided not to interfere directly unless Jedediah neglected to find himself a good foster home. In sum, then, the role of the Court with regard to specific cases of this type, was quite limited. The laws on the matter should be viewed as expressing broad and basic values rather than an actual pattern of intervention in the day-to-day affairs of Old Colony households. In fact, most parents must have tried to define and enforce their authority very much on an individual basis. Quite likely an appeal to the Courts was a last resort, to be undertaken only with a keen sense of failure and personal humiliation.

The innermost dimensions of these vital intrafamily relationships cannot really be traced. But two particular matters seem noteworthy. Questions of inheritance were more closely intertwined with discipline in that period than is generally the case now. In some of the wills bequests to certain children were made contingent on their maintaining the proper sort of obedience. Thus, for example, Thomas Hicks of Scituate left most of his lands to "my two sonnes Daniell and Samuell upon this proviso that they bee Obedient unto theire mother and carrye themselves as they ought soe as they may live comfortably together but if the one or both live otherwise then they ought and undewtyfully and unquietly with theire Mother . . . then hee that soe carryeth himselfe shall Disinheritt himselfe of his pte of this land." The effectiveness of this kind of sanction among the settlers at large is difficult to assess. In many cases, of course, the point was never rendered so explicit as in the will of Thomas Hicks; but it must often have loomed in the background when conflict between parents and children reached a certain degree of intensity.

The same model of filial behavior seems to have obtained for grown as well as for young children, though perhaps in a somewhat attenuated form. In 1663, for example, the Court summoned Abraham Pierce, Jr. "to answare for his abusive speeches used to his father." The younger Pierce was at this time twenty-five years old and married. Another Court case of a different sort involved a question of disputed paternity. Martha, wife of Thomas Hewitt, gave birth shortly—*too* shortly—after their marriage: her husband contended that he could not have been the child's father and so persuaded the Court. Instead suspicion pointed toward Martha's own father, Christopher Winter, raising thereby the awful specter of incest. Among the evidence presented was "Winters acknowlidgment, that after hee had had knowlidge of his said daughters being with child,—being, as hee said, informed by Hewitt,—hee did not bring them together and enquire into it, nor reprove or beare witnes against her wickednes, as would have become a father that was innosent." Apparently then, a parent would normally continue to concern himself directly in the personal affairs of his children, even when they had become adult and were involved with families of their own. And, by implication, the children should listen to his counsel and respond accordingly.

But if the child owed his parents an unceasing kind of obedience and respect, there were other obligations which applied in the reverse direction. The parent for his part must accept responsibility for certain basic needs of his children—for their physical health and welfare, for their education (understood in the broadest sense), and for the property they would require in order one day to "be for themselves." There were, moreover, legal provisions permitting the community to intervene in the case of parents who defaulted on these obligations. One statute affirmed that when "psons in this Gourment are not able to provide Competent and convenient food and raiment for theire Children," the latter might be taken in hand by local officials and placed in foster families where they would be more "comfortably provided for." Another, more extended set of enactments dealt with the whole educational side of the parental role. Children should be taught to read, "at least to be able duely to read the Scriptures." They should be made to understand "the Capital Laws" and "the main Grounds and Principles of Christian Religion." And they should be trained "in some honest lawful calling, labour or employment, that may be profitable for themselves, or the Country." Parents who neglected any of this were subject to fines; and once again the ultimate recourse of transferring children into new families might be applied if the neglect were habitual. Unfortunately we cannot discover how often these procedures were actually set in motion. The responsibility for specific cases was assigned to local authorities in the various towns, and records of their actions have not survived. But the basic intent behind the laws which covered such matters is clear—and in itself significant.

The obligation to provide a "portion" of property for children when they attained maturity was nowhere expressed in formal, legal terms. But it can certainly be inferred from other types of evidence. Many wills made specific mention of previous bequests to grown children—real or personal property, or both. Deeds of apprenticeship and adoption sometimes included the promise of a portion as one of the essential terms. This responsibility might, it seems, be transferred from a child's natural parents to his new master, but it could not be overlooked altogether. Some men gained the assistance of the government in arranging portions for their young, witness the following type of Court Order: "Libertie is graunted unto Mr. John Alden to look out a portion of land to accomodate his sons withall." Indeed the fundamental laws of the Colony recognized a special claim to such "accomodation" for "such children as heere born and next unto them such as are heere brought up under their parents and are come to the age of discretion."

More often, however, portions were managed on a purely private basis. One of the rare personal documents to survive from the Old Colony, a letter written by Benjamin Brewster, describes the process as it operated in a particular case: "Being at the hose of Gorge Geres upon the first of may in the yere of our Lord: 1684 then and there was a discorse betwene the aforesayd Geres and his son Jonathan he then being of age to be for him selfe: upon som consederation mofeing the sayd Geres there to he then declared what he would gefe his son Jonathan as the full of his porshon except ypon his sons better behaver should desarve more which was: 130: akers of Land that his father had of Owanneco up in the contre: and: 2: best of 2 yere old [horse?]: 1: stere of: 4: yer old and a cow."

DOCUMENTS

Two Poems, 1678

To My Dear and Loving Husband

If ever two were one, then surely we;
If ever man were loved by wife, then thee;
If ever wife was happy in a man,
Compare with me, ye women, if you can.
I prize thy love more than whole mines of gold,
Or all the riches that the East doth hold.

My love is such that rivers cannot quench,
Nor aught but love from thee give recompense.
Thy love is such I can no way repay;
The heavens reward thee manifold, I pray.
Then while we live in love let's so persevere
That when we live no more we may live ever.

Before the Birth of One of
Her Children

All things within this fading world have end.
Adversity doth still our joys attend;
No ties so strong, no friends so dear and sweet,
But with death's parting blow are sure to meet.
The sentence passed is most irrevocable,
A common thing, yet, oh, inevitable.
How soon, my dear, death may my steps attend,
How soon it may be thy lot to lose thy friend,
We both are ignorant; yet love bids me
These farewell lines to recommend to thee,
That when that knot's untied that made us one
I may seem thine who in effect am none.
And if I see not half my days that are due,
What nature would God grant to yours and you.
The many faults that well you know I have
Let be interred in my oblivion's grave;
If any worth or virtue were in me,
Let that live freshly in thy memory,
And when thou feelest no grief, as I no harms,

SOURCE: Anne Bradstreet, *Poems of Mrs. Anne Bradstreet* (Boston, 1758).

Yet love thy dead, who long lay in thine arms;
And when thy loss shall be repaid with gains
Look to my little babes, my dear remains,
And if thou love thyself, or lovedst me,
These oh protect from stepdam's injury.
And if chance to thine eyes shall bring this verse,
With some sad sighs honor my absent hearse;
And kiss this paper for thy love's dear sake,
Who with salt tears this last farewell did take.

The Duty of Children toward Their Parents, 1727

God hath commanded saying, Honour thy Father and Mother, and whoso curseth Father or Mother, let him die the Death. Mat. 15. 4.

Children obey your Parents in the Lord, for this is right.

2. Honour thy Father and Mother, (which is the first Commandment with Promise).

3. That it may be well with thee, and that thou mayst live long on the Earth.

Children, obey your Parents in all Things, for that is well pleasing unto the Lord. Col. 3, 20.

The Eye that mocketh his Father, and despiseth the Instruction of his Mother, let the Ravens of the Valley pluck it out, and the young Eagles eat it.

Father, I have sinned against Heaven, and before thee. Luke 15, 10.

I am no more worthy to be called thy Son.

No man ever hated his own flesh, but nourisheth and cherisheth it. Ephes. 5, 19.

I pray thee let my Father and Mother come and abide with you, till I know what God will do for me. I Sam. 22, 3.

My Son, help thy Father in his Age, and grieve him not as long as he liveth.

And if his Understanding fail, have patience with him, and despise him not when thou art in thy full Strength.

Whoso curseth his Father or his Mother, his Lamp shall be put out in obscure Darkness. Prov. 20, 20.

SOURCE: Paul Leicester Ford, ed., *The New England Primer* (New York: Dodd, Mead & Co., 1899). Facsimile reprinting of 1727 edition, pp. 20–22.

Good Manners for Colonial Children, 1772

When at Home

1. Make a bow always when you come home, and be immediately uncovered.
2. Be never covered at home, especially before thy parents or strangers.
3. Never sit in the presence of thy parents without bidding, tho' no stranger be present.
4. If thou passest by thy parents, and any place where thou seest them, when either by themselves or with company, bow towards them.
5. If thou art going to speak to thy parents, and see them engaged in discourse with company, draw back and leave thy business until afterwards; but if thou must speak, be sure to whisper.
6. Never speak to thy parents without some title of respect, viz., Sir, Madam, &c.
7. Approach near thy parents at no time without a bow.
8. Dispute not, nor delay to obey thy parents commands.
9. Go not out of doors without thy parents leave, and return within the time by them limited.
10. Come not into the room where thy parents are with strangers, unless thou art called, and then decently; and at bidding go out; or if strangers come in while thou art with them, it is manners, with a bow to withdraw.
11. Use respectful and courteous but not insulting or domineering carriage or language toward the servants.
12. Quarrel not nor contend with thy brethren or sisters, but live in love, peace, and unity.
13. Grumble not nor be discontented at anything thy parents appoint, speak, or do.
14. Bear with meekness and patience, and without murmuring or sullenness, thy parents reproofs or corrections: Nay, tho' it should so happen that they be causeless or undeserved.

In Their Discourse

1. Among superiors speak not till thou art spoken to, and bid to speak.
2. Hold not thine hand, nor any thing else, before thy mouth when thou speakest.
3. Come not over-near to the person thou speakest to.

SOURCE: Eleazer Moody, *The School of Good Manners. Composed for the Help of Parents in Teaching Their Children How to Carry It in Their Places During Their Minority* (Boston: Fleets, 1772), 17–19.

4. If thy superior speak to thee while thou sittest, stand up before thou givest any answer.
5. Sit not down till thy superior bid thee.
6. Speak neither very loud, nor too low.
7. Speak clear, not stammering, stumbling nor drawling.
8. Answer not one that is speaking to thee until he hath done.
9. Loll not when thou art speaking to a superior or spoken to by him.
10. Speak not without, Sir, or some other title of respect.
11. Strive not with superiors in argument or discourse; but easily submit thine opinion to their assertions.
12. If thy superior speak any thing wherein thou knowest he is mistaken, correct not nor contradict him, nor grin at the hearing of it; but pass over the error without notice or interruption.
13. Mention not frivolous or little things among grave persons or superiors.
14. If thy superior drawl or hesitate in his words, pretend not to help him out, or to prompt him.
15. Come not too near two that are whispering or speaking in secret, much less may'st thou ask about what they confer.
16. When thy parent or master speak to any person, speak not thou, nor hearken to them.
17. If thy superior be relating a story, say not, "I have heard it before," but attend to it as though it were altogether new. Seem not to question the truth of it. If he tell it not right, snigger not, nor endeavor to help him out, or add to his relation.
18. If any immodest or obscene thing be spoken in thy hearing, smile not, but settle thy countenance as though thou did'st not hear it.
19. Boast not in discourse of thine own wit or doings.
20. Beware thou utter not any thing hard to be believed.
21. Interrupt not any one that speaks, though thou be his familiar.
22. Coming into company, whilst any topic is discoursed on, ask not what was the preceding talk but hearken to the remainder.
23. Speaking of any distant person, it is rude and unmannerly to point at him.
24. Laugh not in, or at thy own story, wit or jest.
25. Use not any contemptuous or reproachful language to any person, though very mean or inferior.
26. Be not over earnest in talking to justify and avouch thy own sayings.
27. Let thy words be modest about those things which only concern thee.
28. Repeat not over again the words of a superior that asketh thee a question or talketh to thee.

CHAPTER 5

Eighteenth-Century Religion: Progress and Piety

Religion was a pervasive influence in the lives of American colonists. Indeed, the New England colonies, Pennsylvania, and Maryland were established by founders with religious purposes in mind. In the other colonies, as well, religion was of central importance.

Eighteenth-century immigration, much of it non-English in origin, served to intensify and diversify the religious climate. German Mennonites, Dunkers, and Moravians established settlements in Pennsylvania. Lutherans from Scandinavia and Germany had, by the time of the Revolution, built some 130 churches throughout the middle and southern colonies. Scotch-Irish settlers brought their Presbyterian faith with them as they settled the western regions of Pennsylvania and moved south along the Appalachian mountain chain. English Baptists established a strong foothold in Philadelphia and eventually spread throughout the colonies, gaining particular strength in the South during the latter half of the century. Because no one group could dominate, religious toleration took root in colonial America.

Patricia Bonomi's essay describes the pervasiveness of churchgoing during the eighteenth century. As you read, notice the variety of ways in which the churches served the colonists, both in settled areas and on the frontier, and particularly among women and the elderly. The essay also discusses initial attempts to convert blacks and Indians to Christianity. The first document provides an example of such endeavors. Why did both masters and slaves respond less than enthusiastically to the efforts of missionaries to convert the slaves?

Many factors created a climate conducive to the advent of the evangelical revivalist movement, known as the Great Awakening: the increase in and growing diversity of America's eighteenth-century population, westward expansion, the appearance of new sects and denominations, and the challenging of religion by secular ideas. The movement, which Bonomi's essay describes, had its beginnings in the middle colonies in the mid-1730s and spread up and down the coast during the following decade. Its leaders divided along sectarian lines but found unity in their belief in the capacity of every individual to cast off sin, attain faith, and seek salvation. These "new light" preachers, often noted more for their piety and oratorical skill than for their learning, appealed to their audiences in colorful, highly emotional sermons. The excitement engendered by these ministers is described in the second document. In it Nathan Cole tells of events surrounding the appearance of the evangelist George Whitefield in Middletown, Connecticut, on October 23, 1740.

The "new light" movement was greeted with less than enthusiasm by members of the social and religious establishment. An "old light" view of the Great Awakening is presented in the final document, an excerpt from Charles Chauncy's sermon, "Enthusiasm Describ'd and Caution'd Against." Chauncy was a leading Boston clergyman.

After reading these documents, what do you think were the factors that led many people, including previously resistant blacks, to embrace the Great Awakening, and others to condemn it strongly?

ESSAY

The Churchgoers

Patricia U. Bonomi

Recent estimates suggest that a majority of adults in the eighteenth-century colonies were regular church attenders. Though the worship of God was no doubt the primary motive for churchgoing, eighteenth-century worshipers, like those of today, found that church attendance served a number of non-spiritual needs. The quest for community, long recognized as an incentive for churchgoing, must have operated with particular force among inhabitants of the dispersed farming society of early America. Churches in both country and town were vital centers of community life, as government proclamations were broadcast from the pulpit and news of prices and politics were exchanged in the churchyard. In a society formed from the uprooted communities of the Old World, moreover, the church congregation served as a primary agency by which immigrants recovered something of what they had left behind. Family tradition was another strong stimulus to churchgoing. Pious colonial parents promoted the religious education of their children and instilled in them habits of regular church attendance. In some congregations the founding elders and their offspring gained such firm control over the church that newcomers or persons not descended from "Godly parents" were made to feel unwelcome. Such "tribalism" apparently characterized the early Puritan churches, and a similar turning inward has been detected among the Quakers of Pennsylvania.

Inhabitants living on the geographic periphery of colonial parishes found their churchgoing practices being shaped by circumstances over which they had little control. As towns expanded, owing to natural increase and in-migration, a rising proportion of the outlivers lost touch with the central church. Distance and bad weather made travel to Sabbath services so hazardous that outlying hamlets frequently were granted "winter privileges," or the right to conduct their own services under lay direction. As peripheral districts gained population additional parishes were formed, and soon the former outlivers emerged as pillars of newly gathered churches.

The factors just noted also were significant determinants of the degree of church adherence, that is, of whether individuals became communicants, half-way members, regular attenders, pew holders, irregular attenders, or in a very few cases "scoffers." In all eighteenth-century churches a minority

SOURCE: *Under the Cope of Heaven: Religion, Society and Politics in Colonial America* by Patricia U. Bonomi. Copyright © 1986 by Patricia U. Bonomi. Reprinted by permission of the author and Oxford University Press, Inc.

of the adherents were communicants.* Self-imposed scrupulosity accounts for some of this, especially in the Congregational churches, where admission standards remained high, and the Anglican church, where the absence of an American bishop meant that only those confirmed in England were canonically qualified to take communion. . . .

The conventional ratio of one communicant for every three or four non-communicating church attenders is probably too low for most colonial churches, at least until the late eighteenth century. However that may be, many non-communicants participated vigorously in church life, serving as deacons or vestrymen and supporting their churches financially through the purchase of pews and contributions to the minister's salary. This probably explains why most ministers habitually referred to churchgoers interchangeably as *parishioners, members, auditors,* and *adherents.* In any case, we cannot restrict our consideration of "churched" Americans to communicants alone, since this not only contradicts eighteenth-century usage but excludes from consideration the majority of colonial churchgoers.

The clergymen have left a good deal of information about local churchgoing practice, the best of it for many denominations coming from the S.P.G. [Society for the Propagation of the Gospel, an Anglican missionary society] correspondence. In describing the religious complexion of their territory, the missionaries had little difficulty identifying most inhabitants with a specific denomination or sect. One writes that of several hundred white people inhabiting a North Carolina parish in 1710, only "five or six [were] of no professed religion"; among 1750 whites in Sussex County, Pennsylvania, a minister reported that 1075 were Anglicans, 600 Presbyterians, and 75 Quakers. . . .

New England was universally regarded as the best churched section. Visitors marveled at the regularity of religious practice in a land where "every five Miles, or perhaps less, you have a Meeting-House." Boston, a city of 15,000 inhabitants, had eighteen churches by 1750—ten of them representing the Congregational establishment. Large church buildings were needed to accommodate city congregations that ranged up to 1500 persons and more by mid-century. Indeed, as early as the 1720s Cotton Mather of Second Church scorned a congregation of a thousand as "Thinner . . . than Ordinary."

Middle-colony church life, though reflecting the rapid changes overtaking that section in the eighteenth century, was anything but moribund. New York, New Jersey, Pennsylvania, and Delaware were collectively subject to a 530-percent white population growth between 1710 and 1760 (nearly double the rate in either New England or the South), which added disproportionately large communities of Germans and Scots to the initial

[*entitled to receive communion—full church members]

Swedish, Dutch, and English populations. Churches, like other middle-colony institutions, experienced strain as new congregations and sects proliferated in the hothouse environment generated by the fierce competition for adherents. By 1750, the middle region had more congregations per capita than any other section, though with the shortage of clergymen many of them were served by itinerant preachers. Philadelphia had twenty principal churches by the 1760s, and New York City eighteen. . . .

The Anglican church in the Chesapeake was settled on a sufficiently solid foundation by 1701 that the newly organized S.P.G. could direct its resources to the needier Carolinas and later Georgia, where dissenters abounded. Religious competition once again stimulated growth in all denominations; by 1750 South Carolina, for example, had almost twice as many churches per capita as did either Virginia or Maryland. Charleston, the South's only city—with a population of around 12,000—boasted a number of fine churches including Anglican St. Philip's, described by one admirer as "the most elegant Religious Edifice in British America." Though one hundred feet long and sixty wide, its congregation was so numerous that a second large church, St. Michael's, was built in 1761. Nonetheless, by mid-century the South as a whole lagged behind the North in congregation formation, opening opportunities for the evangelical Presbyterian and Baptist preachers who appeared in increasing numbers from that time forward. . . .

"Daughters of Zion"

By the second half of the eighteenth century mothers were becoming the primary custodians of the family's religious heritage, and in genteel households they took significant responsibility for the children's religious education, often in conjunction with a private tutor. A number of wealthy women also left substantial legacies to their churches. . . .

Besides spiritual refreshment, religion offered women of energy and intellect an outlet to the wider world, as well as opportunities for self-expression, personal growth, and even leadership. Many women spoke with authority about complex theological issues. William Byrd II recorded that his wife and sister-in-law spent one evening at Westover [his home] in "fierce dispute about the infallibility of the Bible." Frances Carter of Nomini Hall discussed with her daughter the question of whether women had souls, and she conversed "with great propriety" about religion to tutor Philip Fithian, demonstrating "a very extensive knowledge." Devereux Jarratt was instructed in vital religion by the New Light wife of the planter whose children he tutored. In New England the religious writings of such pious matrons as Elizabeth Cotton and Jerusha Mather Oliver were incorporated into sermons or published for the enlightenment of a wider audience.

.Women of middle and lower status also found that religious activity offered them a wider stage. The Society of Friends in America defined women and men as equal in the sight of God, opening to females a prominent role in their public ministry. . . . A number of them gained approval from their meetings to leave home and family for extended periods in the eighteenth century to spread the Quaker message. For those at home the Women's Meeting in each congregation exercised significant powers, disciplining female members, regulating marriages, and overseeing church attendance by both men and women. No other denomination matched the Friends in opening opportunities to women, though New Light and especially Baptist meetings sometimes allowed them a voice in church government and a vote on new members.

Occasionally a woman appeared with sufficient self-confidence to test the boundaries of women's religious sphere. . . . [S]uch a one was an elderly parishioner of [Lutheran clergyman] Henry Muhlenberg in mid-eighteenth-century Pennsylvania. This unnamed woman did not shrink from challenging Muhlenberg on such theological points as original sin and conversion, and was much distressed at his seeming to teach that the Jews were under sentence of damnation. Muhlenberg clearly found her conversation edifying, and used her as a "bellwether" of the congregation. Another was the Congregationalist Sarah Haggar Osborne of Newport, Rhode Island. Mrs. Osborne started conventionally enough as leader of a young women's prayer society, following the scriptural rule that older women might instruct the younger. But for some reason this modest venture began to take on the most gratifying momentum. Slaves, male and female, took to attending the Sunday evening prayer meetings; on other evenings came "Little white Lads" and girls from the neighborhood; and during the revival of 1766–1767 between 300 and 500 persons were crowding into the Osborne house every week. For Sarah Osborne it was all wonderfully inspiring. Languor and sick spells faded away; she now slept well, had a good appetite, and knew "nothing about weariness." . . .

The relief that religion brought to the ordinary colonial woman's life of toil, especially on the frontier, is frequently noted in Henry Muhlenberg's record of his pastoral encounters. Muhlenberg tells of aged and ill women who found their only solace in God, of widows with large families rising above adversity through Christian faith, and of women afflicted with melancholia who found surcease from it in religion. One Pennsylvania frontierswoman gave her husband some concern from the frequency with which she would go off to sit in the woods by herself, and he spoke to the pastor about it. But the reason should have been obvious. She was "somewhat weak physically and always had a flock of children around her"; she was not really "melancholy," just worn out—and when things got too much, the best restorative she could think of was a session of solitary prayer.

The sisterhood of the Ephrata cloister at Lancaster, Pennsylvania, offers the most striking case of an institutional haven for women who believed themselves, from whatever causes, to have reached the end of their earthly tether. This Seventh Day Baptist community—which had male as well as female houses—was headed by Conrad Beissel, who believed in a life of celibacy and regarded marriage as the penitentiary of carnal man. A number of women joined the Ephrata cloister when they were quite young. Life in the Saron, or sisterhouse, took many of its features from the nunneries of Europe, a circumstance that provided a satiric foil for Ephrata's critics. The sisters' habit consisted of a vest and long skirt, belted at the waist and covered with a large apron that resembled a monk's scapulary. Their heads were covered by a rounded hood. The sisters' dedication to a "modest, quiet, tranquil and retired" life was regulated by a hierarchy of overseers, sub-prioress, and prioress. Whereas some young women found the regimen too harsh or finally rejected the celibate life, a number of others remained in the Saron, some for forty or fifty years. . . .

The Ephrata experience represents an extreme of female piety in colonial America. Most women followed the more orthodox path of participation with their families in local religious institutions. Yet the rising proportion of women associated with a number of churches and sects suggests that religion offered them satisfactions that nothing else in their existence could provide. Starting from their customary if circumscribed role as guardians of family piety and teachers of the young, many women sought and found in religious life a larger scope for their energy and talents. . . .

Young and Old

Churchgoing was largely an adult activity in colonial America, especially where homesteads were widely scattered. Parents simply would not expose small children to the long journeys and extreme temperatures that churchgoing entailed in rural areas. Anglican parish reports indicate that older youths concentrated their attendance in the Lenten period when rectors gave instruction in the catechism, though schoolmasters regularly catechized young people and parents also were encouraged to do so. Devereux Jarratt recalled that his parents taught their children short prayers and "made us very perfect in repeating the Church Catechism." With no bishop resident in the colonies confirmation in accordance with church canons was impossible, but ministers apparently examined youths at about age sixteen or older and, when satisfied with their level of understanding, admitted them to communion. The sons of Robert Carter III, eighteen-year-old Ben and sixteen-year-old Bob, often "begged" Philip Fithian to let them go to church despite poor weather, and occasionally the boys attended even when their parents would not venture forth. This along with similar evidence from William Byrd's diaries suggests that Sunday was an important day on the social calendar of Virginia's young people.

Middle-colony Lutherans and German Reformed often traveled ten or fifteen miles to worship, which generally restricted churchgoing to adults. The Presbytery of Hanover County, Virginia, noted as late as 1775 that its boundaries were so extensive that "women, children, and servants" often could not attend church. One consequence was that baptism of colonial children was often delayed, less through parental neglect—though that was sometimes a factor—than the inaccessibility of churches and ministers. When clergymen traveled out to such areas, children were brought to them by the score, even by the hundreds, to be baptized. "Baptized Children till was weary" was a familiar comment from frontier itinerants.

In the towns and cities youths participated more regularly in church life. The Anglican rector at Philadelphia, for example, organized a society of young men which met on Sunday evenings to hear sermons, read Scripture, and sing psalms. Henry Muhlenberg provides an unusually full picture of the religious training given children at the Philadelphia Lutheran church. Sunday morning catechism classes, or *Kinderlehre*, were held in the schoolhouse adjacent to the church. (Muhlenberg's notation on a three-year-old child who got lost on her way to *Kinderlehre* suggests that instruction began at an early age.) Muhlenberg often undertook that catechizing himself, leaving morning church service to an assistant pastor. He advocated that children be confirmed by age fourteen, observing that some German and English sects were "sharply critical of us because they consider that we take them too young." Though a few Lutheran children were confirmed at fourteen, or even thirteen in a case or two, admission was more commonly delayed until age sixteen and seventeen and many persons were confirmed only after marriage. Owing to the paucity of Lutheran clergy in the early eighteenth century, Muhlenberg frequently found himself instructing both young and old. During a 1752 sojourn in New York City—where the Lutheran church was often bereft of a regular minister and many adults never had received instruction—Muhlenberg reported that "a number of young people and at least as many adults, some sixty, seventy, and more years of age, came to *Kinderlehre*."

New England children below the age of seven or eight rarely attended the Congregational churches, though religious education certainly went on at home. Churchgoing boys in the mischievous pre-adolescent years were herded into "boys pews" or ranged along the gallery stairs where appointed monitors watched over them, dealing out "raps and blows" to those making "Indecent Gestures and Wry Faces" during service. The more decorous girls sat on little stools in the pews or aisles. Judging from the diary of eleven-year-old Anna Green Winslow, the religious training of young females was well advanced by eleven or twelve. Anna solemnly recorded the biblical texts and applications of the Reverend Mr. Beacon's sermons at Boston's Old South Church, especially those directed to "the young people." She also read daily from the Bible and regularly attended Thursday lecture and catechism. . . .

Congregationalists became formal church members at a later age than did Anglicans, Lutherans, and most others, perhaps because of stricter admission standards. In the early eighteenth century, Andover females and males joined as half-way members around ages twenty and twenty-four, respectively. Before 1730, Andover women delayed entry into full communion until ages twenty-six to twenty-eight, while men did not become full members until their middle to late 30s. At Norton and Middleborough, and in the Connecticut town of Milford, males admitted to full communion before 1740 averaged between twenty-eight and thirty-nine years of age. At Woodbury, Connecticut, where admission policies were quite lenient, women joined the church in their early to middle twentys whereas men were about five years older.

Thus in most denominations prior to the Great Awakening maximum involvement in the church's life was delayed until late adolescence or young adulthood, when religious matters might, presumably, be approached with greater maturity.

If churches were not the terrain of the very young they were certainly familiar ground to the aged. Sermons were regularly directed to elderly churchgoers, and ministers spent a large part of their time visiting aged parishioners who were too feeble to travel to church. In both North and South piety was expected to intensify as men and women moved into old age. Being closer to the eternal resolution, the elderly were presumed to possess a sharpened religious sensibility. . . .

The aged appear to have been disproportionately represented in the congregations of colonial America—a fact of religious sociology that is evident in all faiths and times.

Blacks, Indians, and Indentured Servants

Blacks, Indians, and white servants could also be found at church, though their involvement, subject to some regional and denominational variation, was for the most part quite restricted. The Church of England encouraged its ministers throughout the eighteenth century to convert the "infidels"— the term commonly applied to Negroes and Indians—and many took the charge seriously. The Reverend Anthony Gavin, who believed that slavery was "unlawfull for any Christian," baptized almost as many blacks as whites on his first tour of the South Carolina backcountry in 1738. Slave-owners often resisted missionary efforts out of fear that Christianity would make their slaves prideful and rebellious, even though many clergymen took care to preach up humility and obedience to their black converts. What conversion to Christianity actually did for them under such circumstances is difficult to judge. Nevertheless when slaves ran away or were suspected of plotting rebellion, local authorities were quick to accuse Christian missionaries of fomenting disorder.

White resistance to slave conversion appears to have fluctuated according to the proportion of blacks in the population. Thus early support for S.P.G. missionaries' work in baptizing and catechizing slaves in South Carolina declined as blacks came to outnumber whites in the colony after about 1708. Virginia rectors reported occasional success in Christianizing slaves, but as blacks rose from less than 10 percent of the population in 1680 to around one-third by 1740 white resistance stiffened. Maryland's population was only 12 to 18 percent black in the first third of the century, which may account for the greater willingness of white masters there to allow slaves to be baptized and catechized.

This shading of attitudes is apparent in the responses of southern rectors to the bishop of London's 1724 questionnaire on the state of the colonial church. All nine respondents from South Carolina reported little or no success in converting Negroes, typically because "their Masters will not consent to Have them Instructed." About half of the twenty-eight Virginia respondents had managed to baptize "several," and in rarer cases "many," Negroes, though only three or four noted that some blacks actually came to church. But in Maryland nearly a third of the rectors had baptized "many" slaves, some of whom attended church and took communion. Though a number of ministers had to "press" masters to instruct their slaves, the tone of the Maryland responses is more sanguine, and one rector stated that slaves in his parish had "free liberty from their masters to attend divine service & other means of instruction." Yet if black conversions were more numerous in Maryland, there is no reason to question the conventional view that the overwhelming majority of southern blacks remained unchurched. As one writer summed it up in 1705: "Talk to a *Planter* of the *Soul of a Negro* . . . [and he will respond that whereas the body is worth £20] the souls of an hundred of them would not yield him one farthing."

Masters were undoubtedly the primary obstacle to slave conversions, but language was a further barrier among first-generation Afro-Americans. Moreover, since Sunday was the slaves' only day off, many spent it cultivating their own garden plots and a few "work[ed] for themselves on hire." Thus, as a rule, southern blacks figured no more than marginally in church life during the first half of the eighteenth century. Even fewer Indians were converted to the white people's religion in the South, most likely because the tribes had a strong religion of their own. Southern ministers, already overtaxed by the demands of their white parishioners, reported uniformly that Indians were averse to the Christian religion.

The lower number of blacks in the North suggests that the white population there should have been more receptive to missionary efforts. And, indeed, only New York and New Jersey, which along with Rhode Island contained the largest proportion of blacks, passed laws stipulating that baptism did not alter the slaves' condition of servitude. Conversion did little to ease the burden of slavery in any northern colony, but it appears that more slaves became church adherents there than in the South. . . .

As was the case in the South, Indians proved more resistant than blacks to the S.P.G.'s attempts to convert them, though one missionary successfully formed a congregation of them at Albany. . . .

In Boston, Cotton Mather organized a Society of Negroes which met on Sunday evenings for religious instruction. That blacks attended Mather's church is evident from the remarks he addressed to them in his printed sermons. Mather's deepest concern for blacks, as for whites, was to get them to Christ. "Oh! That more pains were taken, to show the *Ethiopians*, their *Sin*, which renders them so much *Blacker* than their *Skin!*" exhorted Mather. Would that he could "lead them unto the Saviour, who will bestow upon them a *Change* of *Soul*, which is much better than a *Change* of *Skin!*" Participation of blacks at other Congregational churches was probably quite limited, though some church records of the pre-Awakening years indicate that a few slaves, and even an occasional Indian "servant," owned the covenant [had been converted]. Still, these converts were barred from most church activities; they sat in the rear of meeting-houses, and their burial plots were segregated from those of white parishioners.

Though the public attitude of the Society of Friends toward both blacks and Indians was remarkably enlightened for the eighteenth century, the number of either group embraced by Quaker meetings was very small. Nor are Negroes often mentioned in Presbyterian, Lutheran, or Reformed records. Thus even in the North only a few Negroes, and even fewer Indians, were brought within the fold of the early eighteenth-century Christian churches.

White servants too were less likely to partake of religious instruction and Sabbath activities, especially in rural sections. . . .

In Congregational New England white servants were catechized along with children during family worship, and they went to church with the family unless the care of small children kept them at home. In the Middle Colonies, where many indentured servants settled after 1720, the picture is more blurred. Lutheran and Reformed ministers expressed much concern about the souls of German servants in the region, especially those placed in English families where their native religion was neglected. Still, servants regularly appear on Henry Muhlenberg's list of confirmands. A Quaker family in Pennsylvania encouraged a devout young woman in its employ to pursue the role of "speaker" in the Society of Friends. And Quakers were expected to include their servants as part of the family when attending meeting. Nonetheless, it seems likely that in America, as in England at this time, servants and the poor made up a disproportionately high percentage of those outside the embrace of some religious community.

The Great Awakening and Church Membership

The Great Awakening of 1739–1745 temporarily altered the pattern of church adherence described above. Indeed this foremost revival, as well as periodic and more localized quickenings, can be defined in part not only by surging church admissions but by heavier concentrations than usual from two constituencies: men and young people. A typical report came from the Reverend Peter Thacher of Middleborough, Massachusetts: "the Grace of God has surprisingly seized and subdued the hardiest men, and more Males have been added here than the tenderer sex." In addition, many youths were "crying and wringing their hands, and bewailing their Frolicking and Dancing." At Woodbury, Connecticut, between 1740 and 1742, First Church added fifty-nine male to forty-six female members. The awakened flocked to their minister in Wrentham, Massachusetts, "especially young People, under Soul Distress." From Natick came word that "Indians and English, Young and Old, Male and Female" had been called to Christ. In New England those who joined the churches during the revival were on average six years younger than members affiliating before the Awakening, a pattern that pertained also in the Middle Colonies. Considering the ministers' perennial concern for the rising generation, this melting of young hearts was especially gratifying. The addition of larger numbers of men also tended, at least temporarily, to slow the feminization of churches.

Women nonetheless continued to be drawn into the churches during the Great Awakening, where they spoke up more confidently than ever before. Boston's anti-revivalist minister Charles Chauncy, alarmed when "FEMALE EXHORTERS" began to appear, declared that "encouraging WOMEN, yea, GIRLS to speak in the assemblies for religious worship" was a clear breach of the Lord's commandment. One Old Light explained the peculiar susceptibility of women and youths to the emotionalism of the revival as follows: "The aptness of Children and Women to weep . . . in greater Abundance than grown Persons and Men is a plain proof . . . that their Fluids are more numerous in Proportion to their Solids, and their Nerves are weak."

The revival's emphasis on the spoken rather than the written word, and its concern for reaching out to new constituencies, gave it a broad social base. Blacks and Indians, groups with an oral tradition, frequently attended revival meetings in the North. George Whitefield, finding that Negroes could be "effectually wrought upon, and in an uncommon manner," developed "a most winning way of addressing them." In New England, blacks and Indians drawn to the Awakening were sometimes brought directly into the body of the church. Plymouth New Lights had among their members at least "a Negro or two who were directed to invite others to come to Christ," and at Gloucester, where a number of blacks joined the church, there was "a society of negroes, who in their meetings behave very seriously and decently." When the New Light preacher Eleazer Wheelock visited Taunton, Massachusetts, in 1741, he left "almost all the negroes in town wounded: three or four converted." And Wheelock's work among the Indians led, of course, to the founding of a school that later became Dartmouth College. David Brainerd gained a number of converts to Christianity among the Indians of New Jersey. James Davenport was responsible for the conversion of Samson Occum, an eighteen-year-old Mohegan from Connecticut. Occum attended Wheelock's school at Lebanon, Connecticut, for four years, was ordained by the Presbyterian Church in 1759, and carried the message of the revival to many of his brethren in Connecticut and New York. Scattered evidence suggests that the Awakening may have had a more significant and long-range impact on blacks than on any other northern group. . . .

Nor can it be doubted that the revival reached out to servants and laborers among the white population. As Dr. Alexander Hamilton commented with typical astringency during a 1744 trip throughout the North, even "the lower class of people here. . . . talk . . . about justification, sanctification, adoption, regeneration, repentance, free grace, reprobation, original sin, and a thousand other such pritty, chimerical knick knacks as if they had done nothing but studied divinity all their life time." Still, the lowly origins of the awakened can easily be overstated. It is quite possible that the likeliest prospects for conversion came, after all, from the growing and varied ranks of the middle class, people who counted just a bit less than they felt they should in church and town, and for whom the revival opened up new possibilities and uncertainties—great hopes, great fears, great expectations.

Religious awakening came later to the colonial South, starting in the mid-1740s with Presbyterian itinerants and reaching full pitch in the 1760s and 1770s with the Baptist and Methodist revivals. How churchgoing was affected by these revivals remains to be explored, though long-standing regional characteristics probably shaped the southerners' response. Men and women may have continued to participate in church life in relatively equal numbers, whereas young people and Indians, pending new evidence, appear to have been only marginally affected by the revival. Negroes were another matter, however, for all evangelical denominations reported growing numbers of blacks among their adherents. Presbyterian Samuel Davies counted several hundred Negroes in his New Side [evangelical, revivalist] congregations in Virginia. The added dimension that religion gave to black lives is implicit in Davies's comment about the slaves' delight in psalmody: "Whenever they could get an hour's leisure from their masters, [they] would hurry away to my house. . . . to gratify their peculiar taste for Psalmody. Sundry of them have lodged all night in my kitchen; and, sometimes, when I have awaked about two or three a-clock in the morning, a torrent of sacred harmony poured into my chamber, and carried my mind away to Heaven. In this seraphic exercise, some of them spend almost the whole night." . . .

To be sure, only a tiny proportion of blacks were active Christians before the Revolution. Yet great changes were in the making. In religion the implied promise of some small measure of fulfillment, in a life that otherwise had little of it, was considerable, and a foundation was being laid upon which future generations would construct the central institution of Afro-American culture.

The Great Awakening caused a visible warp in the configuration of colonial church adherence. True, for most groups the change was no more than temporary, as pre-Awakening patterns reemerged once the revival subsided. One continuing legacy of the Awakening, however, was that it stimulated a rise in the number of preachers, especially lay preachers, thereby facilitating the extension of religion to the frontier and other underserved sections. Individuals who had been beyond the reach of ministers and churches—owing more to circumstances than choice—were now brought within the purview of a structured religious community. That this previously isolated constituency tended to have a higher proportion of young people, immigrants, and economically marginal persons than were located in the longer settled towns and cities goes far to explain the popular overtones of the revival. The growth of religious institutions was not dependent, of course, on the Great Awakening or any other revival. Far from reviving a languishing church life, the Awakening bespoke the vitality and widening reach of an expanding religious culture. . . .

DOCUMENTS

A New York Act to Encourage the Baptizing of Negro, Indian, and Mulatto Slaves, 1706

Whereas divers of her Majesty's good Subjects, Inhabitants of this Colony now are and have been willing that such Negro, Indian and Mulatto Slaves who belong to them and desire the same, should be Baptized, but are deterr'd and hindered therefrom by reason of a Groundless opinion that

SOURCE: Hugh Hastings, ed., *Ecclesiastical Records of the State of New York* (Albany: State of New York, 1902), 3:1673.

hath spread itself in this Colony, that by the Baptizing of such Negro, Indian or Mulatto slave they would become free and ought to be sett at Liberty. In order therefore to put an end to all such Doubts and Scruples as have or hereafter at any time may arise about the same. Be it Enacted by the Governour Council and Assembly and it is hereby Enacted by the authority of the same, That the Baptizing of any Negro, Indian or Mulatto Slave shall not be any Cause or reason for the setting them or any of them at Liberty.

And be it declared and Enactecd by the Governour Council & Assembly and by the Authority of the same, That all and every Negro, Indian, Mulatto and Mestee* and Bastard Child & Children who is, are, and shall be born of any Negro, Indian, Mulatto or Mestee, shall follow ye State and Condition of the Mother & be esteemed reputed taken & adjudged a Slave & Slaves to all intents & purposes whatsoever.

Provided, always & be it declared & Enacted by ye said Authority That no slave whatsoever in this Colony shall Att any time be admitted as a witness for, or against, any Freeman, in any Case matter or Cause, Civill or Criminal whatsoever.

The Great Awakening in Connecticut, 1740

Now it pleased God to send Mr. Whitefield into this land; and my hearing of his preaching at Philadelphia, like one of the old apostles, and many thousands flocking to hear him preach the Gospel, and great numbers were converted to Christ, I felt the Spirit of God drawing me by conviction; I longed to see and hear him and wished he would come this way. I heard he was come to New York and the Jerseys and great multitudes flocking after him under great concern for their souls which brought on my concern more and more, hoping soon to see him; but next I heard he was at Long Island, then at Boston, and next at Northampton. Then on a sudden, in the morning about 8 or 9 of the clock there came a messenger and said Mr. Whitefield preached at Hartford and Wethersfield yesterday and is to preach at Middletown this morning at ten of the clock. I was in my field at work. I dropped my tool that I had in my hand and ran home to my wife, telling her to make ready quickly to go and hear Mr. Whitefield preach at Middletown, then ran to my pasture for my horse with all my might, fearing that I should be too late. Having my horse, I with my wife soon mounted the horse and went forward as fast as I thought the horse could

[*Mestizo—a person of mixed European and Indian ancestry]

SOURCE: Nathan Cole, ms. cited in Leonard W. Labaree, "George Whitefield Comes to Middletown," *William and Mary Quarterly*, 3d ser. 7 (1950): 590–91.

bear; and when my horse got much out of breath, I would get down and put my wife on the saddle and bid her ride as fast as she could and not stop or slack for me except I bade her, and so I would run until I was much out of breath and then mount my horse again, and so I did several times to favour my horse. We improved every moment to get along as if we were fleeing for our lives, all the while fearing we should be too late to hear the sermon, for we had twelve miles to ride double in little more than an hour and we went round by the upper housen parish. And when we came within about half a mile or a mile of the road that comes down from Hartford, Wethersfield, and Stepney to Middletown, on high land I saw before me a cloud of fog arising. I first thought it came from the great river, but as I came nearer the road I heard a noise of horses' feet coming down the road, and this cloud was a cloud of dust made by the horses' feet. It arose some rods into the air over the tops of hills and trees; and when I came within about 20 rods of the road, I could see men and horses slipping along in the cloud like shadows, and as I drew nearer it seemed like a steady stream of horses and their riders, scarcely a horse more than his length behind another, all of a lather and foam with sweat, their breath rolling out of their nostrils every jump. Every horse seemed to go with all his might to carry his rider to hear news from heaven for the saving of souls. It made me tremble to see the sight, how the world was in a struggle. I found a vacancy between two horses to slip in mine and my wife said "Law, our clothes will be all spoiled, see how they look," for they were so covered with dust that they looked almost all of a colour, coats, hats, shirts, and horse. We went down in the stream but heard no man speak a word all the way for 3 miles but every one pressing forward in great haste; and when we got to Middletown old meeting house, there was a great multitude, it was said to be 3 or 4,000 of people, assembled together. We dismounted and shook off our dust, and the ministers were then coming to the meeting house. I turned and looked towards the Great River and saw the ferry boats running swift backward and forward bringing over loads of people, and the oars rowed nimble and quick. Everything, men, horses, and boats seemed to be struggling for life. The land and banks over the river looked black with people and horses; all along the 12 miles I saw no man at work in his field, but all seemed to be gone. When I saw Mr. Whitefield come upon the scaffold, he looked almost angelical; a young, slim, slender youth, before some thousands of people with a bold undaunted countenance. And my hearing how God was with him everywhere as he came along, it solemnized my mind and put me into a trembling fear before he began to preach; for he looked as if he was clothed with authority from the Great God, and a sweet solemn solemnity sat upon his brow, and my hearing him preach gave me a heart wound. By God's blessing, my old foundation was broken up, and I saw that my righteousness would not save me.

Opposition to the Great Awakening, c. 1742

The cause of this enthusiasm is a bad temperament of the blood and spirits; 'tis properly a disease, a sort of madness, and there are few, perhaps none at all, but are subject to it; though none are so much in danger of it as those in whom melancholy is the prevailing ingredient in their constitution. In these it often reigns, and sometimes to so great a degree that they are really beside themselves, acting as truly by the blind impetus of a wild fancy, as though they had neither reason nor understanding.

And various are the ways in which their enthusiasm discovers itself.

Sometimes, it may be seen in their countenance. A certain wildness is discernable in their general look and air, especially when their imaginations are moved and fired.

Sometimes, it strangely loosens their tongues and gives them such an energy, as well as fluency and volubility in speaking, as they themselves, by their utmost efforts, can't so much as imitate, when they are not under the enthusiastic influence.

Sometimes, it affects their bodies, throws them into convulsions and distortions, into quakings and tremblings. This was formerly common among the people called Quakers. I was myself, when a lad, an eye-witness to such violent agitations and foamings in a boisterous female speaker as I could not behold but with surprise and wonder.

Sometimes, it will unaccountably mix itself with their conduct and give it such a tincture of that which is freakish or furious as none can have an idea of, but those who have seen the behavior of a person in a frenzy.

Sometimes, it appears in their imaginary peculiar intimacy with heaven. They are, in their own opinion, the special favorites of God, have more familiar converse with Him than other good men, and receive immediate, extraordinary communications from Him. The thoughts which suddenly rise up in their minds, they take for suggestions of the Spirit; their very fancies are divine illuminations; nor are they strongly inclined to anything, but 'tis an impulse from God, a plain revelation of His will.

And what extravagances, in this temper of mind, are they not capable of, and under the specious pretext, too, of paying obedience to the authority of God? Many have fancied themselves acting by immediate warrant from heaven, while they have been committing the most undoubted wickedness. There is indeed scarce anything so wild, either in speculation or practice, but they have given in to it. They have, in many instances, been blasphemers of God and open disturbers of the peace of the world.

SOURCE: Charles Chauncy, *Enthusiasm Describ'd and Caution'd Against* (Boston: J. Draper, 1742), 3–7.

But in nothing does the enthusiasm of these persons discover itself more than in the disregard they express to the dictates of reason. They are above the force of argument, beyond conviction from a calm and sober address to their understandings. As for them, they are distinguished persons; God himself speaks inwardly and immediately to their souls. "They see the light infused into their understandings, and cannot be mistaken; 'tis clear and visible there, like the light of bright sunshine; shows itself and needs no other proof but its own evidence. They feel the hand of God moving them within and the impulses of His Spirit, and cannot be mistaken in what they feel. Thus they support themselves, and are sure reason hath nothing to do with what they see and feel. What they have a sensible experience of, admits no doubt, needs no probation." And in vain will you endeavor to convince such persons of any mistakes they are fallen into. They are certainly in the right, and know themselves to be so. They have the Spirit opening their understandings and revealing the truth to them. They believe only as he has taught them: and to suspect they are in the wrong is to do dishonor to the Spirit; 'tis to oppose his dictates, to set up their own wisdom in opposition to his, and shut their eyes against that light with which he has shined into their souls. They are not, therefore, capable of being argued with; you had as good reason with the wind. . . .

They are likewise positive and dogmatical, vainly fond of their own imaginations, and invincibly set upon propagating them; and in the doing of this, their powers being awakened and put as it were, upon the stretch, from the strong impressions they are under that they are authorized by the immediate command of God himself, they sometimes exert themselves with a sort of ecstatic violence; and 'tis this that gives them the advantage, among the less knowing and judicious of those who are modest, suspicious of themselves, and not too assuming in matters of conscience and salvation. The extraordinary fervor of their minds, accompanied with uncommon bodily motions and an excessive confidence and assurance, gains them great reputation among the populace, who speak of them as men of God in distinction from all others, and too commonly hearken to and revere their dictates, as though they really were, as they pretend, immediately communicated to them from the Divine Spirit.

This is the nature of Enthusiasm, and this its operation, in a less or greater degree, in all who are under the influence of. 'Tis a kind of religious frenzy, and evidently discovers itself to be so whenever it rises to any great height. . . .

CHAPTER 6

Urban Life in the Eighteenth Century

Although colonial American society was overwhelmingly agrarian—throughout the eighteenth century, farmers and their families represented over 90 percent of the population—cities also prospered during this period. The very success of agriculture ensured their growth, for the primary function of Boston, Newport, New York, Philadelphia, Baltimore, and Charleston was to gather for export the surplus products of the farms and forests and to import and market manufactured goods. As centers of commerce and political, social, and cultural life, cities played a crucial role in shaping the character of the emerging nation.

In her essay "Boston and New York in the Eighteenth Century," Pauline Maier discusses the functions and characteristics common to American colonial cities. She describes and explains in detail what made New York and Boston unique in many ways, and very different from one another by the end of the eighteenth century. As you read, observe how the different reasons for the founding of these two cities had a lasting influence on them. Notice in each case the impact of geography, war, social class, and political structure. How does Maier's essay help to explain why

Boston, America's third city in population and prosperity by 1775, was in the forefront of events leading to the Revolutionary War?

The documents following the essay provide a view of a third colonial city. By the outbreak of the Revolution, Philadelphia had become colonial America's largest city and was second only to London within the British Empire in population and prestige. In cities as well as on the frontier, colonial Americans learned the value of cooperative effort; voluntary militias, barn raisings, and husking bees are examples. One of the chief advocates of cooperative ventures in an urban setting was Benjamin Franklin. He is credited with organizing America's first cooperative lending library, the first adult self-improvement group (the Junto), and, described in the initial document, the first volunteer fire department.

Visitors to Philadelphia found things to admire other than the city's cooperative spirit. The second document gives the impressions of Swedish botanist Peter Kalm in 1748 during his visit to Philadelphia. What factors did Kalm appear to believe were most significant in accounting for Philadelphia's rapid rise to prominence?

Philadelphia also serves to illustrate a fact of early American urban life that often goes unnoticed. City dwellers had to overcome numerous hazards: fires, street crime, primitive sanitary facilities, and epidemics of cholera, malaria, and yellow fever. The final document describes the yellow-fever epidemic that struck Philadelphia in 1793, resulting in the deaths of more than 5,000 of the city's approximately 55,000 inhabitants. What does the document reveal about the state of medical knowledge in the late eighteenth century?

ESSAY

Boston and New York in the Eighteenth Century
Pauline Maier

My title was inspired by George Rudé's *Paris and London in the Eighteenth Century*, though my concerns were not his. In the course of working on urban politics in the Revolutionary period I became aware of how remarkably different were Boston and New York—different not just in their people and politics but in feeling, in character, in that wonderfully all-encompassing thing called culture. Their differences were neither incidental nor ephemeral: to a remarkable extent the distinctive traits each city had developed by the end of the eighteenth century survived into the

SOURCE: Pauline Maier, "Boston and New York in the Eighteenth Century," *Proceedings of the American Antiquarian Society* 91, Part 2 (Oct. 21, 1981): 177–95.

nineteenth and even the twentieth century. And so I propose to consider those differences, how they began and persisted over time, and their more general importance in American history.

Any such exercise assumes that the subjects of inquiry were comparable, that is, that they had some essential identity in common upon which distinctions were grafted. The existence of such a common identity for two early American ports on the Atlantic seaboard is in part obvious. But there remains a problem relevant to their comparability that is worth beginning with, one that has troubled me and, I suppose, other students of the period since first encountering Carl Bridenbaugh's path-breaking books *Cities in the Wilderness* and *Cities in Revolt*. That is, by what right do we classify together Boston, New York, and similar communities as 'cities' before 1800?

Consider the gulf between Rudé's subjects and mine. He wrote about two of the greatest cities in the Western world, population centers that no one hesitates to call urban. Paris already had over a half million people in 1700. It grew only modestly over the next century, while London expanded at a quick pace—from 575,000 people in 1750 to almost 900,000 fifty years later. By contrast Boston's population stood at 6,700, New York's nearer 5,000 when the eighteenth century began. One hundred years later New York had over 60,000 and Boston almost 25,000 people. It takes no very sophisticated statistical analysis to suggest that a 'city' of 6,700 was something very different from one of a half million, that New York at its eighteenth-century peak was still in many ways distinct from London, whose population was some fifteen times greater. If 'city' denotes a community's size, Boston and New York would not qualify.

The word 'city' has not, however, distinguished places by size so much as by function. Historically it designated independent communities that served as centers for a surrounding countryside and as points of contact with the outside world. The word derives from the Latin word *civitas*, which the Romans used, as it happens, for a colonial situation—for the separate states or tribes of Gaul, and then for their most important towns. They were also *civitates* in Roman Britain, but the Angles and Saxons used instead the word *burh* or *borough*, adopting *city* in the thirteenth century for foreign or ancient cities, for large indigenous communities such as London, and later for the chief boroughs of a diocese, those that became cathedral towns.

Cities perform their centralizing function in many ways, most of which were exercised by Boston and New York. Like other major colonial cities, they were provincial capitals as well as important cultural centers where newspapers and pamphlets were published, discussed, and distributed. But above all they were commercial centers, Atlantic coastal ports where the produce of the countryside was collected and shipped to the West Indies, Africa, or Europe and exchanged for products or credits that could in turn be exchanged for goods of foreign origin needed by colonists in both city and country. Later cities became the merchandising centers for manufactures of either rural or urban origin, whose 'reach' and therefore whose volume of business grew with the development of more advanced transportation systems; they became the homes of banks, of insurance companies, of stock exchanges. As they did so, they drew upon the efforts of increasing numbers of people. But it was not the size of their populations that made them cities so much as the functions Boston and New York shared with Paris and London even when their people were counted in thousands, not tens or hundreds of thousands.

From the beginning, moreover, colonial cities had a cosmopolitan character that distinguished them from more rural towns, of whose people it could be said, as [historian] George Homans wrote of thirteenth-century English villagers, that they 'had upon the whole more contact with one another than they had with outsiders.' While their ships traded at ports-of-call in the Caribbean and the larger Atlantic world, the cities played host to numbers of transients or 'strangers,' whether in the laboring force or among the more substantial persons of affairs who found business to transact at Boston or New York. Already in the seventeenth century Boston merchants found themselves in conflict with their colony's Puritan leaders, whose effort to isolate Massachusetts from Old World contamination proved incompatible with the demands of commerce. 'The well-being of trade,' [historian] Bernard Bailyn has observed, 'demanded the free movement of people and goods.' In the end the merchants won, but their victory was never such as made Boston altogether hospitable to new immigrants, particularly those of non-English origin. Only the French Huguenots—the Faneuils, Bowdoins, Rivoires, and their like—found a welcome there and were easily assimilated.

New York's population was more diverse in origin, including persons of Dutch as well as of French and English origin along with lesser numbers of Germans, Irishmen, Jews, and other Europeans as well as substantial numbers of Africans. Manhattan and the nearby counties of Long Island had the largest concentration of blacks anywhere in North America above the plantation colonies. The city also absorbed substantial numbers of migrants from New England.

The diversity of New York's peoples has, however, often been exaggerated, for they were, like Boston's people, predominantly Northern European Calvinists who shared, out of diverse historical experiences, a militant hostility to 'papism' and to Catholic Absolutism in France and Spain. Even Manhattan's Sephardic [of Spanish or Portuguese origin] Jews shared in some measure this 'Protestant' culture, for they had suffered from the same forces that the Dutch had fought in their long struggle for national independence—the Spanish monarchy and the Catholic Church. With people already so alike, the 'melting pot' could melt: by the mid-eighteenth century . . . younger persons of Dutch descent, particularly on Manhattan, spoke mostly English, attended the English church,'and would even take it amiss if they were called Dutchmen and not Englishmen.' French Huguenots [Protestants] who first arrived at New York in the seventeenth century also gradually became Anglicans, helping to make the city by the late eighteenth century far more culturally unified than it had been one hundred years earlier or would be a century later, when Italian Catholics, the Ashkenazic Jews of Eastern Europe, and other decidedly alien people were added in great numbers to the older 'native stock.'

In the course of the eighteenth century, Boston and New York also gave evidence of a new anonymity among their people that reflected the growth of their populations. That development was slow in coming. Certainly there remained much of the small town about Philadelphia, the largest of American cities in 1771 when Esther DeBerdt Reed reported to her father in London that 'the people must either talk of their neighbors, of whom they know every particular of what they both do and say, or else of marketing. . . . We hardly dare tell one another our thoughts,' she added, 'lest it should spread all over town; so, if anybody asks you how we like Philadelphia, you must say very well.' The newspapers published in colonial cities in their very dearth of local news also testify to the way eighteenth-century urban people knew their news without reading about it. There were, however, signs of change. [Historian] Thomas Bender cites the appearance of craftsmen's ads in New York newspapers of the 1750s as evidence that artisans were finding it necessary to announce their existence to townsmen who might in an earlier day have known of it without such formal notice. The publication of city directories at New York in 1786 and Boston in 1789 attests again to an increasing unfamiliarity of city people with each other. Soon thereafter authorities addressed themselves to the problem of locating people within the increasingly anonymous urban masses. In 1793 New York's Common Council ordered that buildings along the streets be numbered according to a prescribed method. From that regulation it was but a short step to the 1811 report of a New York commission that surveyed the island and planned the expanse of practical if monotonously regular numbered streets that would in time stretch from the old and irregular colonial city on the lower tip of Manhattan up toward the Harlem River, and which has been logically taken as the beginning of New York's emergence as a 'modern' city.

In all these ways—in the functions that marked them as cities, in their relative cosmopolitanism and common Protestant culture, in the gradual development by the late eighteenth century of a social anonymity that has since become so much a part of urban life—Boston and New York were almost interchangeable. And yet they had acquired, like children, distinctive traits that they would carry with them into later life. The appearance of differences early in the cities' histories is striking, their persistence over time the more so. Both need to be explained. Their reasons lie, I suggest, in the ideals or purposes of the cities' founders, and in the peculiar, unpredictable way those early traditions were reinforced by eighteenth-century circumstances.

Boston's Puritan fathers came to America with a mission defined against the avarice and corruption of contemporary England. They sought to establish close-knit communities where love of God and concern for neighbor took precedence over selfish gain. Their ideology proved well suited to the business of colonizing. Because the Puritans sought to found permanent homes in America, whole families migrated, not the men alone. The population of New England therefore grew naturally at a far faster rate than elsewhere in seventeenth-century North America. The Puritans' commitment to their 'callings' and their emphasis on industry also contributed to the cause of success in this world as much as in the next, and Boston became the premier city of British North America.

Its early achievement proved impossible to sustain, however, and as the eighteenth century proceeded Boston gradually yielded its leadership to Philadelphia and New York. It is commonplace to say that geography determined Boston's destiny: the proximity of the Appalachian mountains to the Atlantic coast in New England, the rocky quality of soil along the coastal belt, the course of its rivers, which too often ran on a north-south axis and so provided no ready path to the interior, all these limited the extent and the richness of that hinterland upon which Boston's importance depended. But its fate, we now know, is not so simply explained. An 'almost biblical series of misfortunes' afflicted Boston in the mid-eighteenth century, most of which were related to the series of colonial wars [with France] that brought disaster to Boston even as they blessed with prosperity the artisans and merchants of New York and Philadelphia. The city contributed heavily to imperial armies, and therefore to the casualty lists, which cut deeply into its male population and so into its tax base. Meanwhile taxes rose to finance the expeditions to Canada and to support the widows and orphans left behind, making Boston (then as now) a particularly expensive place to live, even in comparison to neighboring towns. Its shipbuilding industry dispersed to Marblehead, Salem, and Newport, and fear of impressment [seizure of sailors for service in the British navy] disrupted its trade. The results could be read in Boston's population figures, which reached 17,000 in 1740, then dropped, and failed to recover completely until after independence; in the striking excess of white adult females to males among Bostonians of 1764 (3,612 to 2,941); in the dense occupancy of Boston's houses, which included about half again as many people as those of New York and Philadelphia at mid-century, a difference [historian] Gary Nash attributes to the practice of taking in boarders by hard-pressed Boston widows; in the emergence of poverty as a serious social problem well before it reached such importance in other colonial ports.

It is too much to say that Boston never recovered, but its record in the late colonial period was overall one of decline. And hard times served the cause of tradition, for the Spartan ideals of the founders could ennoble necessity by calling it virtue. New England's ministers continued to cite the first generation of settlers as a model of achievement, as they had done from the late seventeenth century, and to chastise the children for failing to take up their fathers' 'Errand into the Wilderness,' explaining the calamities that fell upon them as punishments for the sinful shortcomings of those who had inherited that New World Israel. The ideals of the fathers provided, in short, a way of understanding and of organizing experience, of ordering history, and so continued to influence the life of the region and of its major city.

New York was founded instead as an outpost of the Dutch West India Company in its search for profit. No greater mission brought the Dutch from Holland: indeed, the Dutch were on the whole unwilling to migrate, finding their homeland hospitable as the English Puritans did not. The Dutch West India Company therefore turned elsewhere for settlers—to the oppressed Protestants of France, to Africa—in the hope that they might help make New Netherland economically viable. The commitment to material gain that marked Company rule continued after the British conquest. The financial needs of the later Stuart kings, the hopes of greater fortunes that motivated the governors appointed by them and their successors, the ambitions of colonists who flattered royal officials in a quest for land grants, contracts, or lucrative appointments, all these only enhanced New York's materialistic bent. The city became a nest of those after profit however won—of pirates and privateers, of slave traders and smugglers—a community whose spokesmen on into the Revolutionary era emphasized interest while those of Boston cultivated virtue.

New Yorkers did well—and then did better. The city sat at the mouth of the great Hudson River, which, with the Mohawk, provided ready access to a rich and extensive market even before the canal era added the trans-Appalachian West to Manhattan's 'back yard.' It benefitted also from wartime contracts and privateering returns, and except for occasional years of recession continued the ascent that would in time make it the foremost American city. The results there could be seen in a sense of widespread opportunity such as possessed the immigrant James Murray in 1737, when he advised a clergyman in his native Northern Ireland to 'tell aw the poor Folk of your place, tha God has open'd a Door for their Deliverance.' In New York there was 'no Scant of Breed'; and it was, 'in short, . . . a bonny Country' where a man could readily make a good life for himself. In his *History of the Province of New-York,* first published in 1757, a more established New Yorker, William Smith, Junior, made much the same point. 'Every man of industry and integrity has it in his power to live well,' he wrote, and many who arrived 'distressed by their poverty . . . now enjoy easy and plentiful fortunes.'

New York's great class distinction

Smith also claimed that there was 'not so great an inequality' of riches among New Yorkers 'as is common in Boston and some other places,' but there he was almost certainly incorrect. The rich of Manhattan combined mercantile wealth with great landed estates in the Hudson Valley in a way unknown among Bostonians. The city's people shared a sense of social distance that also distinguished it from its urban neighbor to the northeast. Some of the most memorable expressions of class consciousness that the Revolutionary era produced came from New York—as in Gouverneur Morris's arrogant description of local mechanics and seamen as 'poor reptiles . . . struggling to cast off their winter slough' who 'bask in the sunshine, and ere noon . . . will bite.' As for Morris's 'riotous mob,' it was characterized by deferential habits such as shocked John Hancock when he visited New York on his way to the Continental Congress. On his arrival there Hancock learned that the city's people intended to remove the horses from his carriage and pull it through the streets themselves, a ritual common enough in the Old World. But Hancock, no modest man but a Bostonian nonetheless, 'would not have had [that] taken place upon any Consideration, not being fond of such Parade.' His efforts to dissuade the crowd were unsuccessful, and he was saved from that 'disagreeable occurrence' only by the intercession of some local gentlemen whose wishes the people of New York were more accustomed to honoring.

Politics moderated the distance between rich and poor in Boston. There the governing town meeting brought together persons of different station and blessed men with power for their eloquence, reason, and character as well as their wealth. Boston had a board of selectmen and a series of other municipal officers who were chosen by the town meeting, and those who sought such preferment learned, if they did not instinctively know, that respect was a prerequisite of political support. New York was governed differently. By the terms of the Montgomery Charter of 1731, the governor and provincial council named the city's mayor, recorder, clerk, and treasurer. Municipal ordinances were passed by a Common Council that consisted of the mayor and recorder along with the city's aldermen, who were elected by voice vote within the several wards into which New York had been divided. Qualified voters also chose a set of assistants, several minor officials, and the vestrymen who cared for the poor. But they had no continuing, direct voice in governing the city as in Boston, where 'the meanest citizen ratable at £20 beside the poll, may deliver his sentiments and give his suffrage in very important matters, as freely as the greatest Lord in the Land,' according to the reports of Dr. Thomas Young, a native of the Hudson Valley who migrated to Boston in the mid-1760s. Political opportunities compensated in some measure for Boston's unpromising economy: 'elevated stations,' Young claimed, were there open 'to every one whose capacity integrity and diligence in the affairs of his country attracts the public attention.' Those avenues of advancement, he wrote correspondents in Manhattan, 'I lament are shut to you. . . .'

The existence of a wealthy upper class with a taste for European ways had, however, some cultural advantages, for its patronage set eighteenth-century New York on its way toward becoming an American center for the performing arts. Manhattan claimed two playhouses in 1732; by the time of the Revolution it had as many as seven. Not that all New Yorkers were free from scruples born of their Protestant heritage. William Hallam's London Company of Comedians, which came to the city in 1753, was denied official permission to perform until after it issued assurances that its members were 'not cast in the same Mould' as their 'Theatrical Predecessors,' that 'in private Life' and 'publick Occupation' they were of a different moral order. In retrospect, however, it seems more important that the company went to New York because people in Virginia predicted a 'genteel and favourable Reception' in Manhattan, where 'the Inhabitants were generous and polite, naturally fond of Diversions rational, particularly those of the Theatre,' and that Hallam's company finally enjoyed a successful and profitable run in the city. New York also saw occasional musical performances, as in January 1737 when the *New-York Gazette* advertised a 'consort . . . for the benefit of Mr. Pachebell, the harpsicord parts performed by himself.' And two years later an advertisement announced 'A New Pantomine Entertainment. . . . To which will be added an Optick,' which was a primitive predecessor of motion pictures. Cock-fighting was also popular, as was horse-racing, with wagers part of the event—all of which remained far from Boston, a city less open to such forms of commercial entertainment. Indeed, theatre was introduced at Boston only during the 1790s, having been earlier outlawed by an act of 1750.

Boston was distinguished instead by its traditional respect for learning and for the printed word. Before the Puritan fathers were more than a decade in America they founded Harvard College and established a printing press in Cambridge. New York City was settled in 1626—four years before Boston—but had no press for almost seventy years, until William Bradford was lured to Manhattan in 1693. Even a casual survey of the Evans bibliography of early American imprints testifies to the immense and continuing superiority of eighteenth-century Boston as a place of publication. Few books and pamphlets came out of New York, and those were heavily weighted toward the official publications of the provincial government. As for newspapers, the first to be published on a continuous schedule in British North America was the *Boston News-Letter*, begun in 1704. And Boston had two other papers, the *Boston Gazette* (1719) and the *New-England Courant* (1721) before the *New-York Gazette* began publication in 1725.

New Yorkers' sense of a good education apparently differed from that of Bostonians: the City of New York was 'so conveniently Situated for Trade and the Genius of the people so inclined to merchandise,' wrote the Rev. John Sharpe in 1713 after some twelve years on Manhattan, 'that they generally seek no other Education for their children than writing and

Arithmetick. So that letters must be in a manner forced upon them not only without their seeking, but against their consent'—a proposal unlikely to meet with success. New Yorkers were in fact bizarrely innocent in the world of learning—or so James Murray suggested when he told of a fellow Scots-Irish immigrant who 'now gets ane Hundred Punds for ane year for teechin a Letin Skulle, and God kens, little he is skilled in Learning, and yet they think him a high learned Man. Ye kin I had but sma Learning when I left ye,' he added—and his primitive phonetic spelling suggests he had accumulated little thereafter. Yet Murray reported that he kept a 'Skulle for wee Weans.' Two decades later William Smith, Junior, concluded that New York's schools were of 'the lowest order' and that their 'instructors want instruction.' 'Through a long shameful neglect of all the arts and sciences,' he added, 'our common speech is extremely corrupt, and the evidences of a bad taste, both as to thought and language, are visible in all our proceedings, publick and private.'

New York was, quite simply, a different kind of place than Boston, shaped by different values that were sustained by economic success. The 'Art of getting money' preoccupied its people and served, according to Cadwallader Colden, as 'the only principle of life propagated among the young People.' New Yorkers of both town and country were 'sober, industrious and hospitable,' Smith noted, 'though intent upon gain.' The city's contemporary reputation reflected those traits. 'Our Neighbours have told us in an insulting Tone, that the Art of getting money is the highest Improvement we can pretend to,' wrote a pamphleteer arguing in 1749 for 'Erecting a College in the Province of New-York.' They say 'that the wisest Man among us without a Fortune, is neglected and despised; and the greatest Blockhead with one, caress'd and honour'd: That, for this Reason, a poor Man of the most shining Accomplishments, can never emerge out of his Obscurity; while every wealthy Dunce is loaded with Honours, and bears down all before him.' Such accusations were made, he thought, out of envy over 'the flourishing Circumstances of this City,' and could be easily refuted. 'But that Learning hath not been encourag'd as it ought, admits of no Controversy.'

These distinctions were reflected in John Adams's perceptions of New York, which he visited on the way to the Continental Congress in Philadelphia, as did Hancock, with eyes fully open and with Boston as a constant standard of comparison. Like all travellers, Adams was impressed by New York's beauty, for it was in ways long since lost a garden city whose clean and spacious streets were lined with trees, and where the noise of frogs, especially on hot nights when rain was expected, provided a major annoyance. He remarked on the striking views or 'prospects' the city offered of the Hudson and East Rivers, of Long Island and what he called the 'Sound River,' and of New Jersey. He found New York's streets 'vastly more regular and elegant than those in Boston, and the houses are more grand, as well as neat.' New Yorkers were as hospitable as Smith—and Madam Sarah Knight before him—indicated they would be, and Adams was struck, too, by the evidence of wealth, as in the costly accoutrements of John Morin Scott's breakfast table, which he inventoried lovingly ('rich plate, a very large silver coffee-pot, a very large silver tea-pot, napkins of the very finest materials'), or the 'rich furniture' at the home of Isaac Low. Still, the continuous socializing he found 'very disagreeable on some accounts.' It seems never to have crossed the New Yorkers' minds that a Bostonian might be more anxious to see the twenty-year-old King's College, or the city's churches, printers' offices, and bookshops. And 'with all the opulence and splendor of this city,' Adams reported that there was 'very little good breeding to be found. . . . I have not seen one real gentleman, one well-bred man, since I came to town.' There was, moreover, 'no conversation that is agreeable' at their 'entertainments': there was 'no modesty, no attention to one another,' for the New Yorkers of that still-pastoral island had already acquired the conversational style of the modern metropolis. 'They talk very loud, very fast, and altogether,' Adams observed. 'If they ask you a question, before you can utter three words of your answer, they will break out upon you again, and talk away.'

There are in these observations testimony not merely to style, but to the pace, the bewildering restlessness that already possessed New Yorkers long before the nineteenth century. Even the sleighs they rode in the winter to friends' homes out of town or to 'Houses of entertainment at a place called the Bowery . . . fly with great swiftness,' Madam Knight noted on her visit there in 1704, 'and some are so furious that they'll turn out of the path for none except a Loaden Cart.' What was the hurry? And why were New Yorkers always building, tearing down, rearranging, reconstructing their city, leaving not even the bones of their ancestors in peace? They seem forever to have done things with what struck outsiders as excess: convinced that 'merchandizing' was a good employment, they went into trade in such numbers, reported the visitor John Miller in 1695, 'that whosoever looks on their shops would wonder'—like a modern stroller down Madison Avenue—'where there are so many to sell, there should be any to buy.' The monumental energy of colonial New Yorkers prefigured that of later Americans, who within a century of winning independence built from thirteen modest colonies a nation whose western boundary had pushed from the Appalachians to the Pacific. The enterprise of New Yorkers contributed generously to that development. Indeed, the very physical circumstances of New Yorkers identified them with the nation in 1776: they were concentrated within the lowest mile of a thirteen-and-a-half-mile-long island much as their countrymen were settled along the eastern edge of a vast continent whose expanses of empty land invited and even demanded expansion. People such as these had no time to celebrate the past. They were too engrossed with inventing the future.

How different the situation of the Bostonians, housed on a modest peninsula already fully settled by the time of the Revolution, suffering from a generation of decline, a people convinced that the model of their future lay in the past. In fact, nineteenth-century Boston, true to its colonial origins, became the literary capital of the new nation and also a financial center whose importance yielded to New York only in the 1840s. Meanwhile New Englanders, fleeing the rural poverty of their native region, settled and populated much of the West. There remains considerable irony none-theless in the fact that Boston served for the generation of 1776 as a model for the new republic. Its democratic politics, tradition of disinterested public service, and modest style, inculcated by Puritanism and continued through hardship, coincided neatly with the demands of classical republicanism—so much so that Samuel Adams could see in the United States a final realization of New England's historic mission. New York played a far more ambiguous role in the politics of the Revolution than did Boston, and the city never took on a similar symbolic importance—perhaps because infinite possibilities are more difficult to comprehend than the limited values of an established and well-defined historical tradition. New York has in fact remained difficult to grasp, to summarize. 'By preference, but also in some degree by necessity,' Nathan Glaze and Daniel Patrick Moynihan observed in *Beyond the Melting Pot*, 'America has turned elsewhere for its images and traditions. Colonial America is preserved for us in terms of the Doric sim-plicity of New England, or the pastoral symmetry of the Virginia country-side. Even Philadelphia is manageable. But who can summon an image of eighteenth-century New York that will *hold still in the mind?*' And yet the importance of openness, optimism, opportunity, and energy, even of ma-terialism and of visual over literary entertainments to the nation that emerged from the American eighteenth century is undeniable. . . .

DOCUMENTS

Benjamin Franklin's
Union Fire Company, 1738

About this time I wrote a paper . . . on the different accidents and care-lessnesses by which houses were set on fire, with cautions against them and means proposed of avoiding them. This was much spoken of as a useful piece, and gave rise to a project which soon followed it of forming a company for the more ready extinguishing of fires, and mutual assistance

SOURCE: John Bigelow, ed., *Works of Benjamin Franklin* (New York: G. P. Putnam's Sons, 1877), 1: 204–5.

in removing and securing of goods when in danger. Associates in this scheme were presently found amounting to thirty. Our articles of agreement obliged every member to keep always in good order and fit for use a certain number of leather buckets with strong bags and baskets (for packing and transporting of goods) which were to be brought to every fire; and we agreed to meet once a month and spend a social evening together in discoursing and communicating such ideas as occurred to us upon the subject of fires as might be useful in our conduct on such occasions. The utility of this institution soon appeared, and many more desiring to be admitted than we thought convenient for one company, they were advised to form another, which was accordingly done. And this went on, one new company being formed after another till they became so numerous as to include most of the inhabitants who were men of property; and now at the time of my writing this [1788], tho' upwards of fifty years since its establishment, that which I first formed, called the Union Fire Company, still subsists and flourishes, tho' the first members are all deceased but myself and one, who is older by a year than I am. The small fines that have been paid by members for absence at the monthly meetings have been applied to the purchase of fire engines, ladders, firehooks, and other useful implements for each company, so that I question whether there is a city in the world better provided with the means of putting a stop to beginning conflagrations; and in fact since those institutions, the city has never lost by fire more than one or two houses at a time, and the flames have often been extinguished before the house in which they began has been half consumed.

Philadelphia, 1748

All the streets except two which are nearest to the river, run in a straight line, and make right angles at the intersections. Some are paved, others are not; and it seems less necessary, since the ground is sandy, and therefore soon absorbs the wet. But in most of the streets is a pavement of flags, a fathom or more broad, laid before the houses, and posts put on the outside three or four fathom asunder. Under the roofs are gutters which are carefully connected with pipes, and by this means, those who walk under them, when it rains, or when the snow melts, need not fear being wet by the dropping from the roofs.

The houses make a good appearance, are frequently several stories high, and built either of bricks or of stone; but the former are more com-

Swedish botanst

SOURCE: Peter Kalm, *Travels in North America*, translated into English by John Reinhold Forester (London: Printed for editor, 1770), Vol. I, 34–45, 58–60.

monly used, since bricks are made before the town, and are well burnt. The stone which has been employed in the building of other houses, is a mixture of black or grey *glimmer*, running in undulated veins, and of a loose, and quite small grained *limestone*, which runs scattered between the bendings of the other veins, and are of a grey colour, excepting here and there some single grains of sand, of a paler hue. The glimmer makes the greatest part of the stone; but the mixture is sometimes of another kind. This stone is now got in great quantities in the country, is easily cut, and has the good quality of not attracting the moisture in a wet season. Very good lime is burnt every where hereabouts, for masonry.

Characteristics of Philadelphians

The town is now quite filled with inhabitants, which in regard to their country, religion, and trade, are very different from each other. You meet with excellent masters in all trades, and many things are made here full as well as in *England*. Yet no manufactures, especially for making fine cloth, are established. Perhaps the reason is, that it can be got with so little difficulty from *England,* and that the breed of sheep which is brought over, degenerates in process of time, and affords but a coarse wool.

Here is great plenty of provisions, and their prices are very moderate. There are no examples of an extraordinary dearth.

Every one who acknowledges God to be the Creator, preserver, and ruler of all things, and teaches or undertakes nothing against the state, or against the common peace, is at liberty to settle, stay, and carry on his trade here, be his religious principles ever so strange. No one is here molested on account of the erroneous principles of the doctrine which he follows, if he does not exceed the above-mentioned bounds. And he is so well secured by the laws in his person and property, and enjoys such liberties, that a citizen of *Philadelphia* may in a manner be said to live in his house like a king.

On a careful consideration of what I have already said, it will be easy to conceive how this city should rise so suddenly from nothing, into such grandeur and perfection, without supposing any powerful monarch's contributing to it, either by punishing the wicked, or by giving great supplies in money. And yet its fine appearance, good regulations, agreeable situation, natural advantages, trade, riches and power, are by no means inferior to those of any, even of the most ancient towns in *Europe*. It has not been necessary to force people to come and settle here; on the contrary, foreigners of different languages have left their country, houses, property, and relations, and ventured over wide and stormy seas, in order to come hither. Other countries, which have been peopled for a long space of time, complain of the small number of their inhabitants. But *Pennsylvania,* which was no better than a desert in the year 1681, and hardly contained five hundred people, now vies with several kingdoms in *Europe* in number of inhabitants. It has received numbers of people, which other countries, to their infinite loss, have either neglected or expelled.

The Scourge of Yellow Fever, Philadelphia, 1793

On the origin of the disorder [yellow fever], there prevails a very great diversity of opinion. Dr. Hutchinson maintained that it was not imported, and stated, in a letter which he wrote on the subject to Captain Falconer, the health officer of the port of Philadelphia, that "the general opinion was, that the disorder originated from some damaged coffee, or other putrified vegetable and animal matters." . . .

Several persons were swept away before any great alarm was excited. . . . About this time began the removals from the city, which were for some weeks so general, that almost every hour in the day, carts, waggons, coachees, and chairs, were to be seen transporting families and furniture to the country in every direction. Business then became extremely dull. Mechanics and artists were unemployed; and the streets wore the appearance of gloom and melancholy.

The first official notice taken of the disorder, was on the 22d of August, on which day, the mayor of Philadelphia, Matthew Clarkson, esq. wrote to the city commissioners, and after acquainting them with the state of the city, gave them the most peremptory orders, to have the streets properly cleansed and purified by the scavengers, and all the filth immediately hawled away. These orders were repeated on the 27th, and similar ones given to the clerks of the market. The 29th the governor of the state, in his address to the legislature, acquainted them, that a contagious disorder existed in the city; and that he had taken every proper measure to ascertain the origin, nature, and extent of it. He likewise assured them that the health officer and physician of the port, would take every precaution to allay and remove the public inquietude.

The 26th of the same month, the college of physicians had a meeting, at which they took into consideration the nature of the disorder, and the means of prevention and of cure. They published an address to the citizens, signed by the president and secretary, recommending to avoid all unnecessary intercourse with the infected; to place marks on the doors or windows where they were; to pay great attention to cleanliness and airing the

SOURCE: Mathew Carey, *A Short Account of the Malignant Fever Lately Prevalent in Philadelphia* (Philadelphia, 1793), 16–17, 20–23, 60–63.

rooms of the sick; to provide a large and airy hospital in the neighbourhood of the city for their reception; to put a stop to the tolling of the bells; to bury those who died of the disorder in carriages and as privately as possible; to keep the streets and wharves clean; to avoid all fatigue of body and mind, and standing or sitting in the sun, or in the open air; to accommodate the dress to the weather, and to exceed rather in warm than in cool clothing; and to avoid intemperance, but to use fermented liquors, such as wine, beer, and cider, with moderation. They likewise declared their opinion, that fires in the streets were very dangerous, if not ineffectual means of stopping the progress of the fever, and that they placed more dependence on the burning of gunpowder. The benefits of vinegar and camphor, they added, were confined chiefly to infected rooms, and could not be too often used on handkerchiefs, or in smelling bottles, by persons who attended the sick.

In consequence of this address, the bells were immediately stopped from tolling, which was a measure very expedient; as they had before been kept pretty constantly going the whole day, so as to terrify those in health, and drive the sick, as far as the influence of imagination could produce that effect, to their graves. An idea had gone abroad, that the burning of fires in the streets, would have a tendency to purify the air, and arrest the progress of the disorder. The people had, therefore, almost every night large fires lighted at the corners of the streets. The 29th, the mayor published a proclamation, forbidding this practice. As a substitute, many had recourse to the firing of guns, which they imagined was a certain preventative of the disorder. This was carried so far, and attended with such danger, that it was forbidden by the mayor's order, of the 4th of September. . . .

On the 16th, the managers of Bushhill [hospital], after personal inspection of the state of affairs there, made report of its situation, which was truly deplorable. It exhibited as wretched a picture of human misery as ever existed. A profligate, abandoned set of nurses and attendants (hardly any of good character could at that time be procured,) rioted on the provisions and comforts, prepared for the sick, who (unless at the hours when the doctors attended) were left almost entirely destitute of every assistance. The dying and dead were indiscriminately mingled together. The ordure and other evacuations of the sick, were allowed to remain in the most offensive state imaginable. Not the smallest appearance of order or regularity existed. It was, in fact, a great human slaughter house, where numerous victims were immolated at the altar of riot and intemperance. No wonder, then, that a general dread of the place prevailed through the city, and that a removal to it was considered as the seal of death. In consequence, there were various instances of sick persons locking their rooms, and resisting every attempt to carry them away. At length, the poor were so much afraid of being sent to Bushhill, that they would not acknowledge their illness, until it was no longer possible to conceal it. For it is to be observed, that the fear of the contagion was so prevalent, that as soon as any one was taken sick, an alarm was spread among the neighbours, and every effort was used to have the sick person hurried off to Bushhill, to avoid spreading the disorder. The cases of the persons forced in this way to that hospital, though labouring under only common colds, and common fall fevers, are numerous and afflicting. There were not wanting instances of persons, only slightly ill, being sent to Bushhill, by their panic-struck neighbours, and embracing the first opportunity of running back to Philadelphia. But the case was soon altered under the direction of the two managers, Girard and Helm. They introduced such order and regularity, and had the patients treated with so much care and tenderness, that they retrieved the character of the hospital; and in the course of a week or two, numbers of sick people, who had not at home proper persons to nurse them, applied to be sent to Bushhill. Indeed, in the end, so many people, who were afflicted with other disorders, procured admittance there, that it become necessary to pass a resolve, that before an order of admission should be granted, a certificate must be produced from a physician, that the patient laboured under the malignant fever.

The committee sat daily at the city hall, and engaged a number of carts to convey the dead to a place of interment, and the sick to the hospital. From their organization to the present time, they have most unremittingly attended to the discharge of the trust reposed in them. Neither the regular increase of deaths till towards the middle of October, nor the afflicting loss of four very active members, in quick succession, appalled them. That the mortality would have been incomparably greater, but for their active interposition, is beyond doubt; as most of those who went to Bushhill, and died there, would have otherwise died in the city, and spread the contagion: and the dead bodies would have remained putrifying in deserted houses in every part of the city, and operated as dreadfully as the plague itself. In fact, at the time they entered on the execution of the dangerous office they undertook, there were found several bodies that had lain in this state for two, three, and four days.

CHAPTER 7

People at War: Society During the American Revolution

The Revolutionary War marked the end of the colonial epoch and the beginning of nationhood. The impact of the Revolution was far ranging, felt not only on the battlefield and in the diplomatic chambers but also on the home front. In the essay that follows, excerpted from Robert Gross's prize-winning The Minutemen and Their World, *we see how the war affected the lives of the citizens of Concord, Massachusetts. Although Concord's role in the events of April 19, 1775, has earned it a special place in America's memory, in its political institutions, social structure, religion, and economy, it was quite similar to hundreds of rural towns that dotted the map of eighteenth-century New England. Thus citizens of other communities in that region and beyond shared similar wartime experiences.*

Indeed, anyone who has experienced or has knowledge of the home front during wartime will be struck by the numerous parallels between events in Concord during the Revolution and civilian life during subsequent wars. Interesting comparisons can be made of the treatment of those suspected of not supporting the war effort, wages and the prices of consumer goods, the impact of war on marriage and child-bearing, and methods of raising troops and supplies.

Active Tory opposition was not a significant factor in either Concord or the rest of New England; however, it was very much a concern further south. Historians estimate that Tories constituted 20 percent of the population in the southern and middle colonies and that approximately 80,000 of them fled the country under pressure from the rebels. The first document reveals a common mode of physical punishment meted out to Tories. The second document, taken from the Pennsylvania Packet of August 5, 1779, is illustrative of the verbal attacks leveled at opponents of the patriot cause. What are your reactions to the steps taken against Tories? Were they justifiable? on what grounds?

Although war brought hostility to the Tories and, as the Gross essay illustrates, resulted in varying degrees of sacrifice and deprivation for the general public, for some it offered opportunity for power or profit, and for others it held out the promise of adventure. The last document is excerpted from the memoirs of Andrew Sherburne, a New Hampshire boy who in 1779, at the age of thirteen and filled with the spirit of adventure and patriotism, left his family farm to enlist in the new United States Navy. What parallels can be drawn between the interests, attitudes, and behavior Sherburne recalled from his youth and those of today's teenagers?

ESSAY

This Bleeding Land

Robert A. Gross

When the shots were fired on April 19 [1775], Concord was already a wartime community. For several months the townspeople had been gearing their lives to the demands of raising and drilling troops, storing supplies, and watching out for Tories and spies. Now they redoubled their efforts. No one expected a long struggle. A siege of Boston, a thrust against Canada: quick, aggressive action would force the British Ministry to terms. Instead, the eight exhausting years that followed the clash at the bridge would mark

SOURCE: Adapted from *The Minutemen and Their World* by Robert A. Gross. Copyright © 1979 by Robert A. Gross. Reprinted by permission of Hill and Wang, a division of Farrar, Straus, and Giroux, Inc.

the longest conflict in American history until Vietnam. The War for Independence imposed heavy sacrifices on nearly every family in Concord and unprecedented burdens on local government as well. This was something more than a costly military contest: it was revolution, a great popular movement for self-determination that unleashed powerful liberating currents in a declining provincial society. The people of Concord had set out only to defend their traditional community life. Now they had to face the consequences of their fervent Whig insistence on the people's right to rule.

Concord's mobilization formed an integral part of a wider war effort. First the Provincial Congress and then the General Court directed military activities in Massachusetts, relying on the towns to execute their orders. Throughout the war local communities were responsible for furnishing men and matériel to the central authorities. Hometowns helped equip their troops, often paid their wages, and supported the needy families of men away at war. They were occasionally called on to intern prisoners of war and to hunt for internal enemies. The General Court even required every town to establish a committee of correspondence, inspection, and safety as a general agency in charge of war. In every case, Concord complied with these instructions. Where town meetings before the Revolutionary crisis had seldom noticed the outside world, after 1775 they often subordinated local needs to broad concerns of state. In the process of fighting the British assault on their autonomy, the townspeople allowed state government to assume extraordinary power over their lives.

In the first years of the war, Concord had to cope with the new military demands amid a major population boom. As the siege of British-held Boston began, thousands of city inhabitants were evacuated from the capital, which became an enclave of Tories and Redcoats, and scattered into the countryside. The Provincial Congress ordered the nearby towns to provide for many of the Boston poor. Concord's quota was sixty-six— the third highest in Middlesex County—but the town eventually admitted and supported eighty-two poverty-stricken Bostonians, all of whom it would promptly have warned out only a few months before. So many refugees of all social classes crowded into town that they held a Boston town meeting there in July 1775 to elect legislative representatives of their own. The Bostonians were soon followed by displaced persons from Charlestown, whose homes had been burned by Redcoats during the Battle of Bunker Hill. . . .

By mid-March of 1776, some nineteen hundred persons were concentrated in Concord, representing an increase of over 25 per cent in little more than a year. Not all of the growth came from newcomers. The outburst of war had put a temporary brake on emigration, as young men stayed in their native town in order to join the fight. With the rapid build-up of numbers, the community's resources underwent serious strain. The mild winter and early spring of 1775 had given way to the worst summer drought in decades, reducing the harvest at the very time that the Army outside Boston added to the civilian demand for provisions. Inevitably, shortages appeared. Meanwhile, the public health was threatened by the close conditions in town. That summer—always a dangerous season—an epidemic of dysentery flared; it was followed by an eruption of "Distemper." . . .

Despite these pressures, Concord responded energetically to the early demands of war. Raising troops posed no problem at all. On the day after the battle in Concord, at least sixty townsmen enlisted for eight months in the Massachusetts Army laying siege to Boston. Within their two companies were nearly half of the Minutemen, whose units were apparently dissolved right after they had completed their assignment on April 19. One Concord company took the brunt of the first two British assaults at Bunker Hill and suffered three dead, the town's first losses in the war. Not long after, along with the rest of the Massachusetts forces, both companies were incorporated into the Continental Army of the United Colonies, under the command of General George Washington. By July 4, 1776, the town had raised 190 men—half of its males over sixteen years old—for service on the Massachusetts coast, in Benedict Arnold's fatal expedition against Quebec, and on the New York frontier. Recruits were naturally the younger men, drawn from all social ranks, but virtually every able-bodied man under forty must have taken up arms for at least a few days, since the entire militia was called out for the Battle of Dorchester Heights in March 1776 when the Americans finally maneuvered the Redcoats into abandoning Boston. . . .

Those who stayed behind in Concord often performed important war-related work. Militiamen were assigned to guard the military stores and to keep watch over prisoners of war in the county jail. Deacon Thomas Barrett and his son Samuel established a gunshop at their millsite and experimented with the use of water power for boring, grinding, and polishing muskets. Many women also assembled supplies, knitting stockings and sewing shirts to fill provincial requisitions. Right after the Battle of Bunker Hill, the "patriotic ladies" of the town donated a chest of clothing and other articles for the wounded to the military hospital in Cambridge. "This instance of their humanity and public spirit," remarked one newspaper, "does honor to the town, and will, we hope, induce others to imitate so good an example."

This outpouring of men and money was greatly facilitated by the absence of an active Tory opposition. In only a few Yankee families was the American Revolution ever an internal civil war. While [Reverend] William Emerson was preaching ardent patriotic sermons, his wife's brothers—the Blisses—divided sharply in their loyalties: attorney Daniel and his merchant brother Samuel had already fled to General Gage's Boston and then to

Canada, there to serve as officers in the British Army; Thomas Theodore, a captain in the Massachusetts forces, was taken prisoner during Benedict Arnold's expedition against Quebec in the winter of 1775–76 and spent the rest of the war being shifted about from one British jail to another; the youngest, Joseph, was an eighteen-year-old clerk in Henry Knox's bookstore in Boston when war began, and he was shortly serving in his employer's famous artillery regiment, rising to the rank of paymaster in the Continental Army.

There were undoubtedly others who harbored doubts about the American resistance but were unwilling to break with family and friends. For the time being they laid low rather than risk the reprisals which Concord's Patriots handed out to suspected Loyalists. Former selectman John Flint was overheard declaring that "For myself I think I shall be neutral in these times," and his name was later stricken from the jury lists. Dr. Joseph Lee, who already had a good many enemies, was a particular target of retaliation.* On the night of April 23, 1775, he was "seized for a Tory while in bed," hustled off to deacon Thomas Barrett's farm, and tried by the committee of correspondence for his political sins. The committee, on which his old rival's son, James Barrett, Jr., sat, ordered Lee confined to his farm on Nashawtuc Hill: ". . . if he should presume to go beyond the bounds and should be killed, his blood be upon his own head." . . .

With so few obstacles in their path, the people of Concord moved easily toward separation from Great Britain. In the summer of 1775, on the advice of the Continental Congress, the Massachusetts General Court reconvened in Watertown and resumed its powers of government under the province charter of 1691, which Parliament had revoked. Declaring the governor's chair vacant, the legislature instructed the council to exercise executive authority. Formally, the province remained loyal to the king. So, too, did the Concord selectmen, who were prudently issuing warrants for town meetings "In his Majesties Name" as late as March 1776. But these tokens of allegiance to the royal sovereign made little sense when the citizens were killing his troops. Even before the Continental Congress acted, people like Captain Joseph Butler were making their own symbolic break with Britain by naming their sons for George Washington. As the first anniversary of the battle in Concord approached, William Emerson preached from the text, "Be ye not again entangled in ye Yoke of Bondage." . . .

In mid-July, acting on an order from the Massachusetts Council, Emerson read the Declaration of Independence from his pulpit, and Ephraim

[*Beginning in 1738, a long-lasting religious controversy broke out between "new light" and "old light' Congregationalists in Concord. Dr. Lee was a prominent spokesman for the embittered minority "old light" faction, which opposed the ministries of the Rev. Daniel Bliss and his successor, the Rev. William Emerson.]

Wood inscribed it for a "permanent memorial" in the town book, to be read by future generations as they paged through minutes of town meetings about roads and schools and pigs. Soon the town was holding its meetings "In the Name of the Government and People of the Massachusetts Bay."

Even as the colonies were boldly embarking on new careers as self-governing states, the practical problems of sustaining and winning the fight for independence were mounting. No end to the war lay in sight. . . .

The darkening military outlook was accompanied by an increasingly desperate financial situation. At the start of the contest in 1775, the Continental Congress faced a dilemma: it had taken charge of the sixteen-thousand-man army outside Boston, but it had no cash to pay the troops and no power to raise any through taxes. The only solution was to turn to the printing press and issue paper money of its own. Congress took the plunge—again and again and again. Meanwhile, every state government was doing the same. And that was not all. Other forms of currency were added to the flood: the interest-bearing bonds that both Congress and states gave in exchange for private loans; the "I.O.U.'s" that Army commissary officers forced on reluctant farmers for supplies; and the counterfeit bills that British agents spread in order to disrupt the American war effort. Until late 1776 this infusion of money, combined with the Army demand for provisions, pumped new life into the state economies and brought good prices and prosperity to town and country alike. But no one bets on a likely loser without demanding higher and higher odds. As American military fortunes deteriorated, paper money inevitably sank in value, and prices and wages soared. Beef cost $.04 a pound in 1777; three years later, it stood at $1.69 and was still rising. Paper money had become simply that—a piece of paper and "not worth a Continental [currency issued by the revolutionary Congress]." In 1780, Congress conceded the obvious: through a drastic devaluation of the dollar, it effectively repudiated its money in which no one believed. Even that didn't work. The new bills it issued sank in value almost as soon as they came off the press.

People in Concord drowned in paper along with everyone else. Runaway inflation disordered the finances of the town and claimed its classic victims: the poor, wage laborers, and all who lived on fixed incomes. Common soldiers suffered especially in their country's service. But even ministers of the gospel struggled to stay afloat. . . .

The skyrocketing prices of food and fuel benefited those farmers who could raise large surpluses for market and satisfy many of their own consumer needs. Self-sufficiency, of course, was never fully possible except at the rudest standard of living. But the war stimulated household industries and thereby saved money that had previously been drained away to the country stores and from there to Boston and beyond the sea. Before the Revolution many families had grown accustomed to buying the latest in imported English and European finery. Now that trade with Britain was proscribed, homespun clothing became the patriotic fashion of the day and women at the loom heroines of the Revolution. On Concord farms, flocks of sheep were once again expanding after several decades of neglect. To be sure, many substitutes for English goods could not be made at home. But skilled country artisans rushed in to fill the void, and they, too, thrived on soaring prices in a captive market. For both farmers and artisans, inflation carried an added advantage. It was easy to pay off old debts by stuffing a creditor's pockets full of paper—that is, if you could catch him.

Yet, for most people in Concord, these were not prosperous times. Many lesser yeomen lacked room to expand; at best, they could drive a few head of cattle a year to market. And even substantial commercial farmers like the Barretts were limited in their ability to reap the harvest of inflated prices. Throughout the war years farm labor was scarce. In this preindustrial society, war, like other human activities, conformed to the changing seasons. Armies normally campaigned during the warmer months, then retired to winter quarters. Men were thus called away to the fields of battle at the very time they were urgently needed in the fields at home. Military quotas remained heavy in Concord through 1778 and were often unpredictable. A sudden alarm could disrupt the farming schedule at its most vulnerable moments: in 1776 men were drafted for White Plains in the middle of the corn harvest. But the manpower shortage did not end after the war moved south. The removal of the British threat to the New England interior released a new wave of migration to the west. At least a fifth of the Concord Minutemen left home between the Battle of Saratoga and the final declaration of peace. Once again farms were exporting their youth to the frontier.

It was not just human labor that was drained away from the land. Stocks of draft animals were depleted, too, as farmers sold off large numbers of horses and oxen to pull teams in the Army or to be slaughtered for meat. Farms consequently continued to deteriorate: with fewer field hands and work animals available, men plowed more shallowly, manured more thinly, and cultivated more carelessly than they had done even before the war. Crop returns fell to new lows, at the same time as the area under tillage contracted. More and more land was put into permanent pasture, which required less labor and helped accommodate the expanding flocks of sheep. But grazing lands were wearing out fast. Men estimated in 1780 that it now took over five acres of pasture to keep a single cow for a year.

Army demands and farming problems led to real scarcities of food, further fueling the raging inflation. The hardships bore with particular severity on women, who often had to run farms while their men were away at war. Mrs. Phebe Bliss, widow of the minister, was left with only a daughter at home when her sons went their separate ways. To make ends meet she took in boarders—among them, British prisoners of war.

Ensign Thomas Hughes came to her house in May 1778 and found the mistress to be "the genteelest woman I have met with in New England." But after several months Hughes was compelled to seek new lodgings. Mrs. Bliss could no longer keep up the boardinghouse, "as she had no man to hunt after provisions which are scarce." But even after the men came home, farm families had to make sacrifices. From October 1780 to July 1781, Concord was called upon to furnish 42,779 pounds of beef for the Army—the equivalent of at least a hundred head of mature cattle. Such animals were not quickly replaced. By 1784 Concord's holdings of oxen, cows, and swine were well below prewar levels. To feed the Army, the townspeople had to take food from their own mouths. "They ate poorer food," said the son of one Revolutionary veteran, and "wore less comfortable clothing."

The uncertainties of war and economic change disrupted basic patterns of social life. This was no time to start a family or plan for the future. Those who did marry waited several years longer than was customary. Because of the declining number of marriages and also because military call-ups took husbands from the home, Concord's birth rate plummeted during the period of most active conflict. After 1780, when the fighting was over in the North, a baby boom began. If nothing else, the temporary slowdown in births slightly eased the pain of wartime shortages: there were thankfully fewer mouths to feed.

The citizens of Concord did not quietly resign themselves to economic distress. Neither did people elsewhere. They looked for villains—for the speculators and price gougers they held responsible for inflation, for the engrossers and hoarders they blamed for shortages. In January 1777 the General Court passed "An Act to Prevent Monopoly and Oppression," fixing ceiling prices and wages on a wide range of goods and services and instructing town selectmen and committees of correspondence to enforce them. The Concord committee tried briefly to carry out the assignment. That spring the members heard at least five complaints against both merchants and farmers but found only one guilty of violating the law—a newcomer named Walker, who was ordered to repay what he had overcharged his customers. In other economic regulations, the committee moved to implement an embargo against exporting scarce goods from the state: in May, it stopped yeoman John Parlin from shipping five barrels of rum to a merchant in Cambridge and launched an investigation into the matter. The inquiry came to nought, as did the entire state anti-inflation program. Without strict, uniform enforcement of prices and wages throughout New England, it remained in the individual's self-interest always to make just one forbidden sale or to charge a little more than going rates as a hedge against future inflation. Country farmers and city merchants were soon bitterly blaming each other for the collapse of controls. In September 1777 the legislature repealed its nine-month-old anti-monopoly law. By then, the act was dead in Concord.

That was not the end of the political struggle against inflation. In mid-1779, prices began one last upward spiral before Continentals lost all value and passed into oblivion. Alarmed by the rising cost of farm produce, Boston merchants launched a drive for voluntary price controls. Through their town meeting, they issued a call for a state convention to meet at Concord in July. Though they had not been consulted, Concordians quickly agreed to play host, pledging themselves to "Heartly Join in any Lawful measures" to stem that great "Evil," depreciation. The convention duly gathered with 171 delegates from all over the state. Concord was represented by its committee of correspondence. On a steamy summer's day the participants produced a detailed list of prices, promised to treat violators as "Enemies to this Country," and denounced the "Tories and Monopolizers" who were supposedly spreading those "Wicked and Malevolent Reports" of jealousy between country and city. Nevertheless, the delegates apparently doubted their handiwork would last. Before dissolving, the convention set the following October as the date for another conclave in Concord.

After the mid-summer convention had ended, Concord set out in earnest to implement its resolves. In a unanimous vote the townsmen accepted a schedule of prices that were actually below those allowed by the convention. A special committee was named to "Inspect and keep a Watchfull eye over the People" and, if need be, to punish transgressors. But neither Concord nor any other town could hold back the inflationary tide. When the second price-control convention assembled on October 6, rural and urban delegates deliberated in an atmosphere of mutual distrust. Joseph Lee, now free to go where he pleased, observed their sessions. The delegates "Dispute, are Divided, Tangle & Labour," he wrote; they even met on the Lord's Day! After a week, a new agreement on prices came forth. ". . . If they have done good," Lee remarked, "it is well." But for all their labors, the convention's issue was stillborn. Although Concordians once again unanimously adopted the convention's resolves, three weeks later they had second thoughts. Merchants in Boston and elsewhere were already violating the official prices. There would be no move to form yet another agreement.

Despite all these troubles, the people of Concord preferred paper money to no money at all, and when the state acted to take it out of circulation, they were quick to protest. Massachusetts kept her own financial house in fairly good order during the war, but through policies that frequently angered farming communities. As early as October 1777 the General Court called in the state's paper bills for redemption in bonds paying 6 per cent interest. Shortly thereafter, Concord was among a small minority of rural communities to petition against the move. It was far better, advised the town, to control inflation through regular taxes than to add the unnecessary burden of interest charges to the enormous cost of the war. The excesses of paper money could be cured. But the legislature eventually opted for radical surgery. In 1781, as the state was being buried under worthless Continentals, the General Court put Massachusetts on a hard-money basis and began imposing heavy taxes in gold and silver to pay off the state debt. These extreme deflationary policies were promoted by representatives of the richest, most commercialized communities of the commonwealth. As a center of trade and credit in central Middlesex, Concord placed solidly in this elite group of towns. But for the most part her delegation to the legislature rejected the alliance of privilege and sided with rural interests. . . .

Cheap money, no matter how inflationary, answered a real economic need. Gold and silver coin had never been plentiful in the rural communities of Massachusetts, but after the legislature imposed its deflationary program, specie became a rare item in most homes. With so little money in circulation, farm prices plunged swiftly downward into a deep depression. Many yeomen were unable to pay their taxes and were in danger of losing their land. As money disappeared, Concord had trouble filling the post of constable. In 1780, even before paper was completely driven out of circulation, it became necessary to ask an unlikely pair of substantial citizens—Stephen Barrett and Jonas Lee, the doctor's son—to take the job after two small farmers flatly refused to make tax collector's rounds. Economic problems would only get worse in the next few years. . . .

Amid the trials of inflation and deflation, good harvests and bad, military victories and defeats, war weariness gradually set in. For four years the calls for troops, for men to serve a few days, a few months, or even a few years, did not let up. 1775: 74 men; 1776: 212; 1777: 174; 1778: 139. Thereafter, the fighting was over for most Concordians, but there were still soldiers to be raised and bounties to be paid at a time when costs were spiraling and willing bodies were getting scarce. In all, Concord was obliged to provide some 875 men for terms of two months or more—a figure more than two and a half times the eligible male population on the eve of the war. And that number does not cover the whole, does not include the men who fought on April 19 or answered later alarms, nor does it count the local citizens who enlisted on their own in units belonging to other towns. The demand for manpower was immense, but the town never failed to meet its quota, one way or another. In the process, though, the very character and social meaning of the war were transformed: from a voluntary struggle to a battle by conscripts and eventually from a community-wide effort to a poor man's fight.

Throughout Massachusetts, voluntary enlistments were sufficient to fight the war until the summer of 1776. Then, with British troops attacking from Canada and Washington's forces beleaguered in New York, the General Court resorted to drafts and stuck to them over the next few years. Militiamen were conscripted for short terms of three or six months in theaters far from home—New York, New Jersey, the "Canady" country—as well as in nearby Rhode Island and in Massachusetts itself. There was often no time for ordinary recruitment campaigns, but even if there had been, men were no longer readily forthcoming in Concord or anywhere else. Enthusiasm could occasionally be whipped up in a sudden emergency. In September 1777, John Buttrick enlisted forty-six volunteers to stop Burgoyne only weeks after sixteen inhabitants had been drafted for the Saratoga campaign. But with few exceptions Concord did only what was required. Between July 1776 and April 1778 three quarters of the town's quotas were filled by pulling names from a hat.

Not everybody who was drafted was expected to go. One could be excused by hiring a substitute or paying a substantial fine. Just to make sure no one forgot his obligation, the law occasionally threatened delinquents with a jail term. Although drafts favored the rich, who could buy their way out, they forced all social groups in Concord to contribute to waging the war. Indeed, conscription was carried out with ruthless efficiency. Half the men under fifty received a draft notice at least once; occasionally even the old, the crippled, and the women were not spared. To furnish men for the New Jersey front in November 1776 three aging deacons—Thomas Barrett, Ephraim Brown, and Simon Hunt—were called up along with sixty-nine-year-old widow Prescott. They presumably found substitutes.

Conscription had long precedent in colonial Massachusetts, and it conformed to the same principles of participation that governed peacetime community life: citizens were expected to serve the public whenever they were asked and in ways appropriate to their social and economic rank. In fact, Concord developed its own supplement to the draft, applying tried and tested techniques of getting men to work. From 1777 to 1780 the selectmen, together with the militia officers, periodically estimated the town's war-related expenses and apportioned the sum to the taxpayers according to their wealth. Every individual was credited for the time he had spent at war or the money he had spent on substitutes or fines. He had to pay the difference; if the balance was in his favor, the surplus rested "in bank," to be deducted from the next year's tax. This was the same system Concord routinely used for building highways and bridges. In effect, the town recognized what many generations of soldiers have known: digging a ditch is still digging a ditch, whether at war or peace. Few men seek out the job.

Through these devices, the military burden was widely shared in the years when demands for manpower were at their height. It was chiefly the old who escaped service and naturally the young who did the bulk of the fighting. Available records do not always distinguish between those who were drafted and those who actually turned out, making calculations uncertain, but in all likelihood most eligible men under forty put in their time. Stephen Barrett started as a Minuteman corporal in 1775 and ended in 1780 with a second lieutenant's commission in the militia. Along the way he helped guard the Massachusetts coast at Nantasket in 1776, where he joined in capturing three hundred Scottish Highlanders as they sailed into Boston, unaware of its evacuation by the forces of the king. The next year he was drafted to answer an alarm in Rhode Island. With a wife and three young children at home by 1780 and a farm to run, Barrett served some six to nine months in all, a little better than average. Most of his contemporaries were credited with under half a year's time. They could count on the younger single men like Purchase Brown to take their places. Still landless and rootless, Brown spent a few weeks in camp at Charlestown in 1775–76, just missing the Battle of Bunker Hill, and made the Ticonderoga expedition later that summer. He had been home only half a year before being drafted with Stephen Barrett for the Rhode Island alarm. 1778 was one long furlough—unless records are missing—before doing guard duty in Boston for several months in 1779 and going off yet again to Rhode Island the next year. A few months here, a few months there, and never far from home for long: by 1780, Brown had accumulated a full year of service.

Those who declined to serve had a variety of reasons. After his hard riding on April 19, Reuben Brown never entered the Army. He was drafted several times but always hired a substitute. Then in his late twenties, the saddler spent two years as a military supplier, employed in outfitting several companies. This could be profitable as well as patriotic work. Brown complained that he ended up losing $1,000 when a government contractor pocketed his pay. Perhaps. But Brown's wartime activities hardly slowed his rise in the world. In 1770 he had been warned out of Concord; by the 1780s he was the most active creditor in town.

Other men were simply not cut out for war. John White, the pious storekeeper, nearly turned pacifist after experiencing combat. Born in Acton, he had moved to Concord about 1773. At age twenty-six he enlisted in the Minutemen to defend his country's cause and participated in the Concord Fight. He then tended his store for a while before marching with Buttrick's volunteers to Saratoga, where he "had the pleasure to see the whole of Burgoyne's [defeated] army parade their arms, and march out of their lines; a wonderful sight indeed; it was the Lord's doing, and it was marvellous in our eyes." That was the end of White's military career. He had found war, even with the Lord's backing, to be "a great calamity" and the life of a soldier uncongenial to his nature. In later years he often said that "though he discharged his musket many times . . . he hoped he had killed none of the enemy."

There are no signs in Concord of opposition to the draft, nothing like the votes the town of Braintree took to idemnify its miltia officers if they were fined for failing to carry out state levies. But after April 1778 the townspeople quietly ignored the General Court's orders to conscript and hired men to fill their quotas. This decision accentuated a change in the social character of recruits that had already begun the previous year. In January 1777, Concord was ordered to raise forty-four men for three-year tours in the Continental Army. These were the first long-term enlistments of the war. They had been persistently urged by General Washington as the only rational basis for running an army. Without them, the Continental forces had to be rebuilt every year almost from scratch, for by the time soldiers were well trained and battle tested, enlistments ran out and the Army melted away. Washington's proposal raised fundamental objections in New England. John Adams argued that respectable Yankee farmers and mechanics would not abandon their lands and shops for more than a year; the Army would be filled up with only "the meanest, idlest, most intemperate and worthless" sort. His moral judgments aside, Adams proved right. From 1777 on, the Continental ranks were manned largely by the lower social orders.

Ezekiel Brown signed up right away. Upon his release from debtor's prison in March of 1776 he promptly turned his jailhouse medical studies to advantage and gained a commission as a surgeon's mate for six months in the regular Army.* He returned to Concord by the following January, just in time for the birth of his third child. He was eking out a living as a schoolmaster when the call came for long-term Continental enlistments. With a growing family of five and only a few acres of land, no chance of resuming his store, and no visible prospects (except on the unprotected Maine frontier), Brown seized what opportunities there were in the Army. Despite his low circumstances, he was able to convert his medical training into a commission as a regimental surgeon—equivalent to a captain's rank—and enlisted not just for three years but "for the duration."

Most of the ordinary Continental privates from Concord were, like Brown, men with little or nothing to lose by going off to war for three years or more. Surprisingly, after 1778, the soldiers hired by the town even for short terms in the militia were of the same sort. No longer did young men of substance volunteer for common duty in any sizable numbers. The war was now being fought principally by landless younger sons, by the permanent poor, and by blacks. In Massachusetts, as in every other state, necessity ultimately overcame prejudice. Concord, with a handful of slaves, hired blacks to fill up some 8 per cent of its Continental quotas. For slaves, army service was tantamount to a grant of freedom, although not always

[* Brown, a failed Concord storekeeper, had been in a Boston jail since the winter of 1773.]

formally so. Squire Cuming's man Brister enlisted in 1779 as Brister Freeman, probably with Cuming's consent. Philip, James Barrett's slave, was still part of his master's estate when the colonel died in April 1779. Philip was then nineteen. By his master's will, he would have to labor for Peter Barrett, the colonel's youngest son, until he was thirty and then would obtain his freedom. But within a year Private Philip Barrett was stationed at West Point, obeying the orders of other superiors. At least one Concord slave definitely seized his freedom by enlisting. In January 1781 an eighteen-year-old black laborer named Richard Hobby was hired for a three-year term in the Continental Army while his owner, a newcomer to town, was out of state. On returning, Jonathan Hobby sued the Army for the release of his slave, on the grounds that his property had been taken without his consent. A military court of inquiry sympathized with this argument; belief in the sancity of property was, after all, what had originally triggered the Americans' rebellion. But the Revolution against British-imposed "slavery" had dramatically undermined the notion that any man was, by right, a slave. Caught in the contradiction between property rights and natural rights, the judges temporized. They conceded master Hobby's claim, insisted on slave Hobby's military obligation, and passed the case up to higher authorities. The final disposition is unknown, but Richard Hobby, like many other blacks, probably gained his freedom by default.

The longer the war went on, the poorer and more degraded in status were the recruits Concord supplied. The "three-year-men" who enlisted in the Continental forces in 1777 were generally poor, but at least they were Concord's poor. Three years later, only eight of the sixteen men who signed up for three-year terms had any known connection to the town. The poor who made up the peacetime army of transients were now welcome in Concord, as long as they stayed only long enough to have a drink, take their bounty, and go off to fight. For Concord, the Revolution was becoming a war by proxy. And it was not surprising that those who went, both the residents and the strangers, were often left by their countrymen to go barefoot, wrap themselves in thin blankets, and hunger in the cold. The soldiers represented the bottom of society, resembling in many ways the rank-and-file "lobsters" whom they fought. . . .

As the sounds of musket-fire grew distant and the character of the Army changed, many Concordians began resisting demands for more troops. At the outset the town had generously opened its treasury to pay for the war. But inflation and the sharp competition for volunteers had bid up enlistment bounties to dizzying heights. One could purchase a month and a half of a man's time with a single pound in 1775; by 1780 that sum commanded little more than a day. Time after time the town instructed its officials to hire men at a given rate, only to have them return with the unhappy report that no one could be gotten for the price. Patience was fast running out. In 1780 the town met its quota "after many Debates."

The next year, as they reeled under the impact of the sudden deflation, the citizens divided sharply over yet another requisition for three-year men. "After many Disputes," the measure finally carried by a narrow margin of nine.

The war, combined with depression, left an exhausted people in its wake. Concord learned the news of the Treaty of Paris in a sour mood. Pausing only briefly to congratulate representative Hosmer on the restoration of peace "to this (of Late) Bleeding Land," the voters instructed him to investigate reports that Massachusetts had paid more than her fair share of the war. The conflict had begun in Concord with brave pledges to "go to the utmost with Lives and Fortunes" to defend the country's freedom. It was now ending in resentful muttering that the town had done too much.

DOCUMENTS

A Tory Punished, 1775

FROM THE RECORDS OF THE COMMITTEE OF SAFETY.

NEW YORK, DECEMBER 28, 1775

The 6th of December, at Quibbletown, Middlesex County, Piscataway Township, New-Jersey, Thomas Randolph, cooper, who had publickly proved himself an enemy to his country, by reviling and using his utmost endeavours to oppose the proceedings of the Continental and Provincial Conventions and Committees, in defence of their rights and liberties; and he, being judged a person of not consequence enough for a severer punishment, was ordered to be stripped naked, well coated with tar and feathers, and carried in a wagon pubickly round the town; which punishment was accordingly inflicted. And as he soon became duly sensible of his offence, for which he earnestly begged pardon, and promised to atone, as far as he was able, by a contrary behaviour for the future, he was released, and suffered to return to his house in less than half an hour. The whole was conducted with that regularity and decorum that ought to be observed in all publick punishments.

SOURCE: Peter Force, ed., *American Archives: Fourth Series* (Washington, D.C.: St. Clair Clarke and Peter Force, 1837–1846), 4: 203.

Tories Vilified, 1779

Rouse, America! your danger is great—great from a quarter where you least expect it. The Tories, the Tories will yet be the ruin of you! 'Tis high time they were separated from among you. They are now busy engaged in undermining your liberties. They have a thousand ways of doing it, and they make use of them all.

Who were the occasion of this war? The Tories! Who persuaded the tyrant of Britain to prosecute it in a manner before unknown to civilized nations, and shocking even to barbarians? The Tories! Who prevailed on the savages of the wilderness to join the standard of the enemy? The Tories! Who have assisted the Indians in taking the scalp from the aged matron, the blooming fair one, the helpless infant, and the dying hero? The Tories! Who advised and who assisted in burning your towns, ravaging your country, and violating the chastity of your women? The Tories! Who are the occasion that thousands of you now mourn the loss of your dearest connections? The Tories! Who have always counteracted the endeavors of Congress to secure the liberties of this country? The Tories!

Who refused their money when as good as specie, though stamped with the image of his most sacred Majesty? The Tories! Who continue to refuse it? The Tories! Who do all in their power to depreciate it? The Tories! Who propagate lies among us to discourage the Whigs? The Tories! Who corrupt the minds of the good people of these States by every species of insidious counsel? The Tories! Who hold a traitorous correspondence with the enemy? The Tories! Who daily send them intelligence? The Tories! Who take the oaths of allegiance to the States one day, and break them the next? The Tories! Who prevent your battalions from being filled? The Tories! Who dissuade men from entering the army? The Tories! Who persuade those who have enlisted to desert? The Tories! Who harbor those who do desert? The Tories! In short, who wish to see us conquered, to see us slaves, to see us hewers of wood and drawers of water? The Tories! . . .

Awake, Americans, to a sense of your danger. No time to be lost. Instantly banish every Tory from among you. Let America be sacred alone to freemen.

Drive far from you every baneful wretch who wishes to see you fettered with the chains of tyranny. Send them where they may enjoy their beloved slavery to perfection—send them to the island of Britain; there let them drink the cup of slavery and eat the bread of bitterness all the days of their existence—there let them drag out a painful life, despised and accursed by those very men whose cause they have had the wickedness to espouse. Never let them return to this happy land—never let them taste the sweets

SOURCE: *Pennsylvania Packet*, August 5, 1779, in Frank Moore, *Diary of the American Revolution* (New York: Scribner's, 1859), 2: 166–68.

of that independence which they strove to prevent. Banishment, perpetual banishment, should be their lot.

A New Hampshire Boy
Joins the Navy, 1779

Ships were building, prizes taken from the enemy unloading, privateers fitting out, standards waved on the forts and batteries, the exercising of soldiers, the roar of cannon, the sound of martial music and the call for volunteers so infatuated me, that I was filled with anxiety to become an actor in the scene of war. . . . Though not yet fourteen years of age, like other boys, I imagined myself almost a man. I had intimated to my sister, that if my father would not consent that I should go to sea, I would run away, and go on board a privateer. My mind became so infatuated with the subject, that I talked of it in my sleep, and was overheard by my mother. She communicated what she had heard to my father. —My parents were apprehensive that I might wander off and go on board some vessel without their consent. At this period it was not an uncommon thing for lads to come out of the country, step on board a privateer, make a cruise and return home, their friends remaining in entire ignorance of their fate, until they heard it from themselves. Others would pack up their clothes, take a cheese and a loaf of bread, and steer off for the army.There was a disposition in commanders of privateers and recruiting officers to encourage this spirit of enterprise in young men and boys. Though these rash young adventurers did not count the cost, or think of looking at the dark side of the picture, yet this spirit, amidst the despondency of many, enabled our country to maintain a successful struggle and finally achieve her independence.

The continental ship of war Ranger, of eighteen guns, commanded by Thomas Simpson, Esq. was at this time shipping a crew in Portsmouth. This ship had been ordered to join the Boston and Providence frigates and the Queen of France of twenty guns, upon an expedition directed by Congress. My father having consented that I should go to sea, preferred the service of Congress [the Continental Navy] to privateering. He was acquainted with Capt. Simpson. —On board this ship were my two half uncles, Timothy and James Weymouth. Accompanied by my father, I visited the rendezvous of the Ranger and shipped as one of her crew. There were probably thirty boys on board this ship. As most of our principal

SOURCE: Andrew Sherburne, *Memoirs*, 2d ed. (Providence: H. H. Brown, 1831), 18–21.

officers belonged to the town, parents preferred this ship as a station for their sons who were about to enter the naval service. Hence most of these boys were from Portsmouth. As privateering was the order of the day, vessels of every description were employed in the business. Men were not wanting who would hazard themselves in vessels of twenty tons or less, manned by ten or fifteen hands. Placing much dependence on the protection of my uncles, I was much elated with my supposed good fortune, which had at last made me a sailor.

I was not yet fourteen years of age. I had received some little moral and religious instruction, and was far from being accustomed to the habits of town boys, or the maxims or dialect of sailors. The town boys thought themselves vastly superior to country lads; and indeed in those days the distinction was much greater than at present. My diffidence and aversion to swearing, rendered me an object of ridicule to those little profane chaps. I was insulted, and frequently obliged to fight. In this I was sometimes victorious. My uncles, and others, prompted me to defend my rights. I soon began to improve in boxing, and to indulge in swearing. At first this practice occasioned some remorse of conscience. —I however endeavored to persuade myself that there was a necessity for it. I at length became a proficient in this abominable practice. To counterbalance my guilt in this, I at the same time became more constant in praying; heretofore I had only prayed occasionally; now I prayed continually when I turned in at night, and vainly imagined that I prayed enough by night to atone for the sins of the day. Believing that no other person on board prayed, I was filled with pride, concluding I had as much or more religion than the whole crew besides. The boys were employed in waiting on the officers, but in time of action a boy was quartered to each gun to carry cartridges. I was waiter to Mr. Charles Roberts, the boatswain, and was quartered at the third gun from the bow. Being ready for sea, we sailed to Boston, joined the Providence frigate, commanded by Commodore Whipple, the Boston frigate and the Queen of France. I believe that this small squadron composed nearly the entire navy of the United States. We proceeded to sea some time in June, 1779. A considerable part of the crew of the Ranger being raw hands and the sea rough, especially in the gulf stream, many were exceedingly sick, and myself among the rest. We afforded a subject of constant ridicule to the old sailors.

PART I

Suggestions for Further Reading

On early developments in the colonies, see Clarence L. Ver Steeg, *The Formative Years, 1607–1763* (1965) and Daniel J. Boorstin, *The Americans: The Colonial Experience* (1958). On the northern colonies, there are a number of good books. Among them are Sumner Powell, *Puritan Village: The Formation of a New Town* (1963); Kenneth A. Lockridge, *A New England Town; The First Hundred Years, Dedham, Massachusetts, 1636–1736* (1970); Bernard Bailyn, *The New England Merchants in the Seventeenth Century* (1955); and T. H. Breen, *From Puritans and Adventurers: Change and Persistence in Early America* (1980).

On the southern colonies, see two works by Wesley Frank Craven: *The Southern Colonies in the Seventeenth Century, 1607–1689* (1949) and *White, Red, and Black: The Seventeenth Century Virginian* (1971). Edmund S. Morgan, *American Slavery, American Freedom: The Ordeal of Colonial Virginia* (1975) provides an exciting, readable treatment of developments in seventeenth-century Virginia. Also recommended are Clarence L. Ver Steeg, *Origin of the Southern Mosaic* (1975) and Carl Bridenbaugh, *Jamestown, 1544–1699* (1980).

On society in the eighteenth century, useful works are Richard Hofstadter, *America at 1750: A Social Portrait* (1971); Michael Zuckerman, *Peaceable Kingdoms: New England Towns in the Eighteenth Century* (1970); Gary Nash, *The Urban Crucible: Social Change, Political Consciousness, and the Origins of the American Revolution* (1979); Jackson Turner Main, *The Social Structure of Revolutionary America* (1965); and James Henretta, *The Evolution of American Society, 1700–1815: An Interdisciplinary Analysis* (1973).

For the racial and ethnic mix of the American population, consult Gary Nash, *Red, White and Black: The Peoples of Early America* (1974). Two excellent books on Europeans and Indians are Francis Jennings, *Invasion of America* (1975) and James Axtell, *The Invasion Within: The Contest of Cultures in Colonial North America* (1985). On the Puritans and Indians, see Alden Vaughan, *New England Frontier: Puritans and Indians* (1965). On immigration, see Thomas Archdeacon, *Becoming American: An Ethnic History* (1983) and Maldwyn Jones, *American Immigration* (1960). On blacks, two books are outstanding: Peter Wood, *Black Majority: Negroes in Colonial South Carolina from 1676 through the Stono Rebellion* (1974) and Gerald Mullin, *Slave Resistance in Eighteenth Century Virginia* (1972). On white racism, Winthrop Jordan, *White over Black: American Attitudes toward the Negro, 1550–1812* (1968) is a classic.

On religious developments in the eighteenth century, refer to Carl Bridenbaugh, *Mitre and Sceptre: Trans-Atlantic Faiths, Ideas, Personalities, and Politics, 1689–1775* (1962). J. M. Bumstead and John E. Van de Wetering, *What Must I Do to Be Saved? The Great Awakening in Colonial America* (1976) provides an excellent introduction to the great revival movement of the colonial period. For the impact of the Great Awakening in Virginia, see Rhys Isaac, *The Transformation of Virginia, 1740–1790* (1982) and Richard Beeman, *The Evolution of the Southern Backcountry: A Case Study of Lunenburg County, Virginia, 1746–1832* (1984).

On women, two general books are helpful: Nancy Woloch, *Women and the American Experience* (1984) and Mary Ryan, *Womanhood in America: From Colonial Times to the Present* (1975). For the colonial period, information about women can be found in Edmund Morgan, *The Puritan Family: Religion and Domestic Relations in Seventeenth-Century New England* (1966) and John Demos, *A Little Commonwealth: Family Life in Plymouth Colony* (1970). On attitudes toward children, see Philip Greven, *The Protestant Temperament: Patterns of Child-Rearing, Religious Experience and the Self in Early America* (1977).

A number of books deal with the social history of the American Revolution. For women, see Mary Beth Norton, *Liberty's Daughters: The Revolutionary Experience of American Women, 1750–1800* (1980) and Linda Kerber, *Women of the Republic: Intellect and Ideology in Revolutionary America* (1980). Among studies of the loyalist side of the conflict are Bernard Bailyn, *The Ordeal of Thomas Hutchinson* (1975); Robert M. Calhoon, *The Loyalists in Revolutionary America, 1760–1781* (1973); and William H. Nelson, *The American Tory* (1961). Regional studies of the war include Robert Gross, *The Minutemen and Their World* (1976) and Robert J. Taylor, *Western Massachusetts in the Revolution* (1954). For a view of the war through the eyes of those who fought, see George F. Scheer and Hugh F. Rankin, *Rebels and Redcoats* (1957.)

PART II

Social Life in a New Nation

1783–1877

THE REVOLUTION CONCLUDED, THE FOUNDING FATHERS turned their attention to forming new state and national governments. By 1789 the federal government was reorganized and ready to operate under the newly ratified Constitution. As important as these political changes were, no less crucial for America's future were the vast social and economic developments that occurred during the first seventy years of the nation's history.

Along the country's frontier, Indians were removed to make way for white men and women heading west in search of a new life. In the North, new factory towns were established and older commercial centers expanded. Northern society also experienced large-scale immigration, especially during the two decades preceding the Civil War. The southern states, on the other hand, attracted few immigrants. There, cotton became "king" and slavery remained well entrenched in the social order. So different were northern and southern development that the nation increasingly appeared to be two societies in conflict. Apparent conflict, of course, eventually led to the very real Civil War, which culminated with the triumph of the North and the destruction of slavery. The Reconstruction period following the war was a time of uneasy stability for the South: relative freedom and opportunity for the freedmen (enforced by Federal bayonets), and growing resentment for the former Confederates, who were determined not to lose the control over the economic and political life of their region that had been theirs for generations.

The essays and documents in Part II deal with industrialization, removal of the Native Americans, and the movement west. They also examine immigration, the status of women, the role of religion in American life, the several reform movements of the first half of the nineteenth century, and the institution of slavery. They conclude by considering the social ramifications of the Civil War and the Reconstruction period that followed.

CHAPTER 8

Industry and Ideology in an Emerging Nation: The Lowell Venture

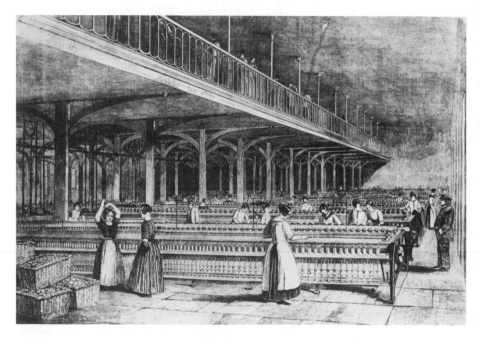

Urban centers in the new nation experienced dramatic changes and growth during the first half of the nineteenth century. Established cities boomed, and new ones were founded, with industry and commerce the focus of endeavor. The building of canals, railroads, and steamboats linked city to city and town to countryside, facilitating the movement of people, products, and ideas within the United States and between it and foreign lands.

The founding fathers had anticipated many of the issues that would confront the post-Revolutionary generation, but their successors nevertheless faced the tasks of developing the nation's economy and shaping its political and social character. What kind of society had the Revolution proclaimed? Conservatives wished to establish a republic of virtue and social stability, directed by men of property and standing. Others insisted that the struggle had been waged to attain a more egal-

itarian society, one offering broad-based participation in the social, political, and economic life of the country.

John F. Kasson's essay describes the establishment of the mill town of Lowell, Massachusetts—a town emblematic of an emerging industrial order that was so central to the dynamic new century. But Lowell also reflects the conflicting views of society in evidence during the period. The founders of Lowell sought to build factories, but also to establish a model, ordered community under their control and direction. As you read, notice how both the supporters and critics of the Lowell system relied on their interpretations of the social goals of the Revolution to support their arguments. What does the essay reveal about the image and status of women and Irish immigrants during this period?

The three documents following the essay illustrate three views of life in the Lowell mills in the mid-1840s. The first, from the Lowell Offering *of June 1844, a paper produced by the mill workers, is written from the perspective of what the mill owners would have viewed as the ideal "cooperative" female worker. (It should be noted that, although the workers produced the* Lowell Offering, *management held the power of approval of its content.) The second document, from testimony before a Massachusetts legislative committee investigating worker grievances in 1845, reflects the viewpoint of what Kasson terms "dissident workers." The final document, also from testimony before the Massachusetts committee, might be termed the "official" or "management" position. How do you explain these varying accounts? What was the impact of the Lowell experience on the lives of the female workers?*

ESSAY

The Factory as a Republican Community
John F. Kasson

As Americans advanced into the nineteenth century, pressures on a deferential society continued and the problems of republican order increased. The whole country surged with dramatic volatility and energy. The nation's population, which had more than doubled every twenty-five years in the eighteenth century, continued to grow at the same phenomenal rate through the first half of the nineteenth. People migrated restlessly not

SOURCE: John F. Kasson, *Civilizing the Machine: Technology and Republican Values in America, 1776–1900* (New York: Grossman Publishers, 1976), 62–79, 85–87, 93–94, 96–100, 102–6.

only along the vast new frontier but within the rapidly mushrooming urban centers as well. And the concept of republicanism, instead of controlling and containing this expansion, became in the hands of new egalitarian forces a weapon with which to challenge established authority in politics, religion, law, commerce—virtually every aspect of society. Social conservatives rubbed their eyes to see a reversion in American life from civilization to barbarism as the whole social order upon which the republican experiment was premised appeared to be collapsing around them. Some recent scholars . . . have in effect supported their perception, arguing that ante-bellum America suffered from a general "institutional breakdown" and "an excess of democracy" which ultimately paved the way for Civil War.

But the ante-bellum period was a time of institution building as well as breaking. Countervailing an intense anti-institutionalism, widespread attempts were made to create *new* institutions capable of dealing with an increasingly complex urban and industrial society and to restore social cohesion and public virtue. The colonial model of a relatively stable, hierarchical community in which each person observed established codes of morality and deference still exerted a powerful influence and appeal over social leaders disturbed about the new direction American society seemed to be taking. Yet at the same time they also wished to grasp the expansive new opportunities which beckoned. They felt with particular intensity the culture's ambivalence toward urbanism and industrialism. In this vision, cities and factories were seen as necessary and laudable agents of prosperity; but they were also viewed as potential tinderboxes of corruption and mob disorder. The promise of increased progress and abundance was far too enticing to allow nostalgia to sweep any significant segment of American society into a reactionary mood. Instead of attempting to solve their dilemma by simply turning back the clock, then, social conservatives concentrated on devising new methods of social improvement and control. They sought to regulate the fluid urban industrial society so as to safeguard their vision of an ordered republic while at the same time enjoying its benefits. In this effort they endeavored to create and harness institutions of moral instruction, rehabilitation, and reform. . . . Studies by a number of historians have documented the range and extent of their efforts: in public education; in support of the fine arts; in Protestant missions; in the treatment of poverty, delinquency, crime, and insanity. Public schools, parks and gardens, art galleries and museums, Sunday schools and tract societies all represented attempts to extend the sphere of republican instruction in the principles of social order and virtue to the maximum number of citizens; to counteract the turbulence and corruption of American life by improving the social environment and establishing monitors over it. In cases where the existing social conditions were potentially most dangerous or the subject most in need of discipline, the commitment to institutional reform was most complete. Thus in the decades after 1820, as David Rothman has shown in his book *The Discovery of the Asylum,* the almshouse, orphanage, penitentiary, reformatory, and insane asylum all were erected and meticulously systematized to deal with the deviant and the dependent. Often established in country settings, these various asylums sequestered inmates from outside influences and organized their lives around a routine of disciplined and officially sanctioned conduct. The order, supervision, industry, and temperance of institutional life, authorities believed, would counteract the chaotic and corrupting forces of the larger society and transform social victims into respectable citizens. More generally, such asylums would stand as models of well-ordered institutions for a society desperately in need of standards and guidance. They were part of an increased reliance in the second quarter of the nineteenth century with what . . . we may call "total institutions"— that is, places "of residence and work where a large number of like-situated individuals, cut off from the wider society for an appreciable period of time, together lead an enclosed formally administered round of life." The total institution represented the ultimate form in this period of the search for institutions of republican community.

To the total institution, then, turned a group of merchants known as the Boston associates, who would become America's leading manufacturers before the Civil War, as they sought an alternative to the poverty and neglect of English industrial conditions and a safeguard against the fluidity and potential corruption of an expanding American society. Beginning in Waltham, Massachusetts, in 1815, they established a successful pattern of textile manufactures and extended it rapidly. By 1850 the Boston associates controlled mills in operation in Chicopee, Taunton, and Lawrence, Massachusetts; Manchester, Dover, Somersworth, and Nashua, New Hampshire; and Saco and Biddeford, Maine; and were making active preparations for new mills in Holyoke, Massachusetts. But the queen city of their system and the leading producer of cotton goods, the nation's largest industry before the Civil War, was Lowell, Massachusetts. Lowell's fame rested not only on its industrial capacity but even more on its reputed social achievement. One of the most important and influential of all total institutions of republican reform in the ante-bellum period, Lowell promised to resolve the social conflict between the desire for industrial progress and the fear of a debased and disorderly proletariat. Its founding sprang from the conviction that, given the proper institutional environment, a factory town need not be a byword for vice and poverty, but might stand as a model of enlightened republican community in a restless and dynamic nation. Lowell offers a dramatic example of the effort to put this conservative faith into practice. Its story is particularly interesting because within a few years of its founding, the basic assumptions of the Lowell factory system and its conception of republican community were challenged both on ideological and institutional grounds by the working class and their spokesmen. . . .

Lowell was conceived in the second decade of the nineteenth century by a trio of innovative and energetic young Boston merchants: Francis Cabot Lowell, Nathan Appleton, and Patrick Tracy Jackson. Touring Great Britain in 1810 and 1811 for his health, F. C. Lowell visited a large iron works in Edinburgh and grew excited over the enormous possibilities such large-scale manufacturing had for America. While in Edinburgh, he also met Nathan Appleton, his friend and fourth cousin, and the two merchants discussed the idea of establishing cotton manufacture employing English technology in the United States. At the same time Lowell was corresponding on the subject with his business partner and brother-in-law, P. T. Jackson, and he determined, before his return to America, to study thoroughly the cotton mills at Manchester and Birmingham. He spent weeks in these factories, applying his keen mathematical and mechanical skill and questioning engineers eager to accommodate a wealthy potential customer. Thus Lowell circumvented stringent regulations against the exportation of English machinery or mechanical drawings and smuggled into America valuable mental baggage. . . .

Shortly after Lowell's return from Europe, he and Jackson bought a water-power site in Waltham, obtained a charter of incorporation from the Massachusetts legislature for their new Boston Manufacturing Company, and sought investors for the enterprise within their circle of friends and relatives among Boston's merchants. . . .

Lowell hired a talented engineer, Paul Moody, and quickly set about a series of reinventions based upon his observations of English machinery and contemporary American developments. Of these the most important was the power loom, which promised to free American mills from dependence on neighborhood weavers and to permit the organization of all manufacturing processes from raw cotton to finished cloth within a single integrated mill complex. When Nathan Appleton first saw Lowell's loom in 1814, he was stupefied by its significance and, in a "state of admiration and satisfaction," sat with Lowell "by the hour, watching the beautiful movement of this new and wonderful machine, destined as it evidently was, to change the character of all textile industry." To exploit the capacity of large-scale mechanized production to its fullest extent while relying on unskilled labor, Lowell decided to concentrate production on standardized inexpensive cotton cloths, sheetings, and shirtings. Later, as new corporations arose at the town of Lowell and elsewhere, each manufactured a different type of cotton goods to avoid duplication and competition with fellow companies. Mills were designed to facilitate the flow of materials from one stage of processing to the next. Cotton was carded on the first floor, spun on the second, woven on the third and fourth, while machine shops resided in the basement. In the next fifteen years New England inventors would build upon this structure and introduce a series of labor-saving technological innovations which equaled or excelled British methods and machinery and mechanized all the basic processes of cloth manufac-turing except spooling and warping. Even before some of these refine-ments, however, Lowell's system achieved dramatic gains in production. According to one technological historian, from its first years of operation the Waltham mill could with the same number of employees produce three and a half times as much as other American factories still operating ac-cording to pre-1812 methods. The achievement of Lowell and his col-leagues, sometimes known as the "Massachusetts system," thus marked a significant stage in the development of modern mass production.

As a final stroke in his grand design, Lowell turned his attention to politics. Competition with British textiles had in the past been the bane of the American industry. Thus when Congress began deliberations over a new tariff measure in 1816, Lowell rushed to Washington to lobby for his cause. He adroitly steered through Congress a minimum valuation tariff which helped to establish the principle of protection to American industry and sheltered his own company's products from foreign competition, while leaving exposed rival manufacturers of more expensive cotton goods. . . .

In the eyes of his contemporaries, however, Lowell's greatest achieve-ment lay in neither his technological success, nor his political skill, nor his business acumen. The special reverence with which his name was spoken in the period before the Civil War emerged from the sense that he had conceived a manufacturing system that concerned itself as much with the health, character, and well-being of its operatives as it did with profits. By allegedly protecting the integrity of America's workers, he had in important measure safeguarded the character of the republic itself. From the begin-ning, Lowell and his associates were mindful of the condition of European workers and particularly concerned to avoid a similar fate here. . . .

Their solution was to organize the factory as a total institution, so that the company might exercise exclusive control over the environment. Unlike most English cotton factories of this time, which were powered by steam, American mills depended upon water power; and the necessity to locate the plant near an important rapids further insured that the community would be placed in the country, apart from urban contamination. But where Lowell's plan differed radically from both earlier English and American factory settlements was in his decision to establish a community with a rotating rather than a permanent population; this was central to the con-ception. Previous American factory settlements had retained the English system of hiring whole families, often including school-aged children. Low-ell and his associates opposed the idea of a long-term residential force that might lead to an entrenched proletariat. They planned to hire as their main working force young, single women from the surrounding area for a few years apiece. For a rotating work force such women were an obvious choice. Able-bodied men could be attracted from farming only with difficulty, and their hiring would raise fears that the nation might lose her agrarian character and promote resistance to manufactures. Women, on the other hand, had traditionally served as spinners and weavers when textiles had been produced in the home, and they constituted an important part of the family economy. However, imports of European manufactured fabrics were eroding American household industry. At the same time, southern New England farmers were gradually shifting from subsistence to commercial agriculture. By employing young farm women in American factories on a relatively short-term basis, the Lowell system in effect extended and preserved the family economy while at the same time avoiding incorporation into the factory of the family as a whole. Factory work, then, would not become a lifetime vocation or mark of caste, passed on from parent to child in the omnipresent shadow of the mill. Rather it might form an honorable stage in a young woman's maturation, allowing her to supplement her family's income or earn a dowry, before assuming what the founders regarded as "the higher and more appropriate responsibilities of her sex" in a domestic capacity. Her factory experience would be a moral as well as an economic boon, numerous spokesmen for American manufactures maintained, rescuing her from idleness, and vice, pauperism, possibly even confinement in an almshouse or penitentiary. Instead, in the cotton mill, under the watchful eyes of supervisors, she would receive a republican education, imbibing "habits of order, regularity and industry, which lay a broad and deep foundation of public and private future usefulness." During her term at Lowell, the worker would be protected *in loco parentis* by strict corporate supervision, lodged in company boardinghouses kept by upright matrons, and provided compulsory religious services. Such stringent standards of moral scrutiny and company control would serve a treble purpose: to attract young women and overcome the reluctance of their parents, most of them farmers; to provide optimal factory discipline and management control of the operatives; and to maintain an intelligent, honorable, and exemplary republican work force. Though Lowell's founders never regarded their efforts as utopian, they aimed to establish an ideal New England community, which would stand not as a blight but a beacon of republican prosperity and purity upon the American landscape. . . .

. . . For the Boston associates and many of their colleagues were in fact both capitalists and concerned citizens, hard-dealing merchants and public-spirited philanthropists, entrepreneurs and ideologues. Even as they helped to transform New England's economy, they sought to preserve a cohesive social order by adhering tenaciously to a rigorous code of ethics and responsibility. They took seriously their role as republican leaders, and the public turned to them for leadership. The Unitarian reformer Theodore Parker expressed the sense of gratitude of many when he praised the

146

development of manufactures and improvements in transportation as help-ing to "civilize, educate, and refine men." "These are men," he concluded, "to whom the public owes a debt which no money could pay, for it is a debt of life." Whether it was sufficient payment or not, obviously these manufacturers received a great deal of money for their services. Never-theless, they insisted both publicly and privately that wealth was not their goal. "My mind has always been devoted to many other things rather than money-making," Nathan Appleton declared toward the end of his life. "Accident, and not effort, has made me a rich man." . . . Boston's leading merchants generally scorned a narrowly acquisitive view of their role and participated in a wide variety of public affairs. They were active and influ-ential in Federalist and later Whig politics and held important offices on both state and national levels. Their contributions to numerous charities and philanthropies, including hospitals, orphanages, and asylums, as well as libraries, historical societies, schools and colleges, helped to make Boston a center of social and cultural institutions in the nineteenth century. Such enterprises, they believed, were essential to the solidity and progress of society. . . .

Concern with the social consequences of Lowell, Massachusetts, as a tight-knit, carefully regulated republican community, then, was certainly consistent with the values and activities of the founders and their associates in a variety of other fields. Moreover, their philanthropic and industrial pursuits were related both historically and institutionally. Nineteenth-century textile mills were direct descendants of the manufacturing societies formed in various American colonies in the eighteenth century and more distant relatives of the work houses of the seventeenth century. Institutions such as the Boston Society for Encouraging Industry and Employing the Poor, established in 1751 and one of the colonies' most important pre-Revolutionary factories, had, as its name indicates, a dual purpose: not only to stimulate American manufactures but to provide work for the des-titute; to encourage industry in both senses of the word, under official supervision. Undoubtedly, with increased mechanization in the textile in-dustry, commercial motives were uppermost in the establishment of Lowell and other mill towns in the nineteenth century, but at the same time one should not lose sight of the social vision that accompanied them. Of course Lowell's founders and directors were not always as idealistic as they pro-fessed. But in instituting their factory system, they did not have to choose between their ethical and ideological convictions and their economic ad-vantage as entrepreneurs—not in the beginning at least. The Lowell system united advanced technology, factory discipline, and conservative repub-licanism; and when it was eventually challenged, protest came on both economic and ideological grounds.

. . . The company's six factory buildings were grouped in a spacious quadrangle bordering the river and landscaped with flowers, trees, and shrubs. They were dominated by a central mill, crowned with a Georgian

147

cupola. Made of brick, with flat, plain walls, and white granite lintels above
each window space, the factories presented a neat, orderly, and efficient
appearance, which symbolized the institution's goals and would be emulated by many of the penitentiaries, insane asylums, orphanages, and
reformatories of the period. Beyond the counting house at the entrance to
the mill yard stretched the company dormitories. Their arrangement reflected a Federalist image of proper social structure. The factory population
of Lowell was rigidly defined into four groups and their hierarchy im-
mutably preserved in the town's architecture. As chief agent for the cor-
poration, most of whose stockholders resided in Boston, [Kirk] Boott* and
the other company agents formed the unquestioned aristocracy of the community; a Georgian mansion with an imposing Ionic portico just below the
original factory in Lowell powerfully symbolized Boott's authority. Beneath
this class stood the overseers, who lived in simple yet substantial quarters
at the ends of the rows of boardinghouses where the operatives resided,
thus providing a secondary measure of surveillance. In the boardinghouses
themselves lived the female workers, who outnumbered male employees
roughly three to one. Originally these apartments were constructed in rows
of double houses, at least thirty girls to a unit, with intervening strips of
lawn. Later, in the 1830s, as companies expanded and proliferated, the
houses were strung together, blocking both light and air. These quarters
were intended to serve essentially as dormitories and offered few amenities
beyond dining rooms and bedrooms, each of the latter shared by as many
as six or eight girls, two to a bed. Boardinghouse keepers were responsible
for both the efficient administration of the buildings and for enforcing
company regulations as to the conduct of the workers. Similar tenements
were provided for male mechanics and their families. At the bottom of this
hierarchy were the Irish day laborers, who built the canals and mills and
made possible the continuing expansion of Lowell. Significantly, no housing had been planned for this group, and they lived in hundreds of little
shanties next to a small Catholic church in an area called "New Dublin"
and the "Acre." This early corporate insensitivity to the needs of the immigrant presaged Lowell's response to the great mass of immigrants
later on.

The adjustment of workers to factory life marked a critical juncture in
America's transition to a mature industrial society. Many of Lowell's operatives had known long hours and hard tasks before in farms or shops;
but the regularity and discipline of factory work were altogether new. They
no longer labored at their own speeds in completing of a task, but to the
clock at the pace of the machine. The employer aimed to standardize irregular labor rhythms and to make time the measurement of work. Thus

[*a trained engineer who had previously served in the British army]

148

the cupolas which crowned Lowell mills were not simply ornamental; their bells insistently reminded workers that time was money. Operatives worked a six-day week, approximately twelve hours a day, and bells tolled them awake to their jobs (lateness was severely punished), to and from meals, curfew, and bed. Other factory owners also demanded long hours, even while they simultaneously claimed that the factory system had in large measure repealed the primeval curse "In the sweat of thy face shalt thou eat bread." In the hands of their operatives, they believed, leisure meant mischief; idleness at best; at worst vicious amusements, drink, gambling, and riot. Hence the resistance to shorter working hours throughout the nineteenth century and into the twentieth: work was a form of social control. Lowell's managers shared this perception and wove it into the entire social order. They established an elaborate structure of social deterrents and incentives, insisting at all times upon "respectability" and defining it to suit their needs. Here the heritage of the Puritan ethic served employers especially well. Many Lowell women had been raised in a strongly evangelical atmosphere which placed heavy emphasis upon personal discipline and restraint. Injunctions to industry and the redemption of time pervaded their home communities, and their reading of popular didactic literature, from Isaac Watts's "How doth the little busy Bee," and Poor Richard's *Way to Wealth*, to the writings of Hannah More, reinforced these teachings. Company officials appropriated these values and adapted them to the imperatives of industrial capitalism. The Lawrence Company regulations, for example, stipulated that all employees "must devote themselves assiduously to their duty during working hours" and "on all occasions, both in their words and in their actions, show they are penetrated by a laudable love of temperance and virtue, and animated by a sense of their moral and social obligations."

A policy of strict social control, implicit in the residential architecture, enforced this code of factory discipline. The factory as a whole was governed by the superintendent, his office strategically placed between the boardinghouses and the mills at the entrance to the mill yard. From this point, as one spokesman enthusiastically reported, his "mind regulates all; his character inspires all; his plans, matured and decided by the directors of the company, who visit him every week, control all." Beneath his watchful eye in each room of the factory, an overseer stood responsible for the work, conduct, and proper management of the operatives therein. Should he choose to exercise it, an overseer possessed formidable power. The various mill towns of New England participated in a "black list" system. A worker who bridled at employers' demands was charged with an offense of character, such as "insubordination," "profanity," or "improper conduct." Issued a "dishonorable discharge," she would be unable to find similar work elsewhere. Supervision was thus constant. If the lines of social division occasionally relaxed on special occasions, it was only because the hierarchical authority of the community, which formed the basis of factory discipline, remained so indisputable.

In addition to these powerful institutional controls, corporate authorities relied upon the factory girls to act as moral police over one another. . . . Declared the Rev. Henry A. Miles of Lowell, "Among the virtuous and high-minded young women, who feel that they have the keeping of their characters and that any stain upon their associates brings reproach upon themselves, the power of opinion becomes an ever-present, and ever-active restraint. A girl, *suspected* of immoralities, or serious improprieties of conduct, at once loses caste." As Miles approvingly described the ostracism, the girl's fellow-boarders would threaten to leave the house unless the housekeeper dismissed the offender. They would shun her on the street, refuse to work with her, and point her out to their companions. "From their power of opinion, there is no appeal." Eventually the outcast would submit to her punishment and leave the community. Even if, as one suspects, Miles overestimated the moral severity of Lowell women, his description nevertheless represented the official standard of behavior. On no account did employers wish to encourage independence of character, for it threatened the stability of the entire factory system.

During its first two decades of operation, Lowell's reputation as a model factory town, offering economic opportunity in a wholesome moral and intellectual atmosphere, proved notably successful in attracting labor. Eager and intelligent young women flocked to the city, mostly from farms in New Hampshire, Vermont, Massachusetts, and Maine. Though their pay was not great and declined relative to the general economy over the years, manufacturing initially offered the greatest income of any occupation open to women at the time; domestic service in particular suffered as a result. Women came for manifold reasons: for money to assist their families, to support a brother's education, or to earn a dowry, and in some cases to gain independence from family life. Often Lowell women offered more romantic explanations as well: a failed family fortune, infidel parents, a cruel mistress, a lover's absence. As Lowell operatives reported their experiences and the community's reputation spread, many came for an informal education and the stimulation of their peers in an urban setting. In addition, company recruiters traveled through New England painting glowing pictures of the life and wages to be enjoyed at Lowell and collecting a commission for each young woman they persuaded. With the construction of new factories and the rise of a middle class in the town to serve the needs of the enterprise, Lowell's population expanded rapidly: From roughly 200 in 1820, it climbed to 6477 in 1830, 21,000 in 1840, and over 33,000 in 1850. For many young women away from home and family for the first time, the factory town appeared overwhelming at first, though most soon adapted to the new industrial environment and institutional life. Some even found the community rather snug and reassuring. . . .

Despite Lowell's swelling population and the lack of public parks until the mid-1840s, the town retained at least suggestions of a rural life. House plants in windows often gave corners of the mills the effect of a bower, and some of the overseers cultivated flower gardens behind the factories as well. . . .

Gradually, most of these young women adjusted to the demands of factory life. Probably the greatest challenge confronting them was the machinery itself. "The buzzing and hissing and whizzing of pulleys and rollers and spindles and flyers"—as one ex-worker described them—often proved bewildering and oppressive for people completely unaccustomed to such devices. As they mastered their machines' intricacies, they learned to defy the noise and tedium by distancing themselves from their work through private thoughts and daydreams. Furthermore, before operatives were given more looms to attend and the machines speeded up in the mid-1840s, they often had long periods of idleness between catching broken threads. Regulations prohibited books in the mill, but women frequently cut out pages or clippings from the newspaper and evaded the edict. Others worked on compositions in their spare moments or spent the time lost in contemplation. Thus they attempted to give meaning to the time that their work denied and to cultivate a mental separation from their activities and surroundings.

In the two or three hours they had remaining at the end of a long working day, and on Sundays, many Lowell women relentlessly pursued an education. They borrowed books from lending libraries, attended the lyceum at which Edward Everett, John Quincy Adams, and Ralph Waldo Emerson spoke, met in church groups, and organized a number of "Improvement Circles," two of which produced their own periodicals, the *Operatives' Magazine* (1841–42) and, most famous, the *Lowell Offering* (1840–45), and its successor, the *New England Offering* (1848–50). Writers in these journals were self-conscious of their position as "factory girls" and eager to vindicate their reputations. As they endeavored "to remove unjust prejudice—to prove that the female operatives of Lowell were, as a class, intelligent and virtuous"—they offered impressive support for the Lowell system as a model republican community. Factory life at Lowell, a number of writers maintained, did not injure their health or degrade their morals. On the contrary, they asserted, the conscientious worker's "intellect is strengthened, her moral sense quickened, her manners refined, her whole character elevated and improved, by the privileges and discipline of her factory life." To those who chafed against this regimen and thought of returning to the country, various authors replied that Lowell presented the most stimulating moral and intellectual climate, the most authentic republican community, in the land. Declared one woman in the *Lowell Offering*: "I believe there is no place where there are so many advantages within the reach of the laboring class of people, as exist here; where there is so much equality, so few aristocratic distinctions, and such good fellowship, as may be found in this community." . . .

As Lowell's fame spread in the 1830s, '40s, and '50s, countless visitors made the pilgrimage to the town, were conducted through its factories by representatives of the corporations, and emerged awe-stricken by its technological splendor and moral sublimity. Their rhapsodic testimonies overwhelmingly endorsed the policies of F. C. Lowell, his associates, and successors. Not only did the town appear to sustain the nation's highest standards of health, intellect, prosperity, and character; its success was such that in many respects it presented a model for American communities. In contrast to the myriad utopian experiments which spread through the country in the decades before the Civil War, only a few of which seriously attempted large-scale manufacturing, here was an experiment of the most practical sort, based not upon a notion of agrarian equality, but rather a paternalist technological order. . . .

Lowell's planners and directors might thus have felt deservedly proud of their accomplishment. For in Lowell and its sister cities—Chicopee, Holyoke, Lawrence, Manchester, Saco, and the rest—they had apparently built a productive, cohesive, and harmonious community based upon the earlier ideological fusion of technology and republicanism. Lowell promised not to compromise the nation's agrarian commitment, but rather to supplement it, to strengthen the country economically, socially, and morally. The factory town ostensibly reconciled the myth of the American garden with a new myth of the machine. . . . Prosperity and republicanism, the directors might have congratulated one another, had—despite John Adams's anguished cry—indeed been reconciled in a temperate and industrious community: This was the stunning achievement of Lowell. But was it?

Alongside the proud affirmations of company officials, the hosannas of industrial spokesmen and technological enthusiasts, and the admiring testimonies of European visitors, the 1830s and 1840s saw an insurgent attack upon the basic assumptions of the Lowell factory system and its conception of republican community. This assault was launched by members of the working class and their spokesmen, who, with the emergence of the labor movement, protested their oppressive working conditions and the hierarchical conception of society which sustained them. Probably their sentiments were not shared by the preponderance of Lowell workers, many of whom shunned political opinions of any sort. But if these dissidents were a minority, they were nonetheless significant. Their very existence contradicted Lowell's image as a uniquely happy and harmonious community, and their arguments brought a radically different perspective to the institutionalization of the Lowell ideology and to the course of American technological development. Instead of remaining content in their station and allowing the social machinery to run smoothly, these workers rejected the notion that they shared a community of interests with mill-owners and called for the secret class war which was being waged against them to be fought in the open. The contrast between American and English factory systems did not appear to them so impressively distinct, and they were hardly inclined to join Whig politicians like Edward Everett in proclaiming Lowell as the fulfillment of the American Revolution and a model of republicanism. Quite the reverse; the more extreme among them charged that the manufacturing elite had betrayed everything the Revolution stood for and were following in the footsteps of the luxury-loving and tyrannical British. Under the guise of humanitarian concern for the republic, they contended, Lowell's supporters were busily erecting a repressive new aristocracy. . . .

The attack against the Lowell factory system gained momentum in the 1830s and '40s and spread within the mills themselves as Lowell women began to demonstrate on behalf of reform. In 1834 they participated in their first "turn-out," a demonstration and short-lived strike. Their numbers were estimated from "nearly eight hundred" (*Lowell Journal*) to two thousand (*The Man*), varying with the sympathies of newspaper reporters. . . .

The immediate occasion of the "turn-out" was the announcement of a 15 per cent reduction in wages, but it represented as well a protest against Lowell's paternalism as unrepublican. As one of the demonstrators announced, "We do not estimate our liberty by dollars and cents; consequently it was not the reduction of wages alone which caused the excitement, but that haughty, overbearing disposition, that purse-proud insolence, which was becoming more and more apparent." Two and a half years later, in October 1836, Lowell women struck against an increase in the price of board in company houses, amounting to a one-eighth cut in wages. Again they fortified their resolution by reminding one another of the Revolutionary struggle against tyranny: "As our fathers resisted unto blood and lordly avarice of the British ministry," they declared, "so we, their daughters, never will wear the yoke which has been prepared for us."

. . . Lowell's directors and other manufacturers were not about to surrender. . . . Prior to 1860 in Massachusetts not a single strike ended in victory for the workers or checked the reduction of wages. . . .

Other obstacles also stood in the way of Lowell's protesting workers. The Panic of 1837 and subsequent depressions threw an estimated one-third of American laborers out of work and seriously damaged the union movement. With jobs scarce, workingmen's organizations came to regard the system of female labor as doubly pernicious; not only did it harm the women themselves, it brought women in competition with men, thereby either throwing the latter out of work or reducing their wages. In light of this situation, the National Trades' Union suggested in 1839 that the solution to the female labor problem might be to keep women at home where they belonged. Women operatives, clearly, could no longer depend upon male labor spokesmen always to uphold their position.

In spite of these impediments, however, resistance to the Lowell factory system gradually increased. By December 1844 Lowell's dissident workers, led by the redoubtable Sarah Bagley, had achieved sufficient strength to form an organization of their own, the Lowell Female Labor Reform Association. Its ranks swelled quickly: within three months it numbered three hundred members and by the end of 1845 it claimed six hundred workers in Lowell alone, plus branches in all major New England textile centers. Now workers were able to establish connections outside Lowell to the labor movement and hence to some degree to subvert institutional pressures. Immediately, they formed their own journal, *Factory Tracts,* and soon formed an alliance with the *Voice of Industry* a new labor weekly newspaper, and brought it to Lowell. Denouncing the *Lowell Offering* as "a mouthpiece of the corporations," these dissident workers powerfully inveighed against the oppressive character of factory life. . . . They pointed with horror to the specter of a degenerate race, spawned in the mills to serve as slaves to a manufacturing aristocracy. And as in earlier appeals to labor, they attempted to rally and organize workers by applying the language and lessons of 1776 to their own times. "Is not," the *Voice of Industry* asked, "the same secret fawning, devouring monster, wilely [sic] drawing his fatal folds around us as a nation which has crushed the freedom, prosperity and existence of other republics whose sad fate, history long ago recorded . . . ?" In such conspiracies, the paper charged, industrious and virtuous labor was inevitably targeted as the first victim. Every year its burdens grew more grievous, and the *Voice of Industry* demanded for all workingmen their God-given right to " 'life, liberty, and the pursuit of happiness.' "

Whatever efficacy the workers' protests had . . . was as symbolic rather than instrumental action; whatever gains they achieved were expressive rather than substantial. Efforts at specific reforms encountered powerful resistance. Workers from several mill towns had petitioned the Massachusetts legislature for establishment of a ten-hour day and other factory reforms as early as 1842, with no response. The petition of 1600 workers from Lowell and elsewhere the next year met a similar fate. In 1844 a third petition was tabled until the next session; so that at last in 1845 a legislative committee held hearings on labor conditions for the first time. In the absence of an existing labor committee, the task was assigned to William Schouler, publisher of the *Lowell Courier* and a staunch supporter of the corporations. Sarah Bagley and the Lowell Female Labor Reform Committee feverishly circulated new petitions to support the ten-hour cause and gained over two thousand signatures, half of them from Lowell. Two conflicting groups of witnesses then paraded before the committee. Spokesmen for the employers defended the healthful environment of the mills, while Miss Bagley and a group of operatives personally testified that Lowell workers endured overlong work days for insufficient pay to the detriment of health, mind, and spirit. To examine conditions firsthand, a portion of the committee went to Lowell, and they returned substantially impressed. Of their visit to the Massachusetts and Boott Mills, they reported, "The rooms are large and well-lighted, the temperature, comfortable, and in most of the window sills were numerous shrubs and plants, such as geraniums, roses, and numerous varieties of the cactus. These were the pets of the factory girls, and they were to the Committee convincing evidence of the elevated moral tone and refined taste of the operatives." Thus Lowell's technological version of pastoral proved remarkably resilient; even in the midst of protest, legislators found confirmation of the essential rightness of the enterprise in a single whiff of a potted flower. . . .

Lowell's leading investors, company agents, and other spokesmen did not reply to protesting workers directly; but beginning in the mid-1840s, they published several books, articles, and pamphlets defending Lowell corporations from their critics. One of the most important of these was *Lowell, As It Was, and As It Is* by Henry A. Miles, a Unitarian minister at Lowell. Plunging into the controversy over the condition of Lowell operatives, Miles presented a detailed justification of Lowell's corporate policies and their beneficent effect upon the community. . . .

Even as Appleton and others defended and memorialized the Lowell system, beginning in the 1840s life in the mills grew increasingly less attractive to young New England women. Previously, in the first two decades after F. C. Lowell returned from Europe transfixed by English textile machinery, enormous strides in productivity had been achieved through rapid technological innovation. After the 1830s, however, the rate of substantial innovation in textile manufacturing slowed considerably. Lowell and other New England textile mills faced increased competition in the sales of their goods and declining prices. Profits and dividends, after hitting their peak in 1845, sagged substantially with only a weak upturn in 1851–53 until the beginning of the Civil War. As a result, companies sought to increase output in relation to labor costs. To boost productivity, New England textile manufacturers constructed larger and larger mills, powered by steam instead of water. The average size of a new mill, about 6000 spindles in 1835, swelled to 18,000 in 1847, and to 50,000 by 1883. At the same time cotton consumption per spindle also increased 50 per cent between 1840 and 1860. The work force in Lowell also expanded in this period, from 8560 in 1837, to 9235 in 1845, to 14,661 in 1855; but the increase in operatives was not proportionate to the increase in mills' capacity. Instead, work assignments were enlarged to include more machines. To stimulate production further, overseers were placed on a premium system and encouraged by bonuses to drive their workers harder, and the comparatively slow pace of the 1820s gave way to a more intense factory discipline. Operatives thus perceived a "speed-up" in which, as output rose, piece-rates dropped. As a result of these changes, workers' average daily earnings increased slightly in the later 1840s, but they did not compensate for wages and conditions that had become increasingly exploitative. The failure of the ten-hour movement added to discontent. When profits declined and new wage-cuts were announced in 1848, the turnover of operatives rose sharply; at one of the most prosperous companies, the Merrimack, average workers' tenure dropped to nine months. In the past, the city's mystique had proved a powerful agent of employee recruitment. Now, as mechanization spread to other industries, such as boots and clothing, and other employment opportunities rivaled the textile mills, Lowell's companies appeared in danger of losing their command over their labor force.

Nevertheless, when the Lowell factory system was suddenly transformed in the late 1840s and 1850s, it was from quite another source than capitulation to workers' demands. At just the moment when company control of its traditional labor pool was growing shaky, Ireland's terrible potato famine that had begun in 1845 and the subsequent eviction of Irish peasants by their landlords triggered a massive immigration to America, over one and a half million people before the Civil War. As a major ship and railroad terminus, Boston received tens of thousands of these Irish immigrants. Upon arriving, however, they encountered a constricted social and economic life with little receptivity to foreigners. Nativist prejudice combined with the newcomers' lack of training and capital to shut them out of all but unskilled occupations. In such a position, Irish immigrants offered textile factories at Lowell and neighboring mill towns a ready and abundant supply of labor, and the incentive to accommodate demands of native workers diminished. Almost immediately, Irish began to take the places of departing New Englanders in the mills; once established, their presence further hastened the flow of native workers to other jobs and discouraged the entrance of other New England women into the industry. Only 7 per cent of the operatives in Lowell mills were Irish in 1845, but by the early 1850s their proportion was estimated as one half, and it grew still higher year by year. Later in the century, the labor force would be supplemented by French-Canadians and other immigrant groups. Instead of predominantly single women, the Irish came as families. As adult males were discriminated against, Irish women and, increasingly, children went to the mills, the last receiving lower wages than ever. High turnover rates thus persisted. But if the work force was not immobile, neither was the work force in Britain; it was certainly not the kind of circulatory labor force able to enter and leave the industrial economy at will with which the Lowell system had begun. Most lived not in company boardinghouses to be supervised by alien authority, but with family or friends in the town at large. With a different culture, training, aspirations, and status from earlier Lowell workers, the Irish obviously did not immerse themselves in improvement circles and literary magazines. And the Lowell mills, which had eagerly received credit for the talents and accomplishments of earlier operatives, now found themselves without their trophies. In less than a decade Lowell lost its prized population of well-educated and temporary New England women and with it the factory system's very rationale. Suddenly the basis that Lowell's founders and most ardent defenders had insisted constituted the principal difference between this city and English manufacturing towns and upon which its welfare would stand or fall—its lack of an established proletariat—was totally overthrown.

Naturally enough, it was a fact Lowell's citizens found difficult to acknowledge. In a handbook and history of Lowell and its businesses published in 1856 when the social transformation was well under way, Charles Cowley insisted that Lowell had no permanent factory population: "This fact, and this alone . . . has saved us from those evils of vice and ignorance, demoralization and misery, which have been engendered by manufactures in some cities in Europe." After a few years in the mills, Cowley maintained, Lowell workers fulfilled the Jeffersonian dictum and returned to agricultural pursuits in the "virtuous rural homes" in which they were born and bred. However, Cowley suddenly abandoned this idyllic picture to warn of the unspeakable evils that would result, should the city ever suffer the "curse" of a permanent factory population. Then "Lowell would become a foul blot upon the face of the country," and its once fair workers would be replaced by a barbaric horde. "Degraded to the level of the Indian Pariahs, their independence would be that of serfs; their liberty, that of prisoners; their leisure, that of workhouse paupers; their education, that of plantation negroes; their health, that of invalids; their chastity, that of harem women; and their wages, like the wages of sin, would be Death." The extraordinary fervor with which Cowley imagined Lowell's possible fate implicitly revealed his awareness of what he would not openly admit. The character of the Lowell community had changed irretrievably, and celebrations inevitably gave way to jeremiads.

The early history of Lowell, like that of other institutional innovations during this period, thus revealed complexities far beyond the shaping powers or expectations of its confident founders. The factory system they established, no matter how benign in intention, was still based upon a hierarchical and manipulative model in which workers were passive agents, tied to the demands of machine production and industrial capitalism as a whole. Ironically, Lowell's very success in attracting educated and independent New England women meant that at least an outspoken minority would refuse to accept the management's conception of "republicanism," inherent in its strict factory discipline, and insist upon a true egalitarian order. Reliance upon temporary workers, in any case, only postponed the question of what accommodations industry should make for a permanent labor force. But the arrival of the Irish triggered not a new concern upon the part of corporate officials and a re-examination of their conception of republican community, but, on the contrary, increased apathy. In this respect, Lowell anticipated or paralleled a number of other total institutions concerned with education or rehabilitation, which in the 1850s and 1860s responded to the Irish presence by dampening their avowed reform expectations and blaming inmates' poor condition, not on an unwholesome environment as before, but on inferior heredity. Just as penitentiary, almshouse, mental hospital, and reformatory gradually moved from a role of rehabilitation to custodianship, so did the factory also move from the notion of a circulatory to a long-term population.

By the 1850s the possibility of an integrated and harmonious republican community seemed further off than ever. Even while Lowell's praises echoed, its founders' optimistic vision lay tarnished, and its most ardent defenders were forced on the defensive. The problems of urban and industrial growth and social disorder which Lowell was established to correct had spread to the community itself.

DOCUMENTS

Lowell: A Cooperative Worker, 1844

DEAR MARY:

In my last I told you I would write again, and say more of my life here; and this I will now attempt to do.

I went into the mill to work a few days after I wrote to you. It looked very pleasant at first, the rooms were so light, spacious, and clean, the girls so pretty and neatly dressed, and the machinery so brightly polished or nicely painted. The plants in the windows, or on the overseer's bench or desk, gave a pleasant aspect to things. You will wish to know what work I am doing. I will tell you of the different kinds of work.

There is, first, the carding-room, where the cotton flies most, and the girls get the dirtiest. But this is easy, and the females are allowed time to go out at night before the bell rings—on Saturday night at least, if not on all other nights. Then there is the spinning-room, which is very neat and

SOURCE: *Lowell Offering* (June, 1844), 169–72.

pretty. In this room are the spinners and doffers. The spinners watch the frames; keep them clean, and the threads mended if they break. The doffers take off the full bobbins, and put on the empty ones. They have nothing to do in the long intervals when the frames are in motion, and can go out to their boarding-houses, or do any thing else that they like. In some of the factories the spinners do their own doffing, and when this is the case they work no harder than the weavers. These last have the hardest time of all—or can have, if they choose to take charge of three or four looms, instead of the one pair which is the allotment. And they are the most constantly confined. The spinners and dressers have but the weavers to keep supplied, and then their work can stop. The dressers never work before breakfast, and they stay out a great deal in the afternoons. The drawers-in, or girls who draw the threads through the harnesses, also work in the dressing-room, and they all have very good wages—better than the weavers who have but the usual work. The dressing-rooms are very neat, and the frames move with a gentle undulating motion which is really graceful. But these rooms are kept very warm, and are disagreeably scented with the "sizing," or starch, which stiffens the "beams," or un-woven webs. There are many plants in these rooms, and it is really a good green-house for them. The dressers are generally quite tall girls, and must have pretty tall minds too, as their work requires much care and attention.

I could have had work in the dressing-room, but chose to be a weaver; and I will tell you why. I disliked the closer air of the dressing-room, though I might have become accustomed to that. I could not learn to dress so quickly as I could to weave, nor have work of my own so soon, and should have had to stay with Mrs. C. two or three weeks before I could go in at all, and I did not like to be "lying upon my oars" so long. And, more than this, when I get well learned I can have extra work, and make double wages, which you know is quite an inducement with some.

Well, I went into the mill, and was put to learn with a very patient girl—a clever old maid. I should be willing to be one myself if I could be as good as she is. You cannot think how odd every thing seemed to me. I wanted to laugh at every thing, but did not know what to make sport of first. They set me to threading shuttles, and tying weaver's knots, and such things, and now I have improved so that I can take care of one loom. I could take care of two if I only had eyes in the back part of my head. . . .

At first the hours seemed very long, but I was so interested in learning that I endured it very well; and when I went out at night, the sound of the mill was in my ears, as of crickets, frogs, and jewsharps, all mingled together in strange discord. After that it seemed as though cotton-wool was in my ears, but now I do not mind it at all. You know that people learn to sleep with the thunder of Niagara in their ears, and a cotton mill is no worse, though you wonder that we do not have to hold our breath in such a noise.

It makes my feet ache and swell to stand so much, but I suppose I shall get accustomed to that too. The girls generally wear old shoes about their work, and you know nothing is easier; but they almost all say that when they have worked here a year or two they have to procure shoes a size or two larger than before they came. The right hand, which is the one used in stopping and starting the loom, becomes larger than the left; but in other respects the factory is not detrimental to a young girl's appearance. Here they look delicate, but not sickly; they laugh at those who are much exposed, and get pretty brown; but I, for one, had rather be brown than pure white. I never saw so many pretty looking girls as there are here. Though the number of men is small in proportion there are many marriages here, and a great deal of courting. I will tell you of this last sometime.

You wish to know minutely of our hours of labor. We go in at five o'clock; at seven we come out to breakfast; at half-past seven we return to our work, and stay until half-past twelve. At one, or quarter-past one four months in the year, we return to our work, and stay until seven at night. Then the evening is all our own, which is more than some laboring girls can say, who think nothing is more tedious than a factory life.

When I first came here, which was the last of February, the girls ate their breakfast before they went to their work. The first of March they came out at the present breakfast hour, and the twentieth of March they ceased to "light up" the rooms, and come out between six and seven o'clock.

You ask if the girls are contented here: I ask you, if you know of *any one* who is perfectly contented. Do you remember the old story of the philosopher, who offered a field to the person who was contented with his lot; and when one claimed it, he asked him why, if he was so perfectly satisfied, he wanted his field. The girls here are not contented; and there is no disadvantage in their situation which they do not perceive as quickly, and lament as loudly, as the sternest opponents of the factory system do. They would scorn to say they were contented, if asked the question; for it would compromise their Yankee spirit—their pride, penetration, independence, and love of "freedom and equality" to say that they were *contented* with such a life as this. Yet, withal, they are cheerful. I never saw a happier set of beings. They appear blithe in the mill, and out of it. If you see one of them, with a very long face, you may be sure that it is because she has heard bad news from home, or because her beau has vexed her. But, if it is a Lowell trouble, it is because she has failed in getting off as many "sets" or "pieces" as she intended to have done; or because she had a sad "break-out," or "break-down," in her work, or something of that sort.

You ask if the work is not disagreeable. Not when one is accustomed to it. It tried my patience sadly at first, and does now when it does not run well; but, in general, I like it very much. It is easy to do, and does not require very violent exertion, as much of our farm work does.

Lowell: A "Dissident Worker", 1845

The first petitioner who testified was *Eliza R. Hemmingway*. She had worked 2 years and 9 months in the Lowell Factories, 2 years in the Middlesex, and 9 months in the Hamilton Corporations. Her employment is weaving,—works by the piece. The Hamilton Mill manufactures cotton fabrics. The Middlesex, woollen fabrics. She is now at work in the Middlesex Mills, and attends one loom. Her wages average from $16 to $23 a month exclusive of board. She complained of the hours for labor being too many, and the time for meals too limited. In the summer season, the work is commenced at 5 o'clock, A.M., and continued till 7 o'clock, P.M., with half an hour for breakfast and three quarters of an hour for dinner. During eight months of the year, but half an hour is allowed for dinner. The air in the room she considered not to be wholesome. There were 293 small lamps and 61 large lamps lighted in the room in which she worked, when evening work is required. These lamps are also lighted sometimes in the morning.—About 130 females, 11 men, and 12 children (between the ages of 11 and 14) work in the room with her. She thought the children enjoyed about as good health as children generally do. The children work but 9 months out of 12. The other 3 months they must attend school. Thinks that there is no day when there are less than six of the females out of the mill from sickness. Has known as many as thirty. She, herself, is out quite often, on account of sickness. There was more sickness in the Summer than in the Winter months: though in the Summer, lamps are not lighted.

Lowell: Management's View, 1845

In Lowell, but very few (in some mills none at all) enter into the factories under the *age of fifteen*. None under that age can be admitted, unless they bring a certificate from the school teacher, that he or she has attended school at least three months during the preceding twelve. Nine-tenths of

SOURCE: Massachusetts House of Representatives, "Report on Hours of Labor, 1845," Doc. 50, in *Documents, 1845* (Boston, 1845), 2–3.

SOURCE: Massachusetts, House, "Report on Hours of Labor, 1845," Doc. 50, in *Documents, 1845* (Boston, 1845), 10.

the factory population in Lowell come from the country. They are farmers' daughters. Many of them come over a hundred miles to enter the mills. Their education has been attended to in the district schools, which are dotted like diamonds over every square mile of New England. Their moral and religious characters have been formed by pious parents, under the paternal roof. Their bodies have been developed, and their constitutions made strong by pure air, wholesome food, and youthful exercise.

After an absence of a few years, having laid by a few hundred dollars, they depart for their homes, get married, settle down in life, and become the heads of families. Such, we believe, in truth, to be a correct statement of the Lowell operatives, and of the hours of labor.

CHAPTER 9

The Cherokee Removal: An American Tragedy

Most people are aware of the fate of Native Americans as white settlement pushed ever westward. However, one episode in the history of white-Indian relations is in many ways unique, and constitutes one of our nation's darkest moments: the forcible removal and transport in 1838–39 of thousands of Cherokees from their ancestral homeland in the Southern uplands.

Ironically, no other Indian nation had responded so fully to Thomas Jefferson's urgings that they abandon their nomadic ways and pattern their life-style after that of the whites. Jefferson had told Congress in 1803, "In leading them [the Indians] thus to agriculture, to manufactures, and civilizations; in bringing together their and our sentiments, and in preparing them ultimately to participate in the benefits of our Government, I trust and believe we are acting for their greatest good." In 1806, Jefferson congratulated the Cherokee chiefs on the progress they had made in farming; "Go on, my children, in the same way and be assured the further you advance in it the happier and more respectable you will be. . . ."

Dee Brown's essay "The Trail of Tears" graphically describes the Cherokees' progress toward "civilization," and the betrayal by both state and federal governments of the assurances and promises made by Jefferson and other national leaders. The Cherokees were not the only Native Americans removed forcibly from their ancestral homes, yet the large measure of sympathy and support on their behalf was atypical. How do you account for the apparent contradiction between the strong sentiment against the removal of the Cherokees and the failure to prevent it?

The three documents following the essay provide eloquent examples of the arguments presented on both sides of the removal controversy. The first is from the "Memorial of the Cherokee Nation" (July 1830) which sets forth the Cherokee view of the removal proposed by President Andrew Jackson. The second is from President Jackson's Second Annual Message to Congress (December 6, 1830). Compare the contrasting descriptions of the life awaiting the Cherokees in the new western territory. Which argument do you find more convincing? How did Jackson respond to those who objected to white encroachment on Indian land?

The task of implementing Jackson's program to remove the Cherokees fell on his successor, President Martin Van Buren. The final document is a letter to Van Buren from Ralph Waldo Emerson, who rarely spoke out on political matters. The letter presents the legal and moral arguments against removal and reveals the mood of those opposed to that policy.

ESSAY

The Trail of Tears

Dee Brown

In the spring of 1838, Brigadier General Winfield Scott with a regiment of artillery, a regiment of infantry, and six companies of dragoons marched unopposed into the Cherokee country of northern Georgia. On May 10 at New Echota, the capital of what had been one of the greatest Indian nations in eastern America, Scott issued a proclamation:

> The President of the United States sent me with a powerful army to cause you, in obedience to the treaty of 1835, to join that part of your people who are already established in prosperity on the other side of the Mississippi. . . . The emigration must be

SOURCE: Dee Brown, "The Trail of Tears," *American History Illustrated*, 7 (June 1972): 30–39. Reprinted through the courtesy of Historical Times, publishers of *American History Illustrated*.

commenced in haste. . . . The full moon of May is already on the wane, and before another shall have passed away every Cherokee man, woman and child . . . must be in motion to join their brethren in the west. . . . My troops already occupy many positions . . . and thousands and thousands are approaching from every quarter to render resistance and escape alike hopeless. . . . Will you then by resistance compel us to resort to arms? Or will you by flight seek to hide yourselves in mountains and forests and thus oblige us to hunt you down? Remember that in pursuit it may be impossible to avoid conflicts. The blood of the white man or the blood of the red man may be spilt, and if spilt, however accidentally, it may be impossible for the discreet and humane among you, or among us, to prevent a general war and carnage.

For more than a century the Cherokees had been ceding their land, thousands of acres by thousands of acres. They had lost all of Kentucky and much of Tennessee, but after the last treaty of 1819 they still had remaining about 35,000 square miles of forested mountains, clean, swift-running rivers, and fine meadows. In this country which lay across parts of Georgia, North Carolina, and Tennessee they cultivated fields, planted orchards, fenced pastures, and built roads, houses, and towns. Sequoya had invented a syllabary for the Cherokee language so that thousands of his tribesmen quickly learned to read and write. The Cherokees had adopted the white man's way—his clothing, his constitutional form of government, even his religion. But it had all been for nothing. Now these men who had come across the great ocean many years ago wanted all of the Cherokees' land. In exchange for their 35,000 square miles the tribe was to receive five million dollars and another tract of land somewhere in the wilderness beyond the Mississippi River.

This was a crushing blow to a proud people. "They are extremely proud, despising the lower class of Europeans," said Henry Timberlake, who visited them before the Revolutionary War. William Bartram, the botanist, said the Cherokees were not only a handsome people, tall, graceful, and olive-skinned, but "their countenance and actions exhibit an air of magnanimity, superiority and independence."

Ever since the signing of the treaties of 1819, Major General Andrew Jackson, a man they once believed to be their friend, had been urging Cherokees to move beyond the Mississippi. Indians and white settlers, Jackson told them, could never get along together. Even if the government wanted to protect the Cherokees from harassment, he added, it would be unable to do so. "If you cannot protect us in Georgia," a chief retorted, "how can you protect us from similar evils in the West?"

During that period of polite urging, a few hundred Cherokee families did move west, but the tribe remained united and refused to give up any more territory. In fact, the council leaders passed a law forbidding any chief to sell or trade a single acre of Cherokee land on penalty of death.

In 1828, when Andrew Jackson was running for President, he knew that in order to win he must sweep the frontier states. Free land for the land-hungry settlers became Jackson's major policy. He hammered away at this theme especially hard in Georgia, where waves of settlers from the coastal lowlands were pushing into the highly desirable Cherokee country. He promised the Georgians that if they would help elect him President, he would lend his support to opening up the Cherokee lands for settlement. The Cherokees, of course, were not citizens and could not vote in opposition. To the Cherokees and their friends who protested this promise, Jackson justified his position by saying that the Cherokees had fought on the side of the British during the Revolutionary War. He conveniently forgot that the Cherokees had been his allies during the desperate War of 1812, and had saved the day for him in his decisive victory over the British-backed Creeks at Horseshoe Bend. (One of the Cherokee chiefs who aided Jackson was Junaluska. Said he afterward: "If I had known that Jackson would drive us from our homes I would have killed him that day at the Horseshoe.")

Three weeks after Jackson was elected President, the Georgia legislature passed a law annexing all the Cherokee country within that state's borders. As most of the Cherokee land was in Georgia and three-fourths of the tribe lived there, this meant an end to their independence as a nation. The Georgia legislature also abolished all Cherokee laws and customs and sent surveyors to map out land lots of 160 acres each. The 160-acre lots were to be distributed to white citizens of Georgia through public lotteries.

To add to the pressures on the Cherokees, gold was discovered near Dahlonega in the heart of their country. For many years the Cherokees had concealed the gold deposits, but now the secret was out and a rabble of gold-hungry prospectors descended upon them.

John Ross, the Cherokees' leader, hurried to Washington to protest the Georgia legislature's actions and to plead for justice. In that year Ross was 38 years old; he was well-educated and had been active in Cherokee government matters since he was 19. He was adjutant of the Cherokee regiment that served with Jackson at Horseshoe Bend. His father had been one of a group of Scottish emigrants who settled near the Cherokees and married into the tribe.

In Washington, Ross found sympathizers in Congress, but most of them were anti-Jackson men and the Cherokee case was thus drawn into the whirlpool of politics. When Ross called upon Andrew Jackson to request his aid, the President bluntly told him that "no protection could be afforded the Cherokees" unless they were willing to move west of the Mississippi.

While Ross was vainly seeking help in Washington, alarming messages reached him from Georgia. White citizens of that state were claiming the homes of Cherokees through the land lottery, seizing some of them by force. Joseph Vann, a hard-working half-breed, had carved out an 800-acre plantation at Spring Place and built a fine brick house for his residence. Two men arrived to claim it, dueled for it, and the winner drove Vann and his family into the hills. When John Ross rushed home he found that the same thing had happened to his family. A lottery claimant was living in his beautiful home on the Coosa River, and Ross had to turn north toward Tennessee to find his fleeing wife and children.

During all this turmoil, President Jackson and the governor of Georgia pressed the Cherokee leaders hard in attempts to persuade them to cede all their territory and move to the West. But the chiefs stood firm. Somehow they managed to hold the tribe together, and helped dispossessed families find new homes back in the wilderness areas. John Ross and his family lived in a one-room log cabin across the Tennessee line.

In 1834, the chiefs appealed to Congress with a memorial in which they stated that they would never voluntarily abandon their homeland, but proposed a compromise in which they agreed to cede the state of Georgia a part of their territory provided that they would be protected from invasion in the remainder. Furthermore, at the end of a definite period of years to be fixed by the United States they would be willing to become citizens of the various states in which they resided.

"Cupidity has fastened its eye upon our lands and our homes," they said, "and is seeking by force and by every variety of oppression and wrong to expel us from our lands and our homes and to tear from us all that has become endeared to us. In our distress we have appealed to the judiciary of the United States, where our rights have been solemnly established. We have appealed to the Executive of the United States to protect those rights according to the obligation of treaties and the injunctions of the laws. But this appeal to the Executive has been made in vain."

This new petition to Congress was no more effectual than their appeals to President Jackson. Again they were told that their difficulties could be remedied only by their removal to the west of the Mississippi.

For the first time now, a serious split occurred among the Cherokees. A small group of subchiefs decided that further resistance to the demands of the Georgia and United States governments was futile. It would be better, they believed, to exchange their land and go west rather than risk bloodshed and the possible loss of everything. Leaders of this group were Major Ridge and Elias Boudinot. Ridge had adopted his first name after Andrew Jackson gave him that rank during the War of 1812. Boudinot was Ridge's nephew. Originally known as Buck Watie, he had taken the name of a New England philanthropist who sent him through a mission school in

Connecticut. Stand Watie, who later became a Confederate general, was his brother. Upon Boudinot's return from school to Georgia he founded the first tribal newspaper, the *Cherokee Phoenix*, in 1827, but during the turbulence following the Georgia land lotteries he was forced to suspend publication.

And so in February 1835 when John Ross journeyed to Washington to resume his campaign to save the Cherokee nation, a rival delegation headed by Ridge and Boudinot arrived there to seek terms for removal to the West. The pro-removal forces in the government leaped at this opportunity to bypass Ross's authority, and within a few days drafted a preliminary treaty for the Ridge delegation. It was then announced that a council would be held later in the year at New Echota, Georgia, for the purpose of negotiating and agreeing upon final terms.

During the months that followed, bitterness increased between the two Cherokee factions. Ridge's group was a very small minority, but they had the full weight of the United States Government behind them, and threats and inducements were used to force a full attendance at the council which was set for December 22, 1835. Handbills were printed in Cherokee and distributed throughout the nation, informing the Indians that those who did not attend would be counted as assenting to any treaty that might be made.

During the seven days which followed the opening of the treaty council, fewer than five hundred Cherokees, or about 2 percent of the tribe, came to New Echota to participate in the discussions. Most of the other Cherokees were busy endorsing a petition to be sent to Congress stating their opposition to the treaty. But on December 29, Ridge, Boudinot and their followers signed away all the lands of the great Cherokee nation. Ironically, thirty years earlier Major Ridge had personally executed a Cherokee chief named Doublehead for committing one of the few capital crimes of the tribe. That crime was the signing of a treaty which gave away Cherokee lands.

Charges of bribery by the Ross forces were denied by government officials, but some years afterward it was discovered that the Secretary of War had sent secret agents into the Cherokee country with authority to expend money to bribe chiefs to support the treaty of cession and removal. And certainly the treaty signers were handsomely rewarded. In an era when a dollar would buy many times its worth today, Major Ridge was paid $30,000 and his followers received several thousand dollars each. Ostensibly they were being paid for their improved farmlands, but the amounts were far in excess of contemporary land values.

John Ross meanwhile completed gathering signatures of Cherokees who were opposed to the treaty. Early in the following spring, 1836, he took the petition to Washington. More than three-fourths of the tribe, 15,964, had signed in protest against the treaty.

When the governor of Georgia was informed of the overwhelming vote against the treaty, he replied: "Nineteen-twentieths of the Cherokees are too ignorant and depraved to entitle their opinions to any weight or consideration in such matters."

The Cherokees, however, did have friends in Congress. Representative Davy Crockett of Tennessee denounced the treatment of the Cherokees as unjust, dishonest, and cruel. He admitted that he represented a body of frontier constituents who would like to have the Cherokee lands opened for settlement, and he doubted if a single one of them would second what he was saying. Even though his support of the Cherokees might remove him from public life, he added, he could not do otherwise except at the expense of his honor and conscience. Daniel Webster, Henry Clay, Edward Everett, and other great orators of the Congress also spoke for the Cherokees.

When the treaty came to a final decision in the Senate, it passed by only one vote. On May 23, 1836, President Jackson signed the document. According to its terms, the Cherokees were allowed two years from that day in which to leave their homeland forever.

The few Cherokees who had favored the treaty now began making their final preparations for departure. About three hundred left during that year and then early in 1837 Major Ridge and 465 followers departed by boats for the new land in the West. About 17,000 others, ignoring the treaty, remained steadfast in their homeland with John Ross.

For a while it seemed that Ross might win his long fight, that perhaps the treaty might be declared void. After the Secretary of War, acting under instructions from President Jackson, sent Major William M. Davis to the Cherokee country to expedite removal to the West, Davis submitted a frank report: "That paper called a treaty is no treaty at all," he wrote, "because it is not sanctioned by the great body of the Cherokees and was made without their participation or assent. . . . The Cherokees are a peaceable, harmless people, but you may drive them to desperation, and this treaty cannot be carried into effect except by the strong arm of force."

In September 1836, Brigadier General Dunlap, who had been sent with a brigade of Tennessee volunteers to force the removal, indignantly disbanded his troops after making a strong speech in favor of the Indians: "I would never dishonor the Tennessee arms in a servile service by aiding to carry into execution at the point of the bayonet a treaty made by a lean minority against the will and authority of the Cherokee people."

Even Inspector General John E. Wool, commanding United States troops in the area, was impressed by the united Cherokee resistance, and warned the Secretary of War not to send any civilians who had any part in the making of the treaty back into the Cherokee country. During the summer of 1837, the Secretary of War sent a confidential agent, John Mason, Jr., to observe and report. "Opposition to the treaty is unanimous and irreconcilable," Mason wrote. "They say it cannot bind them because they did not make it; that it was made by a few unauthorized individuals; that the nation is not party to it."

The inexorable machinery of government was already in motion, however, and when the expiration date of the waiting period, May 23, 1838, came near, Winfield Scott was ordered in with his army to force compliance. As already stated, Scott issued his proclamation on May 10. His soldiers were already building thirteen stockaded forts—six in North Carolina, five in Georgia, one in Tennessee, and one in Alabama. At these points the Cherokees would be concentrated to await transportation to the West. Scott then ordered the roundup started, instructing his officers not to fire on the Cherokees except in case of resistance. "If we get possession of the women and children first," he said, "or first capture the men, the other members of the same family will readily come in."

James Mooney, an ethnologist who afterwards talked with Cherokees who endured this ordeal, said that squads of troops moved into the forested mountains to search out every small cabin and make prisoners of all the occupants however or wherever they might be found. "Families at dinner were startled by the sudden gleam of bayonets in the doorway and rose up to be driven with blows and oaths along the weary miles of trail that led to the stockades. Men were seized in their fields or going along the road, women were taken from their spinning wheels and children from their play. In many cases, on turning for one last look as they crossed a ridge, they saw their homes in flames, fired by the lawless rabble that followed on the heels of the soldiers to loot and pillage. So keen were these outlaws on the scent that in some instances they were driving off the cattle and other stock of the Indians almost before the soldiers had fairly started their owners in the other direction."

Long afterward one of the Georgia militiamen who participated in the roundup said: "I fought through the Civil War and have seen men shot to pieces and slaughtered by thousands, but the Cherokee removal was the cruelest work I ever knew."

Knowing that resistance was futile, most of the Cherokees surrendered quietly. Within a month, thousands were enclosed in the stockades. On June 6 at Ross's Landing near the site of present-day Chattanooga, the first of many departures began. Eight hundred Cherokees were forcibly crowded onto a flotilla of six flatboats lashed to the side of a steamboat. After surviving a passage over rough rapids which smashed the sides of the flatboats, they landed at Decatur, Alabama, boarded a railroad train (which was a new and terrifying experience for most of them), and after reaching Tuscumbia were crowded upon a Tennessee River steamboat again.

Throughout June and July similar shipments of several hundred Cherokees were transported by this long water route—north on the Tennessee River to the Ohio and then down the Mississippi and up the Arkansas to their new homeland. A few managed to escape and make their way back to the Cherokee country, but most of them were eventually recaptured. Along the route of travel of this forced migration, the summer was hot and dry. Drinking water and food were often contaminated. First the young children would die, then the older people, and sometimes as many as half the adults were stricken with dysentery and other ailments. On each boat deaths ran as high as five per day. On one of the first boats to reach Little Rock, Arkansas, at least a hundred had died. A compassionate lieutenant who was with the military escort recorded in his diary for August 1: "My blood chills as I write at the remembrance of the scenes I have gone through."

When John Ross and other Cherokee leaders back in the concentration camps learned of the high mortality among those who had gone ahead, they petitioned General Scott to postpone further departures until autumn. Although only three thousand Cherokees had been removed, Scott agreed to wait until the summer drought was broken, or no later than October. The Cherokees in turn agreed to organize and manage the migration themselves. After a lengthy council, they asked and received permission to travel overland in wagons, hoping that by camping along the way they would not suffer as many deaths as occurred among those who had gone on the river boats.

During this waiting period, Scott's soldiers continued their searches for more than a thousand Cherokees known to be still hiding out in the deep wildernesses of the Great Smoky Mountains. These Cherokees had organized themselves under the leadership of a chief named Utsala, and had developed warning systems to prevent captures by the bands of soldiers. Occasionally, however, some of the fugitives were caught and herded back to the nearest stockade.

One of the fugitive families was that of Tsali, an aging Cherokee. With his wife, his brother, three sons and their families, Tsali had built a hideout somewhere on the border between North Carolina and Tennessee. Soldiers surrounded their shelters one day, and the Cherokees surrendered without resistance. As they were being taken back toward Fort Cass (Calhoun, Tennessee) a soldier prodded Tsali's wife sharply with a bayonet, ordering her to walk faster. Angered by the brutality, Tsali grappled with the soldier, tore away his rifle, and bayoneted him to the ground. At the same time, Tsali's brother leaped upon another soldier and bayoneted him. Before the remainder of the military detachment could act, the Cherokees fled, vanishing back into the Smokies where they sought refuge with Chief Utsala. Both bayoneted soldiers died.

Upon learning of the incident, Scott immediately ordered that Tsali must be brought in and punished. Because some of his regiments were being transferred elsewhere for other duties, however, the general realized that his reduced force might be occupied for months in hunting down and capturing the escaped Cherokee. He would have to use guile to accomplish the capture of Tsali.

Scott therefore dispatched a messenger—a white man who had been adopted as a child by the Cherokees—to find Chief Utsala. The messenger was instructed to inform Utsala that if he would surrender Tsali to General Scott, the Army would withdraw from the Smokies and leave the remaining fugitives alone.

When Chief Utsala received the message, he was suspicious of Scott's sincerity, but he considered the general's offer as an opportunity to gain time. Perhaps with the passage of time, the few Cherokees remaining in the Smokies might be forgotten and left alone forever. Utsala put the proposition to Tsali: If he went in and surrendered, he would probably be put to death, but his death might insure the freedom of a thousand fugitive Cherokees.

Tsali did not hesitate. He announced that he would go and surrender to General Scott. To make certain that he was treated well, several members of Tsali's band went with him.

When the Cherokees reached Scott's headquarters, the general ordered Tsali, his brother, and three sons arrested, and then condemned them all to be shot to death. To impress upon the tribe their utter helplessness before the might of the government, Scott selected the firing squad from Cherokee prisoners in one of the stockades. At the last moment, the general spared Tsali's youngest son because he was only a child.

(By this sacrifice, however, Tsali and his family gave the Smoky Mountain Cherokees a chance at survival in their homeland. Time was on their side, as Chief Utsala had hoped, and that is why today there is a small Cherokee reservation on the North Carolina slope of the Great Smoky Mountains.)

With the ending of the drought of 1838, John Ross and the 13,000 stockaded Cherokees began preparing for their long overland journey to the West. They assembled several hundred wagons, filled them with blankets, cooking pots, their old people and small children, and moved out in separate contingents along a trail that followed the Hiwassee River. The first party of 1,103 started on October 1.

"At noon all was in readiness for moving," said an observer of the departure. "The teams were stretched out in a line along the road through

172

a heavy forest, groups of persons formed about each wagon. The day was bright and beautiful, but a gloomy thoughtfulness was depicted in the lineaments of every face. In all the bustle of preparation there was a silence and stillness of the voice that betrayed the sadness of the heart. At length the word was given to move on. Going Snake, an aged and respected chief whose head eighty summers had whitened, mounted on his favorite pony and led the way in silence, followed by a number of younger men on horseback. At this very moment a low sound of distant thunder fell upon my ear . . . a voice of divine indignation for the wrong of my poor and unhappy countrymen, driven by brutal power from all they loved and cherished in the land of their fathers to gratify the cravings of avarice. The sun was unclouded—no rain fell—the thunder rolled away and seemed hushed in the distance."

Throughout October, eleven wagon trains departed and then on November 4, the last Cherokee exiles moved out for the West. The overland route for these endless lines of wagons, horsemen, and people on foot ran from the mouth of the Hiwassee in Tennessee across the Cumberland plateau to McMinnville and then north to Nashville where they crossed the Cumberland River. From there they followed an old trail to Hopkinsville, Kentucky, and continued northwestward to the Ohio River, crossing into southern Illinois near the mouth of the Cumberland. Moving straight westward they passed through Jonesboro and crossed the Mississippi at Cape Girardeau, Missouri. Some of the first parties turned southward through Arkansas; the later ones continued westward through Springfield, Missouri, and on to Indian Territory.

A New Englander traveling eastward across Kentucky in November and December met several contingents, each a day apart from the others. "Many of the aged Indians were suffering extremely from the fatigue of the journey," he said, "and several were quite ill. Even aged females, apparently nearly ready to drop into the grave, were traveling with heavy burdens attached to their backs—on the sometimes frozen ground, and sometimes muddy streets, with no covering for the feet except what nature had given them. . . . We learned from the inhabitants on the road where the Indians passed, that they buried fourteen or fifteen at every stopping place, and they make a journey of ten miles per day only on an average. They will not travel on the Sabbath . . . they must stop, and not merely stop—they must worship the Great Spirit, too; for they had divine service on the Sabbath—a camp meeting in truth."

Autumn rains softened the roads, and the hundreds of wagons and horses cut them into morasses, slowing movement to a crawl. To add to their difficulties, tollgate operators overcharged them for passage. Their horses were stolen or seized on pretext of unpaid debts, and they had no recourse to the law. With the coming of cold damp weather, measles and whooping cough became epidemic. Supplies had to be dumped to make room for the sick in the jolting wagons.

By the time the last detachments reached the Mississippi at Cape Girardeau it was January, with the river running full of ice so that several thousand had to wait on the east bank almost a month before the channel cleared. James Mooney, who later heard the story from survivors, said that "the lapse of over half a century had not sufficed to wipe out the memory of the miseries of that halt beside the frozen river, with hundreds of sick and dying penned up in wagons or stretched upon the ground, with only a blanket overhead to keep out the January blast."

Meanwhile the parties that left early in October were beginning to reach Indian Territory. (The first arrived on January 4, 1839.) Each group had lost from thirty to forty members by death. The later detachments suffered much heavier losses, especially toward the end of their journey. Among the victims was the wife of John Ross.

Not until March 1839 did the last of the Cherokees reach their new home in the West. Counts were made of the survivors and balanced against the counts made at the beginning of the removal. As well as could be estimated, the Cherokees had lost about four thousand by deaths—or one out of every four members of the tribe—most of the deaths brought about as the direct result of the enforced removal. From that day to this the Cherokees remember it as "the trail where they cried," or the Trail of Tears.

DOCUMENTS

Memorial of the Cherokee Nation, 1830

We are aware, that some persons suppose it will be for our advantage to remove beyond the Mississippi. We think otherwise. Our people universally think otherwise. Thinking that it would be fatal to their interests, they have almost to a man sent their memorial to congress, deprecating the necessity of a removal. This question was distinctly before their minds when they signed their memorial. Not an adult person can be found, who has not an opinion on the subject, and if the people were to understand distinctly, that they could be protected against the laws of the neighboring states, there is probably not an adult person in the nation, who would think it best to remove; though possibly a few might emigrate individually. There are doubtless many, who would flee to an unknown country, how-

SOURCE: *Nile's Weekly Register*, 38 (August 21, 1830): 454–57.

ever beset with dangers, privations and sufferings, rather than be sentenced to spend six years in a Georgia prison for advising one of their neighbors not to betray his country. And there are others who could not think of living as outlaws in their native land, exposed to numberless vexations, and excluded from being parties or witnesses in a court of justice. It is incredible that Georgia should ever have enacted the oppressive laws to which reference is here made, unless she had supposed that something extremely terrific in its character was necessary in order to make the Cherokees willing to remove. We are not willing to remove; and if we could be brought to this extremity, it would be not by argument, not because our judgment was satisfied, not because our condition will be improved; but only because we cannot endure to be deprived of our national and individual rights and subjected to a process of intolerable oppression.

We wish to remain on the land of our fathers. We have a perfect and original right to remain without interruption or molestation. The treaties with us, and laws of the United States made in pursuance of treaties, guaranty our residence and our privileges, and secure us against intruders. Our only request is, that these treaties may be fulfilled, and these laws executed.

But if we are compelled to leave our country, we see nothing but ruin before us. The country west of the Arkansas territory is unknown to us. From what we can learn of it, we have no prepossessions in its favor. All the inviting parts of it, as we believe, are preoccupied by various Indian nations, to which it has been assigned. They would regard us as intruders, and look upon us with an evil eye. The far greater part of that region is, beyond all controversy, badly supplied with wood and water; and no Indian tribe can live as agriculturists without these articles. All our neighbors, in case of our removal, though crowded into our near vicinity, would speak a language totally different from ours, and practice different customs. The original possessors of that region are now wandering savages lurking for prey in the neighborhood. They have always been at war, and would be easily tempted to turn their arms against peaceful emigrants. Were the country to which we are urged much better than it is represented to be, and were it free from the objections which we have made to it, still it is not the land of our birth, nor of our affections. It contains neither the scenes of our childhood, nor the graves of our fathers.

The removal of families to a new country, even under the most favorable auspices, and when the spirits are sustained by pleasing visions of the future, is attended with much depression of mind and sinking of heart. This is the case, when the removal is a matter of decided preference, and when the persons concerned are in early youth or vigorous manhood. Judge, then, what must be the circumstances of a removal, when a whole community, embracing persons of all classes and every description, from the infant to the man of extreme old age, the sick, the blind, the lame, the improvident, the reckless, the desperate, as well as the prudent, the considerate, the industrious, are compelled to remove by odious and intolerable vexations and persecutions, brought upon them in the forms of law, when all will agree only in this, that they have been cruelly robbed of their country, in violation of the most solemn compacts, which it is possible for communities to form with each other; and that, if they should make themselves comfortable in their new residence, they have nothing to expect hereafter but to be the victims of a future legalized robbery!

Such we deem, and are absolutely certain, will be the feelings of the whole Cherokee people, if they are forcibly compelled, by the laws of Georgia, to remove; and with these feelings, how is it possible that we should pursue our present course of improvement, or avoid sinking into utter despondency? We have been called a poor, ignorant, and degraded people. We certainly are not rich; nor have we ever boasted of our knowledge, or our moral or intellectual elevation. But there is not a man within our limits so ignorant as not to know that he has a right to live on the land of his fathers, in the possession of his immemorial privileges, and that this right has been acknowledged and guaranteed by the United States; nor is there a man so degraded as not to feel a keen sense of injury, on being deprived of this right and driven into exile. . . .

Removal Defended, 1830

It gives me pleasure to announce to Congress that the benevolent policy of the Government, steadily pursued for nearly thirty years, in relation to the removal of the Indians beyond the white settlements is approaching to a happy consummation. Two important tribes [the Choctaws and the Chickasaws] have accepted the provision made for their removal at the last session of Congress, and it is believed that their example will induce the remaining tribes also to seek the same obvious advantages.

The consequences of a speedy removal will be important to the United States, to individual States, and to the Indians themselves. The pecuniary advantages which it promises to the Government are the least of its recommendations. It puts an end to all possible danger of collision between the authorities of the General and State Governments on account of the Indians. It will place a dense and civilized population in large tracts of country now occupied by a few savage hunters. By opening the whole territory between Tennessee on the north and Louisiana on the south to

SOURCE: Andrew Jackson, "Second Annual Message to Congress" (December 6, 1830) in J. D. Richardson, ed., *A Compilation of the Messages and Papers of the Presidents,* 2 (Washington, D.C.: Government Printing Office, 1896): 519–22.

the settlement of the whites it will incalculably strengthen the southwestern frontier and render the adjacent States strong enough to repel future invasions without remote aid. It will relieve the whole State of Mississippi and the western part of Alabama of Indian occupancy, and enable those States to advance rapidly in population, wealth, and power. It will separate the Indians from immediate contact with settlements of whites; free them from the power of the States; enable them to pursue happiness in their own way and under their own rude institutions; will retard the progress of decay, which is lessening their numbers, and perhaps cause them gradually, under the protection of the Government and through the influence of good counsels, to cast off their savage habits and become an interesting, civilized, and Christian community. These consequences, some of them so certain and the rest so probable, make the complete execution of the plan sanctioned by Congress at their last session an object of much solicitude.

Toward the aborigines of the country no one can indulge a more friendly feeling than myself, or would go further in attempting to reclaim them from their wandering habits and make them a happy, prosperous people. I have endeavored to impress upon them my own solemn convictions of the duties and powers of the General Government in relation to the State authorities. For the justice of the laws passed by the States within the scope of their reserved powers they are not responsible to this Government. As individuals we may entertain and express our opinions of their acts, but as a Government we have as little right to control them as we have to prescribe laws for other nations.

With a full understanding of the subject, the Choctaw and the Chickasaw tribes have with great unanimity determined to avail themselves of the liberal offers presented by the act of Congress, and have agreed to remove beyond the Mississippi River. Treaties have been made with them, which in due season will be submitted for consideration. In negotiating these treaties they were made to understand their true condition, and they have preferred maintaining their independence in the Western forests to submitting to the laws of the States in which they now reside. These treaties, being probably the last which will ever be made with them, are characterized by great liberality on the part of the Government. They give the Indians a liberal sum in consideration of their removal, and comfortable subsistence on their arrival at their new homes. If it be their real interest to maintain a separate existence, they will there be at liberty to do so without the inconveniences and vexations to which they would unavoidably have been subject in Alabama and Mississippi.

Humanity has often wept over the fate of the aborigines of this country, and Philanthropy has been long busily employed in devising means to avert it, but its progress has never for a moment been arrested, and one by one have many powerful tribes disappeared from the earth. To follow

177

to the tomb the last of his race and to tread on the graves of extinct nations excite melancholy reflections. But true philanthropy reconciles the mind to these vicissitudes as it does to the extinction of one generation to make room for another. In the monuments and fortresses of an unknown people, spread over the extensive regions of the West, we behold the memorials of a once powerful race, which was exterminated or has disappeared to make room for the existing savage tribes. Nor is there anything in this which, upon a comprehensive view of the general interests of the human race, is to be regretted. Philanthropy could not wish to see this continent restored to the condition in which it was found by our forefathers. What good man would prefer a country covered with forests and ranged by a few thousand savages to our extensive Republic, studded with cities, towns, and prosperous farms, embellished with all the improvements which art can devise or industry execute, occupied by more than 12,000,000 happy people, and filled with all the blessings of liberty, civilization, and religion?

The present policy of the Government is but a continuation of the same progressive change by a milder process. The tribes which occupied the countries now constituting the Eastern States were annihilated or have melted away to make room for the whites. The waves of population and civilization are rolling to the westward, and we now propose to acquire the countries occupied by the red men of the South and West by a fair exchange, and, at the expense of the United States, to send them to a land where their existence may be prolonged and perhaps made perpetual. Doubtless it will be painful to leave the graves of their fathers; but what do they more than our ancestors did or than our children are now doing? To better their condition in an unknown land our forefathers left all that was dear in earthly objects. Our children by thousands yearly leave the land of their birth to seek new homes in distant regions. Does Humanity weep at these painful separations from everything, animate and inanimate, with which the young heart has become entwined? Far from it. It is rather a source of joy that our country affords scope where our young population may range unconstrained in body or in mind, developing the power and faculties of man in their highest perfection. These remove hundreds and almost thousands of miles at their own expense, purchase the lands they occupy, and support themselves at their new homes from the moment of their arrival. Can it be cruel in this Government when, by events which it can not control, the Indian is made discontented in his ancient home to purchase his lands, to give him a new and extensive territory, to pay the expense of his removal, and support him a year in his new abode? How many thousands of our own people would gladly embrace the opportunity of removing to the West on such conditions! If the offers made to the Indians were extended to them, they would be hailed with gratitude and joy.

And is it supposed that the wandering savage has a stronger attachment to his home than the settled, civilized Christian? Is it more afflicting to him to leave the graves of his fathers than it is to our brothers and children? Rightly considered, the policy of the General Government toward the red man is not only liberal, but generous. He is unwilling to submit to the laws of the States and mingle with their population. To save him from this alternative, or perhaps utter annihilation, the General Government kindly offers him a new home, and proposes to pay the whole expense of his removal and settlement.

In the consummation of a policy originating at an early period, and steadily pursued by every Administration within the present century—so just to the States and so generous to the Indians—the Executive feels it has a right to expect the cooperation of Congress and of all good and disinterested men. . . .

The "Crime" of Removal, 1838

Sir, [President Van Buren] my communication respects the sinister rumors that fill this part of the country [New England] concerning the Cherokee people. The interest always felt in the aboriginal population—an interest naturally growing as that decays—has been heightened in regard to this tribe. Even in our distant State [Massachusetts] some good rumor of their worth and civility has arrived. We have learned with joy their improvement in the social arts. We have read their newspapers. We have seen some of them in our schools and colleges. In common with the great body of the American people, we have witnessed with sympathy the painful labors of these red men to redeem their own race from the doom of eternal inferiority, and to borrow and domesticate in the tribe the arts and customs of the Caucasian race. And notwithstanding the unaccountable apathy with which of late years the Indians have been sometimes abandoned to their enemies, it is not to be doubted that it is the good pleasure and the understanding of all humane persons in the Republic, of the men and the matrons sitting in the thriving independent families all over the land, that they shall be duly cared for; that they shall taste justice and love from all to whom we have delegated the office of dealing with them.

The newspapers now inform us that, in December, 1835, a treaty contracting for the exchange of all the Cherokee territory was pretended to be made by an agent on the part of the United States with some persons appearing on the part of the Cherokees; that the fact afterwards transpired

SOURCE: Ralph Waldo Emerson, "Letter to President Van Buren," in Ralph Waldo Emerson, *Complete Works* (Boston: Houghton Mifflin, 1903–4), 11: 89–96.

that these deputies did by no means represent the will of the nation; and that, out of eighteen thousand souls composing the nation, fifteen thousand six hundred and sixty-eight have protested against the so-called treaty. It now appears that the government of the United States choose to hold the Cherokees to this sham treaty, and are proceeding to execute the same. Almost the entire Cherokee Nation stand up and say, "This is not our act. Behold us. Here are we. Do not mistake that handful of deserters for us"; and the American President and the Cabinet, the Senate and the House of Representatives, neither hear these men nor see them, and are contracting to put this active nation into carts and boats, and to drag them over mountains and rivers to a wilderness at a vast distance beyond the Mississippi. And a paper purporting to be an army order fixes a month from this day as the hour for this doleful removal.

In the name of God, sir, we ask you if this be so. Do the newspapers rightly inform us? Men and women with pale and perplexed faces meet one another in the streets and churches here, and ask if this be so. We have inquired if this be a gross misrepresentation from the party opposed to the government and anxious to blacken it with the people. We have looked at the newspapers of different parties and find a horrid confirmation of the tale. We are slow to believe it. We hoped the Indians were misinformed, and that their remonstrance was premature, and will turn out to be a needless act of terror.

The piety, the principle that is left in the United States, if only in its coarsest form, a regard to the speech of men, forbid us to entertain it as a fact. Such a dereliction of all faith and virtue, such a denial of justice, and such deafness to screams for mercy were never heard of in times of peace and in the dealing of a nation with its own allies and wards, since the earth was made. Sir, does this government think that the people of the United States are become savage and mad? From their mind are the sentiments of love and a good nature wiped clean out? The soul of man, the justice, the mercy that is the heart's heart in all men, from Maine to Georgia, does abhor this business.

In speaking thus the sentiments of my neighbors and my own, perhaps I overstep the bounds of decorum. But would it not be a higher indecorum coldly to argue a matter like this? We only state the fact that a crime is projected that confounds our understandings by its magnitude, a crime that really deprives us as well as the Cherokees of a country for how could we call the conspiracy that should crush these poor Indians our government, or the land that was cursed by their parting and dying imprecations our country, any more? You, sir, will bring down that renowned chair in which you sit into infamy if your seal is set to this instrument of perfidy; and the name of this nation, hitherto the sweet omen of religion and liberty, will stink to the world.

You will not do us the injustice of connecting this remonstrance with any sectional and party feeling. It is in our hearts the simplest commandment of brotherly love. We will not have this great and solemn claim upon national and human justice huddled aside under the flimsy plea of its being a party act. Sir, to us the questions upon which the government and the people have been agitated during the past year, touching the prostration of the currency and of trade, seem but motes in comparison. These hard times, it is true, have brought the discussion home to every farmhouse and poor man's house in this town; but it is the chirping of grasshoppers beside the immortal question whether justice shall be done by the race of civilized to the race of savage man, whether all the attributes of reason, of civility, of justice, and even of mercy, shall be put off by the American people, and so vast an outrage upon the Cherokee Nation and upon human nature shall be consummated.

One circumstance lessens the reluctance with which I intrude at this time on your attention my conviction that the government ought to be admonished of a new historical fact, which the discussion of this question has disclosed, namely, that there exists in a great part of the Northern people a gloomy diffidence in the *moral* character of the government.

On the broaching of this question, a general expression of despondency, of disbelief that any good will accrue from a remonstrance on an act of fraud and robbery, appeared in those men to whom we naturally turn for aid and counsel. Will the American government steal? Will it lie? Will it kill?—We ask triumphantly. Our counsellors and old statesmen here say that ten years ago they would have staked their lives on the affirmation that the proposed Indian measures could not be executed; that the unanimous country would put them down. And now the steps of this crime follow each other so fast, at such fatally quick time, that the millions of virtuous citizens, whose agents the government are, have no place to interpose, and must shut their eyes until the last howl and wailing of these tormented villages and tribes shall afflict the ear of the world.

I will not hide from you, as an indication of the alarming distrust, that a letter addressed as mine is, and suggesting to the mind of the Executive the plain obligations of man, has a burlesque character in the apprehensions of some of my friends. I, sir, will not beforehand treat you with the contumely of this distrust. I will at least state to you this fact, and show you how plain and humane people, whose love would be honor, regard the policy of the government, and what injurious inferences they draw as to the minds of the governors. A man with your experience in affairs must have seen cause to appreciate the futility of opposition to the moral sentiment. However feeble the sufferer and however great the oppressor, it is in the nature of things that the blow should recoil upon the aggressor. For God is in the sentiment, and it cannot be withstood. The potentate and the people perish before it; but with it, and its executor, they are omnipotent.

I write thus, sir, to inform you of the state of mind these Indian tidings have awakened here, and to pray with one voice more that you, whose hands are strong with the delegated power of fifteen millions of men, will avert with that might the terrific injury which threatens the Cherokee tribe.

With great respect, sir, I am your fellow citizen.

RALPH WALDO EMERSON.

CHAPTER 10

Moving West

The westward movement of American settlement, which spanned a large part of the nineteenth century, to this day continues to stir the imagination. Covered wagons by the hundreds have crossed motion picture and television screens and the dust jackets of books. Daniel Boone, Kit Carson, and Buffalo Bill are widely recognized names. Even so, the popular media have not revealed much about the personal dimension of the westward movement of the families in those wagons.

In "Women and Their Families on the Overland Trail to California and Oregon, 1842–1867," Johnny Faragher and Christine Stansell explore the realities of life on the trail during the movement westward, focusing on prevailing notions of the status and roles of women in the mid-nineteenth century. How do the authors explain the emergence of a separate woman's sphere during the nineteenth century?

The contrast between romantic views of westward migration and actual experiences on the trail is apparent in the first two documents. The first is a description by the editor of the **Missouri Expositor** (May 3, 1845) of the wagon trains passing through Independence, Missouri, a jumping-off point for the long journey to Oregon. Next is an excerpt from Frederick Law Olmsted's **A Journey Through Texas** (1857), in which the author describes caravans of Southerners emigrating to Texas.

(Olmsted, a famous landscape architect, wrote a number of works describing his extensive travels throughout the South.) How do you account for the striking differences in the two descriptions? Is one view more accurate than the other?

The existence of sexual spheres had positive as well as negative implications for women, according to Faragher and Stansell, and they refer to Catharine Beecher (1800–1878), one of the foremost advocates of the ennobling aspects of women's domestic roles. Accepting women's separateness in economic, social, and political matters—she was opposed to women's suffrage—Beecher devoted much of her life to speaking out on behalf of the importance of women's special tasks and to promoting women's education in the domestic arts. An example of her argument is found in the last document, from The American Women's Home *(1869), written with her sister, Harriet Beecher Stowe, author of* Uncle Tom's Cabin. *How do you believe women on the Overland Trail might have responded to what the Beecher sisters advocated as the proper role of women?*

ESSAY

Women and Their Families on the Overland Trail to California and Oregon, 1842–1867

Johnny Faragher and Christine Stansell

From 1841 until 1867, the year in which the transcontinental railroad was completed, nearly 350,000 North Americans emigrated to the Pacific coast along the western wagon road known variously as the Oregon, the California, or simply the Overland Trail. This migration was essentially a family phenomenon. Although single men constituted the majority of the party which pioneered large-scale emigration on the Overland Trail in 1841, significant numbers of women and children were already present in the wagon trains of the next season. Families made up the preponderant proportion of the migrations throughout the 1840s. In 1849, during the overwhelmingly male Gold Rush, the number dropped precipitously, but after 1851 families once again assumed dominance in the overland migration. The contention that "the family was the one substantial social institution" on the frontier is too sweeping, yet it is undeniable that the

SOURCE: Reprinted from Johnny Faragher and Christine Stansell, "Women and Their Families on the Overland Trail to California and Oregon, 1842–1867," *Feminist Studies* 2 (1975): 155–66, by permission of the publisher, *Feminist Studies*, Inc., c/o Women's Studies Program, University of Maryland, College Park, MD 20742.

white family largely mediated the incorporation of the western territories into the American nation.

The emigrating families were a heterogeneous lot. Some came from farms in the midwest and upper South, many from small midwestern towns, and others from northeastern and midwestern cities. Clerks and shopkeepers as well as farmers outfitted their wagons in Independence, St. Louis, or Westport Landing on the Missouri. Since costs for supplies, travel, and settlement were not negligible, few of the very poor were present, nor were the exceptionally prosperous. The dreams of fortune which lured the wagon trains into new lands were those of modest men whose hopes were pinned to small farms or larger dry-goods stores, more fertile soil or more customers, better market prospects and a steadily expanding economy.

For every member of the family, the trip West was exhausting, toilsome, and often grueling. Each year in late spring, westbound emigrants gathered for the journey at spots along the Missouri River and moved out in parties of ten to several hundred wagons. Aggregates of nuclear families, loosely attached by kinship or friendship, traveled together or joined an even larger caravan. Coast-bound families traveled by ox-drawn wagons at the frustratingly slow pace of fifteen to twenty miles per day. They worked their way up the Platte River valley through what is now Kansas and Nebraska, crossing the Rockies at South Pass in southwestern Wyoming by mid-summer. The Platte route was relatively easy going, but from present-day Idaho, where the roads to California and Oregon diverged, to their final destinations, the pioneers faced disastrous conditions: scorching deserts, boggy salt flats, and rugged mountains. By this time, families had been on the road some three months and were only at the midpoint of the journey; the environment, along with the wear of the road, made the last months difficult almost beyond endurance. Finally, in late fall or early winter the pioneers straggled into their promised lands, after six months and over two thousand miles of hardship.

As this journey progressed, bare necessity became the determinant of most of each day's activities. The primary task of surviving and getting to the coast gradually suspended accustomed patterns of dividing work between women and men. All able-bodied adults worked all day in one way or another to keep the family moving. Women's work was no less indispensable than men's; indeed, as the summer wore on, the boundaries dividing the work of the sexes were threatened, blurred, and transgressed.

The vicissitudes of the trail opened new possibilities for expanded work roles for women, and in the cooperative work of the family there existed a basis for a vigorous struggle for female-male equality. But most women did not see the experience in this way. They viewed it as a male enterprise from its very inception. Women experienced the breakdown of the sexual division of labor as a dissolution of their own autonomous "sphere." Bereft of the footing which this independent base gave them, they lacked a cultural rationale for the work they did, and remained estranged from the possibilities of the enlarged scope and power of family life on the trail. Instead, women fought *against* the forces of necessity to hold together the few fragments of female subculture left to them. We have been bequeathed a remarkable record of this struggle in the diaries, journals, and memoirs of emigrating women. In this study, we will examine a particular habit of living, or culture, in conflict with the new material circumstances of the Trail, and the efforts of women to maintain a place, a sphere of their own.

The overland family was not a homogeneous unit, its members imbued with identical aspirations and desires. On the contrary, the period of westward movement was also one of multiplying schisms within those families whose location and social status placed them in the mainstream of national culture. Child-rearing tracts, housekeeping manuals, and etiquette books by the hundreds proscribed and rationalized to these Americans a radical separation of the work responsibilities and social duties of mothers and fathers; popular thought assigned unique personality traits, spiritual capacities, and forms of experience to the respective categories of man, woman, and child. In many families, the tensions inherent in this separatist ideology, often repressed in the everyday routine of the East, erupted under the strain of the overland crossing. The difficulties of the emigrants, while inextricably linked to the duress of the journey itself, also revealed family dynamics which had been submerged in the less eventful life "back home."

A full blown ideology of "woman's place" was absent in preindustrial America. On farms, in artisan shops, and in town marketplaces, women and children made essential contributions to family income and subsistence; it was the family which functioned as the basic unit of production in the colony and the young nation. As commercial exchanges displaced the local markets where women had sold surplus dairy products and textiles, and the workplace drifted away from the household, women and children lost their breadwinning prerogatives.

In Jacksonian America, a doctrine of "sexual spheres" arose to facilitate and justify the segregation of women into the home and men into productive work. While the latter attended to politics, economics, and wage-earning, popular thought assigned women the refurbished and newly professionalized tasks of child-rearing and housekeeping. A host of corollaries followed on the heels of these shifts. Men were physically strong, women naturally delicate; men were skilled in practical matters, women in moral and emotional concerns; men were prone to corruption, women to virtue; men belonged in the world, women in the home. For women, the system of sexual spheres represented a decline in social status and isolation from political and economic power. Yet it also provided them with a psychological power base of undeniable importance. The "cult of true womanhood" was more than simply a retreat. Catharine Beecher, one of the chief theorists of "woman's influence," proudly quoted Tocqueville's observation that "in no country has such constant care been taken, as in America, to trace two clearly distinct lines of action for the two sexes, and to make them keep pace with the other, but in two pathways which are always different." Neither Beecher nor her sisters were simply dupes of a masculine imperialism. The supervision of child-rearing, household economy, and the moral and religious life of the family granted women a certain degree of real autonomy and control over their lives as well as those of their husbands and children.

Indeed, recent scholarship has indicated that a distinctly female subculture emerged from "woman's sphere." By "subculture" we simply mean a "habit of living"—as we have used "culture" above—of a minority group which is self-consciously distinct from the dominant activities, expectations, and values of a society. Historians have seen female church groups, reform associations, and philanthropic activity as expressions of this subculture in actual behavior, while a large and rich body of writing by and for women articulated the subcultural impulses on the ideational level. Both behavior and thought point to child-rearing, religious activity, education, home life, associationism, and female communality as components of women's subculture. Female friendships, strikingly intimate and deep in this period, formed the actual bonds. Within their tight and atomized family households, women carved out a life of their own.

At its very inception, the western emigration sent tremors through the foundations of this carefully compartmentalized family structure. The rationale behind pulling up stakes was nearly always economic advancement; since breadwinning was a masculine concern, the husband and father introduced the idea of going West and made the final decision. Family participation in the intervening time ran the gamut from enthusiastic support to stolid resistance. Many women cooperated with their ambitious spouses: "The motive that induced us to part with pleasant associations and the dear friends of our childhood days, was to obtain from the government of the United States a grant of land that 'Uncle Sam' had promised to give to the head of each family who settled in this new country." Others, however, only acquiesced. "Poor Ma said only this morning, 'Oh, I wish we never had started,' " Lucy Cooke wrote her first day on the trail, "and she looks so sorrowful and dejected. I think if Pa had not passengers to take through she would urge him to return; not that he should be so inclined." Huddled with her children in a cold, damp wagon, trying to calm them despite the ominous chanting of visiting Indians, another woman wondered "what had possessed my husband, anyway, that he should have thought of bringing us away out through this God forsaken country." Similar alienation from the "pioneer spirit" haunted Lavinia Porter's leave-taking:

> I never recall that sad parting from my dear sister on the plains of Kansas without the tears flowing fast and free. . . . We were the eldest of a large family, and the bond of affection and love that existed between us was strong indeed . . . as she with the other friends turned to leave me for the ferry which was to take them back to home and civilization, I stood alone on that wild prairie. Looking westward I saw my husband driving slowly over the plain; turning my face once more to the east, my dear sister's footsteps were fast widening the distance between us. For the time I knew not which way to go, nor whom to follow. But in a few moments I rallied my forces . . . and soon overtook the slowly moving oxen who were bearing my husband and child over the green prairie . . . the unbidden tears would flow in spite of my brave resolve to be the courageous and valiant frontierswoman.

Her dazed vacillation soon gave way to a private conviction that the family had made a dire mistake: "I would make a brave effort to be cheerful and patient until the camp work was done. Then starting out ahead of the team and my men folks, when I thought I had gone beyond hearing distance, I would throw myself down on the unfriendly desert and give way like a child to sobs and tears, wishing myself back home with my friends and chiding myself for consenting to take this wild goose chase." Men viewed drudgery, calamity, and privation as trials along the road to prosperity, unfortunate but inevitable corollaries of the rational decision they had made. But to those women who were unable to appropriate the vision of the upwardly mobile pilgrimage, hardship and loss only testified to the inherent folly of the emigration, "this wild goose chase."

If women were reluctant to accompany their men, however, they were often equally unwilling to let them go alone. In the late 1840s, the conflict between wives and their gold-crazed husbands reveals the determination with which women enforced the cohesion of the nuclear family. In the name of family unity, some obdurate wives simply chose to blockbust the sexually segregated Gold Rush: "My husband grew enthusiastic and wanted to start immediately," one woman recalled, "but I would not be left behind. I thought where he could go I could and where I went I could take my two little toddling babies." Her family departed intact. Other women used their moral authority to smash the enterprise in its planning stages. "We were married to live together," a wife acidly reminded her spouse when he informed her of his intention to join the Rush: "I am willing to go with you to any part of *God's Foot Stool* [the Earth] where you think you can do best, and under these circumstances you have no right to go where I cannot, and if you do you need never return for I shall look upon you as dead." Roundly chastised, the man postponed his journey until the next season, when his family could leave with him. When included in the plans, women seldom wrote of their husbands' decisions to emigrate in their diaries or memoirs. A breadwinner who tried to leave alone, however, threatened the family unity upon which his authority was based; only then did a wife challenge his dominance in worldly affairs.

There was an economic reason for the preponderance of families on the Trail. Women and children, but especially women, formed an essential supplementary work force in the settlements. The ideal wife in the West resembled a hired hand more than a nurturant Christian housekeeper. Narcissa Whitman wrote frankly to aspiring settlers of the functional necessity of women on the new farms: "Let every young man bring a wife, for he will want one after he gets here, if he never did before." In a letter from California, another seasoned woman warned a friend in Missouri that in the West women became "hewers of wood and drawers of water everywhere." Mrs. Whitman's fellow missionary Elkanah Walker was unabashedly practical in beseeching his wife to join him: "I am tired of keeping an old bachelor's hall. I want someone to get me a good supper and let me take my ease and when I am very tired in the morning I want someone to get up and get breakfast and let me lay in bed and take my rest." It would be both simplistic and harsh to argue that men brought their families West or married because of the labor power of women and children; there is no doubt, however, that the new Westerners appreciated the advantages of familial labor. Women were not superfluous; they were workers. The migration of women helped to solve the problem of labor scarcity, not only in the early years of the American settlement on the coast, but throughout the history of the continental frontier.

In the first days of the overland trip, new work requirements were not yet pressing and the division of labor among family members still replicated familiar patterns. Esther Hanna reported in one of her first diary entries that "our men have gone to build a bridge across the stream, which is impassable," while she baked her first bread on the prairie. Elizabeth Smith similarly described her party's day: "rainy . . . Men making rafts. Women cooking and washing. Children crying." When travel was suspended, "the men were generally busy mending wagons, harnesses, yokes, shoeing the animals etc., and the women washed clothes, boiled a big mess of beans, to warm over for several meals, or perhaps mended clothes." At first, even in emergencies, women and men hardly considered integrating their work. "None but those who have cooked for a family of eight, crossing the plains, have any idea of what it takes," a disgruntled woman recalled: "My sister-in-law was sick, my niece was much younger than I, and consequently I had the management of all the cooking and planning on my young shoulders." To ask a man to help was a possibility she was unable even to consider.

The relegation of women to purely domestic duties, however, soon broke down under the vicissitudes of the Trail. Within the first few weeks, the unladylike task of gathering buffalo dung for fuel (little firewood was available *en route*) became women's work. As one traveler astutely noted, "force of surroundings was a great leveler"; miles of grass, dust, glare, and mud erased some of the most rudimentary distinctions between female and male responsibilities. By summer, women often helped drive the wagons and the livestock. At one Platte crossing, "the men drawed the wagons over by hand and the women all crossed in safety"; but at the next, calamity struck when the bridge collapsed, "and then commenced the hurry and bustle of repairing; all were at work, even the women and children." Such crises, which compounded daily as the wagons moved past the Platte up the long stretches of desert and coastal mountains, generated equity in work; at times of Indian threats, for example, both women and men made bullets and stood guard. When mountain fever struck the Pengra family as they crossed the Rockies, Charlotte relieved her incapacitated husband of the driving while he took care of the youngest child. Only such severe afflictions forced men to take on traditionally female chores. While women did men's work, there is little evidence that men reciprocated.

Following a few days in the life of an overland woman discloses the magnitude of her work. During the hours her party traveled, Charlotte Pengra walked beside the wagons, driving the cattle and gathering buffalo chips. At night she cooked, baked bread for the next noon meal, and washed clothes. Three successive summer days illustrate how trying these small chores could be. Her train pulled out early on a Monday morning, only to be halted by rain and a flash flood; Mrs. Pengra washed and dried her family's wet clothes in the afternoon while doing her daily baking. On Tuesday the wagons pushed hard to make up for lost time, forcing her to trot all day to keep up. In camp that night there was no time to rest. Before going to bed, she wrote, "Kept busy in preparing tea and doing other things preparatory for the morrow. I baked a cracker pudding, warm biscuits and made tea, and after supper stewed two pans of dried apples, and made two loaves of bread, got my work done up, beds made, and child asleep, and have written in my journal. Pretty tired of course." The same routine devoured the next day and evening: "I have done a washing. Stewed apples, made pies and baked a rice pudding, and mended our wagon cover. Rather tired." And the next: "baked biscuits, stewed berries, fried meat, boiled and mashed potatoes, and made tea for supper, afterward baked bread. Thus you see I have not much rest." Children also burdened women's work and leisure. During one quiet time, Helen Stewart retreated in mild defiance from her small charges to a tent in order to salvage some private time: "It exceeding hot . . . some of the men is out hunting and some of them sleeping. The children is grumbling and crying and laughing and howling and playing all around." Although children are notably absent in women's journals, they do appear, frightened and imploring, during an Indian scare or a storm, or intrude into a rare and precious moment of relaxation, "grumbling and crying."

Because the rhythm of their chores was out of phase with that of the men, the division of labor could be especially taxing to women. Men's days were toilsome but broken up at regular intervals with periods of rest. Men hitched the teams, drove or walked until noon, relaxed at dinner, traveled until the evening camp, unhitched the oxen, ate supper, and in the evening sat at the campfire, mended equipment, or stood guard. They also provided most of the labor in emergencies, pulling the wagons through mires, across treacherous river crossings, up long grades, and down precipitous slopes. In the pandemonium of a steep descent,

> you would see the women and children in advance seeking the best way, some of them slipping down, or holding on to the rocks, now taking an "otter slide," and then a run til some natural obstacle presented itself to stop their accelerated progress and those who get down safely without a hurt or a bruise, are fortunate indeed. Looking back to the train, you would see some of the men holding on to the wagons, others slipping under the oxen's feet, some throwing articles out of the way that had fallen out, and all have enough to do to keep them busily occupied.

Women were responsible for staying out of the way and getting themselves and the children to safety, men for getting the wagons down. Women's work, far less demanding of brute strength and endurance, was nevertheless distributed without significant respite over all waking hours: mealtimes offered no leisure to the cooks. "The plain fact of the matter is," a young woman complained,

> we *have no time for sociability*. From the time we get up in the morning, until we are on the road, it is hurry scurry to get breakfast and put away the things that necessarily had to be pulled out last night—while under way there is no room in the wagon for a visitor, nooning is barely long enough to eat a cold bite—and at night all the cooking utensils and provisions are to be gotten about the camp fire, and cooking enough to last until the next night.

After supper, the men gathered together, "lolling and smoking their pipes and guessing, or maybe betting, how many miles we had covered during the day," while the women baked, washed, and put the children to bed before they finally sat down. Charlotte Pengra found "as I was told before I started that there is no rest in such a journey."

Unaccustomed tasks beset the travelers, who were equipped with only the familiar expectation that work was divided along gender lines. The solutions which sexual "spheres" offered were usually irrelevant to the new problems facing families. Women, for example, could not afford to be delicate: their new duties demanded far greater stamina and hardiness than their traditional domestic tasks. With no tradition to deal with the new exigencies of fuel-gathering, cattle-driving, and cooking, families found that "the division of labor in a party . . . was a prolific cause of quarrel." Within the Vincent party, "assignments to duty were not accomplished without grumbling and objection . . . there were occasional angry debates while the various burdens were being adjusted," while in "the camps of others who sometimes jogged along the trail in our company . . . we saw not a little fighting . . . and these bloody fisticuffs were invariably the outcome of disputes over division of labor." At home, these assignments were familiar and accepted, not subject to questioning. New work opened the division of labor to debate and conflict.

By midjourney, most women worked at male tasks. The men still retained dominance within their "sphere," despite the fact that it was no longer exclusively masculine. Like most women, Lavinia Porter was responsible for gathering buffalo chips for fuel. One afternoon, spying a grove of cottonwoods half a mile away, she asked her husband to branch off the trail so that the party could fell trees for firewood, thus easing her work. "But men on the plains I had found were not so accomodating, nor so ready to wait upon women as they were in more civilized communities." Her husband refused and Porter fought back: "I was feeling somewhat under the weather and unusually tired, and crawling into the wagon told them if they wanted fuel for the evening meal they could get it themselves and cook the meal also, and laying my head down on a pillow, I cried myself to sleep." Later that evening her husband awakened her with a belated dinner he had prepared himself, but despite his conciliatory spirit their relations were strained for weeks: "James and I had gradually grown silent and taciturn and had unwittingly partaken of the gloom and somberness of the dreary landscape." No longer a housewife or a domestic ornament, but a laborer in a male arena, Porter was still subordinate to her husband in practical matters.

Lydia Waters recorded another clash between new work and old consciousness: "I had learned to drive an ox team on the Platte and my driving was admired by an officer and his wife who were going with the mail to Salt Lake City." Pleased with the compliment, she later overheard them "laughing at the thought of a woman driving oxen." By no means did censure come only from men. The officer's wife as well as the officer derided Lydia Waters, while her own mother indirectly reprimanded teenaged Mary Ellen Todd. "All along our journey, I had tried to crack that big whip," Mary Ellen remembered years later:

Now while out at the wagon we kept trying until I was fairly successful. How my heart bounded a few days later when I chanced to hear father say to mother, "Do you know that Mary Ellen is beginning to crack the whip." Then how it fell again when mother replied, "I am afraid it isn't a very lady-like thing for a girl to do." After this, while I felt a secret joy in being able to have a power that set things going, there was also a sense of shame over this new accomplishment.

To understand Mrs. Todd's primness, so incongruous in the rugged setting of the Trail, we must see it in the context of a broader struggle on the part of women to preserve the home in transit. Against the leveling forces of the Plains, women tried to maintain the standards of cleanliness and order that had prevailed in their homes back East.

Our caravan had a good many women and children and although we were probably longer on the journey owing to their presence— they exerted a good influence, as the men did not take such risks with Indians . . . were more alert about the care of teams and seldom had accidents; more attention was paid to cleanliness and sanitation and, lastly, but not of less importance, meals were more regular and better cooked thus preventing much sickness and there was less waste of food.

Sarah Royce remembered that family wagons "were easily distinguished by the greater number of conveniences, and household articles they carried." In the evenings, or when the trains stopped for a day, women had a chance to create with these few props a flimsy facsimile of the home.

Even in camp women had little leisure time, but within the "hurry scurry" of work they managed to recreate the routine of the home. Indeed, a female subculture, central to the communities women had left behind, reemerged in these settings. At night, women often clustered together, chatting, working, or commiserating, instead of joining the men: "High teas were not popular, but tatting, knitting, crochetting, exchanging recipes for cooking beans or dried apples or swopping food for the sake of variety kept us in practice of feminine occupations and diversions." Besides using the domestic concerns of the Trail to reconstruct a female sphere, women also consciously invoked fantasy: "Mrs. Fox and her daughter are with us and everything is so still and quiet we can almost imagine ourselves at home again. We took out our Daguerrotypes and tried to live over again some of the happy days of 'Auld Lang Syne.' " Sisterly contact kept "feminine occupations" from withering away from disuse: "In the evening the young ladies came over to our house and we had a concert with both guitars. Indeed it seemed almost like a pleasant evening at home. We could none of us realize that we were almost at the summit of the Rocky Mountains." The hostess added with somewhat strained sanguinity that her young daughter seemed "just as happy sitting on the ground playing her guitar as she was at home, although she does not love it as much as her piano." Although a guitar was no substitute for the more refined instrument, it at least kept the girl "in practice with feminine occupations and diversions"; unlike Mary Ellen Todd, no big whip would tempt her to unwomanly pleasure in the power to "set things going."

But books, furniture, knick-knacks, china, the daguerrotypes that Mrs. Fox shared, or the guitars of young musicians—the "various articles of ornament and convenience"—were among the first things discarded on the epic trash heap which trailed over the mountains. On long uphill grades and over sandy deserts, the wagons had to be lightened; any materials not essential to survival were fair game for disposal. Such commodities of woman's sphere, although functionally useless, provided women with a psychological lifeline to their abandoned homes and communities, as well as to elements of their identities which the westward journey threatened to mutilate or entirely extinguish. Losing homely treasures and memorabilia was yet another defeat within an accelerating process of dispossession.

The male-directed venture likewise encroached upon the Sabbath, another female preserve. Through the influence of women's magazines, by mid-century Sunday had become a veritable ladies' day; women zealously exercised their religious influence and moral skill on the day of their families' retirement from the world. Although parties on the Trail often suspended travel on Sundays, the time only provided the opportunity to unload and dry the precious cargo of the wagons—seeds, food, and clothing—which otherwise would rot from dampness. For women whose creed forbade any worldly activity on the Sabbath, the work was not only irksome and tedious but profane.

> This is Sabath it is a beautiful day but indeed we do not use it as such for we have not traveled far when we stop in a most lovely place oh it is such a beautiful spot and take everything out of our wagon to air them and it is well we done it as the flower was damp and there was some of the other ones flower was rotten . . . and we baked and boiled and washed oh dear me I did not think we would have abused the sabeth in such a manner. I do not see how we can expect to get along but we did not intend to do so before we started.

Denied a voice in the male sphere that surrounded them, women were also unable to partake of the limited yet meaningful power of women with homes. On almost every Sunday, Helen Stewart lamented the disruption of a familiar and sustaining order of life, symbolized by the household goods strewn about the ground to dry: "We took everything out the wagons and the side of the hill is covered with flower biscut meat rice oat meal clothes and such a quantity of articles of all discertions to many to mention and childre[n] included in the number. And hobos that is neather men nor yet boys being in and out hang about."

The disintegration of the physical base of domesticity was symptomatic of an even more serious disruption in the female subculture. Because the wagon trains so often broke into smaller units, many women were stranded in parties without other women. Since there were usually two or more men in the same family party, some male friendships and bonds remained intact for the duration of the journey. But by midway in the trip, female companionship, so valued by nineteenth-century women, was unavailable to the solitary wife in a party of hired men, husband, and children that had broken away from a larger train. Emergencies and quarrels, usually between men, broke up the parties. Dr. Powers, a particularly ill-tempered man, decided after many disagreements with others in his train to make the crossing alone with his family. His wife shared neither his misanthropy nor his grim independence. On the day they separated from the others, she wrote in her journal: "The women came over to bid me goodbye, for we were to go alone, all alone. They said there was no color in my face. I felt as if there was none." She perceived the separation as a banishment, almost a death sentence: "There is something peculiar in such a parting on the Plains, one there realizes what a goodbye is. Miss Turner and Mrs. Hendricks were the last to leave, and they bade me adieu the tears running down their sunburnt cheeks. I felt as though my last friends were leaving me, for what—as I thought then—was a Maniac." Charlotte Pengra likewise left Missouri with her family in a large train. Several weeks out, mechanical problems detained some of the wagons, including those of the other three women. During the month they were separated, Pengra became increasingly dispirited and anxious: "The roads have been good today—I feel lonely and almost disheartened. . . . Can hear the wolves howl very distinctly. Rather ominis, perhaps you think. . . . Feel very tired and lonely—our folks not having come—I fear some of them ar sick." Having waited as long as possible for the others, the advance group made a major river crossing. "Then I felt that indeed I had left all my friends," Pengra wrote, "save my husband and his brother, to journey over the dreaded Plains, without one female acquaintance even for a companion—of course I wept and grieved about it but to no purpose."

Others echoed her mourning. "The whipporwills are chirping," Helen Stewart wrote, "they bring me in mind of our old farm in pensillvania the home of my childhood where I have spent the happiest days I will ever see again. . . . I feel rather lonesome today oh solitude solitude how I love it if I had about a dozen of my companions to enjoy it with me." Uprootedness took its toll in debilitation and numbness. After a hard week, men "lolled around in the tents and on their blankets seeming to realize that the 'Sabbath was made for man,' " resting on the palpable achievements of miles covered and rivers crossed. In contrast, the women "could not fully appreciate physical rest, and were rendered more uneasy by the continual passing of emigrant trains all day long. . . . To me, much of the day was spent in meditating over the past and in forebodings for the future."

The ultimate expression of this alienation was the pressure to turn back, to retrace steps to the old life. Occasionally anxiety or bewilderment erupted into open revolt against going on.

> This morning our company moved on, except one family. The woman got mad and wouldn't budge or let the children go. He had the cattle hitched on for three hours and coaxed her to go, but she wouldn't stir. I told my husband the circumstances and he and Adam Polk and Mr. Kimball went and each one took a young one and crammed them in the wagon, and the husband drove off and left her sitting. . . . She cut across and overtook her husband. Meantime he sent his boy back to camp after a horse he had left, and when she came up her husband said, "Did you meet John?" "Yes," was the reply, "and I picked up a stone and knocked out his brains." Her husband went back to ascertain the truth and while he was gone she set fire to one of the wagons. . . . He saw the flames and came running and put it out, and then mustered spunk enough to give her a good flogging.

Short of violent resistance, it was always possible that circumstances would force a family to reconsider and turn back. During a cholera scare in 1852, "women cried, begging their men to take them back." When the men reluctantly relented, the writer observed that "they did the hooking up of their oxen in a spiritless sort of way," while "some of the girls and women were laughing." There was little lost and much regained for women in a decision to abandon the migration.

Both sexes worked, and both sexes suffered. Yet women lacked a sense of inclusion and a cultural rationale to give meaning to the suffering and the work; no augmented sense of self or role emerged from augmented privation. Both women and men also complained, but women expanded their caviling to a generalized critique of the whole enterprise. Margaret Chambers felt "as if we had left all civilization behind us" after crossing the Missouri, and Harriet Ward's cry from South Pass—"Oh, shall we ever live like civilized beings again?"—reverberated through the thoughts of many of her sisters. Civilization was far more to these women than law, books, and municipal government; it was pianos, church societies, daguerrotypes, mirrors—in short, their homes. At their most hopeful, the exiles perceived the Trail as a hellish but necessary transition to a land where they could renew their domestic mission: "Each advanced step of the slow, plodding cattle carried us farther and farther from civilization into a desolate, barbarous country. . . . But our new home lay beyond all this and was a shining beacon that beckoned us on, inspiring our hearts with hope and courage." At worse, temporary exigencies became in the minds of the dispossessed the omens of an irrevocable exile: "We have been travelling with 25-18-14-129-64-3 wagons—now all alone—how dreary it seems. Can it be that I have left my quiet little home and taken this dreary land of solitude in exchange?"

Only a minority of the women who emigrated over the Overland Trail were from the northeastern middle classes where the cult of true womanhood reached its fullest bloom. Yet their responses to the labor demands of the Trail indicate that "womanliness" had penetrated the values, expectations, and personalities of midwestern farm women as well as New England "ladies." "Woman's sphere" provided them with companionship, a sense of self-worth, and most important, independence from men in a patriarchal world. The Trail, in breaking down sexual segregation, offered women the opportunities of socially essential work. Yet this work was performed in a male arena, and many women saw themselves as draftees rather than partners.

Historians have generally associated "positive work roles" for women with the absence of narrowly defined notions of "woman's place." In the best summary of literature on colonial women, for example, the authors of *Women in American Society* write: "In general, neither men nor women seemed concerned with defining what women were or what their unique contribution to society should be. . . . Abstract theories about the proper role of women did not stand in the way of meeting familial and social needs." Conversely, the ascendancy of "true womanhood" and the doctrine of sexual spheres coincided with the declining importance of the labor of middle- and upper-class women in a rapidly expanding market economy. On the Overland Trail, cultural roles and self-definitions conflicted with the immediate necessities of the socioeconomic situation. Women themselves fought to preserve a circumscribed role when material circumstances rendered it dysfunctional. Like their colonial great-grandmothers on pre-market subsistence farms, they labored at socially indispensable tasks. Yet they refused to appropriate their new work to their own ends and advantage. In their deepest sense of themselves they remained estranged from their function as "able bodies."

It could be argued that the time span of the trip was not long enough to alter cultural values. Yet there is evidence that the tensions of the Trail haunted the small and isolated market farms at the journey's end. Women in the western settlements continued to try to reinstate a culture of domesticity, although their work as virtual hired hands rendered obsolete the material base of separate arenas for women and men.

The notion of subculture employed in this and other studies of nineteenth-century women is hazy and ill-defined. We need to develop more rigorous conceptions of society, culture, and subculture, and to clarify the paradoxes of women's position, both isolated and integrated, in the dominant social and cultural movements of their time. Nonetheless, the journals of overland women are irrefutable testimony to the importance of a separate female province. Such theorists as Catharine Beecher were acutely aware of the advantages in keeping life divvied up, in maintaining "two pathways which are always different" for women and men. The women who traveled on the Overland Trail experienced firsthand the tribulations of integration which Beecher and her colleagues could predict in theory.

DOCUMENTS

Oregon Fever, 1845

Even while we write, we see a long train of wagons coming through our busy streets; they are hailed with shouts of welcome by their fellow voyagers, and, to judge from the pleased expression on every face, it "all goes merry as a marriage bell." On looking out at the passing train, we see among the foremost a very comfortably covered wagon, one of the sheets drawn aside, and an extremely nice looking lady seated inside very quietly sewing; the bottom of the wagon is carpeted; there are two or three chairs, and at one end there is a bureau, surmounted by a mirror; various articles of ornament and convenience hang around the sides—a perfect prairie boudoir. Blessed be woman! Shedding light and happiness where'er she goes; with her the wild prairie will be a paradise! Blessed be him who gave us this connecting link between heaven and man to win us from our wilder ways. Hold on there; this is getting entirely too sentimental; but we don't care who laughs, we felt better and happier when we looked on this picture than we may express. That fine manly fellow riding along by the side of the wagon, and looking in so pleasantly, is doubtless the lady's husband; we almost envy him. But they are past, and now comes team after team, each drawn by six or eight stout oxen, and such drivers! positively sons of Anak! not one of them less than six feet two in his stockings. Whoo ha! Go it boys! We're in perfect *Oregon fever.* Now comes on a stock of every description; children, niggers, horses, mules, cows, oxen; and there seems to be no end of them. From present evidences, we suppose that not less than two or three thousand people are congregating at this point previous to their start upon the broad prairie, which will be on or about the 10th of May.

SOURCE: *Nile's National Register*, May 21, 1845, quoting the *Missouri Expositor*, May 3, 1845, 203.

Emigrants to Texas, c. 1857

We overtook, several times in the course of each day, the slow emigrant trains, for which this road, though less frequented than years ago, is still a chief thoroughfare. Inexorable destiny it seems that drags or drives on, always Westward, these toil-worn people. Several families were frequently moving together, coming from the same district, or chance met and joined, for company, on the long road from Alabama, Georgia, or the Carolinas. Before you come upon them you hear, ringing through the woods, the fierce cries and blows with which they urge on their jaded cattle. Then the stragglers appear, lean dogs or fainting negroes, ragged and spiritless. An old granny, holding on, by the hand, a weak boy—too old to ride and too young to keep up. An old man, heavily loaded, with a rifle. Then the white covers of the wagons, jerking up and down as they mount over a root or plunge into a rut, disappearing, one after another, where the road descends. Then the active and cheery prime negroes, not yet exhausted, with a joke and a suggestion about tobacco. Then the black pickininnies, staring, in a confused heap, out at the back of the wagon, more and more of their eyes to be made out among the table legs and bedding as you get near; behind them, further in, the old people and young mothers, whose turn it is to ride. As you get by, the white mother and babies, and the tall, frequently ill-humored master, on horseback, or walking with his gun, urging up the black driver and his oxen. As a scout ahead is a brother, or an intelligent slave, with the best gun, on the look-out for a deer or a turkey. We passed in the day perhaps one hundred persons attached to these trains, probably an unusual number; but the immigration this year had been retarded and condensed by the fear of yellow fever, the last case of which, at Natchitoches, had indeed begun only the night before our arrival. Our chances of danger were considered small, however, as the hard frosts had already come. One of these trains was made up of three large wagons, loaded with furniture, babies, and invalids, two or three light wagons, and a gang of twenty able field hands. They travel ten or fifteen miles a day, stopping wherever night overtakes them. The masters are plainly dressed, often in home-spun, keeping their eyes about them, noticing the soil, sometimes making a remark on the crops by the roadside; but, generally, dogged, surly, and silent. The women are silent, too, frequently walking, to relieve the teams, and weary, haggard, mud-bedraggled, forlorn, and disconsolate, yet hopeful and careful. The negroes, mud-incrusted, wrapped in old blankets or gunny-bags, suffering from cold, plod on, aimless, hopeless, thoughtless, more indifferent than the oxen to all about them.

SOURCE: Frederick Law Olmsted, *A Journey through Texas* (New York: Dix, Edwards & Co., 1857), 55–57.

Woman's Profession, 1869

Introduction

The authors of this volume, while they sympathize with every honest effort to relieve the disabilities and sufferings of their sex, are confident that the chief cause of these evils is the fact that the honor and duties of the family state are not duly appreciated, that women are not trained for these duties as men are trained for their trades and professions, and that, as the consequence, family labor is poorly done, poorly paid, and regarded as menial and disgraceful.

To be the nurse of young children, a cook, or a housemaid, is regarded as the lowest and last resort of poverty, and one which no woman of culture and position can assume without loss of caste and respectability.

It is the aim of this volume to elevate both the honor and the remuneration of all the employments that sustain the many difficult and sacred duties of the family state, and thus to render each department of woman's true profession as much desired and respected as are the most honored professions of men.

When the other sex are to be instructed in law, medicine, or divinity, they are favored with numerous institutions richly endowed, with teachers of the highest talents and acquirements, with extensive libraries, and abundant and costly apparatus. With such advantages they devote nearly ten of the best years of life to preparing themselves for their profession; and to secure the public from unqualified members of these professions, none can enter them until examined by a competent body, who certify to their due preparation for their duties.

Woman's profession embraces the care and nursing of the body in the critical periods of infancy and sickness, the training of the human mind in the most impressible period of childhood, the instruction and control of servants, and most of the government and economics of the family state. These duties of woman are as sacred and important as any ordained to man; and yet no such advantages for preparation have been accorded to her, nor is there any qualified body to certify the public that a woman is duly prepared to give proper instruction in her profession. . . .

There is at the present time an increasing agitation of the public mind, evolving many theories and some crude speculations as to woman's rights and duties. That there is a great social and moral power in her keeping, which is now seeking expression by organization, is manifest, and that resulting plans and efforts will involve some mistakes, some collisions, and some failures, all must expect.

SOURCE: Catharine Beecher and Harriet Beecher Stowe, *The American Woman's Home* (New York: J. B. Ford and Co., 1869), 13–14, 16–19.

But to intelligent, reflecting, and benevolent women—whose faith rests on the character and teachings of Jesus Christ—there are great principles revealed by Him, which in the end will secure the grand result which He taught and suffered to achieve. It is hoped that in the following pages these principles will be so exhibited and illustrated as to aid in securing those rights and advantages which Christ's religion aims to provide for all, and especially for the most weak and defenseless of His children.

The Christian Family

It is the aim of this volume to elevate both the honor and the remuneration of all employments that sustain the many difficult and varied duties of the family state, and thus to render each department of woman's profession as much desired and respected as are the most honored professions of men.

What, then, is the end designed by the family state which Jesus Christ came into this world to secure!

It is to provide for the training of our race to the highest possible intelligence, virtue, and happiness, by means of the self-sacrificing labors of the wise and good, and this with chief reference to a future immortal existence.

The distinctive feature of the family is self-sacrificing labor of the stronger and wiser members to raise the weaker and more ignorant to equal advantages. The father undergoes toil and self-denial to provide a home, and then the mother becomes a self-sacrificing laborer to train its inmates. The useless, troublesome infant is served in the humblest offices; while both parents unite in training it to an equality with themselves in every advantage. Soon the older children become helpers to raise the younger to a level with their own. When any are sick, those who are well become self-sacrificing ministers. When the parents are old and useless, the children become their self-sacrificing servants.

Thus the discipline of the family state is one of daily self-devotion of the stronger and wiser to elevate and support the weaker members. Nothing could be more contrary to its first principles than for the older and more capable children to combine to secure to themselves the highest advantages, enforcing the drudgeries on the younger, at the sacrifice of their equal culture. . . .

The family state then, is the aptest earthly illustration of the heavenly kingdom, and in it woman is its chief minister. Her great mission is self-denial, in training its members to self-scacrificing labors for the ignorant and weak: if not her own children, then the neglected children of her Father in heaven. She is to rear all under her care to lay up treasures, not on earth, but in heaven. All the pleasures of this life end here; but those who train immortal minds are to reap the fruit of their labor through eternal ages.

To man is appointed the out-door labor—to till the earth, dig the mines, toil in the foundries, traverse the ocean, transport merchandise, labor in manufactories, construct houses, conduct civil, municipal, and state affairs, and all the heavy work, which, most of the day, excludes him from the comforts of a home. But the great stimulus to all these toils, implanted in the heart of every true man, is the desire for a home of his own, and the hopes of paternity. Every man who truly lives for immortality responds to the beatitude, "Children are a heritage from the Lord: blessed is the man that hath his quiver full of them!" The more a father and mother live under the influence of that "immortality which Christ hath brought to light," the more is the blessedness of rearing a family understood and appreciated. Every child trained aright is to dwell forever in exalted bliss with those that gave it life and trained it for heaven.

CHAPTER 11

Paths to Salvation: Revivalism and Communitarianism

During the first decades of the nineteenth century, a wave of evangelical revivalism began in upstate New York, western New England, and frontier Kentucky and Tennessee. Between 1820 and 1860 this Second Great Awakening swept the nation. Like its mid-eighteenth-century predecessor, the revival was initiated by clergymen concerned with what they perceived to be a climate of moral laxity and religious decline. America, as they viewed it, had paid a price for its rapid growth and expansion: rootlessness, Godlessness, and drunkenness, which too often afflicted both frontier settlements and urban centers. Contributing to these conditions, they believed, were the intellectualism and mechanistic view of the universe spawned by the Englightenment philosophy of the Revolutionary era; what was needed was a return to spiritual values, to faith in God's guiding hand.

In many respects similar in style to the first Great Awakening, the nineteenth-century revival was even less constrained by theological orthodoxy. Its clergy placed *less emphasis on threats of damnation for sin, and more on preaching a message of God's love, which, if freely accepted, offered both a better life on earth and eternal salvation. Appealing to the emotions of their listeners, using words all could understand, revivalist preachers found enthusiastic audiences. The essay that follows, from Bernard A. Weisberger's study of revivalism* They Gathered at the River, *provides a striking picture of frontier religion and reveals a great deal about the leadership, objectives, and consequences of the movement. What attractions did camp meetings like that described by Weisberger have for the thousands of frontier people who attended? Revivalism has been described as a movement blending religion and democracy in its methods and its goals. What evidence can be drawn from Weisberger's essay in support of this view?*

The first document presents a vivid, though unflattering, view of an Indiana camp meeting in 1829, witnessed by an English visitor, Mrs. Frances Trollope, and described in her book Domestic Manners of the Americans. *Why would European travelers in America be attracted to revivalist camp meetings?*

Some Americans in this period believed that the ideal community could be created only by removing themselves from society and building anew. Prominent among several religious communitarian sects were the Shakers. By 1830, they had gathered themselves into over twenty communities throughout the East and Midwest to await what they believed was Christ's imminent return and rule on earth. In anticipation of this event, they forsook private ownership of property and practiced celibacy. The second document provides a view of this sect by a Lowell mill girl who paid two visits to a New York Shaker community. Does your previous reading about Lowell suggest why this young woman found Shaker village life so appealing?

From the 1820s through the 1840s, a number of predominantly secular utopian experiments in communal living were initiated, with the goal of serving as models of nobler, purer ways of life. One of the most famous was the Brook Farm community established in West Roxbury, Massachusetts, under the leadership of George Ripley, a New England Transcendentalist. Among its participants were some of the leading New England intellectuals, including Nathaniel Hawthorne, Margaret Fuller, and Charles A. Dana. The final document is from a letter Hawthorne wrote to his sister Louisa a few weeks after he arrived at Brook Farm in April 1841. How do you account for his enthusiasm for the agrarian, communitarian life? Despite his initial sentiments, six months later, after deciding that he could not be both farmer and writer, he left the community. Other members made similar decisions. In 1847, after six years of existence, the Brook Farm experiment ended. The farm's short life was a fate shared by most other utopian communities. Can you identify examples of communitarian societies in our own day? What led to their establishment, and how successful have they been?

Walking and Leaping and Praising God

Bernard Weisberger

The preachers congregated [on August 6, 1801] at Cane Ridge had never seen anything like it. Some of them guessed that 20,000 people were on hand. One put it as high as 25,000, a fantastic total in view of the fact that in 1800 there were not more than a quarter of a million people in Kentucky, so scattered that Lexington, the state's largest city, had only 1795 residents. But all the figures were somewhat imprecise. One man counted 147 wagons on the ground Saturday morning, and even allowing for horseback riders and those on foot, that would have meant a much smaller meeting.

Whatever the numbers, there was abundant confusion. Technically, the meeting was Presbyterian, but Baptist and Methodist preachers had come to join in, and there was room for them. Even a Boanerges, a "son of thunder," could not reach a mob of such dimensions alone, so several preaching stands were set up. At eleven on Saturday morning two Presbyterian ministers were holding forth in the meetinghouse. One hundred and fifty yards away, another Presbyterian brought the good news of salvation to a crowd around his feet. Off in another direction a Methodist had an audience pressing close to him. Nearby was a knot of Negroes, one of them loudly exhorting the others. Besides the preachers, some of the worshipers, undistracted by the competition, were telling private gatherings of *their* experiences. One account said there were as many as 300 of these laymen "testifying." The ministers were handing out lead tokens to admit people to the communion, with no questions asked about denomination, and on Saturday morning alone 750 were distributed.

The crowds were without form and void. They collected, listened, shouted "Amen!" and "Hallelujah!" and then broke up and drifted away to find friends, or refreshment, or more preaching. The din must have been enormous; the "stricken" were groaning, the preachers shouted, crowds of the unredeemed contributed a number of hecklers, children unquestionably cried, and horses stamped their hoofs and whinnied. There was a sound like the "roar of Niagara." At night, when campfires threw grotesque shadows of trees across the scene, the whole crowd seemed "agitated as if by a storm." It rained and thundered, to make things more spectacularly impressive. Those without tents got drenched, but the work went on.

It was a time to improvise. Exhorters who could not find a preaching stand climbed onto stumps or wagons. The Reverend William Burke, a Methodist, could find no regular spot unoccupied on Sunday morning, but he discovered a fallen tree on which he could stand fifteen feet above the ground. A brother Methodist tied an umbrella to a pole and held it over his head while he spoke. In moments, Burke claimed, ten thousand people were massed before him. . . .

The Methodist preacher William Burke, speaking from beneath his umbrella, said that under the word of God, hundreds fell prostrate on the ground before him, and lay in agonies of distress, with a sinner occasionally jumping to his feet to give vent to "shouts of triumph." These were probably believers. But scoffers, too, were affected. One man, a "blasphemer," sat mounted on a horse, smiling at these unbridled religious passions, when he suddenly reeled and fell from his saddle, where he lay unconscious for thirty hours. When awakened, he could not account for anything that had occurred during his trance. Little children, too, were brought visibly into the kingdom of God, like the seven-year-old girl, sitting on her father's shoulder, who exhorted the crowd for a time and then slumped with weariness. "Poor thing, she had better be put down," a bystander said. The child roused herself and said, "Don't call me poor, for Christ is my brother, God my father, and I have a kingdom to inherit, therefore don't call me poor, for I am rich in the blood of the Lamb."

Some of these stories were tricks of memory, probably, played on men who had been giddy with piety. But strange things were unquestionably happening. James B. Finely was a witness who learned at firsthand of the tremendous, churning emotional pressures of the great meeting. Finley became a Methodist minister later in life, but in 1801 he was an unlikely candidate for godly exercises. Although his father was a Presbyterian minister, the young Finley liked to whirligig at a dance, and he could hold his own in a bare-knuckle fight and take his dram of raw spirits—all these being mortal sins to frontier churchmen. He had been twenty in 1800, bred up for a doctor by his father, but seduced from his Latin, Greek and mathematics by a passionate love of hunting in the wilderness, then alive with game. Now he was living in a bark-covered cabin in southwestern Ohio, on a tract which he had grubbed clear with his ax and planted in Indian corn. Except for a slight advantage in education, he was a typical young man of the frontier.

He went to Cane Ridge out of curiosity, determined that this wild-eyed religion should not move him. His father was a Princeton graduate, and he himself had book learning and a stout constitution—enough, surely, to allow him to resist any mere "nervous excitability." Yet as he watched the meeting he suddenly became aware that his heart was thundering. His knees became jellylike, and, sitting down on a log, he looked on wide-eyed as five hundred people collapsed with "shrieks and shouts that rent the very heavens" under the spell of an exhorter. Finley scrambled to his feet and rushed back into the woods, with a feeling of suffocation. He found a log hut where liquors were kept, and at this "tavern" he had a nerve-stiffening shot of brandy. So fortified, he went back to the meeting and wandered from crowd to crowd, but it seemed that his mind insisted on raking up every sin he had ever committed, until he felt that he would die if he did not get relief. After a night spent sleeping in a haystack with his guilt for company, he started back home, and burst into an irrational fit of crying on the way. The next day at evening he crept into the woods to pray, but when his knees touched the ground, he gave a shout and fell prostrate. Neighbors found him and put him to bed. When he awoke, he had a sudden feeling of release, and he went on home, uncontrollably laughing, weeping and shouting most of the way. That was how the Kentucky revival worked on one man who was neither a mystic nor a zealot.

Under such compulsions, the neuromuscular system suddenly chose to render its own testimony. At Cane Ridge and elsewhere in the frontier world, during these years, men and women were suddenly swept up in various "exercises" which reflected, to the backwoods mind, especially bountiful gifts of the Holy Spirit.

There was, for one thing, catalepsy, as in the case of Rachel Martin. She was a Kentucky girl who was smitten with a sense of her lost estate and lay for nine days, neither moving, nor uttering speech, nor taking food, until she obtained blessed assurance.

Then, most spectacularly, there were the "jerks," a spasmodic twitching of the entire body of the transported penitent. Richard McNemar said that the victim bounced about like a ball, or hopped from place to place with head, limbs and trunk shaking "as if they must . . . fly asunder." Sometimes the movement would be so quick that the kerchiefs on women's heads would be snapped off. Peter Cartwright, an Illinois Methodist parson, said that even the hairpins flew out, but Cartwright was not above the frontier trick of embroidering a story. . . .

Many stories of unusual transports of holy joy and anguish were undoubtedly stretched. Some came from supporters of the revivals, accepting all that they heard in the firm belief that "with God nothing shall be impossible." Others were planted by opponents, who were trying to underscore the element of caricature in the meetings. But there was good evidence that the spirit often overcame the believers in one way or another. The Reverend Archibald Alexander, in a dignified Connecticut church publication, said that "falling down" created a problem at first during the Cane Ridge affair, but later on grew so familiar that it disturbed nobody. A Kentucky gentleman wrote to his brother in Virginia that he had seen a meeting where hundreds lay prostrate on the ground, and no mere uneducated riffraff or hysterical children, either, but "the learned pastor, the steady patriot, and the obedient son . . . the honorable matron and the virtuous maiden crying, Jesus, thou son of the most high God, have mercy on us."

Claims were made that not all of the ecstasy was spiritual. A conservative Presbyterian minister noted rancorously in his diary of Cane Ridge, "Becca Bell—who often fell, is now big with child to a wicked trifling school master of the name of Brown. . . . Raglin's daughter seems careless. . . . Kitty Cummings got careless. . . . Polly Moffitt was with child to Petty and died miserably in child bed." Finley, too, remembered later that men "furious with the effects of the maddening bowl" would outrage all decency by their conduct. There was plenty of the wherewithal to fill the bowl, too. Some men brought their own supplies, and some of "Satan's emissaries," with a shrewd sense of business, set up barrels as close as they could get to the meeting and went into business. There were enemies of the camp meetings who were quick to sneer that "more souls were begot than saved" as the intoxication of the gatherings whirled away restraint after restraint.

There was, however, no way to prove that the emotional exhilaration of camp-meeting religion was the undoing of frontier virgins. The crowds were composed both of worshippers and of numbers of families who came merely to enjoy the show. When several hundred lonely men and women were brought together for three or four days in an informal outdoor setting, nature took its course among the awakened and the unredeemed alike. As time went on, the meetings were organized and policed, so that temptations were reduced and suspicious characters discouraged away. Once the novelty wore off, the gatherings were dominated beyond challenge by the God-fearing.

It was just as difficult to support the claim that the revival alone elevated the frontier's moral tone. The sins which McGready, Stone, McNemar and the others scourged were mostly personal and sumptuary—gambling, drinking, horse racing, cockfighting, swearing and dueling. As churches grew in number, the practice of these arts declined. But as churches multiplied, so did schoolhouses, courts of law, newspapers and other tranquilizing agencies. All played a part in sanding the ragged edges off the backwoods character.

With or without dancing, laughing, singing, rolling, barking and jerking, revivalism rolled over Kentucky, Tennessee and southern Ohio between 1800 and 1804, and thence spread elsewhere. At Waxhaws, in South Carolina, in 1801, there was a monster meeting with three thousand souls and twenty ministers looking up to the Southern skies for grace. . . .

So the great revival rolled its turbulent way across the frontier world, a crude triangle of rugged territory and hard-working people, its base running from western New England to Georgia, its apex thrust deep into the valley of the Ohio and its tributaries.

The revival should have brought unanimous rejoicing in the religious world. The "unchurched" Western territory, the cause of so much despair and so many missionary societies, now seemed to be ablaze with piety. Thousands were listening eagerly to the gospel and crowding to enroll themselves among the saved. It was easy to thank the Lord enthusiastically for such undeserved, but welcome, mercies.

Yet from the very start there was another side to revivalism. It brought important innovations with it—fiery preaching, and meetings that lasted for whole days and nights together, and tumultuous emotional outbursts by the congregation. These could be dangerous. The revival was a medicine for ailing frontier denominations, starved for support. Yet like most frontier remedies, it was "heroic." It could kill as well as cure, and at the very least it was liable to rack the patient with spasms, purges and sweats. In a church, these symptoms took the form of schisms. They were not long in showing up after the Kentucky revival. By 1809, the Presbyterian Church in the West had split asunder, not once, but twice.

The Presbyterians were vulnerable, because there were, at this time, two Presbyterian worlds. The Presbyterianism of New England and the mid-Atlantic states was the child of seventeenth-century Puritanism. It was intellectually majestic, training its ministers, mainly at Princeton and Yale, to deliver sermons heavily weighted with learning in ancient and modern tongues. Its congregations were drawn from the successful classes of the countryside and supporting towns.

But as one moved southward and westward, one found Presbyterian flocks gathered mostly from the Scotch-Irish who were taming the frontier. Their pastors were educated usually at backwoods "log colleges." The learning of these men was far from contemptible, but their congregations were less contented with the dry bones of theology, hungrier to be stirred up in their worship. These differences were a mirror of a gap dividing two Americas—a settled and orderly one, facing the Atlantic, and another across the Appalachians which was crude, restless and more than a little violent. The two were constantly blending and acting upon each other.

The revival, however, was a wedge driven sharply between the two Presbyterian universes. Suddenly, contrasts between them stood out in unmistakable relief. There was, for one thing, the matter of homiletic technique—the question of how to preach. The established method in the East was to choose a text, deduce a doctrine from it, and lead the doctrine through an hour or two of "application," honeycombed with theological pits and snares. But the revivalists believed that the word of God should be "quick and powerful"—in Saint Paul's language, "sharper than any two edged-sword, piercing even to the dividing asunder of the soul and the spirit, and of the joints and marrow." To camp-meeting apostles, an "intellectual" sermon left "the heart without interest and the conscience without alarm."

And that was the battle—between preaching aimed at the head and at the "joints and marrow." The revivalist thought that his whole duty was to convulse the conscience. He sharpened the message of man's guilt to a point, by repetition, and drove it into the sinner's heart. The prophets of the Kentucky awakening believed in "experimental" religion. Today, the word would be "experiential" or "experienced," but the point was that the sinner had to *feel* in his very bones the smoldering of guilt, abasement, hope and assurance.

Conservative Presbyterians did not see it that way. "I would not give this old handkerchief for all the experimental religion in the world," one of them said. Others distrusted the acrobatics of the jerks. Satan, too, could make men and women dance a frenzied jig. There were ministers who were wary of "protracted meetings, night meetings . . . weeping in the pulpit . . . singing hymns, all noise—shouting, groaning, or crying out for mercy." Some of them, trained in medicine, outraged revivalists by treating fallen "mourners" like victims of a fit, instead of rejoicing over the imminent conversion. It rankled a preacher like Stone or McGready, after he had exhorted a man halfway to salvation, to see someone else hold a bottle of camphor under his nose and open one of his veins. Between the believers in "experimental religion" and their conservative brethren a gap began to widen.

The breach gaped even more when the two groups read the Westminster Confession, which governed the Presbyterian Church. At that time, the confession held closely to the Calvinistic doctrine of election, which stated that God had chosen only a small part of mankind to be saved and had determined beforehand who these "saints" would be. Those elected were "predestined"—certain to go to heaven. All others were just as certainly doomed. Nothing—no effort of will or agony of repentance—could change the awful decree.

A belief like that was a millstone around a revivalist's neck. To be aroused, sinners in his audience simply *had* to feel that there was more hope for them than predestination allowed, *some* reasonable chance that salvation was available. Bit by bit, revival-minded Presbyterians drifted from the "pessimism" of ultraorthodoxy. Frontiersmen, who often took land without asking and lifted their caps to nobody, were apt to lose interest altogether in a heaven whose gates were barred to all except a small aristocracy of "saints." By 1803, Stone and McNemar were concerned lest the narrow view of election should be "the means of strengthening sinners in their unbelief." Eventually, they feared, even preachers might stop worrying about that tiny and unknowable chance of conversion, and take their comfort in the empty outward observances of religion. And that would be an end of the evangelical spirit.

From here it was an easy step to the devaluation of a learned ministry. Better a humble, but converted, pastor than one who was brilliant but not saved. What was the point, anyway, of scholarly sermons to explain the ways of righteousness? A converted heart did what was right instinctively, by reflex. After all, the apostles had known less of the law than the scribes and Pharisees.

The seeds of separation were planted, then. A new group was emerging in the West. They had come to believe that a guilty sinner might well roar, faint, leap and twitch, as he struggled toward the light. They also believed that election might be more freely accessible than the confession allowed— that the kingdom of heaven was really democratic, as frontiersmen had a right to expect.

It was not long before the harvest of controversy was gathered in. The Presbyterian Church operated under a federal organization, so that its internal conflicts had a tendency to show up along geographical lines. Congregations were grouped together under presbyteries, which were governing bodies composed of laymen and ministers. The presbyteries were linked in regional associations, with ruling boards known as synods. Periodically, the synods met in a general assembly of the entire church. In 1801, the Kentucky Synod set up a new presbytery in southwestern Kentucky, where McGready's fires were burning. This Cumberland Presbytery promptly used its authority to ordain a number of new preachers who were something unusual in Presbyterian ministerial circles. They had no seminary training and were established men, with farms and families, who had taught themselves to "exhort." They were all ardent revivalists. Conservatives in the synod branded them as "illiterate," and began a long, bitter battle to dissolve the new presbytery. Finally, in 1809 the general assembly, which was the Presbyterian Congress and Supreme Court, agreed to doom the new body. Thereupon, the Cumberland men seceded and organized separately as the Cumberland Presbyterian Church. It remained a separate church until 1906.

Meanwhile, the Kentucky Synod turned its attention to the north, and began to prepare charges of heresy against Stone, McNemar and three other revivalists. The "heretics" did not wait for trial. They withdrew and organized an independent Springfield Presbytery. Popularly named "New Lights," they soon controlled more than fifteen congregations. By 1804, however, the New Lights were moving too fast even for nominal Presbyterianism. They dissolved their organization and proclaimed a new church, carrying the simple name of "Christian." Its only creed was to be the Bible. Congregations would choose their own ministers and support them by voluntary offerings. Those ministers were to be selected only on the basis of their "soundness in the faith, acquaintance with experimental religion, gravity and aptness to teach," and their sermons were to avoid "philosophy, vain deceit," and "traditions of men." In short, they were to be a band of revivalistic brothers.

Even then, some of the New Lights could find no resting place for the soles of their feet. In 1805, McNemar and some of his associates went over to the Shakers, a small sect whose members lived in little communistic commonwealths, where they practiced celibacy and worshipped the Lord with vigorous bodily exercises which gave them their name. Stone, meanwhile, remained in the Christian Church, which was fortified by union with certain dissenting Methodists and Baptists. In time, he became interested in the teachings of the Campbellites, or Disciples of Christ, another small, Bible-centered body founded in the West. In 1832 he led some of his fellow Christians over to a union with the followers of Thomas and Alexander Campbell, and became, at last, a patriarch among the Disciples.

McGready himself was not a seceder. In 1809 he came before the Transylvania Presbytery to make "due submission to the discipline of our church in every point of view." . . .

At any rate, by 1809 the fight was in the open and the problem was clear, if not easy. Revivalism was a blessing in the number and vigor of its converts. Yet its ecstasies and its short-circuiting of doctrine could lead whole congregations into the quicksands of heresy. Was there some way to save the energy of revivalism and yet purge away its grossness and discipline its results? Conservative evangelical ministers throughout the country would long grapple with this question.

In the interim of hesitation the revival would not cool down. An agency was busily at work institutionalizing it and spreading it over the entire West—an agency so perfectly fitted to that job that it might have been designed for the purpose. Its name was the Methodist Episcopal Church.

Presbyterianism had trouble containing the passions of the revival. Methodism was made for it. Methodist theology was more hospitable to its central ideas. The social classes from whom early Methodism recruited were less rattled by its turbulence. The Methodist plan of organization was ideally suited for making the church a transmission belt of religious values in the West.

The strict Calvinism of the Presbyterian and Congregational churches in that day was a tightly closed system. The elect were foreordained from eternity. The unregenerate could not change their fate. Even their attempts to repent were not signs of holiness, but arose out of mere selfish fear. On the other hand, the elect could not resist salvation, and once touched with grace, they could not backslide. In ministerial shorthand, "predestination, unconditional election, irresistibility, and perseverance" were formidable walls, sheltering the small community of "saints."

The Methodists, in clear contrast, believed in a modified kind of Arminianism, a doctrine taking its name from Jacobus Arminius, a seventeenth-century Dutch theologian. In their view, God would save "those whom He foresaw would persevere to the end," and damn "those who should continue in their unbelief." So election and reprobation were, in a measure, *conditional*, dependent partly on the behavior of the sinner. In addition, the death of Christ made atonement for the whole human race, but only those who believed in Him could enjoy its benefits. Redeeming grace could "be resisted and rendered ineffectual by perverse *will* of the impenitent sinner," and, once regenerated, even saints might relapse and "die in their sins."

Thus fortified with "conditional election" and "free will," the Methodists had a head start in adopting the revival tradition. Salvation was *potentially* available to all. The sincere penitent might expect that the help of the Holy Spirit would not be denied to him. The miscreant who grew old in his sins might be passing up a genuine chance at heaven, not merely a speculative and unlikely one. On this basis it made sense to exhort the crowd to repent, to believe, to wriggle free of the suction of hell.

Besides this, a doctrine which allowed an individual some say in his (or her) eternal destiny harmonized better with democratic theory, and Methodism was thus several steps ahead in the race for converts in the new and professedly equalitarian America. As it happened, Methodists worked mostly among the pushing lower classes neglected by the successful colonial churches. They were a new church in 1800, only thirty-five years old in America, in need of converts, and quite willing to "make Methodists of the raw materials which the frontier presented."

Nor did Methodists fear "enthusiasts." They were fighting in England and America against what they considered heartless and cold formality, and they recruited among the lowly, where the belief in supernatural doings reigned, uncorrupted by the educated rationalism of the Enlightenment. . . .

But the Methodists had something more than democracy and enthusiasm on their side. Western Baptists, too, were down-to-earth in their membership, to name only one example. The Methodists had an extra advantage in a unique scheme of organization both flexible and autocratic. They had few seminaries and widely scattered flocks, so they recruited untrained preachers and kept them on the move. Individual Methodist congregations, called "classes," were linked into "circuits," which embraced a number of classes close enough together to be reached by a man on horseback in a circular tour of two or three months. Circuits were gathered into "districts," and districts into regional "conferences," which were represented in a general conference of the entire church every four years.

The wheel horse of the system was the traveling minister, or circuit rider. A class member with some speaking talent could be licensed as an "exhorter," to try his abilities on friends and neighbors. He could then advance to become a circuit rider. Eventually, he might rise to be a district superintendent, or "presiding elder." At the general conferences, the presiding elders elected bishops from among themselves from time to time, though not many—only twelve in the first fifty years of the church in America.

The circuit riders were a superbly mobile force, ready to go anywhere, at any time, where sinners were in need of the saving word. No settlement was too rundown or too remote for them. They roughed it along the trails in snow and rain, taking their chances on bears, wolves, cutthroats and Indians. They put up where they could find local hospitality, which usually meant corn bread and pork and a spot for sleeping on the dirt floor by the fire. They spent a good part of their lives hungry, wet, cold, verminous and saddlesore, and if they did not die young of consumption, they could expect an old age of rheumatism and dyspepsia. . . .

Yet the "Methodist preachers" were part of a well-disciplined force. The circuit riders were chosen by the presiding elders, and new presiding elders were made by the bishops. Approval came from the top down. Besides this, elders continually visited their subordinate circuits, and bishops wore themselves into exhaustion by constant rounds of inspection covering whole conferences. The traveling was miserable, and the pay, for a long time, sixty-four dollars a year. The reward, however, was not only a harvest of souls for the Lord, but a solid church. Circuit riders could not strike off into schismatic paths, carrying faithful congregations after them. Bishops and elders were always appearing to test classes for doctrinal soundness. In addition, the circuit riders themselves were shifted to a new circuit every year or two by the inflexible command of the *Discipline*, the Methodist rulebook. So in spite of the fact that frontier Methodist ministers were completely on their own for months at a time, the church had a remarkable unity. Until the trouble over slavery broke it apart in 1844, it suffered only two extremely minor secessions, both of them over questions of organization.

The American Wesleyans, therefore, had nothing to fear from the heat and fury of the revival. It worked on their side, as the sinners of the clearings, roused from their indifference, were collected wholesale into Methodist classes by the tireless circuit riders. The Methodists had grown from 15,000 souls in 1785 to 850,000 by 1840, in good part because of their identification with the revivalist viewpoint. The contribution was not all one-sided, however. From bishops to exhorters, the Methodists, in turn, were wide-ranging salesmen of the revival point of view, and they froze into revivalism itself a number of practices which lingered long after the last circuit rider had hung up his saddlebags. Things that were novelties in 1800 came to be at home in American religious life when the evangelists of circuit, district and conference were through with them.

For one thing, they brought the supernatural world close. It was easy for them, countrymen as they were. Frontier boys grew up believing that Satan was as real as General Washington, and hell as palpable as Pittsburgh. Dreams had meaning, and the activities of beasts were oracles to the knowing. Birth, love and death were assisted or held back by incan-

214

tations. When a boy raised in this way became a preacher, it was not hard to reconcile his folk inheritance and his Christianity. . . .

. . . Revivalists would talk easily of Jesus, leaning over the battlements of heaven to see how individual sinners reacted to sermons. Or they would dramatize conversations between the Devil and backsliders, or dying children and choirs of angels. When they did so, they were awakening old ghosts. Long after popular education had limited the role of superstition, they played on half-conscious memories of a time when circuit riders taught that God and His hosts were very near.

Another thing the mounted Methodist clergymen did to perfection was to raise the emotional content of preaching to excruciating levels. For them, the "new birth" had pangs which cut to the bone, and they meant for their listeners to share the intensity. . . . They spread the spirit of the Kentucky awakenings across an entire section of the country. In time to come, the revival as a kind of theatrical excitement in religious dress would rest on foundations which they helped to set in place.

Above all, the Methodist itinerants liked plain talk. Their sermons were short and pungent, aimed at holding crowds which were quick to show scorn or boredom. Proudly, the circuit riders boasted that they read nothing but the Bible, the hymnbook and the *Discipline.* . . .

The legacies of the circuit riders endured long after the spread of settlement and education made their calling obsolete. They had spread the potent, pervasive, democratic and irresistible Arminian theology up and down the West, and it was to be the hallmark of revival preaching ever after. Because their lack of education made them laymen in all but name, they had proved by their work that laymen could be the backbone of evangelism, and the revivalists who came after them were for the most part innocent of formal theological training, though they might acquire degrees of divinity in the course of their labors.

They created an atmosphere of intensity and zeal which lingered after them, and they gave respectability, of a sort, to plain, ungrammatical and almost chatty talk about eternal concerns. They turned Jesus, the hosts of heaven and the powers of hell into villains and heroes as recognizable as Indians and claim-jumpers. The revival of the nineteenth century finally came to be a series of mass meetings addressed in plain language with emotional zest by a man untutored in technical divinity. Such meetings first took place on the frontier under the revivalistic Presbyterians; such meetings were riveted into American experience by the traveling Methodists. . . .

DOCUMENTS

A Camp Meeting, 1829

It was in the course of this summer that I found the opportunity I had long wished for, of attending a camp-meeting, and I gladly accepted the invitation of an English lady and gentleman to accompany them in their carriage to the spot where it is held; this was in a wild district on the confines of Indiana.

The prospect of passing a night in the back woods of Indiana was by no means agreeable, but I screwed my courage to the proper pitch, and set forth determined to see with my own eyes, and hear with my own ears, what a camp-meeting really was. I had heard it said that being at a camp-meeting was like standing at the gate of heaven, and seeing it opening before you; I had heard it said, that being at a camp-meeting was like finding yourself within the gates of hell; in either case there must be something to gratify curiosity, and compensate one for the fatigue of a long rumbling ride and a sleepless night.

We reached the ground about an hour before midnight, and the approach to it was highly picturesque. The spot chosen was the verge of an unbroken forest, where a space of about twenty acres appeared to have been partially cleared for the purpose. Tents of different sizes were pitched very near together in a circle round the cleared space; behind them were ranged an exterior circle of carriages of every description, and at the back of each were fastened the horses which had drawn them thither. Through this triple circle of defence we distinguished numerous fires burning brightly within it; and still more numerous lights flickering from the trees that were left in the enclosure. The moon was in meridian splendour above our heads. . . .

When we arrived, the preachers were silent; but we heard issuing from nearly every tent mingled sounds of praying, preaching, singing, and lamentation. . . .

We made the circuit of the tents, pausing where attention was particularly excited by sounds more vehement than ordinary. We contrived to look into many; all were strewed with straw, and the distorted figures that we saw kneeling, sitting, and lying amongst it, joined to the woeful and convulsive cries, gave to each, the air of a cell in Bedlam [Bethlehem Hospital, an insane asylum in London]. . . .

At midnight a horn sounded through the camp, which, we were told, was to call the people from private to public worship; and we presently

SOURCE: Frances Trollope, *Domestic Manners of Americans* (London: Whittaker, Treacher & Co., 1832), 229–41.

saw them flocking from all sides to the front of the preachers' stand. Mrs. B. and I contrived to place ourselves with our backs supported against the lower part of this structure, and we were thus enabled to witness the scene which followed without personal danger. There were about two thousand persons assembled.

One of the preachers began in a low nasal tone, and, like all other Methodist preachers, assured us of the enormous depravity of man as he comes from the hands of his Maker, and of his perfect sanctification after he had wrestled sufficiently with the Lord to get hold of him, *et caetera.* The admiration of the crowd was evinced by almost constant cries of "Amen! Amen!" "Jesus! Jesus!" "Glory! Glory!" and the like. But this comparative tranquility did not last long: the preacher told them that "this night was the time fixed upon for anxious sinners to wrestle with the Lord;" that he and his brethren "were at hand to help them," and that such as needed their help were to come forward into "the pen." . . . "The pen" was the space immediately below the preachers' stand; we were therefore placed on the edge of it, and were enabled to see and hear all that took place in the very centre of this extraordinary exhibition.

The crowd fell back at the mention of the *pen*, and for some minutes there was a vacant space before us. The preachers came down from their stand and placed themselves in the midst of it, beginning to sing a hymn, calling upon the penitents to come forth. As they sung they kept turning themselves round to every part of the crowd, and, by degrees, the voices of the whole multitude joined in chorus. This was the only moment at which I perceived any thing like the solemn and beautiful effect, which I had heard ascribed to this woodland worship. It is certain that the combined voices of such a multitude, heard at dead of night, from the depths of their eternal forests, the many fair young faces turned upward, and looking paler and lovelier as they met the moon-beams, the dark figures of the officials in the middle of the circle, the lurid glare thrown by the altar-fires on the woods beyond, did altogether produce a fine and solemn effect, that I shall not easily forget; but ere I had well enjoyed it, the scene changed, and sublimity gave place to horror and disgust. . . .

. . . Above a hundred persons, nearly all females, came forward, uttering howlings and groans, so terrible that I shall never cease to shudder when I recall them. They appeared to drag each other forward, and on the word being given, "let us pray," they all fell on their knees; but this posture was soon changed for others that permitted greater scope for the convulsive movements of their limbs; and they were soon all lying on the ground in an indescribable confusion of heads and legs. They threw about their limbs with such incessant and violent motion, that I was every instant expecting some serious accident to occur.

But how am I to describe the sounds that proceeded from this strange mass of human beings? I know no words which can convey an idea of it.

217

Hysterical sobbings, convulsive groans, shrieks and screams the most appalling, burst forth on all sides. I felt sick with horror. As if their hoarse and overstrained voices failed to make noise enough, they soon began to clap their hands violently. . . .

One woman near us continued to "call on the Lord," as it is termed, in the loudest possible tone, and without a moment's interval, for the two hours that we kept our dreadful station. She became frightfully hoarse, and her face so red as to make me expect she would burst a blood-vessel. Among the rest of her rant, she said, "I will hold fast to Jesus, I never will let him go; if they take me to hell, I will still hold him fast, fast, fast!" . . .

Visiting the Shakers, c. 1841

Sometime in the summer of 18—, I paid a visit to one of the Shaker villages in the State of New York. Previously to this, many times and oft had I (when tired of the noise and contention of the world, its erroneous opinions, and its wrong practices) longed for some retreat, where, with a few chosen friends, I could enjoy the present, forget the past, and be free from all anxiety respecting any future portion of time. And often had I pictured, in imagination, a state of happy society, where one common interest prevailed—where kindness and brotherly love were manifested in all of the every-day affairs of life—where liberty and equality would live, not in name, but in very deed—where idleness in no shape whatever would be tolerated—and where vice of every description would be banished, and neatness, with order, would be manifested in all things.

Actually to witness such a state of society, was a happiness which I never expected. I thought it to be only a thing among the airy castles which it has ever been my delight to build. But with this unostentatious and truly kind-hearted people, the Shakers, I found it; and the reality, in beauty and harmony, exceeded even the picturings of imagination.

No unprejudiced mind could, for a single moment, resist the conviction that this singular people, with regard to their worldly possessions, lived in strict conformity to the teachings of Jesus of Nazareth. There were men in this society who had added to the common stock thousands and tens of thousands of dollars; they nevertheless labored, dressed, and esteemed themselves as no better and fared in all respects, like those who had never owned, neither added to the society, any worldly goods whatever. The cheerfulness with which they bore one another's burdens, made even the

SOURCE: "Visit to the Shakers," *Lowell Offering* (1841): 279–81, and "A Second Visit to the Shakers," *Lowell Offering* (1841): 337–40.

temporal calamities, so unavoidable among the inhabitants of the earth, to be felt but lightly. . . .

In whatever light it may appear to others, to me it appears beautiful indeed, to see a just and an impartial equality reign, so that the rich and the poor may share an equal privilege, and have all their wants supplied. That the Shakers are in reality what they profess to be, I doubt not. Neither do I doubt that many, very many lessons of wisdom might be learned of them, by those who profess to be wiser. And to all who wish to know if "any good thing can come out of Nazareth," I would say, you had better "go and see."

I was so well pleased with the appearances of the Shakers, and the prospect of quietness and happiness among them, that I visited them a second time. I went with a determination to ascertain as much as I possibly could of their forms and customs of worship, the every-day duties devolving on the members, &c.; and having enjoyed excellent opportunities for acquiring the desired information, I wish to present a brief account of what "I verily do know" in relation to several particulars.

First of all, justice will not permit me to retract a word in relation to the industry, neatness, order, and general good behavior, in the Shaker settlement which I visited. In these respects, that singular people are worthy of all commendation—yea, they set an example for the imitation of Christians every-where. Justice requires me to say, also, that their hospitality is proverbial, and deservedly so. They received and entertained me kindly, and (hoping perhaps that I might be induced to join them) they extended extra-civilities to me. I have occasion to modify the expression of my gratitude in only one particular—and that is, one of the female elders made statements to me concerning the requisite confessions to be made, and the forms of admission to their society, which statements she afterwards denied, under circumstances that rendered her denial a most aggravated insult. Declining farther notice of this matter, because of the indelicacy of the confessions alluded to, I pass to notice,

1st. The domestic arrangements of the Shakers. However strange the remark may seem, it is nevertheless true, that our factory population work fewer hours out of every twenty-four, than are required by the Shakers, whose bell to call them from their slumbers, and also to warn them that it is time to commence the labors of the day, rings much earlier than our factory bells; and its calls were obeyed, in the family where I was entertained, with more punctuality than I ever knew the greatest "workey" among my numerous acquaintances (during the fourteen years in which I have been employed in different manufacturing establishments) to obey the calls of the factory-bell. And not until nine o'clock in the evening were the labors of the day closed, and the people assembled at their religious meetings.

Whoever joins the Shakers with the expectation of relaxation from toil, will be greatly mistaken, since they deem it an indispensable duty to have every moment of time profitably employed. The little portions of leisure which the females have, are spent in knitting—each one having a basket of knitting-work for a constant companion.

Their habits of order are, in many things, carried to the extreme. The first bell for their meals rings for all to repair to their chambers, from which, at the ringing of the second bell, they descend to the eating-room. Here, all take their appropriate places at the tables, and after locking their hands on their breasts, they drop on their knees, close their eyes, and remain in this position about two minutes. Then they rise, seat themselves, and with all expedition swallow their food; then rise on their feet, again lock their hands, drop on their knees, close their eyes, and in about two minutes rise and retire. Their meals are taken in silence, conversation being prohibited.

Those whose chambers are in the fourth story of one building, and whose work-shops are in the third story of another building, have a daily task in climbing stairs, which is more oppressive than any of the rules of a manufacturing establishment.

2d. With all deference, I beg leave to introduce some of the religious views and ceremonies of the Shakers.

From the conversation of the elders, I learned that they considered it doing God service, to sever the sacred ties of husband and wife, parent and child—the relationship existing between them being contrary to their religious views—views which they believe were revealed from heaven to "Mother Ann Lee," the founder of their sect, and through whom they profess to have frequent revelations from the spiritual world. These communications, they say, are often written on gold leaves, and sent down from heaven to instruct the poor, simple Shakers in some new duty. They are copied, and perused, and preserved with great care. I one day heard quite a number of them read from a book, in which they were recorded, and the names of several of the brethren and sisters to whom they were given by the angels, were told me. One written on a gold leaf, was (as I was told) presented to Proctor Sampson by an angel, so late as the summer of 1841. These "revelations" are written partly in English, and partly in some unintelligible jargon, or unknown tongue, having a spiritual meaning, which cannot be understood only by those who possess the spirit in an eminent degree. They consist principally of songs, which they sing at their devotional meetings, and which are accompanied with dancing, and many unbecoming gestures and noises.

Often in the midst of a religious march, all stop, and with all their might set to stamping with both feet. And it is no uncommon thing for many of the worshipping assembly to crow like a parcel of young chanticleers, while others imitate the barking of dogs; and many of the young

(margin, handwritten) Celibacy

women set to whirling round and round—while the old men shake and clap their hands; the whole making a scene of noise and confusion, which can be better imagined than described. The elders seriously told me that these things were the outward manifestations of the spirit of God.

Apart from their religious meetings, the Shakers have what they call "union meetings." These are for social converse, and for the purpose of making the people acquainted with each other. During the day, the elders tell who may visit such and such chambers. A few minutes past nine, work is laid aside; the females change, or adjust, as best suits their fancy, their caps, handkerchiefs, and pinners, with a precision which indicates that they are not *altogether* free from vanity. The chairs, perhaps to the number of a dozen, are set in two rows, in such a manner that those who occupy them may face each other. At the ringing of a bell, each one goes to the chamber where either he or she has been directed by the elders, or remains at home to receive company, as the case may be. They enter the chambers *sans ceremonie*, and seat themselves—the men occupying one row of chairs, the women the other. Here, with their clean, checked, home-made pocket-handkerchiefs spread in their laps, and their spitboxes standing in a row between them, they converse about raising sheep and kine, herbs and vegetables, building wall and raising corn, heating the oven and pearing apples, killing rats and gathering nuts, spinning tow and weaving sieves, making preserves and mending the brethren's clothes—in short, every thing they do will afford some little conversation. But beyond their own little world, they do not appear to extend scarcely a thought. And why should they? Having so few sources of information, they know not what is passing beyond them. They however make the most of their own affairs, and seem to regret that they can converse no longer, when, after sitting together from half to three-quarters of an hour, the bell warns them that it is time to separate, which they do by rising up, locking their hands across their breasts, and bowing. Each one then goes silently to his own chamber.

It will readily be perceived, that they have no access to libraries, no books, excepting school-books, and a few relating to their own particular views; no periodicals, and attend no lectures, debates, Lyceums, &c. They have none of the many privileges of manufacturing districts—consequently their information is so very limited, that their conversation is, as a thing in course, quite insipid. The manner of their life seems to be a check to the march of mind and a desire for improvement; and while the moral and perceptive faculties are tolerably developed, the intellectual, with a very few exceptions, seem to be below the average.

Secular utopian communal experiment

A Letter from Brook Farm, 1841

As the weather precludes all possibility of ploughing, hoeing, sowing and other such operations, I bethink me that you may have no objection to hear something of my whereabout and whatabout. You are to know then, that I took up my abode here on the 12th ultimo, in the midst of a snow-storm, which kept us all idle for a day or two. At the first glimpse of fair weather, Mr. Ripley summoned us into the cowyard and introduced me to an instrument with four prongs, commonly called a dung-fork. With this tool, I have already assisted to load twenty or thirty carts of manure, and shall take part in loading nearly three hundred more. Besides, I have planted potatoes and peas, cut straw and hay for the cattle, and done various other mighty works. This very morning, I milked three cows; and I milk two or three every night and morning. The weather has been so unfavorable, that we have worked comparatively little in the fields; but, nevertheless, I have gained strength wonderfully—grown quite a giant, in fact—and can do a day's work without the slightest inconvenience. In short, I am transformed into a complete farmer.

This is one of the most beautiful places I ever saw in my life, and as secluded as if it were a hundred miles from any city or village. There are woods, in which we can ramble all day, without meeting anybody, or scarcely seeing a house. Our house stands apart from the main road; so that we are not troubled even with passengers looking at us. Once in a while, we have a transcendental visitor, such as Mr. [Bronson] Alcott; but, generally, we pass whole days without seeing a single face, save those of the brethren. At this present time, our effective force consists of Mr. Ripley, Mr. Farley (a farmer from the far west) Rev. Warren Burton (author of various celebrated works), three young men and boys, who are under Mr. Ripley's care, and William Allen, his hired man, who has the chief direction of our agricultural labors. In the female part of the establishment there is Mrs. Ripley and two women folks. The whole fraternity eat together; and such a delectable way of life has never been seen on earth, since the days of the early Christians. We get up at half-past four, breakfast at half-past six, dine at half-past twelve, and go to bed at nine.

The thin frock, which you made for me, is considered a most splendid article; and I should not wonder if it were to become the summer uniform of the community. I have a thick frock, likewise; but it is rather deficient in grace, though extremely warm and comfortable. I wear a tremendous pair of cow-hide boots, with soles two inches thick. Of course, when I come to see you, I shall wear my farmer's dress.

SOURCE: Nathaniel Hawthorne to Louisa Hawthorne, cited by Richard B. Morris and James Woodress, eds., *Voices from America's Past* (New York: E. P. Dutton & Co., 1961, 1962, 1963), 2: 46–47.

We shall be very much occupied during most of this month, ploughing and planting; so that I doubt whether you will see me for two or three weeks. You have the portrait by this time, I suppose; so you can very well dispense with the original. When you write to me (which I beg you will do soon) direct your letter to West Roxbury, as there are two post offices in the town. I would write more; but William Allen is going to the village, and must have this letter; so good-bye.

NATH HAWTHORNE
PLOUGHMAN

CHAPTER 12

New People in a New Land

RIOT IN PHILADELPHIA
JULY 7ᵗʰ 1844.

Central to the story of America's growth from the seventeenth century forward was the influx of people from abroad. In the 1830s, 1840s, and 1850s this immigration reached massive proportions: over 4.5 million people arrived from the Old World. They sought a better life and escape from economic deprivation, religious persecution, and political oppression. The overwhelming majority of these newcomers were non-English in origin; approximately one-third were from Germany, and 40 percent were Irish Catholics. The Germans, as had their predecessors in eighteenth-century Pennsylvania, experienced some prejudice, but, as in the past, their ability to settle quickly and prosper as farmers, merchants, and craftsmen helped curtail nativist (antiforeign) attacks. The Irish experience was quite different: they were desperately poor; they settled mostly in cities, although they were not accustomed to urban living; and they were steadfastly Catholic in a land that was overwhelmingly Protestant. As a result, they suffered as no prior immigrants had in the land of promise.

Religious and cultural differences, as well as economic competition, evoked fear and mistrust of Irish Catholics, which led to discrimination and even violence. In 1834 an anti-Catholic mob burned the Ursuline Convent in Charlestown, Massachusetts. Ten years later, in Philadelphia, controversy between Irish Catholics and native-born Americans over Bible reading and religious exercises in the public schools erupted into mob riots that turned whole sections of the city into battlegrounds.

Michael Feldberg's essay "The Philadelphia Native American Riots of 1844" explores the riots and the events leading up to them, and discusses the root causes of the enmity between the immigrants and the natives. What appear to have been the major cultural and religious issues that led to friction? Philadelphia, a city whose population was approaching half a million, continued to rely heavily on voluntary fire, police, and militia organizations, as it had in Benjamin Franklin's day. In what ways did the riots reveal the limitations of urban volunteerism?

The documents reveal divergent views of the Irish. The Irish, the most destitute of all immigrant groups, took up pick and shovel and performed the miserable, back-breaking work of building America's canals, railroads, and urban structures. When the famous Irish actor Tyrone Power toured the South in the 1830s, he came upon a work force of Irish immigrants engaged in digging a canal that would connect Lake Pontchartrain and New Orleans. The second document, from the diary of George Templeton Strong, from an elite and prosperous New York family, reveals the ugliness and intensity of hostility toward the Irish and other immigrants. How do Strong's views of the Irish compare with those of Power and with those expressed in the Feldberg essay?

ESSAY

The Philadelphia Native American Riots of 1844

Michael Feldberg

By February 1844, Louisa Bedford had finally run out of patience. She was having a difficult enough time teaching elementary school in Kensington, a working-class suburb just north of Philadelphia. Now her job was made even more trying because of hard feelings between the parents of both her

SOURCE: From *The Turbulent Era: Riot and Disorder in Jacksonian America*, 9–23, 27–32, by Michael Feldberg. Reprinted by permission of the author and Oxford University Press, Inc.

Why did Catholism seem alien + undemoratn ?

immigrant Irish Catholic students and her native-born Protestant students. The problem revolved around the use of the Bible as a reading book in the Philadelphia county public schools. Two years earlier, in 1842, the Philadelphia County Board of School Controllers had ordered that the King James, or Protestant, version of Holy Scripture be used as a basic reading text in all Philadelphia public-school classes. Upon hearing this, the Catholic Bishop of Philadelphia, the Reverend Francis Patrick Kenrick, asked that Catholic children be allowed to read the Douay, or authorized Catholic, version of Scripture, and that Catholic teachers not be compelled to read from the King James during reading exercises. The controllers denied Kenrick's request.

During the 1840s many American Protestants feared Catholicism because it seemed alien and anti-democratic. Protestants believed that the pope and his priests controlled the minds of their followers, and that the papacy was dedicated to overthrowing the American way of life. Because of this widely held prejudice, the Philadelphia School Controllers were afraid to grant equal status to the Douay Bible by allowing it in the schools. They feared that angry Protestant voters would turn them out of office at the next election, and no controller wanted to volunteer for political extinction. Yet to ease Bishop Kenrick's objections to an obvious injustice, the Board of School Controllers saw fit to offer a compromise solution: Catholic children could leave their classrooms while Bible-reading exercises were conducted, but the Douay version was still not to be admitted into the schools.

This compromise pleased almost no one. Catholics believed that the plan ignored their bishop's plea for justice and equality; evangelical Protestants felt that Catholic children should be compelled to read the King James version as an antidote to their "priestly dictated" and "popish" beliefs. The solution also failed to please teachers like Louisa Bedford, who could not tolerate the disruption caused by her Catholic students waiting noisily outside her door until the Bible-reading session was over. To remedy this situation, Bedford took actions which, in a short time, led to the great Philadelphia riots of 1844.

Louisa Bedford was a Protestant, although not a militant evangelical. Seriously committed to teaching the working-class children of Kensington to read and write, she resented the chaos caused by the controllers' policy. Thus when School Controller and Irish Catholic politician Hugh Clark was making his weekly tour of Kensington's public schools, Bedford asked Clark if she could have a word with him. She explained her unhappiness to the politically astute Clark who, one suspects, was waiting for just such a moment. Clark then sympathetically offered an alternative to sending Catholic students out of her room: She could suspend *all* Bible reading in her class until such time as the School Controllers devised a better method for excusing Catholic students from the exercise. Clark volunteered to

what was the name given to all those who openly opposed

all alien elements such as (Catholics, Immigrants, Mormons, etc.?

assume responsibility should she decide to follow this course. Bedford chose to accept Clark's offer and told her students that, for the time being, they would not have to do their Bible reading. Much to her relief, she turned to teaching other subjects.

While Louisa Bedford's discomfort was eased, severe problems for Hugh Clark and Philadelphia's Irish-Catholic community were just beginning. Word of Clark's decision to "kick the Bible out of the schools," as his enemies inaccurately described it, spread like wildfire throughout the city. Evangelical Protestants, most of them native-born Americans and the remainder immigrant Irish Protestants, had been organizing in Philadelphia for nearly a decade. The evangelicals were alarmed by what they believed to be the growing political and religious influence of Catholics, particularly Irish Catholic immigrants. Nativists, a name given to those who openly opposed all "alien" elements such as Catholics, immigrants, Mormons, and others who did not conform to the dominant white Protestant religious and cultural values of the era, had especially feared the political activism of the Irish Catholic clergy. Three years earlier, New York Bishop John Hughes had supported Catholic candidates for public office because the city's school board had refused to excuse Catholics from paying their school taxes. Hughes argued that Catholics should not be forced to support schools that were teaching Catholic students that the pope was "Antichrist" and that the Church of Rome was "The Whore of Babylon." Now Bishop Kenrick and Irish politicians like Hugh Clark were trying to meddle with Philadelphia's public schools. Perhaps, people believed, these Catholic efforts were nothing less than a dastardly plot to overthrow the public schools or turn them into centers for converting Protestant children.   *Sounds like I an Paisley*

To counter this threat to American religious, educational, and political institutions, Philadelphia's evangelicals organized a cluster of religiously oriented "reform" organizations: the American Protestant Association, which was a coalition of the city's Baptist, Methodist, and Presbyterian ministers who lectured on the "evils" and "dangers" of Roman Catholic "superstition"; the Sabbatarian movement, which hoped to promote Protestant church attendance by suppressing Sunday amusements and diversions such as picnics, fairs, train travel, sporting events (especially boxing matches and horse races), gambling, Sunday mail deliveries, and the serving of alcohol in public places; and the colportage movement, which tried to place a free King James Bible in the hand of anyone who promised to read it.

Most important, Protestants concerned with the increasing influence of Catholics and immigrants in American life joined a new political movement known as the American Republican party, which had branches in Philadelphia, New York, Boston, Baltimore, and New Orleans. The American Republicans held rallies and ran candidates to oppose the influence of immigrants in local politics. While they did not call for a halt to foreign immigration, they stood on a three-plank platform that demanded (1) an extension to twenty-one years of the waiting period for naturalization (that is, the granting of citizenship and the right to vote); (2) the election of none but native-born Americans to public office; and (3) the rejection of "foreign interference" in the social, political, and religious institutions of the country, especially the public schools. As one Philadelphia nativist put it:

> The day must come, and, we fear, is not too far distant, when most of our offices will be held by foreigners—men who have no sympathy with the spirit of our institutions, who have done aught to secure the blessings they enjoy, and instead of governing ourselves, we shall be governed by men, many of whom, but a few short years previously, scarcely knew of our existence.

For the most part, American Republican leadership in Philadelphia was composed of "middling" and "respectable" men: lawyers, doctors, clergymen, newspaper editors, shopkeepers, craftsmen, printers, barbers, dentists, and teachers. These individuals were neither numbered in the ranks of the city's traditional upper classes—wealthy merchants, bankers, manufacturers, and gentlemen farmers—nor drawn from the ranks of the struggling poor. Rather, these American Republicans had formerly provided the bulk of middle-class voters for the Whig and Democratic parties. With their wives they filled the pews of Philadelphia's Methodist, Baptist, and Presbyterian churches. By their own description they saw themselves as the "bone and sinew" of society, the hard-working silent majority who, while never independently wealthy and secure like the upper classes, would never allow themselves to fall to the level of the impoverished or degenerate immigrants.

Because they saw themselves as the nation's only "real" Americans, nativists could not stand to see their public schools, or the political system in general, "captured" by persons who spoke with a foreign accent— especially an Irish brogue. The social isolation of America's Irish immigrants and their continued loyalty to their native land particularly worried American nativists. They believed that the typical Irish immigrant would never become a loyal American citizen, freed of his allegiance to Ireland or to the Roman Catholic Church. They did not realize that the experiences of Irish Catholic immigrants with English-speaking Protestants had convinced the Irish to cling to their religion and to their nationalism.

For almost two centuries before their arrival in Jacksonian America, Irish Catholics had been fighting against their Protestant English rulers for the right to political independence and religious liberty. Even after transplanting themselves in American soil, Irish immigrants lost little dedication to the cause of Irish freedom. Catholic priests who migrated with their flocks kept alive the memory of injustices inflicted by the Protestant ruling class on Ireland's Catholic majority: military occupation; government by the English Parliament rather than by Irish home rule; the suspension of the right of Irish children to receive a Catholic education. Thus for the immigrant Irish, the cause of a free Ireland and the cause of the Irish Catholic Church were inseparable.

To maintain their solidarity, to resist integration into a Protestant-dominated society such as the one they had fled, the American Irish tended to cluster in self-imposed ghettos, to socialize in their own taverns, to attend mass in their own parish churches, and to meet in their own political and nationalist clubs. Such self-inflicted isolation upset Protestant American nativists, but the apparent political control that the Irish-born Catholic clergy seemed to exercise over their immigrant followers appeared to bother them even more. Nativists convinced one another that the American Irish voted overwhelmingly for the Democratic party, not because the Jacksonian political platform or personal style appealed to the newcomers, but because corrupt Roman Catholic priests "dictated" voting orders from Rome to their sheeplike parishioners. Nativists believed that such bloc voting threatened to turn American elections into mindless displays of numerical strength rather than expressions of reasoned judgment on issues or candidates.

The American Republicans determined to fight the power of the Catholic Church in the nation's political life. Their own forefathers had fought to drive foreign tyranny from the nation's shores during the American Revolution, and the American Republicans of 1844 would not stand idly by while the Roman Catholic Church attempted to substitute a new foreign tyranny in its place. The nativists based their ideology on two foundations: George Washington's famous Farewell Address, which urged his countrymen to "Beware of Foreign Influence"; and the concept of "Eternal Vigilance," or the principle that Americans, because their example of successful republicanism posed a threat to the kings and hereditary rulers of Europe, had to be on constant guard against attempts to subvert the American government.

Philadelphia American Republicanism was closely allied with the most popular reform movement of the era, the temperance crusade. . . . Somewhat unfairly,* it [alcoholism] was also closely associated with urban immigrant communities: gin and rum with the Irish, beer with the Germans, and wine with the French and Italians. Since nativists considered immigrant groups, and especially the Irish, responsible for most of the nation's poverty, crime, and prostitution, their interest in temperance reflected their critical attitudes toward the life styles of America's urban immigrant populations. . . .

[*Drinking to excess was a universal problem that crossed ethnic and class boundaries.]

The conversion of Philadelphia's temperance movement to a prohibitionist stance was tied in important ways to the American Republican and evangelical Protestant movements of the era. Closing bars and rum shops could have important social and political implications for immigrant communities. Taverns were one of the focal points in working-class Irish and German neighborhoods, and they often served as social and political centers. Their patrons did not usually welcome native Protestant—or even other ethnic—outsiders, and many a Philadelphia brawl was started when an unwitting stranger of the wrong ethnic background violated the sanctity of a German or Irish saloon. Particularly in Irish neighborhoods, taverns became symbols of Irish-Catholic separatism and Irish immigrant rejection of integration into wider American culture.

But nativists had political as well as cultural objections to the immigrants' fondness for alcoholic beverages. They argued that just as priests could control the consciences of immigrant Catholics through the religious doctrine of papal infallibility, so could tavern owners manipulate the political loyalties of immigrants by trading liquor for votes. Nativist temperance advocates feared an unholy alliance between Catholic priests and ambitious tavern-owning politicians that would maintain the immigrants' dependence on the Church and the bottle. The battle against liquor, then, was in part a battle to preserve American political freedom from Catholic-sponsored conspiracies. . . .

Unfortunately for Bishop Kenrick and the rest of Philadelphia's Catholics, the school Bible issue stirred intense hatred in the "City of Brother Love." The city's nativists chose (deliberately or otherwise) to interpret Kenrick's request to grant equality to the Douay Bible as a demand that the King James Bible be *removed* from the public schools. They claimed that the bishop was plotting to make the schools "Godless," a prelude to rendering Protestant students ripe for conversion to the "superstition" of Catholicism. And it may well be that, in his heart, Bishop Kenrick would have preferred to see no Bible read at all in the school than to see Catholic children being forced to read the King James version. He may even have had doubts about their reading the Douay at school with no priest to officiate over the reading. But the bishop had the political wisdom not to call for Bibleless schools in Philadelphia's heated evangelical atmosphere. Instead, he chose to ask only that the Douay version be admitted to the classroom or that Catholic children be excused during Bible reading, regardless of the difficulties that such a practice might cause. Yet nativists continued to believe that Kenrick was planning to make the schools Bibleless, irreligious, and a breeding ground for a Catholic conspiracy to capture the souls of America's Protestant youth.

Thus it is clear why Hugh Clark's suggestion to Louisa Bedford that she suspend Bible reading in her Kensington classroom caused such upheaval throughout Philadelphia. It was as if the bishop's alleged conspiracy had finally come out in the open. The first word of Clark's actions was carried by Henry Moore, a Methodist minister who burst into a prayer meeting at his Kensington church to inform the congregation that Clark had forced Miss Bedford against her will to "kick the Bible out of her classroom." Word spread rapidly throughout the city's nativist network, and Philadelphia's American Republican leaders and evangelical Protestant clergymen convened a series of mass rallies in mid-March to protest Catholic attempts to "trample our free Protestant institutions in the dust." . . .

Their enthusiastic reception at the city-wide rallies encouraged the American Republicans to carry their crusade right to the lair of the beast, the very neighborhood that symbolized Irish Catholic solidarity in Philadelphia: Third Ward, Kensington. The community was long and widely recognized as immigrant Irish "turf." It was dominated by Irish handloom weavers, dock laborers, teamsters, and other semi-skilled workers who held little love for their native Protestant neighbors in adjoining wards. The neighborhood had been the scene of several riots in recent years. . . . It was in this neighborhood of militant and aggressive Irish immigrants that the American Republicans chose to hold a rally on Friday afternoon, May 3, 1844, and invite the general public to attend.

That Friday meeting might well have been calculated to provoke a fateful confrontation with Kensington's immigrant Irish. The American Republicans chose to hold their rally in a schoolyard at Second and Master streets. When the American Republican spokesmen began their speeches, they were heckled, booed, and pelted with rocks and garbage by a crowd of several hundred, and eventually driven from the speaker's platform they had erected earlier in the afternoon. Undaunted (and quite self-righteously), the party decided to reconvene the meeting in the schoolyard on Monday, May 6, and placarded the city with notices urging every American Republican loyalist to attend. This time a large crowd of 3,000 turned out. Around 3:00 P.M., while noted temperance lecturer and political nativist Lewis C. Levin was arousing the crowd's interest, a sudden rainstorm erupted and the crowd moved spontaneously in search of shelter toward the Nanny Goat Market.

Relocating the rally in the market proved catastrophic. The Nanny Goat Market was the hub of the Third Ward Irish community. An open-sided, block-long covered shed at Third and Master streets, the market house served as a shopping center, a meeting place, and a social center for local residents. When the noisy but peaceable nativists arrived, a group of thirty or so Irish locals was waiting there to greet them. One Irishman was heard to proclaim, "Keep the damned natives out of our market house; this ground don't belong to them, it's ours!" Lewis Levin tried to continue his speech from a vendor's stand but hecklers drowned him out. Pushing and shoving began, someone pulled a pistol, a rival dared him to shoot, he did, and panic erupted under the shed. The Irish residents fled to their nearby homes, but the nativists were trapped in the open-sided shed with few places to hide. A rain of gunfire poured down on them from surrounding buildings, most of it from the Hibernia Hose House, the headquarters of an Irish volunteer fire company. The first nativist killed in the shooting, nineteen-year-old George Schiffler, became a martyr to the cause. . . .

The initial advantage possessed by the Irish snipers was soon balanced by the arrival of approximately eighteen nativist reinforcements who brought rifles and shotguns with them. Protected by the fire of their own sharpshooters, nativists began making forays out of the Nanny Goat Market, breaking windows and doors of the houses from which gunfire had been coming and scattering the inhabitants. Several Irishmen were badly beaten and left for dead as others saw their homes and furniture wrecked by the furious nativists. Finally, after two hours of heavy fighting, Sheriff Morton McMichael and a posse of two hundred deputies arrived and the fighting subsided.

That night, when darkness descended on Kensington, nativists from every corner of Philadelphia found their way to the neighborhood around the Nanny Goat Market. Around 10:00 P.M. a crowd "collected in the vicinity of Franklin and Second streets," marched toward the Nanny Goat Market, and on the way "commenced breaking into the houses on both sides of the street, destroying the furniture, demolishing the windows, and rendering the houses completely uninhabitable." The crowd then arrived at the gates of the seminary of the Catholic Sisters of Charity and were threatening to burn it down when a group of Irish defenders "advanced from above and fired a volley of ball and buckshot into the crowd." One nativist attacker died instantly, a second lingered for a month before dying of a chest wound, and several others were injured. On this note, Monday night's fighting in Kensington drew to a close.

Philadelphians awakened Tuesday morning, May 7, to find their city plastered with printed calls to a rally protesting the murder of George Schiffler. The message ended with the inflammatory words, "LET EVERY MAN COME PREPARED TO DEFEND HIMSELF." That morning, the nativist press was filled with militant cries for revenge. The daily *Native American* proclaimed:

> Another St. Bartholomew's day has begun in the streets of Philadelphia. The bloody hand of the Pope has stretched forth to our destruction. Now we call on our fellow-citizens, who regard free institutions, whether they be native or adopted, to arm. Our liberties are to be fought for—let us not be slack in our preparation.

By 3:30 P.M. that Tuesday afternoon, more than 3,000 persons had gathered behind Independence Hall to hear speeches condemning Kensington's Irish. Despite the fact that the call to the meeting had broadly implied that those attending should carry arms, neither Sheriff McMichael nor the commander of the state militia in Philadelphia, General George Cadwalader, had gathered his forces in anticipation of more fighting. Kensington's Irish, on the other hand, seemed better prepared for what was to come.

When the speeches were finished and the American Republicans called for the meeting to adjourn, a voice in the crowd shouted, "Adjourn to Kensington right now!" The crowd took up the call, marched in loose military fashion out of the meeting ground, and turned northward to Kensington. When they arrived in the neighborhood of Second and Master, the marchers found that many of Kensington's Irish had fled the neighborhood and taken their belongings with them. Other inhabitants simply waited at home with their loaded guns. This time, the nativist procession did not pause to convene a meeting and hear speeches, but immediately attacked the Hibernia Hose House. Armed defenders there and in some of the houses along the street immediately opened fire, and in the few moments of shooting four nativists lay dead and eleven others fell wounded. The remaining nativists with a stomach for a fight retreated to the Nanny Goat Market for shelter, and it seemed that the pattern of the day before would repeat itself. This time, however, the nativists changed their tactics. Rather than try to shoot it out with the well-concealed Irish, the nativists snuck out of the market building and set fire to each of the houses from which gunfire had been coming. This tactic proved successful as hidden Irish snipers came tumbling out of the flaming buildings. They made easy targets for nativist gunners, and only poor nativist marksmanship explains why no Irishmen were killed. It was not until 5:00 P.M., nearly an hour after the shooting started, that General Cadwalader, previously unprepared, arrived with several militia companies to restore order in the neighborhood.

The use of fire struck panic in the hearts of the remaining Kensington Irish, and by Wednesday morning most of them had packed their possessions and gone elsewhere to stay with friends and relatives, or to camp in the woods on the outskirts of Philadelphia. The militia was left to guard their abandoned homes, but the outnumbered soldiers were inadequate for the task. Roving bands of nativists snuck from house to house in the vicinity of the Nanny Goat Market and set each on fire. The city's volunteer firefighters, mostly native-born Americans, had little enthusiasm for fighting the flames. In addition, after setting up a diversion to draw the militia away, a group of arsonists gained access to St. Michael's Roman Catholic Church, whose priest had been an outspoken foe of nativism, and set it to the torch. Flames rapidly devoured the wooden structure, and as the cross fell from the toppling steeple the crowd cheered loudly. Volunteer firefighters, arriving on the scene, determined that the gathering would never permit them to extinguish the fire, so they contented themselves with hosing down nearby buildings to keep the flames from spreading. Other rioters completed the day's work by ransacking two stores that had been selling ammunition to Irish marksmen, and eventually they invaded the home of Hugh Clark, the man whose decision to suspend Bible reading in Louisa Bedford's class had provided the pretext for the fighting. The invaders threw Clark's valuable books and furniture into the street and used them to start a bonfire. Finally, several hours after the arson had begun in Kensington, General Cadwalader and Sheriff McMichael arrived with reinforcements and brought the wandering rioters under control.

Thus blocked, the angry nativists simply transferred their field of activity to downtown Philadelphia. By 10:30 that Wednesday night, a huge crowd had gathered in front of St. Augustine's Roman Catholic Church in the heart of that city. Although the mayor stood on the building's front steps and pleaded with the crowd to disperse, his appeals went unheard. Someone knocked him down by heaving a stone against his chest, and a young boy managed to sneak past the constables at a rear door and set the church afire. Within half an hour the $45,000 brick structure was a total loss. As the steeple fell, the crowd cheered as it had done at St. Michael's. Again the volunteer firemen dared only hose down nearby buildings.

The burning of St. Augustine's marked the last major violence in the Kensington phase of the Native American Riots. Governor David R. Porter placed Philadelphia under martial law, and the chief commander of the Pennsylvania militia, General Robert Patterson, took complete command of the city's government. More than 2,000 soldiers from across the state patrolled the streets of Philadelphia, and General Patterson banned all meetings and demonstrations. Patterson instructed his men that they were "to use all force at their disposal to protect public and private property," that they were to "clear and occupy any street, alley, or private property to prevent riot, disturbance, or destruction." If the soldiers encountered resistance they were to issue a warning to the offenders, and then the streets were to be "cleared forcibly." The general closed his instructions with a clear threat to future rioters:

> Order must be restored, life and property rendered secure. The idle, the vicious, the disorderly must be curbed and taught to understand and respect the supremacy of the law and, if they do not take warning, on their own heads be the consequences.

Martial law remained in effect for a week without a serious confrontation between troops and civilians, after which civilian government was restored to Philadelphia. Thus ended the Kensington phase of the 1844 Native American Riots. . . .

That the school Bible controversy shifted from a battle of petitions before the School Controllers to a battle of weapons in the streets of Kensington is stark testimony to the power of ethnic and religious issues to stir the passions of Philadelphians in 1844. It is also indicative, however, of . . . the inability of public officials to prevent or suppress riots before they required the intervention of military troops. . . . The current form of urban policing, in which uniformed officers actively patrol the streets searching out crime and disorder, and in which the police routinely patrol any political or protest rally prepared to disperse the crowd at the first sign of violence, was simply unknown in Jacksonian America.

"Preventive policing," as Jacksonians came to call it, was not introduced in Philadelphia until the 1850s. Like its sister cities Boston and New York, Philadelphia in 1844 still maintained public order through a system of constables, watchmen, and sheriff's posses whose origins dated back to the Middle Ages. The constables and watchmen, who neither pursued a preventive patrol strategy nor were given many incentives to control disorder, were ineffective against all but the smallest riots. . . .

When the American Republican Party announced that it would hold a gala parade to celebrate the Fourth of July, Philadelphians anxiously awaited the day—either in anticipation of a great outpouring of patriotism or in fear of renewed fighting and violence between nativists and the immigrant Irish. Catholics, of course, feared that bitter nativists would use the holiday as a pretext for burning more churches. The American Republicans, however, were quite sensitive to their new reputation as "church burners," and they worked hard to see that the day was not marred by disorder. Sheriff McMichael, General Cadwalader, and other friends of public order prepared for potential violence by readying deputies, militiamen, and citizen volunteers to patrol the streets and nip any outbreak of violence before it blossomed into a riot. One such preventive step—a fateful one, it turned out—was taken by the parishioners of St. Philip de Neri Roman Catholic Church in Southwark, a district just south of central Philadelphia. Its pastor, Father Peter Dunn, had heard a rumor that nativists were planning to attack the church on the Fourth, and so Father Dunn's brother William quietly approached Governor Porter for permission to form the Catholic men of Southwark into a volunteer militia company. The governor agreed, and as was common practice at the time, Dunn and his men were allowed to draw rifles from the state arsenal.

The Fourth itself passed peacefully, much to the relief of everyone involved. . . . Unfortunately, though, the fifth was not to pass as quietly. That morning, the rifles ordered for the defense of St. Philip de Neri Church were seen arriving at the building's rear door, and word spread quickly through Southwark that the church was being armed in preparation for a Catholic attack on native Americans. A crowd quickly gathered and demanded that the arms be removed. Sheriff McMichael hurried to the scene with two local aldermen, entered the church, and learned that William Dunn was indeed authorized to arm a volunteer militia company. Mc-

Michael persuaded Dunn that his safest course was to calm the crowd by depositing the guns in the nearby Southwark Commissioners' Hall. Dunn agreed, and when the guns were carried off, most of those gathered dispersed. McMichael gathered some friends into a posse to guard the church, and General Cadwalader sent a company of soldiers to reinforce the men during the night.

Saturday morning, the soldiers and deputies faced an ever-enlarging crowd of curious and suspicious onlookers. At 2 P.M., General Cadwalader appeared in person at the church and ordered the throng to disperse. When those assembled hooted him down, Cadwalader lost his temper and huffed off, threatening to return with a major show of force. The crowd scoffed at him and continued to mill peacefully outside the church building. True to his word, Cadwalader indeed returned with several companies of soldiers and three light cannons. He ordered his men to fix bayonets and clear the streets. While the troops herded the crowd, some of the bolder protestors started throwing rocks at them and loudly proclaimed their right to gather in the public streets. Cadwalader issued a final warning for the crowd to disperse at once or face the blasts of his soldiers' cannons and rifles. He then gave the order to "ready, aim, fire!" At that very moment, Southwark politician Charles Naylor stepped forward, stood before the pointed rifles and yelled, "My God, don't shoot! Don't shoot!"

Distracted by Naylor's plea, Cadwalader's men refrained from firing, and the crowd had a chance to melt away. But the general was furious. He immediately ordered Naylor and twenty straggling protestors placed under arrest and held in the church basement. Thus Saturday night, July 5, ended without bloodshed, but only by the narrowest of margins. Sunday was to prove less fortunate.

Trouble was renewed on Sunday morning when a group of nativists, led by two Southwark aldermen, appeared at St. Philip's to demand the release of Naylor and his fellow prisoners. Two companies of militia—one composed of Irish immigrants and the other of native Americans—had been left to guard the prisoners, but the soldiers were badly outnumbered by the crowd. After sending Cadwalader a plea for reinforcements—which did not arrive for several hours—Captain John Colahan, the commander of the Irish company (who was in charge of the entire operation), agreed to let the prisoners, including Naylor, be released into the custody of the aldermen. Colahan did not trust the willingness of the soldiers in the native American company to protect the church, and he feared that if he did not meet the protestors' demands and if reinforcements did not arrive, his men would be overwhelmed and perhaps killed. Colahan was then persuaded to remove his men from the church and to turn it over for safekeeping to volunteer American Republican activists, who swore to guard the building against all harm. As the Irish soldiers withdrew, portions of the crowd pelted them with rocks, and in response one of the soldiers opened fire.

He was beaten by the crowd and mistakenly left for dead. The other soldiers ran, escaping without serious injury. The area around the church remained crowded with curious onlookers, mostly nativists, but the church itself was securely guarded by a group of American Republican volunteers. Again, the party was trying to live down its "church burners" reputation, and so the most widely known American Republicans made it their business to stand watch over St. Philip's while the crowd surged outside the building.

As darkness fell on this turbulent but nonviolent scene, General Cadwalader arrived with the heavily armed reinforcements that Captain Colahan had requested. To his surprise, Cadwalader found not Colahan's soldiers but a group of American Republicans in charge of the church, and that his prisoners, especially Charles Naylor, were gone. Outraged, he commanded the American Republicans out of the building and called on his troops to clear the streets. With swords drawn and bayonets fixed, the soldiers began to push the crowd away from the church. The civilians answered with rocks, brickbats, and occasional gunshots. Cadwalader ordered his men to return the fire. This time no one stepped forward to save the crowd. The soldiers' first volley killed two men and wounded four others. The crowd fled in terror. Some went to their homes, many to return with guns in order to seek revenge on Cadwalader and his men. Under the cover of night a group of young men went to a nearby dock and removed two cannons from a Navy ship anchored at the federal dockyard, fully prepared to do battle with the soldiers.

The nativists' cannons proved effective for a while. The first blast killed two soldiers and injured several more. The next time the insurgents fired at the troops, though, Cadwalader called for cavalry reinforcements, and a detachment of horsemen quickly galloped up, killed two of the gunners, and captured the weapon. After that the nativists were afraid to fire the other cannon for fear of revealing its position, and while the soldiers supposedly rode past it several times during the night, the weapon lay idle. Instead, the nativists kept up a sporadic rifle fire until dawn, but the major fighting had ceased. The military had suffered two dead and twenty-three wounded, the rioters approximately ten dead and twenty or more injured.

Once again Governor Porter imposed martial law on Philadelphia and soldiers occupied the streets of Southwark. Nativist hatred of the soldiers was unbounded; as soldiers fainted from thirst in the intense July heat, no Southwark residents offered them water. As General Cadwalader later recalled, "the houses of the people were closed against us." The nativist dead of Southwark were buried with great fanfare and honor by local residents, and relations between the military and civilians were at the flash point. Acting on the advice of the Southwark commissioners, General Patterson, under whose command the district was placed, agreed to withdraw the troops and restore civilian government. The troops left, no further violence occurred, and St. Philip's church was no longer threatened.

Respectable Philadelphians of all religions and political beliefs were left in a state of shock by their realization that civil war between the military and citizens had broken out on the city's streets. The deaths of soldiers and civilians seemed to sober Irish and nativists alike. There was no more rioting in Philadelphia over the issue of the Bible in the public schools after July 7, 1844, although street fighting between native and Irish gangs and fire companies did continue until the eve of the Civil War. Thus ended the great Philadelphia Native American Riots of 1844.

DOCUMENTS

Irish Immigrants: A Sympathetic View, c. 1833

One of the greatest works now in progress here, is the canal planned to connect Lac Pontchartrain with the city [New Orleans]. In the month of February it was completed to within three miles of the lake; and as it was a pleasant ride to the point where the digging was in progress, I two or three times visited the scene, after its bearings had been explained by the two intelligent persons under whose guidance I first penetrated the swamp.

I only wish that the wise men at home who coolly charge the present condition of Ireland upon the inherent laziness of her population, could be transported to this spot, to look upon the hundreds of fine fellows labouring here beneath a sun that at this winter season was at times insufferably fierce, and amidst a pestilential swamp whose exhalations were foetid to a degree scarcely endurable even for a few moments; wading amongst stumps of trees, mid-deep in black mud, clearing the spaces pumped out by powerful steam-engines; wheeling, digging, hewing, or bearing burdens it made one's shoulders ache to look upon; exposed meantime to every change of temperature, in log-huts, laid down in the very swamp, on a foundation of newly-felled trees, having the water lying stagnant between the floor-logs, whose interstices, together with those of the side-walls, are open, pervious alike to sun or wind, or snow. Here they subsist on the coarsest fare, holding life on a tenure as uncertain as does the leader of a forlorn hope; excluded from all the advantages of civilization; often at the mercy of a hard contractor, who wrings his profits from their blood; and all this for a pittance that merely enables them to exist, with little power to save, or a hope beyond the continuance of the like exertion.

Such are the labourers I have seen here, and have still found them civil and courteous, with a ready greeting for the stranger inquiring into their

SOURCE: Tyrone Power, *Impressions of America during the Years 1833, 1834, and 1835* (London: R. Bentley, 1836), 2: 238–44.

condition, and a quick jest on their own equipment, which is frequently, it must be admitted, of a whimsical kind.

Here too were many poor women with their husbands; and when I contemplated their wasted forms and haggard sickly looks, together with the close swamp whose stagnant air they were doomed to breathe, whose aspect changeless and deathlike alone met their eyes, and fancied them, in some hour of leisure, calling to memory the green valley and the pure river, or the rocky glen and sparkling brook of their distant home, with all the warmth of colouring the imaginative spirit of the Irish peasant can so well supply, my heart has swelled and my eyes have filled with tears.

I cannot hope to inspire the reader with my feelings upon a mere sketch like this; but if I could set the scene of these poor labourers' exile fairly forth, with all the sad accompaniments detailed; could I show the course of the hardy, healthy pair, just landed, to seek fortune on these long-sighed-for shores, with spirits newly lifted by hope and brighter prospects from the apathy into which compulsory idleness and consequent reck-lessness had reduced them at home; and then paint the spirit-sinking felt on a first view of the scene of their future labour,—paint the wild revel designed to drown remembrance, and give heart to the newcomers; de-scribe the nature of the toil where exertion is taxed to the uttermost, and the weary frame stimulated by the worst alcohol, supplied by the con-tractor, at a cheap rate for the purpose of exciting a rivalry of exertion amongst these simple men.

Next comes disease, either a sweeping pestilence that deals, wholesale on its victims, or else a gradual sinking of mind and body; finally, the abode in the hospital, if any comrade is interested enough for the sufferer to bear him to it; else, the solitary log-hut and quicker death. Could these things with their true colours be set forth in detail before the veriest grinder of the poor that ever drove the peasant to curse and quit the soil of his birth, he would cover his eyes from the light of heaven, and feel that he yet possessed a heart and human sympathy.

At such works all over this continent the Irish are the labourers chiefly employed, and the mortality amongst them is enormous,—a mortality I feel certain might be vastly lessened by a little consideration being given to their condition by those who employ them. At present they are, where I have seen them working here, worse lodged than the cattle of the field; in fact, the only thought bestowed upon them appears to be, by what expedient the greatest quantity of labour may be extracted from them at the cheapest rate to the contractor. I think, however, that a better spirit is in progress amongst the companies requiring this class of labourers; in fact it becomes necessary this should be so, since, prolific as is the country from whence they are drawn, the supply would in a little time cease to keep pace with the demand, and slave labour cannot be substituted to any extent, being much too expensive; a good slave costs at this time two hundred pounds sterling, and to have a thousand such swept off a line of canal in one season, would call for prompt consideration.

Independent of interest, Christian charity and justice should alike suggest that the labourers ought to be provided with decent quarters, that sufficient medical aid should always be at hand, and above all, that the brutalizing, accursed practice of extorting extra labour by the stimulus of corn spirit should be wholly forbidden.

Let it be remembered that, although rude and ignorant, these men are not insensible to good impressions, or incapable of distinguishing between a kindly and paternal care of their well-doing, and the mercenary cold-blooded bargain which exacts the last scruple of flesh it has paid for. . . .

At present the priest is the only stay and comfort of these men; the occasional presence of the minister of God alone reminds them that they are not forgotten of their kind: and but for this interference, they would grow in a short time wholly abandoned and become uncontrollable; unfortunately of these men, who conscientiously fulfill their holy functions, there are but too few,—the climate, and fatigue soon incapacitates all but the very robust. Those who follow the ministry of God in the swamp and in the forest must have cast the pride of flesh indeed out from them, since they brave the martyr's fate without a martyr's triumph. . . .

The gloomy picture of the labourer's condition, which my mention of this canal has drawn from me, may by some be considered overcharged; but I protest I have, on the contrary, withheld details of suffering from heat, and cold, and sickness, which my heart at this moment aches when I recall. . . .

A Native-born American's Response to the Irish Immigrants, 1838–1857

NOVEMBER 6 [1838]. It was enough to turn a man's stomach—to make a man adjure republicanism forever—to see the way they were naturalizing this morning at the *Hall*. Wretched, filthy, bestial-looking Italians and Irish, and creations [creatures] that looked as if they had risen from the lazarettos of Naples for this especial object; in short, the very scum and dregs of human nature filled the clerk of C[ommon] P[leas] office so completely that I was almost afraid of being poisoned by going in. A dirty Irishman is bad enough, but he's nothing comparable to a nasty French or Italian loafer. . . .

APRIL 13 [1842]. We had some hard fighting yesterday in the Bloody Sixth [Ward], and a grand no-popery riot last night, including a vigorous

SOURCE: Allan Nevins and Milton H. Thomas, eds., *The Diary of George Templeton Strong* (New York: Macmillan, 1952), 1: 94, 177–78, 318, and 2: 197, 348.

attack on the Roman Catholic Cathedral with brick bats and howls, and a hostile demonstration on Hughes's* episcopal palace, terminating in broken windows and damaged furniture. Also the Spartan Band got into the Sixth Ward Hotel, as the no-popery rioters of old did into "the Maypole," and "made a noise and broke things." . . .

APRIL 28 [1848]. Orders given to commence excavating in Twenty-first Street Wednesday night. . . . Hibernia came to the rescue yesterday morning; twenty "sons of toil" with prehensile paws supplied them by nature with evident reference to the handling of the spade and the wielding of the pickaxe and congenital hollows on the shoulder wonderfully adapted to make the carrying of the hod a luxury instead of a labor. . . .

NOVEMBER 13 [1854]. Met a prodigious Know-Nothing** procession moving uptown, as I omnibussed down Broadway to the vestry meeting; not many banners and little parade of any kind, but a most emphatic and truculent demonstration. Solid column, eight or ten abreast, and numbering some two or three thousand, mostly young men of the butcher-boy and *prentice* type . . . marching in quick time, and occasionally indulging in a very earnest kind of hurrah. They looked as if they might have designs on St. Patrick's Cathedral, and I think the Celts of Prince and Mott Streets would have found them ugly customers. . . .

JULY 7 [1857]. Yesterday morning I was spectator of a strange, weird, painful scene. Certain houses of John Watts DePeyster are to be erected on the northwest corner of this street and Fourth Avenue, and the deep excavations therefor are in progress. Seeing a crowd on the corner, I stopped and made my way to a front place. The earth had caved in a few minutes before and crushed the breath out of a pair of ill-starred Celtic laborers. They had just been dragged, or dug, out, and lay white and stark on the ground where they had been working, ten or twelve feet below the level of the street. Around them were a few men who had got them out, I suppose, and fifteen or twenty Irish women, wives, kinfolk or friends, who had got down there in some inexplicable way. The men were listless and inert enough, but not so the women. I suppose they were "keening"; all together were raising a wild, unearthly cry, half shriek and half song, wailing as a score of daylight Banshees, clapping their hands and gesticulating passionately. Now and then one of them would throw herself down on one of the corpses, or wipe some trace of defilement from the face of the dead man with her apron, slowly and carefully, and then resume her lament. It was an uncanny sound to hear. . . . Our Celtic fellow citizens are almost as remote from us in temperament and constitution as the Chinese. . . .

[*Bishop John Hughes of New York]
[**Know-Nothing (or American) party, a nativist political movement.]

CHAPTER 13

The Age of Reform

Economic growth, territorial expansion, and a spirit of democracy characterized the second quarter of the nineteenth century, a time of great optimism. Americans believed their institutions, know-how, and values could overcome all problems. Revivalism and the founding of utopian communities were manifestations of this seemingly boundless perfectionist faith, and so, too, were the great reform movements that began to emerge after the War of 1812, reaching their peak during the 1830s and 1840s before gradually declining in the 1850s. Wherever people perceived problems, they organized to do battle. They formed societies to promote such ideals as temperance, world peace, the abolition of slavery, women's rights, and prison reform, as well as to support public institutions such as libraries, hospitals for the mentally ill, and schools.

The temperance movement, described in Ronald G. Walters's essay "Strong Drink," illustrates the blend of concern and optimism that motivated reformers. As Walters points out, the temperance crusade differed from other reform movements in two ways: in its longevity, and in its appeal in all regions of the country and to people representing a broad spectrum of class and political affiliations. How does the author account for this success? What evidence can you offer in support of Walters's contention that the crusade against alcohol has continued to the present day?

The documents in the chapter reflect the scope of causes promoted during the great reform era and the fervent dedication of their adherents. No other reform movement proceeded with more ardor or was met with more resistance than that for the abolition of slavery. This is evident in the first document, an excerpt from the first edition of abolitionist leader William Lloyd Garrison's newspaper, The Liberator (January 1, 1831). Notice that opposition to an organized abolition movement was by no means restricted to the South. What evidence do you find that the abolition movement, like the temperance crusade, had its moderate and radical wings?

Horace Mann, foremost leader of the movement for universal, free, public schools, had been a successful politician-reformer in Massachusetts prior to being appointed secretary of the Massachusetts Board of Education. He had also spoken out and legislated on behalf of temperance, civil rights for blacks, prison reform, the prevention of pauperism, and better care of the mentally ill. The second document is a selection from Mann's twelfth, and final, Annual Report as secretary. How does the document help explain why he viewed public education as the hub of all reform?

Long before the establishment of the International Court of Justice, the League of Nations, or the United Nations, William Ladd of Maine issued a call for a congress of nations and a world court of arbitration. In 1828 he helped to organize and then became the leader of the American Peace Society. The third document is from Thoughts and Things at Home and Abroad (1854), a book by one of Ladd's closest associates in the movement, Elihu Burritt. Readers may find that Burritt's sentiments have a modern ring. For example, to what contemporary movements has the term passive resistance been applied? Civil Right

The final document is an excerpt from the 1855 wedding vows of Henry B. Blackwell and Lucy Stone, both active reformers. Stone was a leader of the wing of the women's movement that demanded social, economic, and political equality of the sexes. The document reveals the many barriers that stood in the way of equality in marriage. Stone kept her maiden name after marriage, a practice not uncommon today but considered rather shocking in the 1850s. The term "Lucy Stone League" came to be applied to other marrying women who followed her lead in this matter.

ESSAY

Strong Drink

Ronald G. Walters

. . . [T]he crusade against alcohol was extremely significant, both for its practical consequences and for its effect on reform tactics. In the 1850s, when slavery overshadowed every other issue on the national scene, the temperance crusade became a major force in state and local politics and achieved remarkable, if temporary, legislative triumphs. In terms of longevity and membership alone, the crusade against alcohol far surpassed abolitionism. It has continued to the present day and, in the antebellum years at least, attracted the largest, most diverse collection of supporters of any reform. They ranged from shy, pious churchwomen to militant feminists, from freethinkers to fundamentalists, from the high and mighty to the lowly and degraded. It was one of the few things that William Lloyd Garrison, the abolitionist, and Robert Barnwell Rhett, a Southerner and a defender of slavery, could agree upon.

William Cobbett, an Englishman who closely observed drinking habits in the United States and Britain, lamented in 1819 that "Americans preserve their gravity and quietness and good-humour even in their drink." He believed "it were far better for them to be as noisy and quarrelsome as the English drunkards; for then the odiousness of the vice would be more visible, and the vice itself might become less frequent." He may or may not have been correct in his comparison, but he was on to something true. Drunkenness is partly what people make it. Even in such closely related societies as America and England, human beings differ in how they act when drunk, in what groups commonly get intoxicated, and in where, when, and why they do it. Equally important, cultures, classes, and generations vary in how they define drunkenness and in what moral judgments they pass upon it.

At the time Cobbett was writing, alcohol was a perfectly acceptable part of life in the United States. "You cannot go into hardly any man's house," he lamented, "without being asked to drink wine, or spirits, even *in the morning*." Men put down beer or harder beverages to fortify themselves for work, to be sociable, or out of habit. Rum was a staple of New England trade and farmers in the West converted their grain to whiskey, a less bulky commodity to transport to market and a convenient medium of barter in a currency-poor region. There are stories of frontier

SOURCE: Selection from *American Reformers, 1815–1860*, 123–43, by Ronald G. Walters. Copyright © 1978 by Ronald G. Walters. Reprinted by permission of Hill and Wang, a division of Fanar, Straus, and Giroux, Inc.

clergymen being paid with jugs of the local product and even New England ministers, the most priggish in the land, were not opposed to taking a drop or two. Alcohol was everywhere; whether it was used for commerce or conviviality, few people were much disturbed by it. That, however, was beginning to change. Before Cobbett put his critical words to paper, some Americans had come to think of drinking as a new, extremely serious problem.

There had been scattered protests against alcohol in the late eighteenth century, most of them coming from within religious groups such as the Quakers and, especially, the Methodists, who after 1780 were often among the more strident opponents of hard liquor. But the most distinguished and persistent early temperance advocate was neither a clergyman nor a Methodist. He was a physician, Dr. Benjamin Rush, signer of the Declaration of Independence and a major figure in the histories of medicine and reform alike. In 1784 he published *An Inquiry into the Effects of Spirituous Liquors on the Human Body and Mind.* Rush accepted the notion that beer, cider, and wine were good for health and well-being, but he put his prestige behind the argument that distilled beverages led straight to physical, mental, and moral destruction. Rush's *Inquiry* was widely distributed (by himself and others) and it continued to be quoted, reprinted, and plagiarized into the middle of the nineteenth century. Rush did generate sentiment against liquor, both by his writings and through personal appeals to influential people; but the process of forming anti-alcohol organizations was slow.

The first seems to have come in Saratoga County, New York, in 1808, when a doctor and a clergyman persuaded over forty of their neighbors to create the Temperance Society of Moreau and Northumberland. Members obliged themselves to forswear use of wine and distilled spirits, "except by advice of a physician, or in case of actual disease." That loophole may have been an act of deference toward the doctor, but it was consistent with Rush's teachings and with temperance activity for the next generation. Up to the late 1820s most reformers would oppose hard liquor while believing that beer and, usually, wine had medicinal value. Some would not even go that far, merely criticizing intoxication, not temperate drinking. The leading lights of one local society reportedly were so relaxed about things that they met in a tavern and drank a toast to their own moderation.

The Moreau and Northumberland society quickly inspired an imitator in nearby Greenfield, New York, but for half a decade little organizational work was done. The cause was carried largely by church groups and individuals, some of them destined to become important later: a young clergyman named Lyman Beecher began to speak out against liquor, and by 1812 the General Assembly of the Presbyterian Church had gone on record against drunkenness, appointing a committee to see what could be done about it. There were similar rumblings from Congregationalists and Methodists.

Finally, in 1813, the year of Rush's death and three decades after his *Inquiry*, two promising organizations were begun with the idea of helping to stamp out intoxication. They were the Massachusetts Society for the Suppression of Intemperance and the Connecticut Society for the Reformation of Morals. Their founders were distinguished clergy and laymen, most of them Federalists. Neither organization bound its members to do much more than agree to lead godly lives, and both engaged only in mild and dignified activities. Cautious though their approach was, it led to the creation of auxiliaries in Massachusetts and Connecticut and it encouraged people elsewhere to form similar groups. For temperance to grow, however, it would have to loosen its association with New England Federalism, already a political dinosaur, shed some of its elitism, and generally become more passionate in seeking a constituency.

Those conditions began to be met in the mid-1820s. Federalism did its part by dying out. Lyman Beecher helped supply the other ingredients, even though he shared many of the narrow prejudices of the other early leaders of temperance. (He hated Unitarianism and described Jefferson's followers as "Sabbath-breakers, rum-sellers, tippling folk, infidels, and ruff-scruff generally.") Whatever support his views cost the movement among political and theological liberals, he made up for with his ability to stir evangelical Protestants. In the fall of 1825, Beecher preached six thunderous sermons on temperance; these were published the following year and had a tremendous influence, both at the time and over the decades.

What Beecher said was not entirely novel, but he said it well and gave a badly needed sharpness to the debate. Moderate drinking, approved by some temperance writers, was anathema to Beecher. According to him, to take any amount was to be intemperate, whether or not it resulted in drunkenness. Having cut away any happy middle ground, Beecher went on to envision a glorious day when there would come "banishment of ardent spirits from the list of lawful articles of commerce"—an omen of the political turn temperance would take in the next generation. Beecher's goal in 1825, nonetheless, was more immediate. He demanded a new, vigorous attack on alcohol to be carried across the land by voluntary associations.

There were, as Beecher knew, many temperance societies at the time he gave his sermons. What he had in mind was increasing the number of them and fashioning a national organization to provide central direction, sponsor publications and speakers, and supervise creation of auxiliaries. Something of an answer to Beecher's call came in February 1826 in the form of the American Society for the Promotion of Temperance (or American Temperance Society). Those who joined it repudiated moderation in favor of abstinence from hard liquor—Beecher's position.

Beecher himself was not present to sign the constitution of the American Temperance Society, but of the sixteen who did, several were confederates of his in various Protestant religious and charitable enterprises. This close connection with the evangelical "benevolent empire" helped the society greatly. Its first secretary, Reverend Justin Edwards, adopted techniques made familiar by the American Bible Society and related organizations. He and the executive committee, moreover, were able to draw upon the churches and laymen who backed other Protestant crusades. The benefits of annexing temperance to the benevolent empire were apparent in the statistics. By 1834 there were estimates that 5,000 state and local societies were promoting the cause, that millions of pieces of propaganda were in circulation, and that a million members had taken some sort of pledge to avoid alcohol.

Even allowing for exaggeration, the figures are impressive. They also are deceptive. Many local groups originated independently of the national society and a majority of them stayed unaffiliated with it. The American Temperance Society acted as a valuable clearinghouse for information, but it could not provide firm direction for the movement. Supporters of the cause in different places continued to interpret their obligations differently and to keep their vows with greater or lesser faithfulness.

In part to bring about a degree of uniformity, the society's executive committee called for a convention to convene in Philadelphia in 1833. The gathering was attended by delegates from throughout the country and they put together a more genuinely national organization, the United States Temperance Union (American Temperance Union after 1836). . . .

By the mid-1830s prospects looked bright. There was still opposition, even within the churches, but much of the weaponry of evangelical Protestantism was in the service of the cause. Temperance had many of the high and mighty behind it and the message seemed to be filtering down to honest workingmen, groups of whom began taking the pledge—like conservatives, they had begun to see drinking as a cause of poverty. There was a national organization, many newspapers, no shortage of pamphlets, and an abundance of grass-roots enthusiasm.

Arguments in favor of temperance had likewise come to maturity. Several lines of attack had developed by the 1830s and, although the supporting evidence and the emphasis would shift, these would last throughout the century with only slight alterations. One sort of appeal was personal and frightening. "The Holy Spirit," according to a circular, "will not visit, much less dwell with him who is under the polluting, debasing effects of intoxicating drink." Intemperance, in short, led to hell. In a more secular vein, temperance writers pictured alcohol as a form of tyranny, resembling slavery in depriving people of their ability to act as morally responsible creatures. Giving in to it meant destruction of one's autonomy.

If damnation and loss of self-control were not terrifying enough, there were other themes in temperance propaganda. Facts and figures demonstrated that alcohol produced insanity, poverty, and crime. It devastated families, thus causing suffering, robbing society of a crucial institution, and sending innocent women and children out into the cruel world. Get rid of liquor and everyone would gain, from the ex-drunkard to the hard-working taxpayer. As a flourish, temperance writers and orators could always play upon a powerful blend of patriotism and fear. They conjured visions of rum-soaked debtors using their votes to take charge of the country (a credible view, given the realities of Jacksonian electioneering). . . .

. . . Although they were often among the more conservative antebellum reformers on social matters, anti-alcohol crusaders were not blue-nosed reactionaries, as twentieth-century critics made them seem. They had a sense of progress and of the nation's potential. As they saw it, prosperity, godliness, and political freedom were to be the fruits of sobriety. Poverty, damnation, and tyranny were the consequences of intemperance.

Between 1835 and 1840 the temperance movement became a victim of its logic, which led to ever more extreme assaults on alcohol. Beecher and the American Temperance Society worked to destroy the notion that moderate drinking was tolerable. They were not entirely successful, although the pledge after 1825 usually did involve agreeing to abstain from "ardent spirits." By implication that exempted wine and beer. Yet the sin was supposed to be in the alcohol, not in distilling, and one could get as drunk on beer as on whiskey. By 1836 a large faction, which included Beecher and Justin Edwards, pressed the American Temperance Union to adopt a "teetotal" pledge, binding signers to abstain from any alcohol. That view prevailed, but it cost the Union some auxiliaries and it continued to meet resistance from people who believed that wine and beer were healthful and useful in weaning tipplers from harder drink. The teetotal position had in its favor the moral purity, or "ultraism," many antebellum reformers insisted upon; yet it raised further problems. What about communion wine? Was it sinful? Some people thought so. That proposition caused dismay among evangelicals, who found their reading of the Bible pitted against the consistency of their reform principles.

Not that teetotalism exhausted the ability of temperance people to quarrel. Like abolitionists, they disagreed among themselves on the role of women in the movement. Unlike abolitionists they usually resolved their differences by not pressing the issue; some societies separated the sexes, others included them both. More divisive was the question whether temperance meant going beyond simply trying to convert individuals. In his sermons of 1825 Beecher had raised the possibility of using legislation to stop the making and selling of liquor. The matter was openly debated in the Philadelphia convention of 1833 and it would continue to be for years afterward.

Battles over such questions alienated temperance advocates from each other and split organizations. The most socially prominent leaders had begun to drift away in reaction against teetotalism, and there was a general decline in membership by 1836. The movement was in the doldrums by the time the financial panic of 1837 cut further into its resources. Within three years temperance would be suddenly revived, but changed. The new inspiration did not come from New England or the saintly folk of evangelical reform.

The setting was Chase's Tavern in Baltimore and the unlikely heroes of the piece were six friends, later to describe themselves as ex-drunkards. Their story was the stuff of which legends are made. They met on the night of April 2, 1840, with anything but sobriety on their minds. Tavern humor being what it was, they delegated a "committee" to attend a nearby temperance lecture, presumably so they might know their enemy. The committee report, duly delivered, was unexpectedly persuasive. The six swore off intoxicants and decided to form an organization, called the Washington Temperance Society in honor of the first President (a drinker but a virtuous man nonetheless). By Christmas there were a thousand Washingtonians in Baltimore and before a year had passed the society established a beachhead in New York City. At the end of three years supporters were claiming—with more enthusiasm than accuracy—pledges from 600,000 intemperate men, 100,000 of them formerly habitual drunkards.

Existing temperance organizations first greeted the Washingtonians as allies, but tensions soon appeared and were based on more than just competition for members. Several things separated the new phase of the movement, begun at Chase's Tavern, from the old one. The first anti-alcohol societies had been dominated by clergy and by wealthy evangelical laymen. The Washingtonians did have help from ministers, and many of their methods were derived from revivalism, but their leaders were neither clergy nor men of social prominence. Of their two greatest lecturers, one had been a hatter and the other a bookbinder and minstrel. Such men were distinctly uninterested in theological niceties; occasionally they were even hostile to the formal trappings of religion, much to the disgust of American Temperance Union officials.

An equally crucial difference between Washingtonians and their predecessors had to do with the people they tried to reach. Older temperance societies had not been eager to deal with drunkards. The Massachusetts Society for the Suppression of Intemperance was candid about its position. "The design of this institution," it admitted in 1814, "is . . . not so much to wrest the fatal cup from those who are already brutalized and ruined, as to keep sober those who are sober." In contrast, the Washington Society had as its chief goal getting tipplers to pledge total abstinence. Not every member was an ex-alcoholic, but many were, and almost all were workingmen or from the bottom ranks of society.

Besides opening membership and leadership to drunks and men of low status, the Washingtonians also helped increase participation by women and children. Some women had been involved in earlier temperance activity, and in 1836 Reverend Thomas Hunt began organizing Sunday-school youth into a Cold Water Army. These efforts were almost tepid compared to those of the Washingtonians. They placed special emphasis on alcohol as a destroyer of families and exhorted females and juveniles to lend the cause a hand, lest they be left helpless by a drunkard. The invitation may have been maudlin, but the response was stirring.

Temperance would never be the same after the Washingtonians. Up to 1840 anti-alcohol crusaders had used a fair number of devices, ranging from the usual sermons and pamphlets to such institutions as temperance hotels for the sober-minded traveler. Leaders of organizations like the American Temperance Union, nevertheless, had primarily worked through religious groups, engaged in fairly rational discourse, corresponded with like-minded people elsewhere in the United States and Britain, and held meetings which, despite sharp debates, were reasonably staid. The Washingtonians adopted many of the same instruments of reform—they also gave lectures, published newspapers, and had conventions. There the resemblance ended. Like their clientele, the Washingtonians' behavior and tactics were not genteel.

Using wit, pathos, and the language of common folk, their orators moved audiences to tears, laughter, and signing the pledge. More unusual, they gave accounts of their own careers as drunkards and demanded similar confessions from those who attended their gatherings, an emotionally charged practice older temperance reformers found vulgar. The Washingtonians also sponsored picnics, parades, and fairs, techniques they learned from political parties and, probably, from abolitionists. They put together grand spectacles like a giant day-long parade in Boston in 1844, which was addressed by the governor of the state, a temperance man. It was an easy step to move from that sort of public festivity to popular entertainment, a transformation best represented in the work of Timothy Shay Arthur. Already a believer in temperance by 1840, Arthur was inspired by the Washingtonians to begin writing fiction for the cause. He was not the first or the last to do so, but his output was formidable and easily translated into stage productions. His enduring reputation rests upon the anti-alcohol equivalent of *Uncle Tom's Cabin, Ten Nights in a Bar-Room* (1853), a novel, a widely produced melodrama, and, for a time in the mid-twentieth century, a staple of drama groups aiming at quaintness. In the 1840s, however, it was the final indignity to the stuffier older leaders when temperance became theater.

The Washingtonian movement was long past its prime when Joe Morgan, the fictitious hero of *Ten Nights,* took the pledge. The Washingtonians could not control their auxiliaries—the typical fate of national organizations in the antebellum period. Growth was as haphazard as it was swift and there was not enough central direction to sustain local societies. Despite their flair for parades and picnics, the Washingtonians had trouble figuring out what to do once the pledge was taken, the confession made, and the first enthusiasm gone. People lost interest or went into newer, more exciting organizations. The Washingtonians also suffered from putting too much faith in men who were better at swearing off alcohol than at staying off. One lecturer was lost for nearly a week in New York City, only to be found sobering up in a bawdy house. Such episodes, combined with institutional weakness, personality conflicts, and disagreements over issues, led to the quick decline of the Washingtonians. Within a few years most of their organizations were dead.

Their influence lingered. The American Temperance Union and other, older organizations took on some of the Washingtonians' fervor, although they found the public confession and the use of popular entertainment hard to swallow. Thanks to the Washingtonians, the drunkard continued to get more attention than he had in the past. . . .

The Washingtonians were valuable to the cause in their failure as well as for their innovations. Several societies begun after 1840 sought to remedy weaknesses obvious in the Washingtonian movement. The majority were similarly non-sectarian, committed to total abstinence, and aimed at common people, but they had the sturdy institutional structure the Washingtonians lacked. The Sons of Temperance, begun in 1843, was the most important of these organizations, although there were others of consequence. With an elaborate hierarchy and centralized control, the Sons recruited a quarter of a million dues-paying brethren by 1850. They exercised discipline over those who took their pledge, adopted the air of a secret fraternal order, and offered important forms of mutual assistance—all things that secured the loyalty of members to a degree unapproached by the Washingtonians.

The magnetism of secular groups like the Washingtonians and the Sons does not mean that religious campaigns against alcohol ended in the 1840s. The evangelical tradition persisted in the American Temperance Union, in churches, and in later organizations like the Woman's Christian Temperance Union (1874). They, too, learned from the Washingtonians, particularly from their tactics, some of which, like the public confession, fit well with the modes of revivalism popular among lower-middle-class folk. . . .

There was one important new tactic in the 1840s that the Washingtonians neither initiated nor accepted with enthusiasm. It was political action. When reformers divided over whether or not to press for temperance legislation, the Washingtonians were often among those most opposed. In that, they were uncharacteristically backward.

Lyman Beecher, in 1825, had spoken of banning the sale of distilled spirits and there were other early indications that political involvement might be on the horizon. In 1833 a group of lawmakers and public officials formed the Congressional Temperance Society. Their avowed purpose was not to legislate alcohol out of existence but rather to provide a sterling moral example, something politicians rarely did. Yet the very existence of the society was a sign that an influential anti-alcohol faction might possibly be put together in Congress. . . .

In the 1830s and 1840s, however, many temperance people had their doubts about prohibition. Some feared casting aspersions on liquor dealers, a few of whom they thought to be pious, if misguided. There was also a feeling, common to many reformers, that politics was degraded and disgusting to moral men. It seemed as if electioneering required appealing to base instincts and putting expediency above virtue. Political action, furthermore, went against the evangelical belief that true goodness could only flow from a converted heart. People had to *want* to behave properly, and that came from enlightenment, not force. It took soul-searching, and a bit of evasion, for many temperance advocates to accept legislation as a legitimate means of reform.

Still, the prohibitionists had arguments in their favor. The liquor trade was licensed by the government and people were under no obligation to let their government license sin. Besides, most reformers agreed that if the public was godly, decent laws would follow as a matter of course. Prohibitionists felt that the process could be speeded up if temperance men engaged in political action (which would serve as a form of propaganda) and if alcohol, which corrupted many voters, were gotten out of the picture. A final argument—although few cared to put it so bluntly—was that prohibition promised to be successful.

Beginning in the 1830s temperance voters agreed not to cast ballots for heavy drinkers, breaking the chains of party loyalty if need be. They also sought, and sometimes got, local-option legislation, which gave communities the power to stop the traffic in liquor within their jurisdictions. The first statewide victory for temperance forces came in 1838, with a Massachusetts law banning the sale of distilled spirits in amounts of less than fifteen gallons, an act which removed hard beverages from taverns and kept them away from poor people, who could not afford such a quantity. The statute inspired civil disobedience from "rum-sellers" and much agitation for and against, during which many temperance people who had opposed political action fell into line behind the law. It was repealed in 1840 and Massachusetts prohibitionists shifted their attention to the towns, persuading about a hundred of them to go dry by 1845. In 1839 Mississippi passed a law like Massachusetts', although more modest. It forbade the sale of less than a gallon of liquor. After intensive lobbying on both sides, New York voters presented prohibitionists with a massive victory in 1846 and a defeat the following year. The Supreme Court gave the movement a boost in 1846 by deciding in favor of the right of states to deny licenses to sell distilled spirits. Reformers were not always so lucky—a disastrous political campaign set the cause in Georgia back for almost a generation—but temperance battles at the ballot box and in the courts were becoming fierce by the mid-1840s. And by that time Maine had begun to lead the nation.

Much of what happened in Maine was due to two circumstances. The first was a strong antislavery movement. Abolitionists joined the fray and their organizational and propaganda skills were a significant addition to temperance firepower in Maine. Prohibitionists had a second advantage in Neal Dow, a wealthy merchant and an ex-Quaker. Born in 1804, he had been converted to temperance in 1827 after exposure to Beecher and to Justin Edwards of the old American Temperance Society. By the early 1830s Dow was a total-abstinence man and before the decade was out he had taken his principles into politics, in part because he found them there already.

At about the time Massachusetts was experimenting with its fifteen-gallon law, Maine's legislature considered, then tabled, similar restrictive legislation. Meanwhile, Dow began to try to move public opinion in Portland, his home town. He and a coalition of groups, the Washingtonians among them, won in 1842, when the Portland electorate voted by an almost two-to-one margin to stop the sale of alcohol in the city. The ban was evaded and temperance men, led by Dow, agitated for statewide, and presumably more effective, legislation. In 1846 they got almost what they wanted—a law forbidding the sale of intoxicating beverages in less than twenty-eight-gallon lots. Enforcement, however, was the responsibility of town selectmen, who often looked the other way at infractions. Partly to remedy the situation, Dow ran for mayor of Portland; in 1851 he won. His office magnified his influence and within a few months Dow and his supporters had prodded the legislature into passing the so-called Maine Law of 1851. It prohibited the sale and manufacture of intoxicating beverages within the state.

. . . After passage [of the Maine Law] the American Temperance Union swung around to endorse prohibition. Within four years, thirteen states had their own versions of it and there were narrow defeats in others. By 1855 all of New England was dry, as was New York and large parts of the Midwest. Those triumphs were swift and encouraging to prohibitionists, but temperance had achieved quieter, perhaps more impressive, objectives well before Maine saw the light. Per capita consumption of alcohol declined sharply between 1830 and 1850; and large parts of several states were dry before 1851, the result of local-option laws. Statewide prohibition legislation in the 1850s, moreover, was usually not well enough drafted (or defended) to survive court challenges. By the Civil War, Maine Laws had virtually disappeared outside New England, gone but—as it turned out—not forgotten. . . .

From the antebellum period on, temperance was to play a great role in American politics. In numerous local elections throughout the nineteenth and early twentieth centuries alcohol mattered more than all the national issues of the day. At times it fractured parties; at other times it formed a sharp division between them, as when wet Democrats ran against dry Republicans. In most instances temperance mingled with religion and ethnicity, and it easily fused with other political crusades—with antimasonry, nativism, antislavery, the Republican Party, and even woman's rights. Yet the crusade against alcohol had a vitality of its own, separate from the fortunes of any party or any other cause, which is partly why it stayed alive so long in American politics.

In itself the hardiness of temperance is remarkable, but the most important thing for the history of reform is that it became political at all. More than antislavery, it convinced reformers not to rely exclusively upon moral suasion. The fifteen-gallon and Maine laws were proof that vices might be legislated away more easily than sinners could be converted. . . .

The most intriguing question is what made temperance so attractive to such a diverse collection of people—men and women, Northerners, Southerners, and Westerners, urban and rural, rich and poor? The easy answer (and there is much to it) is that America had a drinking problem. . . . Yet temperance was more than a response to rampant intoxication. The real rise in drunkenness must have gone back into the last half of the eighteenth century, when Americans improved their ability to make rum and whiskey. That was more than a generation before the first anti-alcohol society was formed. Much the same thing happened in England, where gin put its stamp upon the working classes long before temperance organizations materialized.

It took social and cultural pressures, combined with that prior increase in intoxication, to make some Americans see alcohol as a problem and temperance as a solution. For the gentlemen and clergy who were prominent in the 1820s and 1830s, the reform was a badge of their own superior virtue and of their disapproval of the antics of poor people, set loose from traditional moral controls by economic and religious changes. If temperance took hold among the masses it would reduce the nastiness of life in the burgeoning cities, elevate the tone of politics, and help preserve the old moral order, which seemed to be rapidly vanishing. If temperance did not take hold, sobriety would be a measure of the social distance between decent folk and others. Changes in the nature of work, moreover, made it desirable that the labor force have the discipline to stay in factories for long hours rather than pursue the traditional course of artisans, who had enjoyed greater independence, conviviality, and tippling. Those calculations swayed some early temperance advocates, as did a genuine hope for human progress, but the majority of men and women who entered the movement in the late 1830s and 1840s were neither wealthy nor distinguished and they clearly had different expectations.

Men with a taste for liquor had the most straightforward reasons for joining, particularly after 1840, when the Washingtonians began to seek them out. Temperance provided self-discipline, moral support, and a way of gaining control over a destructive impulse. Yet ex-drunkards never were a majority in the movement and certainly there were few of them among the thousands of women attracted to the crusade. More likely, temperance provided them with unique opportunities. It was far less threatening to the social order than antislavery, woman's rights, and most other antebellum reforms. If anything, it promised to defend the status quo against the forces of dissipation. Even though it attracted militant feminists, its respectability made it equally acceptable to timid or conservative women who feared or rejected radical agitation but who nevertheless wanted a place for themselves in public life. Temperance could also be a way to reproach males. Anti-alcohol propaganda, like the sentimental fiction American females read and wrote, consisted of a catalogue of awful sufferings men inflicted upon their loved ones. It was almost always the father (or son, or brother) who brought grief to his wife (or mother, or sister) and his innocent children. If he was redeemed, it was often through the agency of a woman (or child, or both) whose natural goodness exorcised the demon rum. These melodramas had a ring of truth—American men were capable of swinish behavior—but such stories also sound like acts of revenge by women against the male world that glorified them, confined them to the home, and failed to live by its own preachings.

That simply makes more curious the matter of what drove thousands of reasonably sober men to sign the pledge after 1840. The evidence is fragmentary, but it gives some hints in their ages, which appear to have clustered in the early twenties, and in their occupations. Many belonged on the fringes of respectability, working in the lesser professions (including teaching), as petty entrepreneurs, or as artisans in skilled trades such as carpentry. These were men making their way in the world (upward, they hoped). An image of propriety could be very important in increasing their prospects. . . .

There were still more reasons for joining temperance societies. Beginning in the late 1830s, they provided important services. The Sons of Temperance were especially strong in that respect, having as one of their primary objectives "mutual assistance in cases of sickness." In fact, they offered life, as well as health, insurance, and the San Francisco branch, perhaps others, acted as an employment agency, posting the names of members who needed work. Those were no mean advantages in days when the government did nothing to help the ill, destitute, and unemployed.

Temperance societies—particularly ones begun after 1840—also provided opportunities for sociability. The Sons of Temperance, with their rituals and regalia, satisfied the same impulses that sent American males into lodges like the Odd Fellows and countless similar voluntary organizations in antebellum America. Throughout the year there were various excuses for getting together—picnics, fairs, and Fourth of July celebrations. These were fine places to enjoy companionship and for decent women and men to court. (A North Carolinian described a neighborhood zealot as "a young widower" who "wanted a wife—and he spoke to show how well he could speak rather than for any immediate practical effect in advertising the cause of temperance.") Besides saving drunkards, the movement redeemed the uncertainty and loneliness of life in antebellum America, and only when it did that could it become a genuine substitute for the solace of alcohol. Like sports and popular stage shows, temperance societies became nineteenth-century alternatives to the camaraderie of the old tavern.

Despite the social and practical advantages of belonging to anti-alcohol organizations, interest waxed and waned. Members acquired families and ceased to participate actively; brethren fell from grace, some to be forgiven, to fall again. But at the core of the movement were dedicated people and they carried it through the years. They were a diverse lot: reformers who saw conquest of alcohol as an important part of some broader program; religious men and women who felt abstinence was a divine command; and those who knew from personal experience the evils of strong drink. . . .

DOCUMENTS

"And I Will Be Heard," 1831

In the month of August, I issued proposals for publishing, *"The Liberator"* in Washington City; but the enterprise, though hailed in different sections of the country, was palsied by public indifference. Since that time, the removal of the *Genius of Universal Emancipation* [an abolitionist newspaper] to the Seat of Government has rendered less imperious the establishment of a similar periodical in that quarter.

During my recent tour for the purpose of exciting the minds of the people by a series of discourses on the subject of slavery, every place that I visited gave fresh evidence of the fact, that a greater revolution in public sentiment was to be effected in the free states—*and particularly in New England*—than at the south. I found contempt more bitter, opposition more active, detraction more relentless, prejudice more stubborn, and apathy

SOURCE: *Liberator*, January 1, 1831, cited by Wendell Phillips Garrison and Francis Jackson Garrison, *William Lloyd Garrison, 1805–1879: The Story of His Life Told by His Children* (Boston: Houghton Mifflin, 1885), 1: 224–25.

more frozen, than among slave owners themselves. Of course, there were individual exceptions to the contrary. This state of things affected, but did not dishearten me. I determined, at every hazard, to lift up the standard of emancipation in the eyes of the nation, *within sight of Bunker Hill and in the birth place of liberty.* That standard is now unfurled; and long may it float, unhurt by the spoliations of time or the missiles of a desperate foe— yea, till every chain be broken, and every bondman set free! Let Southern oppressors tremble—let their Northern apologists tremble—let all the ene- mies of the persecuted blacks tremble.

I deem the publication of my original Prospectus unnecessary, as it has obtained a wide circulation. The principles therein inculcated will be steadily pursued in this paper, excepting that I shall not array myself as the political partisan of any man. In defending the great cause of human rights, I wish to derive the assistance of all religions and of all parties.

Assenting to the "self evident truth" maintained in the American Dec- laration of Independence, "that all men are created equal, and endowed by their Creator with certain inalienable rights—among which are life, liberty and the pursuit of happiness," I shall strenuously contend for the immediate enfranchisement of our slave population. In Park Street Church [Boston], on the Fourth of July, 1829, in an address on slavery, I unreflect- ingly assented to the popular but pernicious doctrine of *gradual* abolition. I seize this opportunity to make a full and unequivocal recantation, and thus publicly to ask pardon of my God, of my country, and of my brethren the poor slaves, for having uttered a sentiment so full of timidity, injustice and absurdity. A similar recantation, from my pen, was published in the *Genius of Universal Emancipation* at Baltimore, in September, 1829. My con- science is now satisfied.

I am aware, that many object to the severity of my language; but is there not cause for severity? I *will* be as harsh as truth, and as uncompro- mising as justice. On this subject, I do not wish to think, or speak, or write, with moderation. No! No! Tell a man whose house is on fire, to give a moderate alarm; tell him to moderately rescue his wife from the hands of the ravisher; tell the mother to gradually extricate her babe from the fire into which it has fallen;—but urge me not to use moderation in a cause like the present. I am in earnest—I will not equivocate—I will not excuse— I will not retreat a single inch—AND I WILL BE HEARD. The apathy of the people is enough to make every statue leap from its pedestal, and to hasten the resurrection of the dead.

It is pretended, that I am retarding the cause of emancipation by the coarseness of my invective, and the precipitancy of my measures. *The charge is not true.* On this question my influence,—humble as it is,—is felt at this moment to a considerable extent, and shall be felt in coming years—not perniciously, but beneficially—not as a curse, but as a blessing; and poster- ity will bear testimony that I was right. . . .

The "Reformatory and Elevating Influences" of the Public Schools, 1848

Under the Providence of God, our means of education are the grand machinery by which the "raw material" of human nature can be worked up into inventors and discoverers, into skilled artisans and scientific farmers, into scholars and jurists, into the founders of benevolent institutions, and the great expounders of ethical and theological science. By means of early education, those embryos of talent may be quickened, which will solve the difficult problems of political and economical law; and by them, too, the genius may be kindled which will blaze forth in the Poets of Humanity. Our schools, far more than they have done, may supply the Presidents and Professors of Colleges, and Superintendents of Public Instruction, all over the land; and send, not only into our sister states, but across the Atlantic, the men of practical science, to superintend the construction of the great works of art. Here, too, may those judicial powers be developed and invigorated, which will make legal principles so clear and convincing as to prevent appeals to force; and, should the clouds of war ever lower over our country, some hero may be found,—the nursling of our schools, and ready to become the leader of our armies,—that best of all heroes, who will secure the glories of a peace, unstained by the magnificient murders of the battle-field. . . .

Without undervaluing any other human agency, it may be safely affirmed that the Common School, improved and energized, as it can easily be, may become the most effective and benignant of all the forces of civilization. Two reasons sustain this position. In the first place, there is a universality in its operation, which can be affirmed of no other institution whatever. If administered in the spirit of justice and conciliation, all the rising generation may be brought within the circle of its reformatory and elevating influences. And, in the second place, the materials upon which it operates are so pliant and ductile as to be susceptible of assuming a greater variety of forms than any other earthly work of the Creator. The inflexibility and ruggedness of the oak, when compared with the lithe sapling or the tender germ, are but feeble emblems to typify the docility of childhood, when contrasted with the obduracy and intractableness of man. It is these inherent advantages of the Common School, which, in our own State, have produced results so striking, from a system so imperfect, and an administration so feeble. In teaching the blind, and the deaf and dumb, in kindling the latent spark of intelligence that lurks in an idiot's mind, and in the more holy work of reforming abandoned and outcast

SOURCE: [Horace Mann], Massachusetts Board of Education, *Twelfth Annual Report of . . . the Secretary of the Board* (Boston, 1849), 32, 37.

children, education has proved what it can do, by glorious experiments. These wonders, it has done in its infancy, and with the lights of a limited experience; but, when its faculties shall be fully developed, when it shall be trained to wield its mighty energies for the protection of society against the giant vices which now invade and torment it;—against intemperance, avarice, war, slavery, bigotry, the woes of want and the wickedness of waste,—then, there will not be a height to which these enemies of the race can escape, which it will not scale, nor a Titan among them all, whom it will not slay.

The Convictions
of a Peace Advocate, 1854

We have considered the power and dignity of passive resistance, when opposed to assaults from without, or oppression from within. We have tried to show that necessity does not make it a virtue in any case; but that its inherent virtue always makes it a necessity. We now proceed to demonstrate its patriotism. We deem it due to the principles and advocates of peace, to rebut the charge that is often brought against them, that they are "the complacent allies of despotism—that they would stand by and see, without concern or remonstrance, communities, peoples, and nations manacled hand and foot, by tyrants; their rights, liberties, hopes, and aspirations, trodden out of existence by the iron heel of oppression." The imputation of cowardice, unmanly imbecility, a crouching, abject spirit, is involved in this charge. "What! would you have us lie down in the dust, and be trampled upon by these despotic powers and governments! Would you have us permit them to enslave us, and hold out our arms and feet to the fettering without a struggle or a murmur?" And then, having filled their bosoms to bursting with patriotic indignation at the course and disposition described interrogatively by these triumphant questions, they exclaim, "No! we would spill the last drop of our blood;—we would see our cities burned with fire;—we would perish with arms in our hands on the battle-field, or pine in exile in Siberia or Botany Bay, before we would tamely submit to be slaves! Liberty or death!" These are the most striking and usual terms of comparison in the vocabulary of martial patriotism. Frequently the sentiments they express take a figurative form more fearful still. We recollect one employed by the editor of an American journal,

SOURCE: Elihu Burritt, *Thoughts and Things at Home and Abroad, with a Memoir by Mary Howitt* (Boston: Phillips, Sampson & Co., 1854), 277–80.

259

pending the Oregon controversy,* to this effect: "Sooner than relinquish our just rights to the disputed territory, we would shed every drop of blood in the heart of the nation!" Mr. Borrow, agent of the Bible Society, records "a broken prayer for my native land, which, after my usual thanksgiving, I breathed forth to the Almighty, ere retiring to rest that Sunday night at Gibraltar"; a prayer *for* his native country which contains this passage— "May'st thou sink, if thou dost sink, amidst blood and flame, with a mighty noise, causing more than one nation to participate in thy downfall!" And these are regarded as the outbursts of a patriotic feeling—of a love of country so intense that they would see it engulfed in fire and blood, and even the last vein of the nation's heart pierced, and its existence extinguished, rather than endure insult, injury, or oppression! They measure their attachment and devotion to their country and its institutions by the awful calamities which they would bring upon it, in defending its honor and rights. What a fearful antithesis of alternatives! How many peoples and nations have "sunk, amidst blood and flame, and with a mighty noise," in the abyss which yawns between these alternative conditions! How many patriots of this order have seen their country a smoking sea of ruin, without finding a bulrush ark in which to float "the immediate jewel of its soul"— the charter of its existence as a nation!

We wish no one to accept or share the responsibility of our convictions, or of the views we wish to express in reference to this aspect of the subject. If peace has its victories no less than war, it has its heroism and its patriotism. The men of peace can find no attribute, in the great Gospel principles of their faith, that can side with despotism, or wink with indifference at oppression. They are not cowards. They counsel no tame, unmanly submission to wrong; but to oppose to wrong a courage of the human will that shall never faint or waver at any extremity of endurance;—aye, to "resist unto blood," if it be unavoidable,—to give their own necks to the axe or to the halter, on the block or the scaffold, but never to shed themselves a single drop, or perpetrate a single act of malevolent injury on any human being, under the severest pressure of despotic rule. Peace has its heroism, serene and dauntless, that neither trembles nor pales before the guillotine, the halter, or the knout. Peace has its patriotism; deep, earnest, unselfish, self-sacrificing, and sensitive,—a love of country that would bleed to the last vein, but never wound, for its rights, honor, and prosperity. Peace has its battle-fields; bloodless, but brave to a degree of heroic endurance of wrong and outrage to which martial courage could never attain.

[*the dispute over the boundary between the United States and British Columbia, resolved by treaty in 1846 as the 49th parallel, which it remains today]

A Feminist Marries, 1855

It was my privilege to celebrate May day by officiating at a wedding in a farm-house among the hills of West Brookfield, [Massachusetts]. The bridegroom was a man of tried worth, a leader in the Western Anti-Slavery Movement; and the bride was one whose fair name is known throughout the nation; one whose rare intellectual qualities are excelled by the private beauty of her heart and life.

I never perform the marriage ceremony without a renewed sense of the iniquity of our present system of laws in respect to marriage; a system by which "man and wife are one, and that one is the husband." It was with my hearty concurrence, therefore, that the following protest was read and signed, as a part of the nuptial ceremony; and I send it to you, that others may be induced to do likewise.

REV. THOMAS WENTWORTH HIGGINSON

While acknowledging our mutual affection by publicly assuming the relation of husband and wife, yet in justice to ourselves and a great principle, we deem it a duty to declare that this act on our part implies no sanction of, nor promise of voluntary obedience to such of the present laws of marriage, as refuse to recognize the wife as an independent, rational being, while they confer upon the husband an injurious and unnatural superiority, investing him with legal powers which no honorable man would exercise, and which no man should possess. We protest especially against the laws which give to the husband:

1. The custody of the wife's person.
2. The exclusive control and guardianship of their children.
3. The sole ownership of her personal, and use of her real estate, unless previously settled upon her, or placed in the hands of trustees, as in the case of minors, lunatics, and idiots.
4. The absolute right to the product of her industry.
5. Also against laws which give to the widower so much larger and more permanent an interest in the property of his deceased wife, than they give to the widow in that of the deceased husband.
6. Finally, against the whole system by which "the legal existence of the wife is suspended during marriage," so that in most States, she neither has a legal part in the choice of her residence, nor can she make a will, nor sue or be sued in her own name, nor inherit property.

SOURCE: Elizabeth Cady Stanton et al., eds., *History of Woman Suffrage* (Rochester, N.Y.: Published for Susan B. Anthony, 1877), 1: 260–61.

We believe that personal independence and equal human rights can never be forfeited, except for crime; that marriage should be an equal and permanent partnership, and so recognized by law; that until it is so recognized, married partners should provide against the radical injustice of present laws, by every means in their power.

We believe that where domestic difficulties arise, no appeal should be made to legal tribunals under existing laws, but that all difficulties should be submitted to the equitable adjustment of arbitrators mutually chosen.

Thus reverencing law, we enter our protest against rules and customs which are unworthy of the name, since they violate justice, the essence of law.

HENRY B. BLACKWELL
LUCY STONE

Worcester Spy, 1855

CHAPTER 14

The Slave Family

By 1850, participants in a number of reform movements could point to some notable achievements. Throughout the Northeast and Midwest, public schools had been established in towns in which none had previously existed, while older systems were receiving substantially greater financial support. The public-library movement was experiencing similar success, and improvements were being made in the treatment of debtors, criminals, and the mentally ill. Despite these and other successes, it is unlikely that any reform leader would have considered the goals of his or her movement attained by the beginning of the 1850s; much remained to be accomplished. As the decade wore on, the spirit of perfectionism was gradually overwhelmed by the bitter divisiveness of sectionalism and slavery—issues that ultimately were resolved by neither moral suasion nor legislation but by war.

During the American Revolution, a number of white Americans had seen the inconsistency in struggling against Great Britain in the name of freedom while holding other people in bondage as slaves. Virginia, North Carolina, and Maryland passed laws making it easier for masters to free their slaves. A few planters released *their slaves outright, and some others, including George Washington, made provisions for manumission in their wills. Gradually the northern states abolished slavery. With the expansion of the cotton kingdom, however, white southerners became increasingly dependent on slave labor. Far from liberalizing their attitudes and practices toward slavery, after 1800 Southern legislatures passed new restrictions, making it extremely difficult for masters to emancipate their bondsmen. In response to abolitionist attacks, many Southerners shifted their public posture on slavery from defending it as a necessary evil to advocating it as a positive good. By the time of the Civil War there were some 4 million slaves in the South, the vast majority of whom lived and worked on the cotton plantations.*

In the eyes of the law, slaves were little more than property, with few legal rights. Yet their individual experiences could vary greatly. In recent years scholars have devoted considerable attention to how blacks survived and created their own distinctive culture within slavery. Loren Schweninger's essay "A Slave Family in the Ante Bellum South" follows a remarkable black family, the Thomas-Rapiers, over three generations and describes how its members, despite innumerable obstacles, maintained their ties with each other. Notwithstanding the difficulties, the Thomas-Rapier family survived. Note how its members managed and what occupations were open to them. The essay suggests that urban slaves fared better than those on plantations. Why was this so? Remember that only a small minority of slaves lived in cities.

The first document, former slave Josiah Henson's account of a slave auction, illustrates vividly why keeping a slave family together was no simple task.

If the lot of slaves and free blacks in the antebellum South was so burdensome, one might ask why more slaves did not flee to the North. Many did, but life in the North was far from easy. There, racism excluded most blacks from voting, limited most of them to menial labor, and channeled their children into segregated schools. The second document demonstrates that even blacks who achieved a measure of economic well-being in the North were victimized by racial prejudice. It is from a letter to white abolitionist Angelina Grimké from black abolitionist Sarah Forten, daughter of a prosperous Philadelphia sailmaker. What does Forten identify as the bases for prejudice against blacks? Forten's discussion of colonization refers to the plans of the American Colonization Society to alleviate racial problems at home by promoting the settlement of freed blacks in Africa. What are the grounds for her hostility to the idea?

Whether in the North or South, the church was a significant institution for blacks. The final document relates a British traveler's impressions of services in two black churches he visited in Savannah, Georgia. How does the document help explain why religion played an important role in the lives of black Americans during this period?

264

ESSAY

A Slave Family in the Ante Bellum South

Loren Schweninger

An investigation of one slave family . . . can only tell us about *a* family, and one that was in many respects very fortunate. The members of the Thomas-Rapier slave family received an education; achieved a degree of economic independence; and eventually became free or at least "quasi-free." Moreover, they belonged to extremely permissive and beneficent masters. They lived in an urban environment (as did only 10% of the South's slave population), and hired out, though it was against the law. But, like many other Blacks in the ante bellum South, they too suffered the pains of separation (living in Alabama, Tennessee, and Canada); sexual exploitation (the slave mother bore three sons by three different white men); and the legal denial of the slave family. Yet, in spite of these institutional barriers or perhaps because of them, the members of the Thomas-Rapier family maintained their integrity. Indeed, as seen in a rare collection of slave letters, notes, and autobiographical reminiscences, they preserved a cohesive family unit for three generations. In a larger sense, then, an investigation of one slave family can perhaps shed some light on the family experiences of many slaves in the ante bellum South.

Born in Albemarle County, Virginia, about 1790, the black slave, Sally, grew up on the 1500-acre tobacco plantation of Charles S. Thomas, a friend and neighbor of Thomas Jefferson. At a young age she was sent to the fields. Working from sun-up to sundown, season to season, and year to year, she (along with forty-one other slaves on the "big gang"), prepared beds, planted seeds, transplanted shoots, "wormed and topped" young plants, hung, and then stripped, sorted and bundled the final product. When she was about eighteen, Sally suffered (or accepted) the sexual advances of a white man (probably John Thomas, the owner's eldest son); and in September 1808, she gave birth to a mulatto boy, John. Some years later she gave birth to a second mulatto child, Henry. As Virginia law required that progeny take the status of the mother, both children were born in bondage, but as part of the Thomas Trust Estate, they were protected against sale or separation. Consequently, when one of the heirs of the estate (again probably John) joined the westward movement of slaveholders across the Appalachians into the Cumberland river valley about 1818, Sally, John and Henry were transported to the fast growing town of Nashville, Tennessee.

SOURCE: Loren Schweninger, "A Slave Family in the Ante Bellum South," *Journal of Negro History*, 60 (January 1975): 29–44.

The city offered many opportunities. With the master's permission, Sally hired out as a cleaning lady, a practice common among urban slaves, and secured an agreement to retain a portion of her earnings. She then rented a two-story frame house on the corner of Deaderick and Cherry Streets in the central business district. Converting the front room into a laundry, and manufacturing her own soap (blending fats, oils, alkali and salt in a small vat in the front room), she established a business of cleaning clothes. She soon built up a thriving trade. At the same time Sally arranged for her eldest son, John, to hire out as a waiter and poll boy to river barge Captain Richard Rapier, who was plying the Cumberland-Tennessee-Mississippi river trade, between Nashville, Florence (Alabama), and New Orleans; and arranged for Henry to hire out as an errand boy to various "white gentlemen" around Nashville. Part of their earnings, along with her own, she saved in a tea cannister, which she hid in the loft, hoping someday to be able to purchase "free papers" [legal proof of free status] for the children. "However, that might cost as much as $2000!" Undeterred, she conscientiously set aside part of her earnings every month, and by early 1826, she had saved over $300.

Though thirty-six years old, Sally was still an attractive woman. In October 1827, in the house on Deaderick Street she gave birth to a third mulatto son, James. The father was the famous ante bellum Judge John Catron, but according to the state law, which, like the law in Virginia, assigned progeny the status of the mother, James was born in bondage. "Now my own father presided over the supreme court of Tennessee [and served as a justice on the United States Supreme Court]," James later recalled, "[but] he had no time to give me a thought. He gave me 25 cents once, [and] if I [were] correctly informed, that is all he ever did for me." With three children, John nineteen, Henry about sixteen, and James, Sally despaired that she might not be able to save enough to free her family.

But her despair soon turned to joy. She received word in 1829 that her eldest son had been emancipated. "I bequeath one thousand dollars to my executors for the purpose of purchasing the freedom of the mulatto boy, John, who now waits on me, and belongs to the Estate of Thomas," Richard Rapier stipulated in his will, and the Alabama General Assembly, the only legal emancipator of slaves in the state, passed a law freeing "a certain male slave by the name of John H. Rapier." Then, she saw an opportunity to free Henry. With the final settlement of the Thomas Estate in 1834, "Sally and the two mulatto boys," reverted to one John Martin, an affable young man who wanted to sell a part of his inheritance for a quick profit. Fearing that her children would be sold "down river to Mississippi," Sally urged Henry to escape. Heeding his mother's advice, Henry fled through upper Tennessee and Kentucky but was captured near Louisville and confined to a guard house. He managed to work off his leg-chains one night, however, steal down to the Ohio River, untie a boat, and drift into the current. "The night was cold," Henry wrote afterwards. "I headed the yawl downstream, sculled over the falls and made for the Indiana shore. There I found a man who freed my hands." Taking the surname Thomas, he travelled to Buffalo, New York, where he opened a barber shop.

Shortly after Henry's escape, Sally went to Ephraim H. Foster, a prominent Tennessee lawyer, and asked for assistance in putting James out of Martin's reach. "Will you talk with him [Martin] and see what he will take for the boy," she asked. "Very well, Aunt Sally," Foster replied, "I will see him and let you know what can be done." A few days later Foster told her that Martin wanted $400. "I have saved only $350," Sally explained, but quickly added: "Now if you, Col. Foster, will pay the fifty and make it four hundred, have the bill of sale made to yourself, you can hold James in trust until I return [the] money. I want you to be his protector." Foster agreed and the bargain was sealed. A short time later, she paid off the debt and received a bill of sale, "free papers," for six-year-old James. Even then, however, he was not free. The law required emancipated Blacks to secure a manumission deed from the county court, and "thereupon immediately leave Tennessee." Thus, despite having "free papers," James was still legally a slave.

But neither the law nor slavery seemed to curtail his activities. As a young boy, he performed a variety of chores for his mother: keeping salt in the hopper for making soap, cutting wood for the fire place, cleaning up around the house, and delivering clothes to customers. He also enrolled in the Nashville school for Blacks. Thomas recalled sitting on splintery benches, in a drafty one-room school house and listening to ill-prepared lessons on such basic subjects as "the fundamentals of reading." In addition, he remembered that the school remained open only a few months each year, the pupils, or "scholars," had to pay a very high $4 tuition fee, and that free Blacks Rufus Conrad, Daniel Watkins and Samuel Lowery taught at the school from time to time. "But often," he said, "there was no school because there was no teacher." In 1836, for instance, a black teacher, described as "a fine scholar," was taken out by whites and whipped nearly to death. "Tennesseans generally opposed educating blacks," he recalled, "they might want the same as whites." But young James had an intense desire to learn and quickly mastered the basics of mathematics, reading and writing.

Having secured a rudimentary education, James hired out as an apprentice barber. Working with bondsman Frank Parrish, who had earlier established a barber shop on Public Square, he quickly learned the trade. "James [is] still with Frank Parrish and has the character of a good barber, So a Gentleman told me," his brother, John Rapier, observed in 1843. "He is well thought of by the Gentlemen. James has manners to please almost anyone who does not let their prejudice go far on account of color." Two years later James was still with Parrish, earned $12 a month, and at the same time had begun violin lessons with one Gordan McGowan. "James will make a man of musick I think. He seems to be very fond of it." Having served a five-year apprenticeship, in 1846, he opened his own barber shop. The nineteen-year-old slave established his shop in the house where he had grown up (and where his mother still operated her cleaning business), at 10 Deaderick Street. The location was ideal. Within a few steps of several banking houses, newspapers, and law firms, as well as the county court house, Market Square, and the Capitol, "the place on Deaderick," he explained, "was convenient to bankers, merchants, lawyers, politicians, and professional men." He counted among his customers six famous Tennesseans: William Carroll, one time governor; E. S. (Squire) Hall, an important businessman; General William Harding, owner of Bellemeade Estate; Ephraim Foster, a Whig political leader; and William G. (Parson) Brownlow, the Civil War governor. Francis Fogg, the well-known Davidson County lawyer, visited the Thomas shop daily. "He returns to us in the evening," Mrs. Fogg noted approvingly, "with face smooth and curls nicely arranged."

While attending to his duties as a barber, James listened attentively to conversations that took place among his customers. "They had time to talk in the barber shop. Nobody seemed in a great hurry. Everything was discussed—social, commercial, political and financial." He remembered conversations about the abolitionists, the advancement of cotton on the Liverpool market, the magnetism and sporting proclivities of Andrew Jackson, plantation acreage along the Mississippi, and fugitive slaves. Once, he recalled being sharply questioned about runaway Blacks. "You have a brother living in Buffalo, New York, I believe," General Harding asked pointedly. "Yes," was the reply. "Well he treated me in a gruff manner. I went to ask him if he knew anything about a boy who ran off from me. I told him I only wanted to see him. I had come to Buffalo for that purpose. I received a very cold and indifferent reply." James could do little but apologize for his brother's "rudeness." Though he usually remained silent when the conversation turned to such controversial issues; at times he ventured an opinion on the slavery question. Once, for example, while shaving a young Virginia lawyer, he defended the Wilmot Proviso, a proposal to prohibit slavery in the newly acquired Mexican territories. "The set back I got caused me to be careful in the future. Among other things he told me I had no right to listen to a gentleman's conversation." Despite such "set backs," James built up a flourishing business. Charging 25 cents for a haircut, 15 cents for a shave, and $1 for occasionally extracting teeth, he operated one of the most prosperous "tonsorial establishments" in Nashville. In the city's first business directory (published in 1853), he advertised in large boldface print: "JAS THOMAS, BARBER SHOP, 10 Deaderick St."

Meanwhile, Sally's other two children, freedman John H. Rapier and fugitive Henry Thomas, were also prospering as barbers. Rapier opened a shop in Florence, Alabama, soon saved over $500, purchased a white frame house on Court Street in the downtown district, and like James, converted the house into a place of business as well as a residence. In 1831, he married Susan, a free Black from Baltimore, Maryland, and in the next decade the couple had four children: Richard, John Jr., Henry and James. After his wife's death in childbirth at the age of twenty-nine, he purchased a sixteen-year-old slave, Lucretia, and between 1848 and 1861, they had five slave children, the youngest named Susan. During the ante bellum period Rapier acquired real estate holdings in Alabama, the Minnesota Territory, and Canada, purchased valuable railroad stock, and saved $2000 in cash. By 1860, he was one of the wealthiest free Blacks in Alabama, with about $10,000.

Henry Thomas also opened a barber shop. Locating in the basement of Buffalo's elegant hotel Niagara, he too built up a lucrative trade. About 1835, he married a black woman, Maria, and they had eleven children, ten boys and a girl, Sarah. In 1852, to avoid apprehension by slave catchers (who were encouraged by the 1850 Fugitive Slave Law), he moved to the black community of Buxton, Canada West. With resources he had saved as a barber, he purchased one hundred acres of wilderness land, built a log house, cleared the trees, and put in a crop of corn, wheat and barley. "The settlement improves slowly, but prospects are good for its success," he noted in 1856. "The lumber mill is making improvements for the neighborhood. Soon the railroad will pass through. The school is flourishing. I have six acres in wheat and 2 in barley." Thus, using one of the few profitable occupations open to ante bellum Blacks, James, John and Henry were all able to achieve a degree of financial independence.

The members of the slave family were also successful at maintaining close family ties. Though separated by hundreds, even thousands of miles, though forbidden to travel in certain regions, and though denied postal privileges, they kept in close touch. As a slave and also when he was a free Black, John Rapier Sr. frequently visited Nashville. And between 1838 and 1846, he arranged for all four of his children to attend school in the Tennessee capital and to stay with their slave uncle and slave grandmother. "John and James are so [well] pleased with their grandmother [and school]," he noted in 1843, "that they do not want to come home, so James writes." A couple of years later he added: "My two sons that are with mother are well when I last hear[d] from them. I entend to go up to Nashville in the course of ten or twelve days and See them all." On that occasion Rapier confessed that he had not been to Tennessee in nearly a year. "I am extremely anxious to See the family again," he said, promising to deliver a letter from his brother, which had been smuggled into the South from the North. After a visit to the Tennessee capital, he wrote to "Brother Henry": "Mother looks as young as she did 8 years ago and works as hard and hardly takes time to talk to you." Forwarding other family news, he said that "Brother James" was doing extremely well as a barber; and of his sons, he proudly observed that Richard wrote in an excellent hand; Henry wanted to continue his education; James read extremely well "for a little boy of his age [6] and training;" and "John has wrote me two letter and writes very plain for a boy of eight, . . . and has as much taste for reading as any child I know off and is very good in arithmetic." Rapier not only journeyed to Tennessee often, but about once a year, he travelled to New York or Canada. After one such sojourn, he expressed concern for Brother Henry's future in the North. "I told him to buy [more] land in that country and to pay the taxes. [But] I am fearful that Brother Henry will come to want in [Canada] as I am of the opinion that [it] is poor farming country." For their parts, Henry and James also expressed a deep concern for the welfare of the slave family. Henry usually concluded his letters with the simple, but significant, line: "All the family is well and wishes to be remembered to you." And James Thomas wrote: "A letter from your hands [John Rapier Jr.] offers me a great deal of pleasure to say nothing of the family news it imparts." It seems that separation, an inherent part of the institution of slavery, had little effect on the spiritual unity of the slave family.

There was also a solidarity among the members of the Rapier family. Deeply concerned about the welfare of his children, John Rapier offered them advice on everything from economic matters to questions of morality: "Settle your debts," "Save your money." "Stay away from liquor," he admonished "The Four Boys." "Stick closer to work and Say nothing and do nothing but what is right and you will do well my sons." In 1845 he wrote Richard, who was attending school in Buffalo and living with Henry Thomas: "Study your books so I can hold you up as an example to your lettle Brothers. You are blessed if you will look at your situation. You have kind relations who are anctious to see you grow up an ornament to society." Perhaps the best expression of the spiritual unity of the Rapier family was written by James Thomas Rapier, James P. Thomas's namesake and one of Sally's twenty-six grandchildren. Also living with fugitive Henry Thomas, and attending school in Buxton, he wrote:

> In our boyhood . . . all four of us boys were together. We all breathed as one. [Now] we are scattered abroad on the face of the Earth. Do you ever expect to see us all together again? I do not. Just look where we are . . . John in [Minnesota]. Myself in the north. Henry and Dick in California. Father in Alabama. Did you ever think how small our family is?

Among the Rapiers, as well as the Thomases, there was an almost religious devotion to the institution of the family.

The ability of the slave family to remain so close seems all the more remarkable in the face of the legal restrictions placed on Blacks. Statutes forbade a free Black from either visiting with slaves, or travelling from one state to another, both on penalty of being sold into slavery. Laws prohibited slaves from owning personal property, renting real estate, earning money, or securing an education. "No person shall hire to any slave," one Tennessee code pronounced, "the time of said slave." Lawmakers prescribed a ten year prison sentence to anyone helping a slave to escape, forging a pass for a slave, harboring a runaway or inciting a Black to defy a white; and laid down the death penalty for Blacks convicted of assaulting or molesting a white woman, maliciously setting fire to a barn, preparing any poison, or conspiring to revolt. "A ring leader or Chief Instigator of any plot to rebel or murder any white," one law stated, "may be lawfully killed [on sight], if it is not practicable, otherwise, to arrest and secure him." Nashville ordinances required free Blacks to pay a capitation (head) tax of $1 or $2, register at the court house, and "carry free papers on their person at all times." Blacks without such papers were to be treated as slaves. Moreover, Negroes were not permitted to walk the streets after dark, enter tippling houses, make weird noises, or gather within the city limits for any purpose, except public worship, and Blacks attending church were to be supervised by whites.

But the slave family disregarded the elaborate code governing Blacks. Sally hired out, earned money, rented a house, and operated a business. "Mother lived so long at the corner of Deaderick and Cherry Streets," James Thomas remarked later, "that the people of Nashville thought she [was free] and owned the property." She moved about the city with little hindrance, boarded her grandchildren as they attended school, and secretly advised Henry to escape to the North. In a similar manner James Thomas hired out, earned money and established a business. He eventually accumulated a large amount of personal property—furniture, mirrors, clothes, and about $1000 in cash, and while still a slave, became the manager of one of the largest barbering establishments in Nashville. He travelled to various parts of the city without a pass, entertained free Blacks in his home, and attended black church meetings. At one such gathering he recalled the black congregation, mostly slaves, singing until 12 o'clock at night. "The owners," he wrote, "seemed to care very little how much religion their servants got. They seemed to encourage it." In much the same way John Rapier and Henry Thomas acquired personal property, hired out, earned as much as $50 a month, and, despite the laws against the movement of Blacks, travelled throughout the South, North, and Canada. Rapier even assisted a slave, Sam Ragland, to escape on one occasion. In short, the slave family was not in the least constrained by the restrictive black codes.

Sally's dream that all of her children secure their freedom finally came true in 1851, when her youngest son, James, asked Ephraim Foster to present a manumission petition to the Davidson County court. The slave and his master appeared at the courthouse in Nashville on March 6. "James has always maintained an exemplary character," Foster told the nine-judge panel hearing the case. "He has been industrious, honest, moral, humble, polite and had conducted himself as to gain the confidence and respect of whites. He is a man of great worth in his place." The testimony of such an eminent Tennessean swayed the magistrates and, after a short deliberation, they ordered "the slave James, otherwise called James [P.] Thomas, emancipated and forever set free." Thomas now addressed the court himself. He requested immunity from the 1831 law requiring manumitted Blacks to leave Tennessee. "I have deported myself in a manner requiring the confidence of whites. I have always earned a good living. I would be greatly damaged having to Start anew in some Strange Country." The judges, after receiving the required $500 good behavior bond, granted the immunity. James P. Thomas thus became the first black man in the county, perhaps the state, under the stringent emigration law of 1831, to gain legally both freedom and residency.

A short time before James gained his freedom, however, Sally died of cholera. A woman of great drive and dedication, she had devoted her life to freeing her children. She had hired out, started a business, and gladly put up her life savings to purchase "free papers" for James. She had also assisted Henry in his quest for freedom. Due in part to her unwavering efforts, the slaves John H. Rapier, Sr., Henry K. Thomas, and James P. Thomas, all gained free status before the Civil War. In addition, the Thomases and Rapiers all found great strength in the slave family. Members of these families were quite successful: John entered politics during Reconstruction; Henry farmed hundreds of acres in Canada; and James acquired property in St. Louis valued at $250,000, while Sarah Thomas became a school teacher, James T. Rapier a Congressman, and John Rapier, Jr. a surgeon, stemmed from the security they found in the slave family. It seems that for the black slave Sally, sexual exploitation, miscegenation, separation, and legal restrictions—the very forces designed, in part, to destroy the black family— gave impetus, *not* to disintegration and disunity, but to an extraordinary feeling of family loyalty, unity, and love. For Sally, her children, and her grandchildren, the slave family was indeed "a refuge from the rigors of slavery."

DOCUMENTS

Sold at Auction, c. 1820

The crowd collected round the stand, the huddling group of Negroes, the examination of muscle, teeth, the exhibition of agility, the look of the auctioneer, the agony of my mother—I can shut my eyes and see them all.

My brothers and sisters were bid off first, and one by one, while my mother, paralyzed by grief, held me by the hand. Her turn came, and she was bought by Isaac Riley of Montgomery county. Then I was offered to the assembled purchasers. My mother, half distracted with the thought of parting forever from all her children pushed through the crowd, while the bidding for me was going on, to the spot where Riley was standing. She fell at his feet, and clung to his knees, entreating him in tones that a mother could only command, to buy her *baby* as well as herself, and spare to her one, at least, of her little ones. Will it, can it be believed that this man, thus appealed to, was capable not merely of turning a deaf ear to her supplication, but of disengaging himself from her with such violent blows and kicks, as to reduce her to the necessity of creeping out of his reach, and mingling the groan of bodily suffering with the sob of a breaking heart? As she crawled away from the brutal man I heard her sob out, "Oh, Lord Jesus, how long, how long shall I suffer this way!" I must have been then between five and six years old. I seem to see and hear my poor weeping mother now. This was one of my earliest observations of men; an experience which I only shared with thousands of my race. . . .

Northern Racism, 1837

PHILADELPHIA [PA.] APRIL 15TH, 1837

TO ANGELINA GRIMKE
ESTEEMED FRIEND,

I have to thank you for the interest which has led you to address a letter to me on a subject which claims so large a share of your attention. In making a reply to the question proposed by you, I might truly advance the excuse of inability; but you well know how to compassionate the weak-

SOURCE: Josiah Henson, *Truth Stranger Than Fiction, Father Henson's Story of His Own Life* (Boston: J. P. Jewett & Co., 1858), 11–13.

SOURCE: Sarah Forten to Angelina Grimké in G. H. Barnes and D. L. Dumond, eds., *Letters of Theodore Dwight Weld, Angelina Grimké Weld, and Sarah Grimké* (New York: American Historical Association, 1934), I: 279–82.

ness of one who has written but little on the subject, and who has until very lately lived and acted more for herself than for the good of others. I confess that I am wholly indebted to the Abolition cause for arousing me from apathy and indifference, shedding light into a mind which has been too long wrapt in selfish darkness.

In reply to your question—of the "effect of Prejudice" on myself, I must acknowledge that it has often embittered my feelings, particularly when I recollect that we are the innocent victims of it; for you are well aware that it originates from dislike to the color of the skin, as much as from the degradation of Slavery. I am peculiarly sensitive on this point, and consequently seek to avoid as much as possible mingling with those who exist under its influence. I must also own that *it* has often engendered feelings of discontent and mortification in my breast when I saw that many were preferred before me, who by education, birth, or worldly circumstances were no better than myself, THEIR sole claim to notice depending on the superior advantage of being White; but I am striving to live above such heart burnings, and will learn to "bear and forbear" believing that a spirit of forebearance under such evils is all that we as a people can well exert.

Colonization is, as you well know, the offspring of Predjudice. It has doubtless had a baneful influence on our People. I despise the aim of that Institution most heartily, and have never yet met one man or woman of Color who thought better of it than I do. I believe, with all just and good persons, that it originated more immediately from prejudice than from philanthropy. The longing desire of a separation induces this belief, and the spirit of "This is not your Country" is made manifest by the many obstacles it throws in the way of their advancement mentally and morally. No doubt but there has always existed the same amount of prejudice in the minds of Americans towards the descendants of Africa; it wanted only the spirit of colonization to call it into action. It can be seen in the exclusion of the colored people from their churches, or placing them in obscure corners. We see it in their being barred from a participation with others in acquiring any useful knowledge; public lectures are not usually free to the colored people; they may not avail themselves of the right to drink at the fountain of learning, or gain an insight into the arts and science of our favored land. All this and more do they feel accutely. I only marvel that they are in possession of any knowledge at all, circumscribed as they have been by an all pervading, all-powerful predjudice. Even our professed friends have not yet rid themselves of it—to some of them it clings like a dark mantle obscuring their many virtues and choking up the avenues to higher and nobler sentiments. I recollect the words of one of the best and least predjudiced men in the Abolition ranks. Ah said he, "I can recall the time when in walking with a colored brother, the darker the night, the better Abolitionist was I." He does not say so now, but my friend, how much of this leaven still lingers in the hearts of our white brethren and sisters is oftentimes made manifest to us; but when we recollect what great sacrifices to public sentiment they are called upon to make, we cannot wholly blame them. Many, very many are anxious to take up the cross, but how few are strong enough to bear it. For our own family, we have to thank a kind Providence for placing us in a situation that has hitherto prevented us from falling under the weight of this evil; we feel it but in a slight degree compared with many others. We are not much dependant upon the tender mercies of our enemies, always having resources within ourselves to which we can apply. We are not disturbed in our social relations; we never travel far from home and seldom go to public places unless quite sure that admission is free to all; therefore, we meet with none of these mortifications which might otherwise ensue. I would recommend to my colored friends to follow our example and they would be spared some very painful realities.

My Father bids me tell you that white and colored men have worked with him from his first commencement in business. One man (a white) has been with him nearly thirty seven years; very few of his hired men have been foreigners; nearly all are natives of this country; the greatest harmony and good feeling exists between them; he has usually 10 or twenty journeymen, one half of whom are white; but I am not aware of any white sailmaker who employs colored men; I think it should be reciprocal—do not you? . . .

Negro Churches in Savannah, c. 1860

I attended afternoon service in a Baptist church at Savannah, in which I found that I was the only white man, the congregation consisting of about 600 negroes, of various shades, most of them very dark. As soon as I entered I was shown to a seat reserved for strangers, near the preacher. First the congregation all joined, both men and women, very harmoniously in a hymn, most of them having evidently good ears for music, and good voices. The singing was followed by prayers, not read, but delivered without notes by a negro of pure African blood, a gray-headed venerable-looking man, with a fine sonorous voice, named Marshall. He, as I learnt afterward, has the reputation of being one of their best preachers, and he concluded by addressing to them a sermon, also without notes, in good style, and for the most part in good English; so much so, as to make me doubt whether a few ungrammatical phrases in the negro idiom might not have been purposely introduced for the sake of bringing the subject home

SOURCE: Charles Lyell, *A Second Visit to the United States of North America* (New York: Harper & Brothers, 1868), 2: 14–15.

to their family thoughts. He got very successfully through one flight about the gloom of the valley of the shadow of death, and, speaking of the probationary state of a pious man left for a while to his own guidance, and when in danger of failing saved by the grace of God, he compared it to an eagle teaching her newly fledged offspring to fly, by carrying it up high into the air, then dropping it, and, if she sees it falling to the earth, darting with the speed of lightning to save it before it reaches the ground. Whether any eagles really teach their young to fly in this manner, I leave the ornithologist to decide; but when described in animated and picturesque language, yet by no means inflated, the imagery was well calculated to keep the attention of his hearers awake. He also inculcated some good practical maxims of morality, and told them they were to look to a future state of rewards and punishments in which God would deal impartially with "the poor and the rich, the black man and the white."

I went afterward, in the evening, to a black Methodist church, where I and two others were the only white men in the whole congregation; but I was less interested, because the service and preaching was performed by a white minister. Nothing in my whole travels gave me a higher idea of the capabilities of the negroes, than the actual progress which they have made, even in a part of a slave state, where they outnumber the whites, than this Baptist meeting. To see a body of African origin, who had joined one of the denominations of Christians, and built a church for themselves— who had elected a pastor of their own race, and secured him an annual salary, from whom they were listening to a good sermon, scarcely, if at all, below the average standard of the compositions of white ministers— to hear the whole service respectably, and the singing admirably performed, surely marks an astonishing step in civilization.

(1) It was not uncommon in the south for white slave owners to bear children by the young black slaves.

(2) Most blacks long before the Civil war viewed colonization as an act of white prejudice

CHAPTER 15

The Soldiers' Civil War

At its outset, the Civil War embodied romantic impulses. Colorful uniforms, martial and sentimental music, promises of adventure, and the certainty of quick victory stirred both sides of the conflict. Instead, the war produced death and destruction on a massive scale (about 1 million casualties and more than 600,000 dead), and its conclusion left a legacy of bitterness that was to last for generations.

James L. McDonough's essay "Glory Can Not Atone, Shiloh—April 6, 7, 1862" looks at battle from the perspective of the participants, and considers examples of these romantic notions of war. Were there any significant differences between the Union and Confederate soldiers described in the essay in terms of their reasons for enlisting, their military skill, and their patriotism?

The initial documents illustrate the mood of the nation during the early stages of the Civil War. The first is an account of the enthusiastic reaction of the citizens of Richmond, Virginia, to news of the capture of Fort Sumter by the Confederates *in April 1861. Compare this account with that in the second document, from a New York woman's description of the North's response to the same event.*

Blacks played more than a passive role in the Civil War; approximately 230,000 of them enlisted in the Union Army and Navy, and many others served the armed forces as laborers, nurses, scouts, cooks, and spies. The third document, a letter from Corporal James Henry Gooding of the Fifty-fourth Massachusetts Infantry Regiment to President Abraham Lincoln, reveals the intense patriotism of his fellow black volunteers and the continuing injustices they suffered. Gooding refers to the Confederacy's position that captured black soldiers would be treated as slaves rather than as prisoners of war, and to the Union's policy of paying black troops less than it paid whites. White privates were paid $13 per month; black soldiers, regardless of rank, received $10, the remaining $3 being deducted for clothing. Congress ultimately voted to equalize the pay of white and black soldiers in July 1864, by chance the month Corporal Gooding died of battle wounds.

The final document was written by the Great American poet, Walt Whitman, who served as a nurse in Union Army hospitals. How do his recollections compare with the romantic visions expressed at the war's outset?

ESSAY

Glory Can Not Atone:
Shiloh—April 6, 7, 1862

James L. McDonough

Will Pope was a young Confederate soldier who suffered a mortal wound at the Battle of Shiloh [Tennessee]. As his life was ebbing away he looked into the eyes of Johnnie Green, one of his comrades in arms from the border state of Kentucky, and earnestly asked the question: "Johnnie, if a boy dies for his country the glory is his forever isn't it?" Indeed it is manifest that the more than 600,000 who died in the most tragic of American wars, at least the most tragic until Viet Nam, have laid claim to a certain glory in the very heart of the America over whose fields and plains they fought, a glory which will endure as long as the annals of America herself shall last. The Battle of Shiloh, in which Will Pope lost his life, was a great part of that tragic war. And the stories of the Will Popes are an indispensable segment in the recounting of that Battle.

SOURCE: James L. McDonough, "Glory Can Not Atone, Shiloh—April 6, 7, 1862," *Tennessee Historical Quarterly* (Fall 1976), 35: 179–95. Reprinted by permission.

Confederate General Basil Duke, who fought at Shiloh, recalled the struggle some years later, and said that "Two great battles of the Civil War seem to command an especial interest denied the others. . . . There yet lingers a wish to hear all that may be told of Shiloh and Gettysburg. . . ." Otto Eisenschiml, newspaperman and Civil War scholar, after extensive study and visits to many of the battlefields of America, wrote of Shiloh: "No novelist could have packed into a space of two days more action, romance, and surprises than history did on that occasion. Of all the battlefields . . . I thought Shiloh the most intriguing."

Certainly Gettysburg has deservedly received widespread attention, but there is still much to be told about Shiloh. Somehow the Battle has been relegated in the literature of the present century to a second priority position. Even though it was the decisive engagement in the struggle for the Mississippi Valley, without which the Rebels could not realistically hope to win the war, and even though it was the biggest and bloodiest fight of the entire war west of the Appalachian Mountains, Shiloh has never received the attention which has often been accorded to lesser battles, some of which have had several books written about them. What has been written about Shiloh has usually dealt with the commanders such as Grant, Sherman, Johnston, Beauregard, etc. The blunders and the missed opportunities have been the focal points. But Shiloh is also intriguing because of the role played by some of the lesser known, even unknown figures; particularly by the common soldiers of both armies.

This article presents some of those little known, and sometimes previously unpublished, human interest occurrences. The Battle can only cease to seem like the movements on a chess board of war when one knows the tangible, flesh and blood characters, the common men of North and South, who fought, suffered, and died at Shiloh. To understand their emotions, and what happened to them, is a large part of understanding the Battle itself. Theirs are the stories which run the gauntlet of human emotions, from pathos to romance, but most of all reveal the tragedy of war.

Many diverse elements composed the Southern army. From New Orleans came the heralded "Crescent Regiment," composed of men 18 to 35 years of age, many of whom regarded themselves as the Bluebloods of Louisiana. Nicknamed the "Kid Glove" regiment, the unit was a colorful, well-drilled outfit, including many members who were equipped with "servants," and enamored with the glory of war. The command impressed a resident of Corinth as one of the finest regiments he ever saw. The Crescents would fight gallantly and be badly cut up at Shiloh. On the other hand there were units like the Sixth Mississippi, which was a ragtag regiment whose men were dressed and equipped with little or no regard for uniformity.

Great numbers of the Southerners who assembled at Corinth were very young. Henry Morton Stanley of the Sixth Arkansas Infantry, the "Dixie Grays," who was nineteen years old, recalled going into battle at Shiloh beside Henry Parker, a boy seventeen. W. E. Yeatman, who fought at Shiloh with the "Cumberland Rifles," Company C., Second Tennessee Infantry (a regiment organized at Nashville which fought at Manassas and claimed to be the first to reenlist for the duration of the war) wrote that his company "mustered with a roll of 80 men, or boys rather, as much the largest number were youths from 16 to 18 years of age.

Willie Forrest, the son of Nathan Bedford Forrest, fought at Shiloh although he was only 15 years old. His father spent part of the night of April 6 searching for Willie among the casualties. The boy later turned up safe, along with two young companions and some Yankee stragglers the three had captured. Brigadier General James R. Chalmers commended two 17-year-old boys, in his official report of the battle, who acted as staff officers for him. He wrote that one of them, Sergeant-major William A. Rains, deserved special notice for carrying an order on Sunday evening "under the heaviest fire that occurred during the whole engagement." Major General B. F. Cheatham told of "a noble boy," John Campbell, who "while acting as my aide-de-camp, fell dead, his entire head having been carried away by a cannon shot."

A colonel of the Fifth Tennessee Infantry was amazed at the "coolness and bravery throughout the entire Shiloh fight" of a private John Roberts who, although knocked down twice by spent balls, and his gun shattered to pieces, continued to push on with his advancing company. He was fifteen years old.

Not all of them were young, or even middle age, however. One man of about 60, who lived near Corinth, came to see his two sons who were in the army. He happened to arrive on the very day their unit was moving out to attack the enemy at Pittsburgh Landing. The father could not resist shouldering his musket and marching into the fight with his sons. He paid for his rashness with the loss of a leg.

A father and son, John C. Thompson, 70, and Flem, 13, enlisted in a north Mississippi company that fought at Shiloh. The old gentleman was a lawyer, who, when asked why he joined up, replied that he had talked and voted for secession and now felt that he ought to fight for the cause. Though wounded, he survived Shiloh only to fall at Chickamauga in the midst of a charge on Snodgrass Hill.

The Southerners were coming to fight for many reasons. Some were romantics. A Tennessean of Patrick Cleburne's command, George T. Blakemore, wrote that he "volunteered to fight in defense of the sunny South, the land of roses, . . . and for my Melissa, Ma and Sister, and all other fair women. . . ." Henry M. Doak described himself as a "soldier of fortune—eager for the fray. . . ." When he heard a great battle was expected near Corinth, so anxious was he for a fight that he arose from a sick bed and headed west on the first train in order not to miss it. He got to Shiloh in time—in time, after six years' instruction on the violin with German and French masters, for a rifle ball to shatter his left hand.

J. M. Lashlee came from Camden, Tennessee, to join the Confederates. He was a man opposed to slavery and to secession, who enlisted with the Rebels, as did many others, only because the Union army had invaded his state. For Lashlee the memory of the second day of the battle would hold an unlikely nostalgia—one all its own. For there on the battlefield, wounded, he would meet a young girl from near Iuka, Mississippi, by the name of Emma Dudley. And he would marry her.

Another soldier who reached Corinth in time to hear the guns of Shiloh but too late to take part in the fight was brief about his reasons for joining the Confederates. He said simply: "Our liberties are threatened, our rights endangered." He was perhaps echoing the Memphis *Daily Avalanche* which was calling forth every armed, able-bodied man to the "scenes of a great and decisive battle" in the struggle for "Southern Independence." The New Orleans *Daily Picayune* was likewise sounding the theme of a great "struggle for independence" without which there would be "nothing left . . . for which a free man would desire to live." The New Orleans paper was in fact running a series of articles under the heading "Chronicle of the Second Armerican Revolution." Its editorials were also fervently declaring that the situation now facing the South was the "crisis of the Confederate cause." Governor Pettus of Mississippi proclaimed that the decision to be faced was "liberty or death."

Many Southerners, of course, fought to protect the "peculiar institution" [slavery]. . . . Some Confederates even took selected Negroes along with them as personal body servants when they went to war. A man who fought at Shiloh later recounted a gory but impressive occurrence he witnessed involving a young Rebel officer and his slave. As the officer rode into battle on the first day of the fight, a cannon shot decapitated the young man. The Negro servant almost immediately caught his master's horse, and put the lifeless body upon it. Then the Black man moved off the battlefield, going slowly to the rear with the remains in the saddle and he behind on the horse, steadying the animal while they made their way back toward Corinth. The witness was convinced that the slave was taking his dead master's body back home for burial.

Every type of man seemed to be represented among the soldiers gathering at Corinth. Like all armies the Confederates had their gamblers. Some had a mania for cockfighting, scouring the country for fighting cocks and whenever the opportunity offered, staging a contest and betting on the outcome. "There were five or six men, mostly officers, who were ring leaders in this sport," remembered James I. Hall, who was convinced that the Almighty took a dim view of their activities. "In the Battle of Shiloh," he wrote, "they were all killed and although I remained in the army three years after this, I do not remember ever seeing or hearing of another cock fight in our regiment. . . ."

Some of those who were coming to join the Rebels were in love. Confederate Captain Benjamin Vickers of Memphis, Tennessee, was no doubt thinking much of the time about his fiance, Sallie Houston, also of Memphis, as he marched to the defense of the South at the Battle of Shiloh. There in the midst of one of the many Rebel charges he suffered a mortal wound. The young lady, even though she knew he was about to die, insisted upon their marriage, which was solemnized ten days after the battle, and a few days before his death.

There were men who came to pillage and plunder. Major General Braxton Bragg, commanding the Confederate Second Corps, was particularly disturbed by "the mobs we have, miscalled soldiers." He complained to General Beauregard that while there was "some discipline left" in those troops from the Gulf (Bragg's own command) there was "none whatever" in the rest of the army. He further stated that "the unrestrained habits of pillage and plunder" by Confederate soldiers about Corinth was making it difficult to get supplies, and, worse yet, reconciling the people to the approach of the Federals "who certainly do them less harm." The troops were even "monopolizing or plundering the eating and sleeping houses" on the railroads. The forty-five-year-old Bragg, with his lowering brow, haggard, austere, no-nonsense appearance, was determined to do something about the pillaging and he quickly gave substance to his growing reputation as a severe disciplinarian. One of the Rebel soldiers wrote that Bragg's name became a "terror to deserters and evil doers," claiming that "men were shot by scores." Another said he hanged sixteen men on a single tree.

The last two statements were, of course, wild exaggerations, but it was soon after the Shiloh campaign, on the retreat from Corinth, that an incident occurred which did much to stamp Bragg as a stern, unreasoning disciplinarian. Bragg gave orders that no gun be discharged lest the retreat route be given away, and set the penalty of death for disobedience. Subsequently a drunken soldier fired at a chicken and wounded a small Negro child. The soldier was tried by court martial, sentenced to be shot, Bragg approved, and the man was executed. Some of the facts of the actual event were soon twisted, or ignored, however, and the story circulated that because a Confederate soldier shot at a chicken Bragg had the soldier shot— a soldier for a chicken. Although he was falsely maligned as a result of this incident there is no denying that many of the soldiers thought he was unreasonably strict. Even in the earlier Mexican War, where Zachary Taylor's statement at the Battle of Buena Vista had helped make Bragg famous ("Give them a little more grape, Captain Bragg") somebody hated Bragg enough to attempt his destruction by planting a bomb under his tent. Bragg was undoubtedly right, however, about the Rebel army at Corinth being in need of more discipline.

Some of those gathering at Corinth were despondent. Jeremy Gilmer wrote of the "confusion and discomfort—dirty hotels, close rooms, hot weather—and many other disagreeable things." And no doubt many were thinking of the possibility of death. One man confided to his diary: "e'er I again write on these pages, I may be sleeping in the cold ground . . . as a battle is daily . . . anticipated."

Although they were a mixed lot, there was one quality shared by nearly every one in the Confederate army and a sizeable part of the Union army also: they had little if any experience as soldiers. It has been stated that "probably 80 percent of each army had never heard a gun fired in hatred." The estimate may be about right for the Rebel army but not for the Union force. Three of the five Federal divisions which fought at Shiloh had also seen action at Forts Henry and Donelson. There was a smattering of men in the Confederate ranks who thought of themselves as veterans, usually because they had been in one battle or heavy skirmish, but most were green. And there would not be enough time or resources to train them properly. General Leonidas Polk, in his official report, stated that one company of artillery, because of "the scarcity of ammunition, had never heard the report of their own guns."

Many of the officers, elected by their soldiers, or appointed by state governors, were not better prepared than the men in the ranks. A Confederate brigadier general said later that before Shiloh he had never heard a lecture or read a book on the science of war, nor seen a gun fired. At least he could appreciate the necessity to learn, whereas among the enlisted men were many who could see no need for target practice; after all, they thought, they already knew how to shoot!

The top Rebel commanders were attempting to bring organization and discipline out of the chaos, but the necessity for haste in attacking the enemy came to seem imperative, finally overriding all other considerations.

Meanwhile, in the Union camp, although the new recruits and even some of the commands that fought at Forts Henry and Donelson were in need of better organization and discipline, most of those gathering in the Blue ranks at Pittsburgh Landing were not short on confidence. Excited by the recent victory at Fort Donelson, which had been climaxed with the surrender of nearly 15,000 soldiers in Gray, some of the Federals believed they were moving in for the *coup de grace*. A feeling of victory was in the air. That some of the Union soldiers coming up the Tennessee River to Pittsburgh Landing had not fought at Fort Donelson made little difference.

The sense of pride in that triumph was contagious, and now the Union army "from private to commanding general" knew, in the words of a soldier in the Sixth Iowa Infantry, that a great battle was shaping up "for the mastery and military supremacy in the Mississippi Valley." With new Springfield muskets, good clothing, fine camp equipage, and wholesale rations, and inspired by music from "splendid bands and drum corps," the troops in his regiment were "happy and supremely confident," he said.

A Northerner in the Fifteen Illinois agreed. "The weather was delightful," he wrote. "Spring had just begun to open. . . . We all knew that a battle was imminent" but the victory at Fort Donelson "had given us great confidence in ourselves. . . ." Alexander Downing of the Eleventh Iowa recorded in his diary: "The boys are getting anxious for a fight." Division Commander Major General Lew Wallace told his wife in a letter that the enemy was disorganized and demoralized and that the war, if pushed, could not last long. General Grant, writing to his wife and obviously misinterpreting the Southern will to resist, said the " 'Sesesch' is . . . about on its last legs in Tennessee. A big fight" would soon occur which, "it appears to me, will be the last in the west." Many a man in the ranks, like William Skinner, was echoing the same sentiment. Skinner wrote his sister and brother on March 27, 1862: "I think the rebellion is getting nearly played out, and I expect we will be home soon." The same theme was found in the letters of some people who were writing to the soliders. Mrs. James A. Garfield, wife of the thirty-two-year-old man then serving in Buell's army who would become the Twentieth President of the United States, was telling her husband: "If our army accomplishes as much this month as during the past month it seems as though there will not be much left of the rebellion."

Some Union men were so confident that the Confederates were demoralized and giving up that they seemed to be looking for a sizeable number of Southerners to swell their ranks. A correspondent travelling with the army wrote, with evident satisfaction, of an alleged 150 or so men from Hardin County who joined the Federal army at Savannah. This does not seem particularly hard to believe since there was much Union sentiment in that county.

If the soldiers read the northern newspapers, and many of them did, (Chicago papers were available at the landing about a week after publication) they would have found it difficult to escape the conclusion that the war was about over. Through the latter part of February and March the headlines were continually recounting dramatic Union successes and some of the editorials were fervent in implying, and occasionally actually stating, that the war could not last much longer. A correspondent of the Chicago *Times* who interviewed Confederate prisoners from Fort Donelson at Camp

Douglas, reported that many of the Confederates were weary of war, that they declared the cause of the Confederacy was lost, and that it was useless to fight any longer. A few days later the same paper was reporting that the administration of Jefferson Davis was being bitterly denounced by even the Richmond newspapers.

The Cincinnati *Gazette*, on April 3, reported a great dissatisfaction in the Rebel ranks. Many Confederates, coming in from Corinth, Mississippi, were deserting to the Union army assembled at Pittsburgh Landing, the *Gazette* observed, and many more would desert if they could. The New York *Times* in big headlines was day after day heralding the triumphs of Union armies, noting that in London the capture of Fort Donelson had caused a change in British opinion and a rise in United States securities. Even the pro-Southern London *Times*, anticipating the demise of the Confederacy, was quoted as saying "There are symptoms that the Civil War can not be very long protracted."

Although Northern papers occasionally carried warnings that some signs indicated that the Confederate will to resist was still alive, such articles were often buried in the corner of a second or third page or else virtually obscured by the general optimism exuding from the continual accounting and recounting of Union triumphs.

Not only were some of the Union soldiers overconfident; there were also men gathering at Pittsburgh Landing who were so inexperienced and naive about war that they seemed to be enjoying a holiday. They banged away at flocks of wild geese from the steamboat decks as they came up the Tennessee River. It was all like "a gigantic picnic," one wrote. And some of them were getting wild, such as those men in the Twenty First Missouri Infantry who were firing from the decks of their steamer as it moved up the river, aiming their guns at citizens on the river banks. Grant labelled the conduct "infamous" and preferred charges against the colonel of the regiment.

A correspondent from the Chicago *Times* traveling with the army thought that some of the soldiers had no respect for anything. He was appalled by their morbid curiosity, when, debarking at Pittsburgh Landing and finding some fresh and rather shallow graves—the evidence of a small skirmish early in March—some of the troops, with pointed sticks and now and then a spade, removed the scanty covering of earth, which in most cases was less than a foot deep, exposing the bodies of the dead, with remarks such as: "He keeps pretty well," and "By golly! What a red moustache this fellow had!"

The Union army, like the Confederate, had many very young soldiers in their ranks. A sixteen-year-old boy in the Union army would remember, sometime during the battle of Shiloh, passing the corpse of a handsome

Confederate, blond hair scattered about his face, with a hat lying beside him bearing the number of a Georgia regiment. Seeing the boy was about his own age, he broke down and cried.

A fourteen-year-old Yankee, Private David W. Camp, of the First Ohio Light Artillery, was said by his captain to deserve particular mention, having served "with the skill and bravery of an old soldier during the entire engagement." The captain further added "I did not for a moment see him flinch."

Years later, Charles W. Hadley of the Fourteenth Iowa recalled one of the most affecting events of his war experience occurring in the area of prolonged and fierce fighting which became known as the "Hornet's Nest." He watched as a small boy, mounted on a fine horse, was suddenly lifted from the saddle by an exploding shell and dropped lifeless upon the ground.

The youngest of all usually were the drummer boys, among whom was Johnny Clem, ten years old, who went along with the Twenty Second Wisconsin Infantry, and whose drum was smashed at Shiloh, the exploit winning him the name "Johnny Shiloh"; he later became still more famous as the drummer boy of Chickamauga and retired from the army in 1916 as a major general.

With the rapid concentration of so many men at Pittsburgh Landing it was inevitable that accidents would occur, some of them fatal. A soldier in the Fourteenth Iowa who had just come up the river on the steamer *Autocrat* watched as a soldier on the *Hiawatha* fell into the Tennessee close to Pittsburgh Landing and drowned before anyone could reach him. He was not the only one to suffer such a fate, for several drownings have been recorded. General Charles F. Smith, a crusty, square-shouldered, old officer who played a leading role at Fort Donelson as a division commander, and for a while afterward replaced Grant as the army's commander, slipped and fell while getting into a row boat and skinned his shin. Infection set in which forced him to relinquish his command while the buildup at Pittsburgh Landing was in process, and in about a month he was dead.

Many of the men in Blue who left records in letters, diaries, and memoirs revealing why they fought, said they did so for the Union. But of course, and again like the Confederates, the Federals had their share of soldiers seeking glory, adventure, and plunder. [Historian] Clement Eaton has suggested that it is "highly probable that the typical soldier, Northern or Southern, had no clear idea why he was fighting." It must have seemed to him, especially when he left for war as many did, with the hometown looking on, bands playing, girls waving, and small boys watching with awe and envy, that he fought for something splendid and glorious. The cheers told him so. And the realization assured him of his own individual worth and greatness; but, at the same time, he fought for something, whether "Southern Rights" or "the Union," that must also, at times, have seemed vague and intangible. Perhaps the most concrete thing for which the soldier fought, mentioned time and time again by the warriors on both sides, was "his country."

Regardless of why they were in the army, many of the Union troops, despite the recent successes and their confidence that more would soon follow, found that army life on the whole was dull, monotonous and unpleasant. When the exhilarating, but all too brief periods of interstate camaraderie through card playing, gambling, wrestling, joking and singing were over, the soldier still brooded, worried, got sick, and thought of loved ones back home. There was too much drill and routine, rain and mud. Sanitation was bad, with logs serving as latrines, and sickness and diarrhea (a correspondent remarked that no person could really claim to be a soldier who had not experienced the latter) were rampant at times.

Perhaps above all there was loneliness. An unknown soldier of "Co. C." of an unknown regiment was keeping a small, pocket-size diary, pathetic in its brief entries revealing utter boredom. Again and again, he set down such comments as: "Weather cold and unpleasant. Nothing of any importance"; "In camp . . . no drill. Nothing new"; "Drill today . . . boys sitting by fires." Toward the latter part of March, entries begin referring to "Beautiful morning," "Beautiful spring day," and "Weather pleasant," but the evidences of loneliness and boredom are still present. The pages are blank after March 29, except for one. There appears a final entry—in a different hand: "Killed in the evening by the exploding of a boomshell from the enemies battery." The entry is on the page for April 6.

One of the men who fought for "his country" at Shiloh and experienced something of the loneliness and sickness which was so common to all was forty-year-old Brigadier General William H. L. Wallace. Recently appointed as leader of the Second Division of the Union army, he was an Ohio-born, Illinois-educated lawyer who had served in the Mexican War as an adjutant. When the Civil War began he entered the service as a colonel of Illinois Volunteers. He fought at Fort Donelson, handled himself well, and was promoted to Brigadier General of Volunteers following that battle. Popular and respected by his men he was a natural choice when Grant had to find a new division commander to replace the ailing General C. F. Smith.

On March 8, Wallace told his wife in a letter that he had been quite ill for several days and prayed for the "strength and wisdom to enable me to do my whole duty toward the country in this her hour of peril." In this and other letters he spoke often of his longing for the war to end, and how much he wanted to see his wife and all the family once more. Ann Dicky Wallace, twelve years younger than her husband, must have found his loneliness especially touching, for she decided to go south and visit him. Wallace had told her not to attempt the trip and friends and relatives warned that she would not be allowed to pass, that all civilians were being turned back. Ann was not easily persuaded to change her course once she had made up her mind.

The daughter of Judge T. Lyle Dicky, one of the most successful lawyers in Illinois, she may have thought her father's influence would help her get through. Most important in her decision, however, was her determination to see "Will" again. She had known her husband since she was just a small girl when Will, as a young lawyer, had visited many times in her father's home. Often he had taken an interest in the bright child, sometimes suggesting books for her to read, sometimes watching her ride her pet pony, or engage in some other sport, and on occasion just sitting and talking to her. When Will returned from the Mexican War he made the pleasant discovery that little Ann had become a charming young lady of fifteen. When she was sixteen he pledged his love and asked her to become his wife. Soon after her eighteenth birthday they were married.

Now, after all the years she had known him, it did not seem right to Ann for Will to be away, undergoing hardship, sickness, facing danger and possible death, while she remained passively at home. "Sometimes, Will, I can hardly restrain myself," she wrote on March 21. "I feel as if I must go to you, more so when I think of you sick. It seems wrong to enjoy every comfort of a good home and you sick in a tent. Is it indeed my duty to stay so far back and wait so anxiously?" Three days later she dispatched another letter in the same vein. And in a few more days she was on her way south.

On the morning of April 6 Ann Wallace was just arriving at Pittsburgh Landing on a steamboat—her coming still unknown to her husband. As she was putting on her hat and gloves, readying to walk from the boat to her husband's headquarters, she could hear a great deal of firing in the distance. It was first explained to her that this probably involved nothing more than the men on picket duty exchanging a few shots with some Rebel patrol. A captain in the Eleventh Illinois who was on board suggested that perhaps it would be better for him to first find out how far it was to General Wallace's headquarters, for it would be better for Mrs. Wallace to ride if the distance were great.

As she waited for the captain to return the sounds of firing seemed to be growing more pronounced. In less than thirty minutes, she thought, the captain was back with news that it looked like a major battle was shaping up. Ann's husband had already taken his command to the front, and now it was too late for her to see him. There seemed to be nothing she could do except settle down on the steamboat and wait—disappointed, frustrated, fearful for Will's safety as well as for her other relatives who were in the army. In addition to her husband, Ann's father, two brothers, two of her husband's brothers, and several more distant relatives were all fighting on the field of Shiloh.

Late in the evening a man from back home in Illinois came up to her. She thought he looked worn and depressed. He had been wounded though not seriously. "This is an awful battle," he said. "Yes, but these fresh troops will yet win the day," she replied. He reminded her that she had many relatives in the battle and could not expect that all of them would come through safely. Ann's reply, as she remembered it, was that they had all come safely through the Battle of Fort Donelson, and her husband, now a division commander, should be in a comparatively safe position. The friend then repeated his earlier comment, "It is an awful battle," and then, looking at him carefully, she realized what he was trying to tell her. Her husband had been stricken down while making the defense at the "Hornet's Nest" which proved to be so vital to the salvation of the Union army.

About that time her brother Cyrus, who had been with her husband when he fell, came in and gave her some of the details. He explained how he and another man tried to bring the body back to the landing, but could not as the Rebels were closing in around them. In her grief Ann, who could not sleep, spent most of the night in helping care for the wounded who lay all about her.

About ten o'clock on Monday morning her spirit was wonderfully lifted as news came that Will had been found on the battlefield, still breathing. She had rushed to the adjoining boat where they had brought him. He was wet and cold, his face flushed, and the wound in his head was awful looking. Ann clasped his hand and, though those standing around doubted, was convinced that he immediately recognized her, if only for a moment. He was removed to Savannah where Ann stayed with him constantly. Her hopes for his recovery grew brighter for a while. But then it gradually became obvious that his condition was growing worse, and he was mortally wounded. He breathed his last on Thursday night. She later wrote how thankful she was that he had not died on the battlefield and that she was able to be with him during those final hours.

When the battle was over the Federal army was forming burial details and digging mass graves into which they were stacking the dead bodies in rows, one on top of another. The stench of the dead was sometimes almost unbearable, and the battlefield was filled with ghastly scenes, like in the Hornet's Nest where fire had taken hold in the leaves and grass, burning the flesh from around the set teeth of some of the dead, leaving them with a horrible grin. There were scenes of wonderment, like that of a big Northerner, still gripping his musket, and a young Southerner, revolver in hand, who lay up against one another in a death embrace, having shot each other at virtually point blank range, yet neither face showing any expression of pain or anger.

But unquestionably, there were feelings of bitterness which would not subside for generations. Among the relatives coming to claim the bodies of their dead kinfolk was Samuel Stokes Rembert, III. He drove a team of horses and a wagon from his farm in Shelby County, north of Memphis, to Shiloh and somehow found the body of his eldest son, Andrew Rembert, a private in the Confederate army. Andrew's body was brought back and buried on the homeplace. Some years later Andrew's brother Sam erected a monument to his memory. That monument, still a striking sight today, is in the form of a kneeling angel, and stands eleven or twelve feet in height. But more startling than the white angel suddenly looming up in the midst of a forested area, is the bitter epitaph, which reads: "Three generations of Remberts. To my dear parents and loving sisters and my noble, gentle, brilliant and brave brother, killed for defending home against the most envious lot of cut throats that ever cursed the face of this earth."

One of the men who was walking over the battlefield in those days immediately after Shiloh was James A. Garfield. Wandering out beyond the Union lines with his pickets he came upon a group of tents in which there were about thirty wounded Rebels, attended by a surgeon and a few soldiers. He found dead men lying right in among the living. Sight and smell, he said, were terrible. It was soon after this that he was moved to write, in a letter sent back home, "The horrible sights that I have witnessed on this field I can never describe. No blaze of glory, that flashes around the magnificent triumphs of war, can ever atone for the unwritten and unutterable horrors of the scene of carnage."

DOCUMENTS

The Fall of Fort Sumter:
The South Celebrates, 1861

The news of the capture of Fort Sumter was greeted with unbounded enthusiasm in this city [Richmond, Virginia]. Everybody we met seemed to be perfectly happy. Indeed, until the occasion we did not know how happy men could be. Everybody abuses war, and yet it has ever been the favorite and most honored pursuit of men; and the women and children admire and love war ten times as much as the men. The boys pulled down the stars and stripes from the top of the Capitol (some of the boys were sixty years old), and very properly run [sic] up the flag of the Southern Confederacy in its place. What the women did we don't precisely know, but learned from rumor that they praised South Carolina to the skies, abused Virginia, put it to the Submissionists hot and heavy with their two-

SOURCE: *Daily Richmond Examiner*, April 15, 1861, in W. J. Kimball, *Richmond in Time of War* (Boston: Houghton Mifflin, 1960), 4.

edged swords, and wound up the evening's ceremonies by playing and singing secession songs until fifteen minutes after twelve on Saturday night.—The boys exploded an infinite number of crackers; the price of tar has risen 25 percent, and sky-rockets and Roman candles can be had at no price, the whole stock in trade having been used up Saturday night. We had great firing of cannon, all sorts of processions, an infinite number of grandiloquent, hifaluting speeches, and some drinking of healths, which has not improved healths; for one half the people we have met since are hoarse from long and loud talking, and the other half have a slight head-ache, it may be, from long and patriotic libations.

The Fall of Fort Sumter: The North Responds, 1861

Inside the parlor windows the atmosphere has been very fluffy, since Sumter, with lint-making and the tearing of endless lengths of flannel and cotton bandages and cutting out of innumerable garments. How long it is since Sumter! I suppose it is because so much intense emotion has been crowded into the last two or three weeks, that the "time before Sumter" seems to belong to some dim antiquity. It seems as if we never were alive till now; never had a country till now. How could we ever have laughed at Fourth-of-Julys? Outside the parlor windows the city is gay and brilliant with excited crowds, the incessant movement and music of marching regiments and all the thousands of flags, big and little, which suddenly came fluttering out of every window and door and leaped from every church tower, house-top, staff and ship-mast. It seemed as if everyone had in mind to try and make some amends to it for those late grievous and bitter insults. You have heard how the enthusiasm has been deepening and widening from that time.

A friend asked an Ohio man the other day how the West was taking it. "The West?" he said, "the West is all one great Eagle-scream!" A New England man told us that at Concord the bells were rung and the President's call read aloud on the village common. On the day but one after that reading, the Concord Regiment was marching into Fanueil Hall [in Boston]. Somebody in Washington asked a Massachusetts soldier: "How many more men of your state are coming?" "All of us," was the answer. One of the wounded Lowell men crawled into a machine shop in Baltimore. An "anti-Gorilla" citizen, seeing how young he was, asked, "What brought you

SOURCE: G. W. Bacon and W. E. Howland, eds., *Letters of a Family during the War for the Union, 1861–1865* (New Haven: Tuttle, Morehouse & Taylor, 1899), 1: 66–71.

here fighting, so far away from your home, my poor boy?" "It was the stars and stripes," the dying voice said. Hundreds of such stories are told. Everybody knows one. You read many of them in the papers. In our own little circle of friends one mother has sent away an idolized son; another, two; another, four. One boy, just getting over diphtheria, jumps out of bed and buckles his knapsack on. One throws up his passage to Europe and takes up his "enfield [rifle]." One sweet young wife is packing a regulation valise for her husband today, and doesn't let him see her cry. Another young wife is looking fearfully for news from Harper's Ferry, where her husband is ordered. He told me a month ago, *before Sumter*, that no Northman could be found to fight against the South. One or two of our soldier friends are surgeons or officers, but most of them are in the ranks, and think no work too hard or too mean, so it is for The Flag. . . .

The Vermont boys passed through this morning, with the "strength of the hills" in their marching and the green sprigs in their button-holes. The other day I saw some companies they told me were from Maine. They looked like it—sun-browned swingers of great axes, horn-handed "breakers of the glebe," used to wintering in the woods and getting frost-bitten and having their feet chopped off and conveying huge fleets of logs down spring-tide rivers in the snow and in the floods.—The sound of the drum is never out of our ears.

Never fancy that we are fearful or gloomy. We think we feel thoroughly that war is dreadful, especially war with the excitement off and the chill on, but there are so many worse things than gun-shot wounds! And among the worst is a hateful and hollow peace with such a crew as the "Montgomery mutineers." There was a dark time just after the Baltimore murders, when communication with Washington was cut off and the people in power seemed to be doing nothing to re-establish it. It cleared up, however, in a few days, and now we don't feel that the "social fabric"—I believe that is what it is called—is "falling to pieces" at all, but that it is getting gloriously mended. So, "Republicanism will wash"—*is* washed already in the water and the fire of this fresh baptism, "clothed in white samite, mystic, wonderful," and has a new name, which is *Patriotism*.

A Black Soldier Writes to President Lincoln, 1863

MORRIS ISLAND, S.C.
SEPTEMBER 28, 1863

YOUR EXCELLENCY, ABRAHAM LINCOLN:

Your Excellency will pardon the presumption of an humble individual like myself, in addressing you, but the earnest solicitation of my comrades in arms besides the genuine interest felt by myself in the matter is my excuse, for placing before the Executive head of the Nation our Common Grievance.

On the 6th of the last Month, the Paymaster of the Department informed us, that if we would decide to receive the sum of $10 (ten dollars) per month, he would come and pay us that sum, but that, on the sitting of Congress, the Regt. [regiment] would, in his opinion, be allowed the other 3 (three). He did not give us any guarantee that this would be, as he hoped; certainly he had no authority for making any such guarantee, and we cannot suppose him acting in any way interested.

Now the main question is, are we Soldiers, or are we Laborers? We are fully armed, and equipped, have done all the various duties pertaining to a Soldier's life, have conducted ourselves to the complete satisfaction of General Officers, who were, if anything, prejudiced against us, but who now accord us all the encouragement and honors due us; have shared the perils and labor of reducing the first strong-hold that flaunted a Traitor Flag; and more, Mr. President, to-day the Anglo-Saxon Mother, Wife, or Sister are not alone in tears for departed Sons, Husbands and Brothers. The patient, trusting descendant of Afric's Clime have dyed the ground with blood, in defence of the Union, and Democracy. Men, too, your Excellency, who know in a measure the cruelties of the iron heel of oppression, which in years gone by, the very power their blood is now being spilled to maintain, ever ground them in the dust.

But when the war trumpet sounded o'er the land, when men knew not the Friend from the Traitor, the Black man laid his life at the altar of the Nation,—and he was refused. When the arms of the Union were beaten, in the first year of the war, and the Executive called for more food for its ravenous maw, again the black man begged the privilege of aiding his country in her need, to be again refused.

And now he is in the War, and how has he conducted himself? Let their dusky forms rise up, out of the mires of James Island, and give the answer. Let the rich mould around Wagner's parapets be upturned, and

SOURCE: James Henry Gooding to Abraham Lincoln in Herbert Aptheker, ed., *A Documentary History of the Negro People in the U.S.* (New York: Citadel Press, 1951), 482–84.

there will be found an eloquent answer. Obedient and patient and solid as a wall are they. All we lack is a paler hue and a better acquaintance with the alphabet.

Now your Excellency, we have done a Soldier's duty. Why can't we have a Soldier's pay? You caution the Rebel chieftain, that the United States knows no distinction in her soldiers. She insists on having all her soldiers of whatever creed or color, to be treated according to the usages of War. Now if the United States exacts uniformity of treatment of her soldiers from the insurgents, would it not be well and consistent to set the example herself by paying all her soldiers alike?

We of this Regt. were not enlisted under any "contraband"* act. But we do not wish to be understood as rating our service of more value to the Government than the service of the ex-slave. Their service is undoubtedly worth much to the Nation, but Congress made express provision touching their case, as slaves freed by military necessity, and assuming the Government to be their temporary Guardian. Not so with us. Freemen by birth and consequently having the advantage of thinking and acting for ourselves so far as the Laws would allow us, we do not consider ourselves fit subjects for the Contraband act.

We appeal to you, Sir, as the Executive of the Nation, to have us justly dealt with. The Regt. do pray that they be assured their service will be fairly appreciated by paying them as American Soldiers, not as menial hirelings. Black men, you may well know, are poor; three dollars per month, for a year, will supply their needy wives and little ones with fuel. If you, as Chief Magistrate of the Nation, will assure us of our whole pay, we are content. Our Patriotism, our enthusiasm will have a new impetus, to exert our energy more and more to aid our Country. Not that our hearts ever flagged in devotion, spite the evident apathy displayed in our behalf, but we feel as though our Country spurned us, now we are sworn to serve her. Please give this a moment's attention.

Recollections of War, 1875

The dead in this war—there they lie, strewing the fields and woods and valleys and battle-fields of the South—Virginia, the Peninsula—Malvern Hill and Fair Oaks—the banks of the Chickahominy—the terraces of Fredericksburg—Antietam bridge—the grisly ravines of Manassas—the bloody

---

SOURCE: *The Complete Works of Walt Whitman* (New York: G. P. Putnam's Sons, 1902), 1: 137–39.

[*fugitive slaves who often worked as laborers for the North] promenade of the Wilderness—the varieties of the *strayed* dead, (the estimate of the War Department is 25,000 national soldiers kill'd in battle and never buried at all, 5,000 drown'd—15,000 inhumed by strangers, or on the march in haste, in hitherto unfound localities—2,000 graves cover'd by sand and mud by Mississippi freshets, 3,000 carried away by caving-in of banks, &c.,)—Gettysburg, the West, Southwest—Vicksburg—Chattanooga—the trenches of Petersburg—the numberless battles, camps, hospitals everywhere—the crop reap'd by the mighty reapers, typhoid, dysentery, inflammations—and blackest and loathsomest of all, the dead and living burial-pits, the prison-pens of Andersonville, Salisbury, Belle Isle, &c., (not Dante's pictured hell and all its woes, its degradations, filthy torments, excell'd those prisons)—the dead, the dead, the dead—*our* dead—or South or North, ours all, (all, all, all, finally dear to me)—or East or West—Atlantic coast or Mississippi valley—somewhere they crawl'd to die, alone, in bushes, low gullies, or on the sides of hills—(there, in secluded spots, their skeletons, bleach'd bones, tufts of hair, buttons, fragments of clothing, are occasionally found yet)—our young men once so handsome and so joyous, taken from us—the son from the mother, the husband from the wife, the dear friend from the dear friend—the clusters of camp graves, in Georgia, the Carolinas, and in Tennessee—the single graves left in the woods or by the roadside, (hundreds, thousands, obliterated)—the corpses floated down the rivers, and caught and lodged, (dozens, scores, floated down the upper Potomac, after the cavalry engagements, the pursuit of Lee, following Gettsyburg)—some lie at the bottom of the sea—the general million, and the special cemeteries in almost all the States—the infinite dead—(the land entire saturated, perfumed with their impalpable ashes' exhalation in Nature's chemistry distill'd, and shall be so forever, in every future grain of wheat and ear of corn, and every flower that grows, and every breath we draw)—not only Northern dead leavening Southern soil—thousands, aye tens of thousands, of Southerners, crumble to-day in Northern earth.

And everywhere among these countless graves—everywhere in the many soldier Cemeteries of the Nation, (there are now, I believe, over seventy of them)—as at the time in the vast trenches, the depositories of slain, Northern and Southern, after the great battles—not only where the scathing trail passed those years, but radiating since in all the peaceful quarters of the land—we see, and ages yet may see, on monuments and gravestones, singly or in masses, to thousands or tens of thousands, the significant word *Unknown.* . . .

CHAPTER 16

Reconstruction and Free Plantation Labor

The Civil War eliminated slavery but left undecided the question of what agrarian labor system would replace it in the devastated South. Peter Kolchin's essay "Free Plantation Labor" describes how Alabama freedmen (former slaves) and their erstwhile masters established relationships by which the productivity of the land could be maintained. As you read, consider the aspirations, fears, and misunderstandings that governed the behavior of blacks, Southern whites, and Southern-based representatives of the federal government working for the Freedmen's Bureau. Although salaried agricultural labor and tenant farming made an appearance on Alabama plantations, it was sharecropping that came to dominate agriculture in that state and much of the rest of the South. Sharecropping ultimately proved to be an unproductive system of land management, crushing black farmers and their families under a yoke of debt and poverty for generations to come. Yet, as Kolchin's essay

points out, both blacks and whites initially found the system attractive. Why was this so?

The first document is a letter from a freed slave to his former master. The letter speaks eloquently of the conditions and humiliations that he had endured in the past and also of the better life that he had built for himself. How would you describe the general tone of the letter?

Although even the most tenacious plantation owners recognized that slavery was finished and that a new system of labor was required, few white Southerners were ready to accept the freedmen as social and political equals. In 1865–66, Southern politicians established Black Codes to ensure the maintenance of white supremacy. The second document is the Black Code of St. Landry's Parish, Louisiana. To what extent does this document support the claim of some Northern Radical Republicans that the Black Codes amounted to nothing less than the continuation of slavery? Reading the code will help explain part of the motivation for the passage of the Reconstruction amendments and laws by the Republican-controlled federal government. It will also provide clues to the fate in store for Southern blacks after 1877, when the last federal troops were removed from the South and Reconstruction came to an end.

The third document consists of letters from two Northern schoolteachers, who were among the hundreds who went south after the war under the auspices of the Freedmen's Bureau and several private philanthropic agencies. What do these documents and the Kolchin essay indicate about the goals of the newly freed blacks? What actions did the freedmen take to achieve their objectives?

Beginning in the 1890s the freedmen lost the rights and opportunities they had won during the ten years following the Civil War, as Southern whites began systematically to disenfranchise blacks and to institutionalize segregationist and discriminatory practices. Whites prohibited blacks from voting, segregated them in public life, denied them justice in the courts, and placed their children in underfunded "colored schools." Though blacks never accepted these conditions as permanent, over half a century would pass before their march toward full equality resumed with the promise of significant success.

ESSAY

Free Plantation Labor

Peter Kolchin

I

Despite the migration of Negroes to Alabama's towns and cities, the most important question to blacks in 1865 concerned the role of the rural freedmen. The end of the Civil War found general confusion as to their status. "You have been told by the Yankees and others that you are free," one planter declared to his Negroes in April 1865. "This may be so! I do not doubt that you will be freed in a few years. But the terms and time of your ultimate freedom is not yet fully and definitely settled. Neither you nor I know what is to be the final result." Even if free, the Negroes' position in society remained to be determined. Presumably they would continue to till the land, for agriculture, especially cotton, was the mainstay of the state's economy and would continue as such for years. But it was not clear under what new system the land would be cultivated.

In the spring of 1865, before the arrival of Freedmen's Bureau officials, Union officers played the greatest role in establishing the new order. Throughout the state, they informed whites that the Negroes really were free and gathered blacks together to tell them of their new rights. "All persons formerly held as slaves will be treated in every respect as entitled to the rights of freedmen, and such as desire their services will be required to pay for them," announced Lieutenant Colonel C. T. Christensen in a typical statement from Mobile.

The army also served as the precursor of the Freedmen's Bureau in establishing the new agricultural labor system, according to which freedmen were to work under yearly contracts with their employers, supervised by federal officials. Varieties of this contract system had already been tested in certain Union-occupied portions of the South before the end of the war, and in April Thomas W. Conway, general superintendent of freedmen for the Department of the Gulf, arrived in Montgomery to inaugurate it in Alabama. But it was late summer before the Freedmen's Bureau was fully established throughout the state, and until then the task of supervising relations between planters and freedmen rested primarily with the army. Officers advised blacks to remain on their plantations "whenever the persons by whom they are employed recognize their rights and agree to compensate them for their services." Similar circulars,

SOURCE: Peter Kolchin, "Free Plantation Labor," in *First Freedom: The Responses of Alabama Blacks to Emancipation and Reconstruction* (Greenwood Press Inc., Westport, Conn.: 1972), 30–48. Copyright © 1972. Reprinted with permission of the author and publisher.

although not always so friendly in tone, were issued from other parts of the state. Brevet Major General R. S. Granger ordered that all contracts between freedmen and planters must be in writing. He added bluntly that "[t]hose found unemployed will be arrested and set to work." But officers were usually vague in recommending what the compensation of the freedmen, or their working relations with planters, should be. Conditions varied widely from one location to another during the first few months after the war as individual army officers, Freedmen's Bureau officials, and planters exercised their own discretion.

Observers generally noted a demoralization of labor during the spring and summer of 1865, which they frequently associated with the early migration of freedmen. Upon his arrival in Montgomery, Conway noted a "perfect reign of idleness on the part of the negroes." Other Bureau officials joined planters in declaring that blacks either would not work or would at best make feeble symbolic gestures toward work. Southern whites, and some Northern ones as well, complained that Negroes refused to work and were "impudent and defiant." In one piedmont county, the commander of the local militia warned that "[t]he negroes are becoming very impudent and unless something is done very soon I fear the consequences." White Alabamians frequently confused black "impudence" with outright revolt, but organized violence did occasionally occur.

Events on the Henry Watson plantation, a large estate in the blackbelt county of Greene, illustrate the behavior of freedmen during the first few months after the war. "About the first of June," wrote John Parrish to his brother-in-law Henry Watson, who was vacationing in Germany, "your negroes rebelled against the authority" of the overseer George Hagin. They refused to work and demanded his removal. As Parrish was ill at the time, he induced a friend of Watson's, J. A. Wemyss, to go to the plantation and attempt to put things in order. "He made a sort of compromise bargain with the negroes," Parrish reported, "agreeing that if they would remain he would give them part of the crop, they should be clothed and fed as usual, and that Mr. Hagan [sic] should have no authority over them. . . . All hands are having a good easy time, not doing half work." Six days later Parrish reported that "they have again rebelled." When Wemyss informed them firmly that they must submit to the overseer's authority, at first they "amiably consented," but soon they once again objected— "their complaints were universal, very ugly"—and seventeen of them left for nearby Uniontown, where a federal garrison was stationed. Meanwhile, a Freedmen's Bureau agent had arrived in Greensboro. Parrish brought him to the plantation, where he "modified the contract in the negroes['] fav[or] & made them sign it with their marks." The modified contract granted the laborers one-eighth of the crop.

When Watson finally returned from Germany to take charge of matters himself, he was totally disgusted with what he found. The Negroes "claim of their masters full and complete compliance on their part," he complained, "but forget that they agreed to do anything on theirs and are all idle, doing nothing, insisting that they shall be fed and are eating off their masters." Finding such a state of affairs more than he could tolerate, he decided to rent the plantation to overseer Hagin and "have nothing to do with the hiring of hands or the care of the plantation." Hagin, in turn, later broke up the plantation and sublet individual lots to Negro families.

II

Southern whites, long accustomed to thinking of their slaves as faithful and docile servants, were quick to blame outsiders for any trouble. As early as April 1862, a north Alabama planter had noted that the Union soldiers "to a great extent demoralized the negroes. . . . The negroes were delighted with them and since they left enough can be seen to convince one that the Federal army[,] the negroes and white Southern people cannot inhabit the same country." After the war, planters continued to complain about the harmful influence of the army. The presence of black troops was especially unpalatable to former slave owners. "[N]egroes will *not work* surrounded [by] black troops encouraging them to insubordination," complained one outraged resident of a blackbelt community.

Although Alabama whites were deeply humiliated by the presence of Yankees and black troops in their midst, there was little foundation to the complaints about outside agitation. Indeed, federal officials often cooperated directly with planters and local authorities in attempting to keep blacks in line. Army officers urged Negroes to stay on their plantations. Freedmen's Bureau agents frequently assisted in keeping order, too. "My predecessors here worked with a view to please the white citizens, at the expense of, and injustice to, the Freedmen," complained a shocked Bureau assistant superintendent shortly after his arrival in Tuskegee. "They have invariably given permission to inflict punishment for insolence or idleness, and have detailed soldiers to tie up and otherwise punish the laborers who have, in the opinion of the employers, been *refractory*." [Freedmen's Bureau] Commissioner [O. O.] Howard later explained that the Bureau "came to the assistance of the Planters" and succeeded in making the blacks "reliable laborers under the free system." He added that "[t]he good conduct of the millions of freedmen is due to a large extent to our officers of the Army and the Bureau."

A more substantial cause of the demoralization of labor was the mistrust existing between freedman and planter. Where this mistrust was minimal— that is, where planters and freedmen had relatively close ties and where planters readily acknowledged the changed condition of their relations— Negroes continued to work well. More often than not it was the small planter, who worked in the field beside his employees and knew them personally, who managed to remain on good terms with them. But few planters were willing to accept all the implications of the overthrow of slavery. "Thus far," pronounced the state's leading newspaper [*Daily Selma Times*] in October, "we are sorry to say that experience teaches that the negro in a free condition will not work on the old plantations." Another newspaper agreed that freedom had made the blacks "dissatisfied, listless, improvident, and unprofitable drones." Throughout the state, whites refused to believe that Negroes would work without the compulsion of slavery.

Some planters continued to hope that emancipation could either be rescinded or delayed, and "consequently told the negroes they were not free." Others recognized the de jure passing of slavery and concentrated on making the condition of the freedmen as near as possible to that of slaves. Upon his arrival in Montgomery, Conway noted that "the Planters appeared disinclined to offer employment, except with guarantees that would practically reduce the Freedmen again to a state of bondage."

Early contracts between planters and freedmen reflected the disbelief of whites in the possibility of free black labor and their desire to maintain slavery in fact, if not in name. Some planters reached "verbal agreements" with freedmen to continue as they had, without recompense. It was also relatively easy, before the Freedmen's Bureau was firmly established, for planters to lure former slaves into signing contracts that essentially perpetuated their condition. "Today I contracted with Jane and Dick to serve the remainder of the year, such being the federal law," Sarah Espy of the mountain county of Cherokee wrote in her diary in July. "I give them their victuals and clothing, the proceeds of their patches[,] and they are to proceed as heretofore." Similar contracts were made in other regions, and numerous Freedmen's Bureau officials reported upon arrival at their posts that Negroes were working without pay. The practice was summarized in a report to [Assistant Commissioner Wager] Swayne: "We find that the agreements they [the freedmen] have been working under (some of them since last April) are merely a paper drawn up by their late owners," wrote Captain J. W. Cogswell, "in which the negro promises to work for an indefinite time for nothing but his board and clothes, and the white man agrees to do nothing."

When some compensation was provided, as was the case more often than not, it almost always involved a share of the crop. There seems to have been little or no experimentation with wage labor during the first few months after the war. The initial reason for the immediate widespread adoption of sharecropping was simple: the defeated South did not have sufficient currency to pay laborers in cash. Cropping provided a convenient mode of paying freedmen without any money transactions.

Partly for the same reason and partly from tradition, most early contracts specified that food and medical care would be provided by the

planter. In addition to being a continuation of the old plantation paternalism, this provision also conformed to the wishes of the Freedmen's
Bureau. Shortly after his arrival in Montgomery, Swayne drew up a list of
proposed labor regulations. One was that "[p]art of the compensation is
required to be in food and medical attendance, lest the improvident leave
their families to suffer or the weak are obliged to purchase at unjust rates
what they must immediately have." The concern of the Freedmen's Bureau
for the welfare of the freedmen, superimposed upon the legacy of slave
paternalism and combined with the shortage of currency, insured that early
contracts would give Negroes, in addition to their share of the crop, "quarters, fuel, necessary clothes, [and] medical attendance in case of sickness."

Although the size of the shares freedmen received in 1865 varied considerably, it was almost always very small. W. C. Penick agreed to pay his
laborers one-quarter of the crop, but such liberality was rare during the
summer of 1865. More typical was the contract between Henry Watson
and his more than fifty adult blacks, which promised them one-eighth of
the crop. In other cases shares varied from one-quarter to one-tenth of the
crop.

In addition to appropriating the greater portion of the freedmen's labor,
planters were concerned with maintaining control over their lives. "I look
upon slavery as gone, gone, gone, beyond the possibility of help," lamented one planter. He added reassuringly, however, that "we have the
power to pass stringent police laws to govern the negroes—This is a blessing—For they must be controlled in some way or white people cannot live
amongst them." Such an outlook did not necessarily represent a conscious
effort to thwart the meaning of freedom, for whites had been conditioned
by years of slavery to look upon subservience as the only condition com-
patible with Negro, or any plantation, labor. Nevertheless, the effect was
the same. Early contracts often included provisions regulating the behavior
of laborers. A typical one provided that "all orders from the manager are
to be promptly and implicitly obeyed under any and all circumstances"
and added "[i]t is also agreed that none of the said negroes will under any
circumstances leave the plantation without a written permission from the
manager." If any of them quit work before the expiration of the contract,
he was to forfeit all his wages. Some contracts gave planters authority to
whip refractory Negroes.

It is only as a response to such attempts to perpetuate slave conditions
that the seeming demoralization of black labor can be understood. Although whites pointed at idle or turbulent Negroes and repeated that they
did not comprehend the meaning of freedom, the lack of comprehension
was on the part of Alabama's whites. Blacks lost little time in demonstrating
their grasp of the essentials of freedom and the tactical flexibility their new
condition provided. Just as many felt compelled to leave their old plantations immediately after the war to prevent old relations from being per-

petuated, so did they find it necessary to establish at the outset that they would not labor under conditions that made them free in name but slave in fact.

III

In December 1865 events reached something of a crisis as planters continued to strive for a return to the methods of prewar days and blacks continued to resist. Planter-laborer relationships were tense during the summer and fall, but with contracts entered into after the war due to expire on 31 December, the approach of the new year heralded an especially difficult time. Negroes now had the experience of over half a year as freedmen in dealing with planters. They also had the backing of the Freedmen's Bureau, which, if generally ambivalent about the precise position of the freedman in Southern society, refused to sanction his essential reenslavement. The culmination of the demoralization of labor and the mass migrations of 1865 was the refusal of many blacks to contract for the following year.

One reason Negroes were slow to contract was that many of them expected the plantations of their ex-masters to be divided among them at the start of the year. While this idea proved to be a total misconception, it was neither so ludicrous nor so far-fetched a notion as white Alabamians portrayed it. Southern whites themselves had contributed greatly to the expectation by warning during the war that defeat would result in the confiscation of their lands. Commissioner Howard had originally intended to turn over confiscated and abandoned lands to the freedmen, and it was only when President Johnson directly countermanded this policy in the autumn of 1865 that the Bureau reversed itself and began restoring the lands in its possession to the original owners. As the end of the year approached, Freedmen's Bureau officials carefully explained to Negroes that they were not to be given land and advised them to contract for moderate wages.

White Alabamians responded to the black desire for land by exaggerating the extent to which the freedmen expected confiscation, playing up every minor incident, and predicting ominously that New Year's would bring a black uprising. They complained of Negroes arming themselves, and in at least one area whites organized armed patrols to defend themselves against an imagined impending Negro insurrection. Other observers, however, denied any threat of an uprising, and according to [reformer] Carl Schurz rumors were "spread about impending negro insurrections evidently for no other purpose than to serve as a pretext for annoying police regulations concerning the colored people."

The refusal of the freedmen to contract in December in no way presaged a rebellion, but merely expressed their reluctance to repeat their unhappy experience of the past half-year. Without careful Freedmen's Bureau supervision, the contract system threatened to become little more than an opportunity for whites to take advantage of illiterate and ignorant blacks. As Swayne wrote, with what turned out to be something of an underestimation of the abilities of the newly freed slaves, "[c]ontracts imply bargaining and litigation, and at neither of these is the freedman a match for his Employer." For this reason, the assistant commissioner [Swayne] reported, planters "so vigorously demanded contracts there was danger they would not undertake to plant at all without them."

That the fears of insurrection consisted chiefly of groundless rumors became evident when New Year's day passed without the slightest hint of trouble. To the astonishment and relief of whites, freedmen rushed to contract during the first few days of 1866 and then settled down to work. "The praiseworthy conduct of the negroes has surprised many," declared the Selma *Morning Times* in an editorial that typified the general white response. The demoralizing effects of emancipation about which whites had complained so bitterly vanished in a matter of days. "One thing is obvious," recorded a surprised planter; "the negroes, who are hired are farming and working much better than any one predicted they would work." Other white Alabamians agreed. From Tuskegee, the local Freedmen's Bureau agent boasted that "the Freedmen have commenced work with such a zeal as to merit the praise and approbation of the Planters. Planters say to me [']my negroes have never done so well as they are doing now[']."

But if planters rejoiced that their laborers were hard at work, the freedmen had won a signal victory that was noticed by the more perceptive whites. "I think the negro hire was very high," complained future Democratic Governor George S. Houston; "[I] never had any idea of paying that much for negroes." He was right. Gone were the days when a typical contract gave the laborers one-eighth of the crop, or merely bed and board. By refusing to contract until the last moment, the freedmen had thrown their prospective employers into a panic and forced a significant alteration in the terms of the ultimate settlement. Although neither so well concerted nor organized, the process had essentially the same effect as a massive general strike.

Aside from the presence of the Freedmen's Bureau, which made blatant cheating by planters more difficult, the prevailing shortage of labor proved an inestimable boon to the freedmen. In 1866, as throughout most of the early postwar period, the pressure was on the planter to find laborers rather than on the Negro to find employment. Freedmen could feel relatively free in refusing to contract on what they regarded as unsatisfactory terms or in leaving employers with whom they were unhappy. Labor stealing, or enticing freedmen to change employers for higher wages, was a persistent complaint among planters. Occasionally, blacks were even able to strike for higher wages, as in the mountain county of Cherokee, "where they bound themselves together, under a penalty of fifty lashes, to be laid on the naked back, not to contract to work for any white man during the present harvest, for less than two dollars per day."

As had been the case in 1865, the terms of working arrangements varied widely among plantations. Both the lower and upper limits of the pay scale, however, were substantially higher than they had been. Half, or perhaps slightly more than half, of the contracts provided for a division of the crop. In such cases, the laborer almost always received a larger share than he had in 1865. Although there are examples of freedmen receiving as little as one-sixth of the crop, the prevailing portion—when, as was usual in 1866, the laborer provided nothing but his own labor—was one-quarter. For the first time, many planters contracted to pay their employees money wages rather than a portion of the crop. A typical small planter recorded that he paid his eight field hands an average of ten dollars per month for men and fifty dollars a year for women, in addition to food. In other cases where Negroes worked for wages, the rate of compensation usually ranged from seven to fifteen dollars per month for men, and somewhat less for women.

IV

The economic disadvantage of sharecropping to the Negro became evident in 1866 as the bright prospects of winter and spring faded in the summer. By August the cotton crop, which once seemed so promising, had been reduced by unseasonal rains to half its usual size, and autumn saw the second straight crop failure. As the extent of the disaster became clear, whites across the state began to decide that free blacks were not working well after all. The *Clarke County Journal*, for example, noted that although freedmen had labored satisfactorily during the winter and spring, now they seemed stubborn and lazy. "What is the matter with the freedmen?" it queried.

The contract system provided innumerable opportunities for friction between planters and freedmen—especially sharecroppers—in time of crisis. True, there were occasional touching instances when planters looked after former slaves. One white wrote to Swayne that an ex-slave of his who had left him after the war "because he would not 'feel free' if he did not" was "about to be imposed upon by an unprincipled man, who is about to employ him for the next year for far less than he is worth. . . . Please write to me," begged the distressed planter in a letter asking the assistant commissioner for advice. "I am willing to put myself to some trouble to protect my former faithful slave." Most planters, however, were primarily interested in receiving the maximum possible labor from the freedmen at minimal cost, even if it involved cheating, violence, and brutality.

The most common complaint of the freedmen was that either after the main labor on the crop was done or when it came time to divide the crop, planters would drive them off the plantations, frequently charging them with some technical violation of contract. Unlike wage earners, who were relatively secure, sharecroppers could be discharged and deprived of any compensation whatsoever. Temporary laborers could then be hired either by the day or week to finish up any remaining work. From Greene County, in the blackbelt, a Freedmen's Bureau agent reported "I find many, many men who employed them [freedmen] are arresting them . . . in a large majority of cases without cause" and sending them to sit in jail until the crop was sold. Although in some instances Bureau officials, or even the courts, mediated between planters and freedmen and were able to se-cure for the latter some payment, many injustices went unnoticed or unredressed.

The cyclical pattern established in 1865–1866 was repeated with some variations the following year. In December 1866, blacks once again were reluctant to contract. Although many of them now had the additional experience of being cheated out of their share of the crop, the absence of any illusions over the possibility of land confiscation enabled most blacks and planters to come to agreements more quickly and with less bitter feeling on both sides than they had the previous year. By spring, whites were rejoicing over Alabama's good fortune and praising her Negroes for their hard work and reliability. "The freedmen, according to universal testi-mony, are working better than they did last year," reported the *Daily Selma Messenger* with satisfaction.

There was an almost universal return to sharecropping in 1867, al-though a very few planters and freedmen continued, despite the shortage of currency, to experiment with wages. Some Freedmen's Bureau officials, who felt that Negroes fared better economically on wages, and some white Alabamians, who supported the system under which blacks were most carefully supervised, continued to advocate wage labor. With very few exceptions, however, planters and freedmen ignored their pleas. Arrange-ments granting the laborers one-quarter of the crop were most widespread, although in a few instances freedmen contracted to provide their own food and receive half the crop.

Sharecropping triumphed because both planters and freedmen favored the system. To the average planter it continued to be a more feasible labor system than wages, if for no other reason than the shortage of currency. In addition, many whites felt that shares gave blacks an interest in the crop, thus providing them with an incentive to work. Most blacks appar-ently preferred cropping, despite the economic disadvantages, because it allowed them greater control of their own lives. Because of his interest in the crop, the sharecropper required less supervision. In contrast to the wage laborer, who was a hired hand clearly in a subordinate position to his employer, the cropper was the partner of the landowner in a joint business venture that provided the freedman with opportunities for greater individual discretion, dignity, and self-respect. For this reason, Negroes considered the cropper a notch above the wage laborer in the social scale. "I am not working for wages," declared one freedman to his employer, as he explained why he had a right to leave the plantation at will to attend political meetings, "but am part owner of the crop and as I have all the rights that you or any other man has I shall not suffer them abridged."

V

As in 1866, the cotton crop of 1867 was a poor one. By fall, planters had once again begun to complain about the inefficiencies of freedmen as laborers. "The cause of the cotton crop being so inferior is the inefficiency of labor and the bad season [is] more on account of labor than anything else," lamented George Hagin, the ex-overseer who had rented Henry Watson's plantation. "There has been a few of the old negroes that lived on the place before that have worked very well but the younger ones are worth nothing." A correspondent of the Union Springs *Times* proclaimed free labor a failure.

Once again, planters drove freedmen from their homes without pay. "Negroes are now being dismissed from the plantations[,] there being nothing more for them to do," explained one blackbelt resident. He added calmly that "[t]hey will all be turned loose without homes[,] money or provisions[;] at least no meat." From the northwest corner of the state, 114 Negroes appealed for assistance to Major General John Pope, who in April had assumed command of the Third Military District, comprising Alabama, Georgia, and Florida. They explained that "unless some person in whom we can place the utmost confidence be appointed to superintend the settling up of our affairs, we do not feel that justice will be done us." In 1867, for the first time, many blacks were also fired for voting Republican or attending political meetings.

Occasionally, through unusual persistence or intelligence, blacks were able to enlist the aid of the Freedmen's Bureau and resist arbitrary discharge. Bernard Houston, a sharecropper on an Athens plantation, told his landlord, "I shall not suffer myself to be turned off[,] and under legal advice and the advice of assistant Commissioner of [the] Freedmans Bureau I shall stay there until the crop is matured[,] gathered and divided according to contract." The planter protested lamely that he objected to the Negro's being "disobedient" and denied that politics had anything to do with the situation, but a month later he complained to Swayne that the freedman was "yet on the place acting in utter and entire disobedience of orders & the necessary discipline of the plantation."

In numerous other cases, freedmen were less fortunate. Freedmen's Bureau agents tried to come to the assistance of persecuted blacks, but there were simply too few agents for the job. Furthermore, since the procedure for handling grievances was not clear, Bureau representatives were not sure how best to dispose of them. Some turned cases over to the civil courts. In general, however, this method proved unsatisfactory. "[B]esides the slow process of the Law, there stands in the way the difficulty of obtaining counsel," explained one Bureau agent. "The Freedmen as a general thing have no mean[s] to pay a fee: consequently they submit to the swindle simply because they cannot purchase justice." The sub-assistant commissioner at Huntsville sent discharged freedmen back to their plantations and told them to stay there. In other locations, officials tried to mediate between laborers and planters. "I notify the parties concerned to appear at this office together, and try either to effect an understanding, or a settlement," explained one Bureau official. He reported that he had "so far been fortunate, to prevent any injustice to be done." But for every such settlement, many other grievances undoubtedly went unheard.

The cumulative effects of three years of substandard crops became increasingly evident during the late autumn and early winter of 1867–1868, a period of considerable tension because of the meeting of the Radical Constitutional Convention in December and the election to ratify the new constitution in February. The problem was no longer that freedmen were reluctant to contract, but rather that planters were unwilling or unable to plant. Their universal reaction to poor crops and low profits was to plan to cut back on planting operations. Unemployment among Negroes threatened to reach serious proportions for the first time since the war. . . .

VI

Hidden behind the daily monotony of agricultural labor, significant changes occurred in the lives of black plantation workers during their first few years of freedom. These changes were evident both in their relations with their employers and in their relations with each other. All of them can, with little inaccuracy and only slight ambiguity, be called moves toward independence. These moves, as much class as racial in nature, represented not only the desire of blacks to be free of white control, but also of ex-slave plantation laborers to be free of planter control.

"Freedom has worked great changes in the negro, bringing out all his inherent savage qualities," proclaimed the Mobile *Daily Register* in 1869. Certainly a growing physical restlessness and self-consciousness among black plantation workers—reinforced by the political emancipation brought about under congressional Reconstruction—were very evident. They were no longer willing to be imposed upon by their former owners. From the end of the war laborers, such as those on the Henry Watson plantation, had revolted against working under their old overseers. But the increasing number of white complaints of Negro "impudence," "insolence," and "insubordination," and the increasing readiness of black laborers to resort to violence and organization when faced with an unpalatable situation, testified to their growing self-assertiveness and confidence. In December 1867, for example, planters in Russell County, who were forced to cut back on planting operations because of poor crops the previous year, complained that their laborers were "seizing and holding property upon some of the places. They are generally armed." A year later, a revolt in the same area had to be put down by military force.

This desire of agricultural laborers for independence, which led them to choose sharecropping over wages even though they usually fared better economically under a wage system, was one of the greatest causes of other changes in modes of life and labor on the plantation. Before the war, field hands on large plantations had usually lived in rows of cabins grouped together. They had worked together in a slave gang, under the authority of an overseer and perhaps a driver. Their lives had been, by and large, collective. After the war, black plantation laborers quickly indicated their preference for a more individual form of life. They objected to working under the control of an overseer. They also objected to the regimented nature of the work gang and the Negro quarters. These had been accepted "in the days of slavery, when laborers were driven by overseers by day, and penned like sheep at night, and not allowed to have any will of their own," reported one Freedmen's Bureau agent. "But now, being *free* to think and act for themselves, they feel their individual responsibility for their conduct, and the importance of maintaining a good character." He noted that fights frequently broke out among Negroes forced to live among others against their will.

Many planters found it necessary or useful to break up the former slave quarters and allow laborers to have individual huts, scattered across the plantations. The process was far from complete by the end of the 1860s, but the trend was unmistakable. As early as the spring of 1867, an article in the Montgomery *Daily Advertiser* described certain changes that had occurred in the appearance of one plantation community. "You do not see as large gangs together as of old times, but more frequently squads of five or ten in a place, working industriously without a driver," wrote the correspondent. "Several large land owners have broken up their old 'quarters' and have rebuilt the houses at selected points, scattered over the plantation. . . ."

Although most black sharecroppers continued to provide only their labor and receive food and clothing in addition to their usual quarter of the crop, the late 1860s saw the introduction of a new cropping arrangement that would, in a matter of years, be widely adopted. Early in 1868, a Freedmen's Bureau official noted that there "does not seem to be as much uniformity in the tenor of contracts as last year." He wrote that although "some give the freedmen one-fourth of the crop and provide rations as was customary last year . . . others give one third of [the] crop, and require the laborers to furnish their own rations; and some give one half, the laborers bearing an equal share of the expense." The result was to remove the cropper still further from the wage laborer, and accentuate his role as a partner of the planter in a joint business venture.

Such changes in working and living conditions were sometimes fostered by planters themselves. Some, like Henry Watson, found it impossible to adjust to a new situation in which they did not have total control over their labor force. Under such circumstances, it was tempting for them to adopt whatever system would permit the least contact between employer and laborer, even if it resulted in more of the very independence that so troubled them. A correspondent from the blackbelt county of Hale reported to the Mobile *Daily Register* in 1869 that "everything appears experimental. . . . Many planters have turned their stock, teams, and every facility for farming, over to the negroes, and only require an amount of toll for the care of their land, refusing to superintend, direct, or even, in some cases, to suggest as to their management."

By the late 1860s, then, old patterns of agricultural relationships had been irreparably shattered, and the outlines of new ones had emerged. The logical culmination of emancipation for the plantation workers—the acquisition of their own land—remained for most an illusory dream. But within the confines of the plantation system great changes had occurred in the lives of the black laborers. They themselves had helped bring about most of these changes by demonstrating that they were not willing to continue in a position of complete subservience to their former owners. As one white planter lamented succinctly of the freedmen, "[T]hey wish to be free from restraint." That wish was a potent one in the years immediately following the Civil War.

DOCUMENTS

A Letter
"To My Old Master . . . ," c. 1865

TO MY OLD MASTER, COLONEL P. H. ANDERSON,
BIG SPRING, TENNESSEE

Sir: I got your letter, and was glad to find that you had not forgotten Jourdon, and that you wanted me to come back and live with you again, promising to do better for me than anybody else can. I have often felt uneasy about you. I thought the Yankees would have hung you long before this, for harboring Rebs they found at your house. I suppose they never

SOURCE: L. Maria Child, *The Freedmen's Book* (1865).

heard about your going to Colonel Martin's to kill the Union soldier that was left by his company in their stable. Although you shot at me twice before I left you, I did not want to hear of your being hurt, and am glad you are still living. It would do me good to go back to the dear old home again, and see Miss Mary and Miss Martha and Allen, Esther, Green, and Lee. Give my love to them all, and tell them I hope we will meet in the better world, if not in this. I would have gone back to see you all when I was working in the Nashville Hospital, but one of the neighbors told me that Henry intended to shoot me if he ever got a chance.

I want to know particularly what the good chance is you propose to give me. I am doing tolerably well here. I get twenty-five dollars a month, with victuals and clothing; have a comfortable home for Mandy—the folks call her Mrs. Anderson—and the children—Milly, Jane, and Grundy—go to school and are learning well. The teacher says Grundy has a head for a preacher. They go to Sunday school, and Mandy and me attend church regularly. We are kindly treated. Sometimes we overhear others saying, "Them colored people were slaves" down in Tennessee. The children feel hurt when they hear such remarks; but I tell them it was no disgrace in Tennessee to belong to Colonel Anderson. Many darkeys would have been proud, as I used to be, to call you master. Now if you will write and say what wages you will give me, I will be better able to decide whether it would be to my advantage to move back again.

As to my freedom, which you say I can have, there is nothing to be gained on that score, as I got my free papers in 1864 from the Provost-Marshal-General of the Department of Nashville. Mandy says she would be afraid to go back without some proof that you were disposed to treat us justly and kindly; and we have concluded to test your sincerity by asking you to send us our wages for the time we served you. This will make us forget and forgive old scores, and rely on your justice and friendship in the future. I served you faithfully for thirty-two years, and Mandy twenty years. At twenty-five dollars a month for me, and two dollars a week for Mandy, our earnings would amount to eleven thousand six hundred and eighty dollars. Add to this the interest for the time our wages have been kept back, and deduct what you paid for our clothing, and three doctor's visits to me, and pulling a tooth for Mandy, and the balance will show what we are in justice entitled to. Please send the money by Adam's Express, in care of V. Winters, Esq., Dayton, Ohio. If you fail to pay us for faithful labors in the past, we can have little faith in your promises in the future. We trust the good Maker has opened your eyes to the wrongs which you and your fathers have done to me and my fathers, in making us toil for you for generations without recompense. Here I draw my wages every Saturday night; but in Tennessee there was never any pay-day for the Negroes any more than for the horses and cows. Surely there will be a day of reckoning for those who defraud the laborer of his hire.

In answering this letter, please state if there would be any safety for my Milly and Jane, who are now grown up, and both good-looking girls. You know how it was with poor Matilda and Catherine. I would rather stay here and starve—and die, if it come to that—than have my girls brought to shame by the violence and wickedness of their young masters. You will also please state if there has been any schools opened for the colored children in your neighborhood. The great desire of my life now is to give my children an education, and have them form virtuous habits.

Say howdy to George Carter, and thank him for taking the pistol from you when you were shooting at me.

FROM YOUR OLD SERVANT,
JOURDON ANDERSON

The Black Code of
St. Landry's Parish, 1865

Whereas it was formerly made the duty of the police jury to make suitable regulations for the police of slaves within the limits of the parish; and whereas slaves have become emancipated by the action of the ruling powers; and whereas it is necessary for public order, as well as for the comfort and correct deportment of said freedmen, that suitable regulations should be established for their government in their changed condition, the following ordinances are adopted, with the approval of the United States military authorities commanding in said parish, viz:

SECTION 1.   *Be it ordained by the police jury of the parish of St. Landry,* That no negro shall be allowed to pass within the limits of said parish without a special permit in writing from his employer. Whoever shall violate this provision shall pay a fine of two dollars and fifty cents, or in default thereof shall be forced to work four days on the public road, or suffer corporeal punishment as provided hereinafter.

SECTION 2.   *Be it further ordained,* That every negro who shall be found absent from the residence of his employer after 10 o'clock at night, without a written permit from his employer, shall pay a fine of five dollars, or in default thereof, shall be compelled to work five days on the public road, or suffer corporeal punishment as hereinafter provided.

SECTION 3.   *Be it further ordained,* That no negro shall be permitted to rent or keep a house within said parish. Any negro violating this provision shall be immediately ejected and compelled to find an employer; and any

SOURCE: U.S. Congress, *Senate Executive Document No. 2* (Washington, D.C., 1865), 93–94.

person who shall rent, or give the use of any house to any negro, in violation of this section, shall pay a fine of five dollars for each offence.

SECTION 4.   *Be it further ordained,* That every negro is required to be in the regular service of some white person, or former owner, who shall be held responsible for the conduct of said negro. But said employer or former owner may permit said negro to hire his own time by special permission in writing, which permission shall not extend over seven days at any one time. Any negro violating the provisions of this section shall be fined five dollars for each offence, or in default of the payment thereof shall be forced to work five days on the public road, or suffer corporeal punishment as hereinafter provided.

SECTION 5.   *Be it further ordained,* That no public meetings or congregations of negroes shall be allowed within said parish after sunset; but such public meetings and congregations may be held between the hours of sunrise and sunset, by the special permission in writing of the captain of patrol, within whose beat such meetings shall take place. This prohibition, however, is not intended to prevent negroes from attending the usual church services, conducted by white ministers and priests. Every negro violating the provisions of this section shall pay a fine of five dollars, or in default thereof shall be compelled to work five days on the public road, or suffer corporeal punishment as hereinafter provided.

SECTION 6.   *Be it further ordained,* That no negro shall be permitted to preach, exhort, or otherwise declaim to congregations of colored people, without a special permission in writing from the president of the police jury. Any negro violating the provisions of this section shall pay a fine of ten dollars, or in default thereof shall be forced to work ten days on the public road, or suffer corporeal punishment as hereinafter provided.

SECTION 7.   *Be it further ordained,* That no negro who is not in the military service shall be allowed to carry fire-arms, or any kind of weapons, within the parish, without the special written permission of his employers, approved and indorsed by the nearest or most convenient chief of patrol. Any one violating the provisions of this section shall forfeit his weapons and pay a fine of five dollars, or in default of the payment of said fine, shall be forced to work five days on the public road, or suffer corporeal punishment as hereinafter provided.

SECTION 8.   *Be it further ordained,* That no negro shall sell, barter, or exchange any articles of merchandise or traffic within said parish without the special written permission of his employer, specifying the articles of sale, barter or traffic. Any one thus offending shall pay a fine of one dollar for each offence, and suffer the forfeiture of said articles, or in default of the payment of said fine shall work one day on the public road, or suffer corporeal punishment as hereinafter provided.

SECTION 9.   *Be it further ordained,* That any negro found drunk within the said parish shall pay a fine of five dollars, or in default thereof shall work five days on the public road, or suffer corporeal punishment as hereinafter provided.

SECTION 10. *Be it further ordained,* That all the foregoing provisions shall apply to negroes of both sexes.

SECTION 11. *Be it further ordained,* That it shall be the duty of every citizen to act as a police officer for the detection of offences and the apprehension of offenders, who shall be immediately handed over to the proper captain or chief of patrol.

SECTION 12. *Be it further ordained,* That the aforesaid penalties shall be summarily enforced, and that it shall be the duty of the captains and chiefs of patrol to see that the aforesaid ordinances are promptly executed.

SECTION 13. *Be it further ordained,* That all sums collected from the aforesaid fines shall be immediately handed over to the parish treasurer.

SECTION 14. *Be it further ordained,* That the corporeal punishment provided for in the foregoing sections shall consist in confining the body of the offender within a barrel placed over his or her shoulders, in the manner practiced in the army, such confinement not to continue longer than twelve hours, and for such time within the aforesaid limit as shall be fixed by the captain or chief of patrol who inflicts the penalty.

SECTION 15. *Be it further ordained,* That these ordinances shall not interfere with any municipal or military regulations inconsistent with them within the limits of said parish.

SECTION 16. *Be it further ordained,* That these ordinances shall take effect five days after their publication in the *Opelousas Courier*.

Dedicated Teachers,
Determined Students, 1869

RALEIGH, N.C., FEB. 22, 1869

It is surprising to me to see the amount of suffering which many of the people endure for the sake of sending their children to school. Men get very low wages here—from $2.50 to $8 per month usually, while a first-rate hand may get $10, and a peck or two of meal per week for rations— and a great many men cannot get work at all. The women take in sewing and washing, go out by day to scour, etc. There is one woman who supports three children and keeps them at school; she says, "I don't care how hard I has to work, if I can only sen[d] Sallie and the boys to school looking respectable." Many of the girls have but one decent dress; it gets washed

SOURCE: Edward L. Pierce, "The Freedmen at Port Royal," *Atlantic Monthly* 12 (September 1869): 306–7.

and ironed on Saturday, and then is worn until the next Saturday, provided they do not tear it or fall in the mud; when such an accident happens there is an absent mark on the register. . . . One may go into their cabins on cold, windy days, and see daylight between every two boards, or feel the rain dropping through the roof; but a word of complaint is rarely heard. They are anxious to have the children "get on" in their books, and do not seem to feel impatient if they lack comforts themselves. A pile of books is seen in almost every cabin, though there be no furniture except a poor bed, a table and two or three broken chairs.

MISS M. A. PARKER

CHARLOTTESVILLE, VA., OCT. 17, 1866

Mrs. Gibbins (a colored native teacher) is very much liked by the colored people here. Her nature is so noble, that she is not so liable to stimulate petty jealousy among her people as many might under similar circumstances. . . . I think she is doing well in her new sphere of duty, especially in the matter of government. She has a kind of magnetism about her which is a good qualification for a teacher. She is really a fine reader of easy readings, and I should choose her to prepare scholars for me in that line, from among nine-tenths of those engaged in this work, so far as I have known her. She intends to pursue her studies in the evening with my help.

ANNA GARDNER

PART II

Suggestions for Further Reading

For general social and economic changes before the Civil War, several books are useful. Among them are Robert Wiebe, *The Opening of American Society: From the Adoption of the Constitution to the Eve of Disunion* (1984); Sean Wilentz, *Chants Democratic: New York City and the Rise of the American Working Class, 1785–1850* (1984); Daniel Walkowitz, *Worker City, Company Town: Iron and Cotton-Worker Protest in Troy and Cohoes, New York, 1855–1884* (1978); Alan Dawley, *Class and Community: The Industrial Revolution in Lynn* (1976); and Howard Gitelman, *Workingmen of Waltham: Mobility in Urban Industrial Development, 1850–1890* (1974).

On the removal policy of American Indians to the West, see Ronald Satz, *American Indian Policy in the Jacksonian Era* (1975). On removal itself, see Arthur DeRosier, *The Removal of the Choctaw Indians* (1970) and Wilkins Thurman, *Cherokee Tragedy: The Story of the Ridge Family and the Decimation of a People* (1970). On assimilation, see Henry E. Fritz, *The Movement for Indian Assimilation, 1860–1890* (1963).

On the westward movement generally, particularly recommended are two studies by Ray Billington: *The Far Western Frontier, 1830–1860* (1956) and *Westward Expansion* (1974). See also John D. Unruh, Jr., *The Plain Across: The Overland Emigrants and the Trans-Mississippi West, 1840–1860* (1979). For women and the West, consult John M. Faragher, *Women and Men on the Overland Trail* (1979) and Julie Roy Jeffrey, *Frontier Women: The Trans-Mississippi West, 1840–1880* (1979).

There is a growing literature on women's history. Two general works of value are Alice Kessler-Harris, *Out to Work: A History of Wage Earning Women in America* (1982) and Carl Degler, *At Odds: Women and the Family from the Revolution to the Present* (1981). On plantation women, see Catherine Clinton, *The Plantation Mistress* (1982) and Ann Firor Scott, *The Southern Lady: From Pedestal to Politics, 1830–1930* (1970). On women in American culture, consult Ann Douglas, *The Feminization of American Culture* (1977); Nancy Cott, *The Bonds of Womanhood: "Woman's Sphere" in New England, 1780–1835* (1977); Mary Ryan, *Cradle of the Middle Class: The Family in Oneida County, New York, 1790–1865* (1981); and Katherine Kish Sklar, *Catharine Beecher: A Study in American Domesticity* (1973). On women factory workers, see Thomas Dublin, *Women at Work: The Transformation of Work and Community in Lowell, Massachusetts, 1826–1860* (1979), and for black women, see Jacqueline Jones, *Labor of Love, Labor of Sorrow: Black Women, Work and the Family from Slavery to the Present* (1985).

For religion in early-nineteenth-century America, an older but useful work is Whitney Cross, *The Burned-Over District: A Social and Intellectual History of Enthusiastic Religion in Western New York, 1800–1855* (1950). See

316

also John B. Boles, *The Great Revival* (1972) and Charles A. John, *The Frontier Camp Meeting* (1955). For a large study of revivalism, consult William McLoughlin, *Modern Revivalism: Charles Grandison Finney to Billy Graham* (1959). A newer view is found in Paul E. Johnson, *A Shopkeepers Millennium: Society and Revivals in Rochester, New York, 1815–1837* (1978).

On immigration before the Civil War, see Jay Dolan, *Immigrant Church: New German Catholics, 1815–1865* (1975); Robert Ernst, *Immigrant Life (in New York City), 1812–1863* (1949); Oscar Handlin, *Boston's Immigrants, 1790–1880: A Study in Acculturation* (1970); and Lawrence McCaffrey, *The Irish Diaspora* (1976). A classic study of anti-immigrant sentiment is Ray Allen Billington, *The Protestant Crusade, 1800–1860: A Study of the Origins of American Nativism* (1938).

For reform movements, useful general works are Alice Felt Tyler, *Freedom's Ferment* (1944) and Ronald G. Walters, *American Reformers, 1815–1860* (1978). On antislavery, see Louis Filler, *The Crusade Against Slavery* (1960); Blanche Glassman Hersh, *The Slavery of Sex: Feminist-Abolitionists in America* (1978); and Eric Foner, *Free Soil, Free Labor, Free Men: The Ideology of the Republican Party Before the Civil War* (1970). On the women's rights movement, the reader will profit from Ellen C. DuBois, *Feminism and Suffrage: The Emergence of an Independent Women's Movement in America, 1848–1869* (1978). Studies of the crusade for public schooling include Carl F. Kaestle, *Pillars of the Republic: Common Schools and American Society, 1780–1860* (1983); Lawrence A. Cremin, *American Education: The National Experience, 1783–1876* (1981); and Frederick M. Binder, *The Age of the Common School: 1830–1865* (1974). An important revisionist view is found in Michael Katz, *The Irony of Early School Reform* (1968).

Surveys of the several utopian movements may be found in Michael Fellman, *The Unbounded Frame: Freedom and Community in Nineteenth Century Utopianism* (1973); Mark Holloway, *Heavens on Earth* (1951); and Raymond Muncy, *Sex and Marriage in Utopian Communities: 19th Century America* (1973).

The literature on antebellum slavery is large. Among the better books are John Blassingame, *The Slave Community: Plantation Life in the Antebellum South (1972);* Eugene D. Genovese, *Roll, Jordan, Roll* (1974); Herbert Gutman, *The Black Family in Slavery and Freedom, 1750–1925* (1976); Kenneth Stampp, *The Peculiar Institution* (1956); and Leslie Owens, *This Species of Property: Slave Life in the Old South* (1976). A newer account of slavery in one community is Charles Joyner, *Down by the Riverside: A South Carolina Slave Community* (1984). For free blacks in the South, consult Ira Berlin, *Slaves Without Masters: The Free Negro in the Antebellum South* (1975) and Michael Johnson and James Roark, *Black Masters: A Free Family of Color in the Old South* (1984), and for the North, Leon Litwack, *North of Slavery: The Negro in the Free States* (1961).

Among studies of the Civil War from the perspective of the fighting men are two by Bell I. Wiley: *The Life of Johnny Reb* (1943) and *The Life of*

Billy Yank (1952). The experiences of black soldiers are described in Dudley R. Cornish, *The Sable Arm* (1966). For treatments of the home front, consult Robert Meyers, *The Children of Pride* (1972) for a Southern view and George Winston Smith and Charles Burnet Judah, *Life in the North During the Civil War* (1966) for the Northern view. For contributions of women to the war effort, see Mary E. Massey, *Bonnet Brigades* (1966). Benjamin Quarles, *The Negro in the Civil War* (1953), reveals the impact of the war on blacks.

On southern black Americans after the Civil War, consult Eric Foner, *Nothing But Freedom: Emancipation and Its Legacy* (1983); John Hope Franklin, *Reconstruction After the Civil War* (1961); Leon Litwack, *Been in the Storm So Long: The Aftermath of Slavery* (1979); and Howard Rabinowitz, *Race Relations in the Urban South, 1865–1890* (1980). On black poverty, see Jay R. Mandle, *The Roots of Black Poverty* (1978). C. Vann Woodward, *The Strange Career of Jim Crow* (1966), remains an important work.

2   3   4   5   6   7   8   9   0